C O R O N A D O

KNIGHT OF PUEBLOS & PLAINS

CORONADO

Knight of Pueblos and Plains

HERBERT E. BOLTON

THE UNIVERSITY OF NEW MEXICO PRESS

ALBUQUERQUE

First published in 1949 by the University of New Mexico Press as Volume I
of the Coronado Cuarto Centennial Publications, 1540-1940, edited by
George P. Hammond, with the title *Coronado on the Turquoise Trail,
Knight of Pueblos and Plains.* Reprinted in 1949 jointly with Whittlesey
House, a division of the McGraw-Hill Book Company, Inc., under the title
Coronado, Knight of Pueblos and Plains. Reprinted in 1964 by the Univer-
sity of New Mexico Press, simultaneously in clothbound and paperbound
editions. Manufactured in the United States of America by the University
of New Mexico Printing Plant, Albuquerque. Library of Congress Catalog
Card No. 64-17854.

Dedicated to all my good companions on the trail and to my many students who vicariously have accompanied me in my ramblings

PREFACE

This book starts off with a conscious falsification, not even calling the principal character by his right name. Arciniegas, in his delightful volume called *The Knight of El Dorado*, confesses to the same crime and explains how it happened. "Throughout the whole conquest of America one never knows who is who. Names are always being changed about. . . . Sebastián de Belalcázar, for example, was named Sebastián Moyano, but historians wrote reams of paper, saying, some, that he was called Belalcázar, and others, Benalcázar. As a matter of fact, he was probably not a Moyano at all but a García. Let the reader go to Quito, Popayán, or Cali, however, and tell residents that the founder of their city was named García Moyano, and they will laugh in his face, if they do not stone him to death." In the same way, the famous pioneer of Arizona, New Mexico, Texas, Oklahoma, and Kansas was Francisco Vázquez de Coronado, but few persons now living in these regions would recognize him under his correct name of Vázquez, and they might assassinate a writer who should insist on being accurate on that point. Not wishing the crown of martyrdom, even for the sake of veracity, I shall conform to well established custom and call him Coronado. The case is similar with García López de Cárdenas, Coronado's ablest lieutenant and discoverer of Grand Canyon. By his contemporaries he was called López, but in this gringo country he is known as Cárdenas, and so he is designated here.

To catch the significance of Coronado he must be seen in perspective. In 1848 gold was discovered at Sutter's Mill in California. The news got out, and within a year fifty thousand Argonauts from all parts of the world found their way to the Promised Land, hoping to make their fortunes, go back home, and live happily ever afterward. In the mines not one in a thousand struck it rich, and the rank and file scarcely averaged a dollar a day for their toil. The California Gold Rush was a typical episode which had been repeated innumerable times in America since Columbus' celebrated voyage. In essence it was not greatly different from the remarkable treasure hunts which swept over a large part of the Western Hemisphere in the second quarter of the sixteenth century. We justly glorify our Forty-niners, but we have customarily applied the term "wild-goose chases" to earlier quests for the Golden Fleece. One of these was the Coronado Expedition, whose four hundredth anniversary we have recently commemorated.

Set in motion by a story not altogether unlike that of Marshall's discovery in California, Coronado and his followers made known the great Southwest and contributed toward its permanent settlement. Leaving Mexico City in 1540 with some three hundred Spaniards and a large body of Indian allies, Don Francisco went west to the Pacific Ocean, ascended the coast through the regions now known as Sinaloa and Sonora, explored Arizona and New Mexico, marched out upon the buffalo-covered plains of Texas, discovered Tule and Palo Duro canyons, turned north through Oklahoma, entered Kansas, reached the Arkansas River near the site of Ford (so designated for the historic crossing there), and followed the stream to Quivira, a name then given to the Wichita Indian settlements between the Arkansas and Smoky Hill rivers. Meanwhile Alarcón with part of Coronado's force ascended the Gulf of California and explored the lower Colorado River. Incidentally, he reached California two years ahead of Cabrillo, the reputed discoverer.

First among Europeans, Coronado and his men saw and described on the basis of eye-witness information the Zuñi Pueblos, the Hopi Pueblos, Colorado River, Grand Canyon, Gila River, and the giant Yuman tribes along the River of the Firebrands. Farther east they were first to see Ácoma, "the Sky City," the upper Rio Grande, the Tiguex Pueblos along its banks, snow-covered Sangre de Cristo Mountains, Pecos River, Canadian River, the vast herds of buffaloes, and the great canyons of the Staked Plains, as later they were miscalled by the Anglo-American pioneers. They first explored the Texas Panhandle, first crossed Oklahoma, the Cimarron and Arkansas rivers, traversed eastern Kansas, and became acquainted with the tattooed Wichitas. These helmet-crested Spanish horsemen saw and made known to the world most of the places visited today by myriad travelers in the region now known in the United States as the Far Southwest.

Coronado thus performed in North America a feat of adventure and discovery comparable to what was done in South America in the same period by Pizarro, Almagro, Belalcázar, or Quesada, and in Middle America by Cortés, Guzmán, or Alvarado. He converted the old trail up the West Coast Corridor of Mexico into a well-known road which is still in use as an automobile highway and as the route of the Southern Pacific Railroad. Historical tradition in the vast area up the Corridor, and all the way from California to Kansas, runs back four centuries to the spectacular expedition made by Don Francisco and his companions.

The impress left by the young Spaniard on the history and lore of the Southwest is patent and still growing. Geographical designations given or first made known to Europeans by Don Francisco and his men are found all over the map. Names reminiscent of his adventure have been assigned to a multitude of places, objects, institutions, and organizations. We find among Arizona place names Alarcón Terrace, Cárdenas Butte, Coronado Park, Conquistador Aisle, Coronado International Memorial Park, Coronado Mesa, Coronado Mountains, Coronado Summit, Coronado Trail (U. S. Highway No. 666), El Despoblado, Fray Marcos Mountain, Padilla Mesa, Tovar Mesa, and Tobar Terrace. In New Mexico, besides the names of many Indian pueblos first made known by Coronado, there are Cíbola National Forest, Coronado State Monument, and Gran Quivira National Monument. In Kansas we encounter Eldorado and Coronado Heights. Coronado City and Coronado Beach in California, it may be noted, get their names not from Coronado the explorer, but from nearby islands whose designation alludes to certain Christian martyrs. Besides geographical names commemorating Coronado's exploit, the Southwest has Coronado motor courts, schools, and theaters, and at least one Coronado cattle ranch. There is a Coronado hotel as far east as Philadelphia. Among commercial and industrial enterprises one finds a Coronado Carbon Company, a Coronado Petroleum Company, and a Coronado Exploration Company, whose business is that of prospecting for oil.

Somewhat more highbrow than any of the foregoing memorials to the explorer is the historical organization called the Quivira Society. In Omaha even the *bon ton* bow to the famous general. There a leading social group styled Ak-Sar-Ben each year commemorates the Coronado Expedition to Quivira, in whose tradition Nebraska claims a share. In 1940 several of the Southwestern states conducted Coronado celebrations in honor of the four hundredth anniversary of the expedition, conspicuous among them being the one held in New Mexico. The legislature of that commonwealth formed a Coronado Cuarto Centennial Commission which carried out an elaborate and state-wide celebration. As a part of the Coronado memorial the University of New Mexico is issuing a series of historical volumes called the Coronado Cuarto Centennial Publications.

The Coronado Expedition shares in the tradition of Mexico as well as of the United States. Don Francisco Vázquez de Coronado was a conspicuous and honored figure at the court of Mendoza, first viceroy of New Spain. His wife, Doña Beatríz de Estrada, was the wealthiest heiress in the Mexico of her day, notable for her piety and charity, and her fame is recorded on her tomb in one of North America's most historic churches. As governor of Nueva Galicia, which then embraced a vast area west of the capital,

Coronado occupies many pages in the annals of Guadalajara, Compostela, Tepic, and Culiacán, those old cities which charm every visitor within their gates. His spectacular expedition is a chapter in the history of the Mexican states of Jalisco, Nayarit, Sinaloa, and Sonora, as well as of our great Southwest. Thus he is an immortal link between the republics of Mexico and the United States. To symbolize this early historic bond the governments of Mexico and the United States have plans for setting aside and developing an area on the Sonora-Arizona boundary line as a Coronado International Monument.

Whatever merit may be claimed for this book must be left to others than myself. But it may be appropriate to say that besides consulting extensive manuscript sources that hitherto have been used little or not at all, I have made a more detailed reconnoissance of Coronado's route of travel and the scenes of his adventure than any of my predecessors, and thereby have been able to vivify the episode, to clear up many obscure or disputed points, and to offer new interpretations.

TABLE OF CONTENTS

TABLE OF CONTENTS

MAPS

CORONADO

KNIGHT OF PUEBLOS & PLAINS

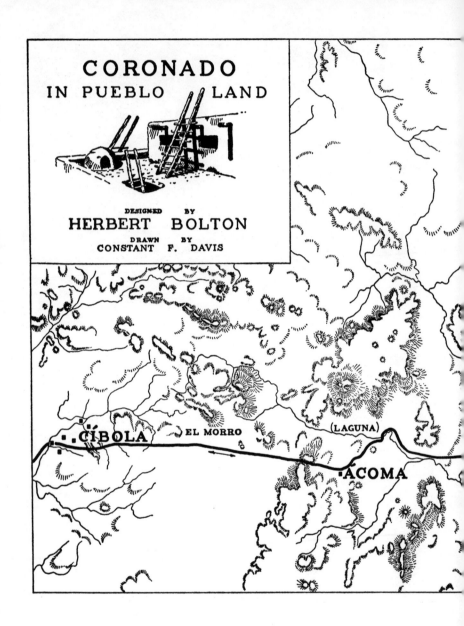

CORONADO
IN PUEBLO LAND

DESIGNED BY
HERBERT BOLTON
DRAWN BY
CONSTANT F. DAVIS

CÍBOLA · EL MORRO · (LAGUNA) · ÁCOMA

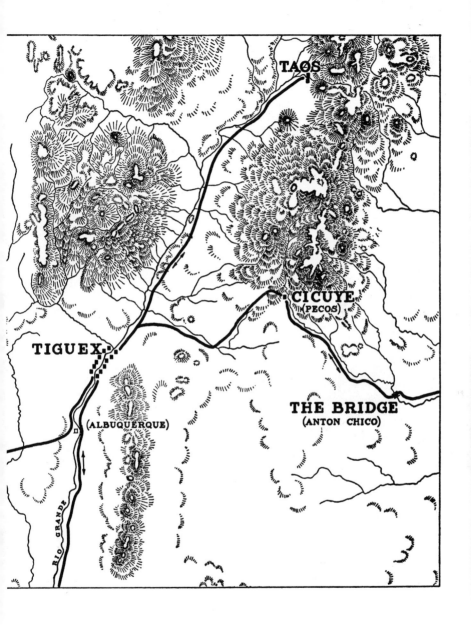

TAOS

CICUYE
(PECOS)

TIGUEX

(ALBUQUERQUE)

THE BRIDGE
(ANTON CHICO)

RIO GRANDE

Chapter I

EL DORADO

The Spanish occupation of mainland America proceeded from an already established base in the West Indies, where Columbus had planted the first European colony in America. Grijalva, sent out to explore by the governor of Cuba, gathered gold on the coast of Mexico and heard of the rich Aztec civilization in the interior. Thereupon Hernando Cortés, with some five hundred men, thirty muskets, a few toy cannons, and sixteen horses, set forth in 1519 from Cuba, a rebel against the island governor, to conquer this land of rumored gold. He arrived on the Vera Cruz coast with sixteen horses and a colt. Here, Grijalva's report was confirmed by the lavish present sent to the bold invader by Montezuma, the frightened ruler at the Aztec capital situated on a lake on the high plateau 250 miles inland.

This astonishing gift was emphatic evidence of the great wealth of Mexico. The present included a gold necklace set with emeralds and hung with pearls, a huge golden disk, as large as a wagon wheel, representing the sun, and another of silver to simulate the moon. There were gold and silver ornaments and toys, feather headdresses decorated with gems, pearl-pointed tridents, amazing feather-work, garments of finely woven cotton, and what were called "books" written in hieroglyphics. The bare list of items comprised in the gift occupies several pages of modern print. It was one of the decisive documents in world history, for it caused a "gold rush" embracing two-thirds of the hemisphere, and brought about revolutionary changes in America, Europe, and Asia.

Montezuma had sent these lavish offerings to induce the unwelcome visitor to depart, but they merely whetted his appetite and fired his imagination. Don Hernando, in turn, sent the treasure to Spain as a bribe to soften the heart of Charles V toward a rebel, and then marched boldly toward the Aztec capital, fighting battles and winning native allies as he went. In spite of a veritable "Dunkirk" in the Noche Triste retreat, he overthrew Montezuma, made himself master of the heart of the country, was forgiven for rebellion, and rewarded by being made captain-general and marquis, with thousands of tributary subjects.

Cortés, by his lucky strike, set everybody in motion. To discover other Mexicos, great prospecting expeditions were organized, some launched in Spain, some in the islands, and others on the mainland of North and South America. As a rule they were privately financed, for the Emperor was thrifty. A typical expedition consisted of a few hundred Spaniards, followed by hordes of natives carrying the baggage, opening roads, performing camp duty, and serving as couriers and interpreters. As far as possible the invaders lived off the country they raided. But in most cases, as a precautionary measure, a commissary department was driven on all fours, and included droves of hogs, herds of cattle, and flocks of sheep and goats, brought from Spain or the West Indies with immeasurable difficulty. Supply ships crossing the ocean with livestock and provisions stank to heaven. Below the Isthmus of Panama, immense droves of llamas were taken along both as pack animals and to serve as food. An airplane view of *Mundus Novus* at almost any time in the two decades after 1520 would have disclosed several different bands of these gold-thirsty prospectors, crawling like armies of ants across the face of the Hemisphere in numerous regions wide apart, all bound on the same errand. In some instances they were able to penetrate the mainland by the great river systems. But whether they traveled by water or by land, their object was the same—wealth and adventure. The ranks of these armies were filled with eager young fellows who had read in Spain or obtained in the book stalls of Mexico and Lima the romances of chivalry just then being published—*Amadís de Gaula, Las Serges de Esplandián, Palmería de Oliva,* and a dozen others, whose influence in the conquest Dr. Irving Leonard has so convincingly set forth.

Many individual soldiers of fortune were ubiquitous, appearing, in spite of the difficulties of travel, here, there, and yonder, now at the top and then at the bottom of the map, like the proverbial prospector who joins every new gold rush. The names of some of these repeaters are familiar to every schoolboy. De Soto pioneered in regions as far apart as Central America, Peru, Florida, and the Mississippi Valley; Pedro de Alvarado in Mexico, Central America, and Ecuador; Cabeza de Vaca in Texas, Mexico, and Paraguay. Las Casas was with the vanguard in Guatemala, Peru, and Mexico; Fray Juan de Padilla in Tehuantepec, Jalisco, New Mexico, and Kansas.

On the mainland the regions inhabited by sedentary natives were usually first to be subjugated, and they became the first centers of permanent Spanish settlement on a considerable scale. The reasons for this are not far to seek. Sedentary people were the easiest to conquer, for they had fixed homes and could not run away. They were the most worth exploiting because they were accustomed to disciplined labor. They had a steady food supply and, in some cases, an accumulation of precious metals. Their daughters were pleasing, so there were many thousands of "Pocahontases" in America long before the days of John Smith of Jamestown. When the Europeans entered the interior they carried with them the extravagant tales they had heard in Europe or the islands, added to their repertoire new ones gathered on the way, and embroidered them with fantastic passementerie of their own fabrication, sometimes with waggish humor. Each track made by the explorers on the enormous map of the New World represents some glowing idea, some feverish quest, and effort to run to its source this or that tale of treasure, some rumored city, some wonder in the country beyond—*mas allá*.

In this expansion the lieutenants of Cortés quickly extended their conquests in all directions from the Aztec capital till most of the sedentary peoples of central and southern Mexico were under Spanish control. Red-headed Pedro de Alvarado pushed into Guatemala, seat of an old civilization, in some respects more remarkable than that of the Aztecs. Panama became a base for expeditions northward into Central America which met and contested the field with the men of Cortés. The fever spread to South America. Panama City was barely three years old when adventurers began to sail down the Pacific coast to investigate rumors of great wealth in Peru. Francisco Pizarro, cousin of Cortés, set forth from the Isthmus to emulate his now millionaire relative. Like Mexico, Peru was easy to conquer because of internal dissensions. Atahualpa, governor of Quito, was in rebellion against the Inca at Cuzco. Pizarro marched inland over the towering Andes and captured Atahualpa, who for his ransom paid a room full of gold and another of silver, the combined value of which has been estimated at several millions of dollars. Pizarro now made himself master of a large part of Peru, founded Lima, and extended his conquest into what are now Bolivia and Chile. Thus Mexico and Lima, established by two humble cousins from rock-strewn Estremadura in Mother Spain, became the capitals of Spanish North and South America.

Settlers at Santa Marta, near the mouth of the great Magdalena River, which pours its waters northward into the Caribbean Sea, heard the legend of the Gilded Man. It told of a tribe in the south, on the high plateau of Bogotá, whose chief was installed by an unusual rite of deep religious significance. He was anointed with oil and sprinkled with gold dust, then, being pushed on a raft out upon the sacred lake of Guatavitá, he dived into the water and washed off the gleaming metal. As part of the ceremony the natives threw into the lake countless gold ornaments and precious stones as offerings to the gods. The gold-sprinkled chief became known to the Spaniards as El Dorado—the Gilded Man. This story inspired a new series of epic marches southward from the Spanish Main, a three-cornered struggle among conquerors, and the founding, by Quesada, of the city of Bogotá, now the cultured capital of the Republic of Colombia. The longest chase of El Dorado was still to come, for when Quesada reached Guatavitá, the Gilded Man was no longer there, so the treasure hunters continued the search eastward over the Andes. In the quest, Orellano navigated the largest river in the world to its mouth. Because of a battle with brawny women on its banks, so the story goes, the river was called and still is known as the Amazon. All this had happened within the space of a few years.

The military success of these small bands of Spaniards—a few hundred in each army at the most—was due to the ability and boldness of their leaders, their possession of gunpowder and horses, and the lack of organization and equipment of the natives. Indians using bows and arrows were as helpless in the face of mounted men and fire-arms as were some of the armies of World War II which, using the weapons of 1914, had to oppose modern tanks and bombing planes. Even more important than the material equipment of the Europeans were the hordes of native allies who joined the invaders. In fact, it might well be said that the Spaniards did not conquer America—the natives, led by the Spaniards, conquered each other.

Cortés, meanwhile, had been active in western Mexico, seeking other El Dorados. He extended the conquest across Michoacán, and, less than a year after the fall of the Aztec capital, his lieutenants reached the Pacific Ocean and there established bases for expansion by sea. A ship sent by Cortés from Zacatula in 1527, safely reached the Moluccas, thus making the first American voyage to the Orient—two and one-half centuries ahead of Robert Gray. Colima, founded on the coast at the foot of the towering volcano, became a base for long strides up the map in pursuit of new and old objectives. The search for slaves, gold, and silver led in that direction. Other lures were reports of a good harbor and tales of Amazons. Native chiefs, said Cortés, "affirm that there is an island inhabited only by women . . . and that at certain times men from the mainland visit them." So the excitement increased.

The conqueror of Mexico was now summoned to Spain to defend his rights in America, and the advance up the west coast was continued by his tough-fibered rival, Nuño de Guzmán.

In 1529 Don Nuño left central Mexico with five hundred Spaniards and several thousand native allies. At Tepic he established a garrison, the germ of the capital of the present state of Nayarit. Going north, and failing to find the Amazons, he turned his attention to a search for the legendary Seven Cities, long famed in European tradition and now transplanted to America. Some time previously, when a conquistador in Pánuco, Don Nuño had contemplated an expedition to the northern interior. An Indian named Tejo told him of a trading jaunt which he had once made with his father in that direction to some rich and populous cities, seven in number. Like the story of the Amazons, this one of Seven Cities came out of the distant past and was brought to America by the discoverers. In the Middle Ages, so the old tale ran, seven Portuguese bishops, pressed by the conquering Mohammedans, fled west into the "Ocean Sea," and founded the Seven Cities of Antilia—hence the name Antilles, given by the Spaniards to the West Indian islands. The story was not confined to Portuguese and Spanish circles. John Cabot, after his celebrated voyage to Newfoundland in 1497 in the service of England, was reputed to have discovered "the isles of Brazil and the Seven Cities," as well as the Kingdom of the Gran Khan of China. Now, if Tejo told the truth, seven cities had been visited not long ago by natives of Mexico. Could these be the same as those of the legend? Whatever they might be, Guzmán decided to seek them by crossing the formidable Sierra Madre Occidental, for it was from Pánuco in the east that Tejo had journeyed north with his father to those terraced towns. The difficult march was made in vain; but, to secure the lands he had conquered on the west coast, Guzmán established the permanent settlement of Culiacán in 1531, just a century before the founding of Boston. Don Nuño himself now withdrew to Tepic, but his colonists extended their explorations and slave hunting raids as far north as the Yaqui River.

This advance into Sinaloa and Sonora by land spurred Cortés to further activities by sea. Returning to Mexico he renewed his expeditions up the coast. Four years later Jiménez, one of his sea captains, discovered pearls on the Peninsula of California, which he thought was an island, and to which the Amazons had retreated. The legend was popularized by Montalvo's best-seller novel of the day in which he wrote: "Know ye that at the right hand of the Indies there is an island called California, very close to that part of the Terrestrial Paradise, which was inhabited by black women without a single man among them, and they lived in the manner of Amazons. They were robust of body with strong, passionate hearts and great virtue. The island itself is one of the wildest in the world on account of its bold and craggy rocks." Two years after its discovery by Jiménez, Cortés himself led a colony to this island of pearls and Amazons. Thus California was brought into history. In that same year, however, Antonio de Mendoza became first viceroy of Mexico, checked the activities of Cortés in the Gulf, caused the withdrawal of the California colony, and sent Guzmán, a prisoner, to Spain.

Chapter II

FOUR RAGGED CASTAWAYS

Meanwhile, from the West Indies, explorers had reconnoitered the vast region then known as La Florida—Land of Flowers—an area lying between the Atlantic Coast and the central prairies, and extending indefinitely northward. This rim of the Caribbean was for a long time the "graveyard of colonies," whether Spanish, French, Dutch, Danish, or English. Ponce de León, seeking among the Bahamas the Fountain of Youth, discovered the Florida Peninsula, and lost his life in an effort to plant a colony there. Ayllón, a solemn judge at Santo Domingo, next threw the dice on the Florida green. Looking for Utopia in Chicora, land of the giant King Datha, he founded a short-lived colony in South Carolina. Story-loving Peter Martyr tells us that King Datha was not naturally monstrous, but in his childhood was merely rubbed with the juice of herbs and stretched. We would now call it a matter of glands. The name Chicora is still preserved in that of a South Carolina college.

Narváez followed—he who had a booming voice which sounded "as if it issued from a cavern." Though he had lost an eye as well as a battle in a contest with Cortés at Vera Cruz, he again gambled with Fate, and again found the cards stacked against him. As governor of Florida he succeeded to more than Ponce's quota of disasters. Landing near Tampa bay, his venturesome band marched boldly north seeking a place called Cale, whose inhabitants were said to wear "golden hats like casques." Cale proved to be anything but golden, so Narváez turned west to look for Apalachen, whose glories the natives had proclaimed. He found it in western Florida, near the site where Tallahassee now stands. Although rich in maize and yellow pumpkins, the province had no gold, and what was worse, the residents were hostile and amused themselves at cracking Spanish heads with war clubs.

So Narváez retreated to the coast and built five horsehide boats, while his followers consumed the flesh of the animals. In this bizarre fleet he set sail with more than 250 disillusioned men, and started down the Gulf shore toward Mexico. The flotilla was first driven out to sea, then wrecked by a storm on the Texas coast. Thus Galveston came into history in a hurricane, as it nearly went out in another some four centuries later. Narváez and most of his companions were drowned, or eaten by cannibal Texans. Four men survived, and after nearly six years among the Indians, much of the time in slavery—a living martyrdom for which they were only partially compensated by becoming known to fame—managed to elude their captors.

Of this quartet the central figure was Alvar Núñez Cabeza de Vaca, treasurer of the Narváez expedition and a man of rare qualities. For more than a year after the shipwreck he was a slave of the natives of Malhado (Galveston) Island and the adjacent Texas coast. He then fled to the interior and became a trader. Meanwhile he acquired fame among the natives as a medicine man, his cures consisting mainly of prayers and the sign of the Cross. Some five lonely years after the shipwreck Vaca met three other survivors of the same expedition who had gone through experiences similar to his own. They were Dorantes, Castillo, and Estevanico, or Stephen, a Moorish slave of Dorantes. Thus, about December, 1533, on Colorado River near the Texas coast, the historic little group laid plans for escape which they put into effect a year later. With many setbacks and vicissitudes, they ascended Colorado River, turned west through the mesquite country, skirted the southern flank of the Llano Estacado, and crossed Pecos River.

Vaca and his companions were sometimes abject slaves carrying heavy loads for cruel masters, but later were revered as Children of the Sun. The stories of the marvelous cures performed by the castaways tax the credulity of a twentieth-century reader. In western Texas their fame as medicine men increased till their progress was seriously impeded by crowds

clamoring to be healed, or even to touch their garments—such
as they had. The Negro Stephen, especially, acquired a mysterious influence over the admiring natives. He quickly learned
their speech and did most of the talking for the party. A gourd
rattle which he obtained along the way gave him added power.
Dorantes also was given a rattle, but it was fashioned of copper
and on it was carved a human face. He was told that the curiosity came from the north where there was much of the same
metal, and it was concluded that where the rattle came from
"there must be foundries, and that the metal was cast in molds."
The travelers were presented with many beads and buffalo
skins, pouches filled with what Vaca called pearls, and powdered
antimony or lead, with which the natives painted their faces.

After many weary months of travel the castaways crossed the
Rio Grande some distance above the place now called El Paso,
where they saw permanent houses whose inhabitants ate beans,
squashes, and maize, and heard of people upstream who had
many cotton fabrics—news which had tremendous consequences.
Here, too, they were told of a famous land of maize "where the
sun sets," and this land became their next objective. At the end
of a difficult and hungry journey lasting more than another
month they reached the Ópata settlements in upper Sonora
Valley—Land of Maize! Their worst trials were over. These
four castaways were the real European pioneers of the great
Southwest. First to see New Mexico and Arizona, they furnished
the immediate cause of the discovery and conquest of the
Pueblo Indians, and of Coronado's great expedition.

In the Sonora Valley the Ópata people welcomed the wayfarers with food and other gifts, many of which they said had
come from distant places. It was the story that Vaca later told
of this rich valley and the things he heard and saw there which
piqued the curiosity of the viceroy and became a decisive factor
in the developments that followed. Continuing south the
travelers threaded the canyon of Sonora River and emerged at
a settlement downstream which Vaca called Corazones, or the
Town of Hearts, because the natives there gave Dorantes "more
than six hundred hearts of deer, of which they always kept a

great store for eating." This generous supply of deer hearts was not for consumption by the four strangers alone, but also for the large band of natives who from here accompanied and guided the pilgrims. Corazones, the gateway to the south, was on Sonora River near Ures at the lower end of the canyon cut by the stream through the ridge that separates the Sonora and Ures valleys. Its inhabitants were not Ópatas, but Lower Pimas, of a different culture.

From Corazones the guides led Vaca and his companions past the sites of present Alamos, Mátape, and Rebeico to Yaqui River, which they apparently struck at Soyopa. Twelve leagues downstream, Vaca writes, "such a rain overtook us that, as the river rose high, we could not cross it, and remained there fifteen days." This halt was probably at Onabas. Vaca was now approaching the "land of his desires," and here on Yaqui River he got his first news of Spaniards on the West Coast. Castillo made the discovery. He "saw on the neck of an Indian a small buckle from a sword belt, and in it was sewed a horseshoe nail." It is not difficult to imagine the excitement which must have followed. Castillo took the buckle from the Indian and inquired about it, "and they said it had come from Heaven." With this view the castaways were disposed to agree, for certainly they could think of nothing more heavenly than a sign of nearby Spaniards. When asked who had brought the buckle to this vicinity, "they answered that some men with beards like ours had come from Heaven to that river; that they had horses, lances, and swords, and had lanced two of the natives," which was not so heavenly after all. These bearded strangers were led by Diego Guzmán, nephew of Don Nuño, who, three years previously, had reached the Yaqui River a short distance downstream. To the pilgrims this story of bearded strangers was the most joyous news they had heard in all the long years since the shipwreck.

The flood subsided, and the travelers continued southward. At Mayo River, Vaca's route joined that of Diego Guzmán. Thus, in the short space of some fifteen years since the men of Cortés first reached the shores of the Pacific Ocean, the Spaniards had opened a continuous road up the West Coast between Colima and the Yaqui Valley, and now it met a trail from the north. Going forward, Vaca saw vestiges of the campsites of Spanish slave catchers, and at Sinaloa River his Indian scouts, hiding behind trees, actually spied mounted Spaniards driving slaves southward. A few days later, says Vaca, "I came upon four Christians on horseback, who, seeing me in such strange attire, and in the company of Indians, were greatly startled. They stared at me speechless; such was their surprise that they could not find words to ask me anything. I spoke first, and told them to lead me to their captain, and we went to Diego Alcaráz, their commander," who seized some of Vaca's followers as slaves. This meeting was in the vicinity of Mocorito.

The wayfarers were now conducted to Culiacán, where they were met by Melchior Díaz, the alcalde mayor, who becomes one of the heroes of our story. He was deeply moved by their account, and righteously angry at Alcaráz for his unfriendly conduct toward the castaways. After a much needed rest the refugees were escorted to Compostela, and there greeted by Governor Nuño de Guzmán, who gave them "what he had" to cover their nakedness. Don Nuño, though a ruthless conqueror, was a gracious host, but his hospitality could not be fully enjoyed by his guests, who had been so long in the wilderness. "For many days," says Vaca, "I could bear no clothing, nor could we sleep, except on the bare floor." Soon the travelers went on their way to Mexico City. They reached the capital on Sunday, eve of the Vespers of St. James, and were warmly welcomed by Viceroy Mendoza and Cortés. Still a true Spaniard, Vaca notes that the day after their arrival there was a church fiesta in honor of Apostle Santiago, with "bullfight and tournament." He felt at home!

CHAPTER III

MENDOZA DECIDES TO GAMBLE

In the capital Vaca became a guest at the viceroy's palace. If the adventurer had not been a gentleman bred he would have felt ill at ease in such surroundings, for young Mendoza held the most exalted office in all North America, over most of which he was now ruler, from the Isthmus to the northernmost borderlands. In the previous November he had entered his capital in great state and with much ceremony. "Trumpeters with gaily colored cloaks and the roll of kettledrums greeted his arrival as the city dignitaries, knights and commoners, went out to meet him arrayed in fiesta attire. Games in the plaza and a repast for the viceroy, his gentlemen, and contestants, following the solemn reading of his commissions by the public crier in the presence of the audiencia, cabildo, and citizens, completed the official ceremonies provided at the cost of the city." So writes Aiton, Don Antonio's biographer. Mendoza set up an impressive household, quite in contrast with the sordid native camps in which Vaca had lived for the past eight years. "Sixty Indian servants were always in attendance on him and his guests in his palace, where he maintained a miniature court. From thirty to forty gentlemen, foot and horse, composed a bodyguard which was always about him, and formed an escort when he went abroad. . . . In the midst of the crowd of retainers and vassals, and with his own family, represented by his son Francisco and his sister María, Mendoza lived in almost regal splendor."

The reports given by Vaca and his companions could not fail to command the viceroy's attention. Beyond the outermost region reached by Diego de Guzmán, they had visited people who lived in permanent houses in a fertile and populous valley.

They raised plentiful maize, squash, and beans, and wore cotton blankets "better than those of New Spain"; they traded parrot plumes for turquoises, emeralds, and buffalo robes with people living still farther north in "very large houses"; and they had easy access to a famous pass into many provinces near the South Sea, where they obtained coral, and on whose shores there were "a thousand leagues of inhabited land," where the natives raised "three crops of beans and maize each year." No one indicated in what direction those thousand leagues ran. Finally, throughout all that country, wherever it was mountainous, Vaca reported "many signs of gold, antimony, iron, copper, and other metals." Could it be another El Dorado of which the refugees had heard? Another Mexico? Or perhaps the Seven Cities which Guzmán had sought in vain?

One would not be surprised under the circumstances if a wild rush to the northwest had occurred. But no such thing happened; and reasons for this can be found. Guzmán was discredited and was fast fading out of the picture. Cortés had just withdrawn from the Island of Pearls under discouraging circumstances. Mendoza had come as viceroy primarily to establish royal authority on this seething American frontier, and to put a check on anybody whose ambitions and power might make him dangerous to the interests of the Crown. He was especially instructed to end rampant Indian slavery and other abuses practiced by the conquistadores, most notably by Guzmán. Altogether, the atmosphere at the moment was not encouraging to swashbucklers.

Mendoza welcomed any real opportunity to discover and exploit new lands beyond the border, for he must enhance as well as preserve the royal patrimony. But when Vaca reached the capital the viceroy had been there less than a year and was just getting a firm seat in a none too easy saddle. So Don Antonio, in keeping with his character, moved cautiously. But he was by no means asleep. He not only gave generous hospitality to Vaca and his ragged companions, but held several conferences with them and listened to their almost incredible tale. As a consequence, he decided to make further inquiry, and, if warranted by the prospects, to enter the field of exploration and "to appropriate to himself the fame of conquering new and rich civilizations for the king." In any case, he had no intention of letting someone else reap the profit and the glory which were due to himself as the highest representative of the Emperor in all North America. But careful investigation was necessary, and Mendoza was immersed in a welter of duties arising from his new and important office.

Vaca and his companions prepared for the viceroy a report of their travels, and, according to Beaumont, a map of the regions they had visited. It has been inferred that Mendoza proposed to Vaca and Dorantes that they should head a further reconnoissance of the regions which they had traversed or had heard of en route. But in the fall of 1536 both of these veteran pedestrians decided to return to Spain. Vaca had plans of his own, and a personality which would give them weight at the royal Court. Stephen was obtained by Mendoza with a view to sending him north as guide when a new inquiry should be undertaken, for obviously the Negro would be useful for such a purpose, he having been everywhere with Vaca, "being an intelligent person," as Mendoza testified, and having a special gift for dealing with Indians. Castillo, weary of travel, married a widow, with her acquired an estate, and remained in Mexico.

After long delays, one false start, and a sea voyage fraught with storms and pirates, Cabeza de Vaca, armed with a letter of recommendation from Mendoza to the Emperor, arrived at last, on August 9, 1537, in Lisbon, Portugal, whence he went to Spain. Behind him were ten as hazardous years as any man ever survived. Alvar Núñez had returned home with a fabulous tale to tell but not to settle down, for he was destined to new exploits equal to any he had experienced in North America. Arrived in Spain, he applied to the Emperor for a commission as conquistador of La Florida in place of long-dead Narváez, only to learn that Hernando de Soto had just been awarded the dangerous honor. One would assume that Vaca had seen enough of that land of his misfortune. But not so. As an alternative to Florida, he was sent as governor and captain-general to rule in Paraguay, South America—so vast already was Spain's reach in the New World.

The more Mendoza thought about the reports brought from the north by Vaca and his companions, the warmer waxed his interest. Learning that Dorantes was in Vera Cruz, awaiting passage for Spain, the viceroy wrote to him there, requesting him to return to the capital. He wished to talk things over. This was sometime after April 10, 1537, a date whose significance will later appear. Don Andrés responded to the summons, and Mendoza proposed that he should lead to the north country a party of friars and soldiers "to find out for certain what was there." This would be a cautious move and not too expensive. Dorantes "gladly" consented, and on December 10, Mendoza reported the plan to the Emperor, estimating that to equip the expedition would cost not more than four thousand pesos. The gamble, he thought, was worth that small sum in a world where everything was a lottery. But the project fell through, and the circumstances, whatever they were, irritated the viceroy, a fact which he did not conceal. To the Emperor he peevishly wrote: "Andrés Dorantes, one of those comprising the army of Pánphilo de Narváez, has come to me, and I have had frequent conferences with him, thinking he might render a great service to your Majesty if I should send him with forty or forty-five horsemen and all the things necessary to explore that country. I have spent a great amount of silver for the expedition, but for reasons unknown to me the affair has come to naught. From all the preparations I have made there are left to me only a Negro who came with Dorantes, some slaves whom I have purchased, and some Indians, natives of the country, whom I have assembled." Don Andrés for the moment was out of the viceroy's favor. It appears that before Vaca and Dorantes separated they had planned a joint enterprise for the land of their adventure, and this may have been Dorantes' reason for not coöperating with Mendoza.

This episode ended the active connection of Dorantes with northern exploration, but it did not by any means terminate his career. The hardy qualities he had shown on the trail with

Vaca still persisted. Like his old companon, Castillo, he remained in Mexico, married a widow, and became a person of importance, esteemed by the viceroy as a *"caballero muy principal."*

Dorantes having proved so disappointing, Mendoza turned elsewhere for help. Friars had shown themselves to be fearless explorers and skillful diplomats among the native tribes of America, for they went armed with gentleness and messages of hope, whereas soldiers carried terrifying weapons and were prone to use them. One such friar, already famous as Protector of the Indians, was the fervent Dominican, Bartolomé de las Casas. Both his zeal and his bravery were proverbial alike in Europe and America. Might there not be found another friar with similar qualities? In fact, just at the psychological moment one such appeared on the scene in the person of Fray Marcos de Niza.

This remarkable missionary-adventurer, and many of the missionaries were adventurers, had lived at Nice, in the Duchy of Savoy, hence his usual designation as Marcos de Niza. Though still a comparatively young man he was already a veteran in the New World. He had crossed the Atlantic when every such voyage required courage. He came in 1531 to Santo Domingo where, as missionary, he took part in the rough and tumble life of that turbulent island. His arrival there was just when Guzmán was founding Culiacán and when Vaca was a slave in Texas. From Santo Domingo he went to Guatemala, thence with Alvarado to South America. In Peru he met Pizarro and is said to have witnessed the execution of the Inca Atahualpa and the division of the fabulous spoils. He was also present when Alvarado sold to Almagro his rights in the conquest of Ecuador, for leaden dollars it has been said. By September, 1536, he was back in Guatemala, whence he wrote to the great Zumárraga, first bishop of Mexico, telling of his experiences in Peru. The prelate replied, urging him to come to Mexico, and he responded to the summons, arriving in the capital before April 4, 1537. It is said that he walked all the way from Guatemala, "barefooted as was his custom." This pedestrian habit may be partly legendary.

Zumárraga's interest now became decisive. He made Fray Marcos his house guest, listened to his story of cruelties to the Indians in South America, had him put the account in writing, and introduced him to the viceroy. Both Mendoza and Zumárraga were shocked at the recital. They sent copies of the narrative to Spain, and it is said to have been incorporated by Las Casas in his sensational book called the *Destruction of the Indies!*

From the foregoing, it is seen that Fray Marcos had just arrived in Mexico and talked with Mendoza when, early in 1537, the viceroy suddenly called Dorantes back from Vera Cruz. Did Fray Marcos suggest the summons, or was it fiery Zumárraga? And was it intended that Fray Marcos should accompany Dorantes to the north country told of by Cabeza de Vaca? It would appear so, for at or about the same time when Mendoza reported the failure of negotiations with Dorantes he asked the Emperor's permission to send Fray Marcos north on the same errand. The friar was already a marked man, and his selection for the adventure is no cause for surprise. "This father," wrote Zumárraga, "is reliable, of approved virtue and fine religious zeal." On April 17, 1538, the desired permission was granted by Charles V, and must have reached Mexico in the summer or early fall. In the interim Marcos and Fray Onorato, his companion, were engaged in missionary work in the west. But Marcos was back in Mexico City in September, and in that month he left the capital for Nueva Galicia, preparatory to his embassy to the far north.

The formal assignment of Fray Marcos to his new duty was made by the Chapter of his Order at the request of Mendoza, Fray Onorato being appointed as his companion in the prospective jaunt. Of the qualifications of Marcos for exploration, Father Ciudad-Rodrigo, then Franciscan Provincial in Mexico, declared in writing that he was "skilled in cosmography and in the arts of the sea, as well as in theology." The viceroy adds his own testimonial to the fitness of the two missionaries chosen for the important task at hand. "These friars have lived in the neighboring country,"—west of the capital—"they are habituated to hardships, experienced in the affairs of the Indies, conscientious, and of exemplary conduct." Brother Marcos had more than this, something that both Zumárraga and Mendoza had already recognized. He had the qualities of a born promoter— physical stamina, imagination, ardor, optimism, and an ability to dramatize himself and everything he touched. He would have made a great movie star.

In preparation for the proposed Dorantes expedition to the north, Mendoza had not only acquired the Negro Stephen, but also had assembled Indians from the country beyond Culiacán, some of whom had been members of Vaca's retinue as he descended the coast. These natives were now assigned to Friar Marcos for the new enterprise. Stephen was to go as guide and diplomat, for he had demonstrated exceptional gifts in dealing with the Indians. He had a way with him, and like a medicine man, he carried a gourd rattle, the one he had obtained in his long march across Texas.

The supervision of the new enterprise which Mendoza now planned was entrusted to young Francisco Vázquez de Coronado. Don Francisco was in many ways a typical Spanish adventurer in the New World. He had come to Mexico at the age of twenty-five as one of the gentlemen in the train of Viceroy Mendoza, to whom he had been favorably known at Court in Old Spain. A native of Salamanca, he was a younger son in a family of lesser nobles, a position not always enviable. Don Francisco's father, as corregidor of Burgos, was wealthy enough to found an entailed estate (*mayorazgo*) by which his eldest son, Gonzalo, inherited the bulk of the family patrimony. Two sisters, with "suitable endowments," were sent to convents to become nuns and thus removed from the matrimonial market.

The rule of primogeniture had consequences not intended, for its results were not wholly conservative. By it, younger sons were driven to initiative—even to revolution. The younger Coronado brothers no doubt cursed their fate when they learned they had been given terminal settlements, without further right of inheritance. Don Juan and Don Francisco came to America to seek their fortunes, as did hundreds of other younger sons of noble families, for the New World was already the land of opportunity. Juan became an official in Costa Rica, there made a good name for himself, and there his descendants still live. Francisco cast his lot with Viceroy Mendoza, and with him entered Mexico City in 1535, amid pageantry and blare of trumpets. He was pioneering *de luxe*.

Coronado rose rapidly, for he was attractive and popular, and, more to the point, he enjoyed the viceroy's favor. We may assume that he was handsome, which we know was true of his brother Juan, of whom we have a portrait. It has been surmised that, like Juan, he was fair-haired, but this is only an idle guess. Francisco's prestige was vastly enhanced when, within two years after his arrival, he married Doña Beatríz, daughter and heiress of wealthy Alonso de Estrada, deceased treasurer of New Spain and a reputed son of King Ferdinand—on the wrong side of the blanket. In this left-handed way, Coronado was now linked with royalty. Castañeda tells us that the bride was beautiful as well as rich, and we know that for her piety and good works she became known as "the Saint." From his capture of a lady possessed of both charm and wealth we must conclude that although impecunious, Coronado had what it takes. The wedding gift from Señora Estrada, the American mother-in-law, was "half of Tlapa," a large and profitable hacienda south of Mexico City. To make life pleasant for daughter and son-in-law, Doña Marina moved out of her city mansion, and the newly-weds moved in.

The Goddess of Fortune continued to smile on Don Francisco. He was sent by Mendoza in 1537 to suppress an uprising outside the capital, a commission which he energetically fulfilled. Next year, again through Mendoza's favor, he became regidor, or member of the city council, in the capital of New Spain. Coronado's next step up the ladder of success was his appointment as governor of Nueva Galicia, the office until recently held by Nuño de Guzmán. He was putting his feet in a big man's shoes. How this came about can be quickly explained.

Don Nuño's harsh policy on the frontier had scandalized nearly everybody, and to fill his place Emperor Charles V appointed Pérez de la Torre (March 17, 1536), with instructions to investigate his predecessor's official conduct. Torre departed from Spain promptly and arrived in Mexico before the end of the year. Scenting danger, Guzmán attempted to escape to Spain, but it was too late. His horse did not show sufficient speed. Pérez met him at Mendoza's palace in Mexico City and had him arrested, while his numerous enemies grinned with satisfaction, at the same time that his henchmen trembled in their boots. For many months Guzmán was kept in prison, and was then sent to Spain for further inquiry by the royal officials. There he spent the next four years cooling his heels and urging his rights to a share in the northern conquests which were stimulated by Vaca's narrative. Pérez was killed in battle by rebellious Indians. Thereupon Mendoza, about the middle of August, 1538, appointed Coronado governor of Nueva Galicia, an action subsequently confirmed by the Emperor Charles V. Of a son of Pérez we shall hear exciting tales.

Thus were heavy responsibilities put upon the shoulders of a youth of twenty-eight. Coronado now occupied the key position with reference to the development of the northwestern frontier. In this capacity he was the successor of two such men of experience, stamina, and initiative as Cortés and Guzmán. He was on a hot spot. The major enterprise in the viceroy's mind when he appointed young Coronado was coöperation with Fray Marcos and Stephen in their projected expedition up the Pacific Coast to check the reports made by Vaca and his companions. At the same time Don Francisco was instructed to succor needy Culiacán, protect the natives there from abuse by the settlers, and suppress a threatened Indian uprising. Moreover, rumors of gold at Topira (Topia), east of Culiacán, demanded investigation. Coronado was ordered to make inquiries concerning this matter, and given authority to utilize the services of Fray Marcos for the purpose. If anything important came of it, Mendoza was ready to go in person to take a hand, and apparently he itched to do so.

The new governor, with official escort, was soon on his way to take charge of the western province and to speed the grey-robed explorer on his journey. At Tonalá, on November 20, 1538, Don Francisco delivered to the friar a copy of Mendoza's instructions regarding his journey to the north. Coronado, Fray Marcos, and Stephen the Moor were at this moment embarking on an adventure which would link their names forever.

The stage was set. Let the curtain rise!

CHAPTER IV

FRAY MARCOS SEEKS THE SEVEN CITIES

Coronado left the capital for Nueva Galicia with a considerable force of "gentlemen," whom he was expected to keep profitably employed and out of mischief. Like himself they were mainly newcomers from Spain, fortune-hunters in the New World. While he was at Tonalá messengers came breathless with a call for help from Culiacán, where staunch Melchior Díaz was alcalde mayor. Ayapín, a rebellious chief, was besieging the town, and the starving inhabitants were threatening to abandon it. So Coronado hurried west, followed by Fray Marcos and his companions. The governor must have traveled *á la ligera*, for by December 15 he had reached Compostela, capital of his province, and moved it from the old site at Tepic to the place it now occupies, a few miles inland. He informed Mendoza by letter that within a week he would go forward to Culiacán. Affairs there could not wait.

When all was ready the caravan set forth—the governor, Fray Marcos, Fray Onorato, Stephen, their Indian companions, the pack train, and an escort of soldiers. In spite of Coronado's glittering armor, the conspicuous figure in the party was sandal-shod Fray Marcos, the man who had seen Pizarro and the Inca in Peru. They made their way past Tepic, down the easy slope to Rio Santiago, and thence to Culiacán, through the dense jungle over trails already opened by Guzmán and his colonists. The enthusiastic reception tendered Marcos by the Indians was recounted by Coronado in communications written to Mendoza on the way. "It is impossible," he says, "to give a better idea of the manner in which he has been welcomed during his journey than I have already set forth in . . . my letters from Compostela

and San Miguel. . . . If they had received him only one-tenth
as warmly it would have been more than enough."

The matter of first concern at Culiacán was the rebellion,
and with the aid of Díaz, Coronado stamped it out with vigor.
He writes: "When Ayapín saw that . . . the people were coming
to me peacefully, he fled to the fastnesses of some very rough
mountains, where, pursuing him relentlessly, I apprehended
him." This was the official "I." It was in fact Díaz who caught
the culprit, under Coronado's orders. "After capturing him I
brought him to trial, where he was found guilty and sentenced
to death, and I ordered him quartered. This execution completed the task of stabilizing and pacifying the land."

Pleasanter things occupied a part of the young governor's
time at Culiacán. In the midst of grim duties he found room
for tender thoughts of Doña Beatríz. Melchior Díaz, as a
knightly gesture, gave him two Indian women to send to her as
servants. Coronado demurred on the ground that Mexico was
far away and the road very difficult—they would probably have
to walk the entire distance. And there were legal aspects of the
problem, for the women were of free status. When Coronado
was being confessed at Culiacán by Father Antonio de Castilblanco, he disclosed his doubts in the case. And of them was relieved by Father Antonio, who charged him to send the women
to Mexico as a matter of conscience. With Doña Beatríz they
would be taught womanly arts and crafts. More important, they
would become Christians, otherwise they might remain in their
heathendom and be lost. So Don Francisco sent the women to
the capital. One of them married but soon died. The other was
still living with Doña Beatríz five years later. Another subject
for reform came to the governor's attention. Finding some
thirty Spaniards at Culiacán living with Indian women, Coronado, seconded by Fray Marcos, required them to be married
in facie ecclesia, and thus legitimatized a goodly infusion of
Indian blood into the pioneer stock on that frontier.

Meanwhile Coronado sounded out the temper of the natives who lived on the road to the north and prepared the way
for the embassy. "When the journey of exploration was thus

assured," he tells us, "Fray Marcos, his friend [Fray Onorato], the Negro, and other slaves and Indians whom I had given them departed, after twelve days devoted to their preparations." It is not clear just how these twelve days were related to the time spent by Marcos on an excursion made at this time into the sierra to check rumors of great wealth in Topira, a matter to which Coronado devoted some time after the friar started north.

The nature of the errand on which Fray Marcos had embarked is set forth in lengthy instructions given to him by Mendoza. The friar's task was one of exploration in general as well as of inquiry into the particular things reported by Cabeza de Vaca, since from the venture Mendoza hoped for enlightenment regarding the whole northwest. Marcos must note the peoples and the natural features of the country through which he passed. He must keep his ears open for news of both the South Sea and the North—that is, both the Pacific and the Atlantic oceans, "since the land might become narrow." A few years previously, Verrazano had crossed the Maryland peninsula and mistaken Chesapeake Bay for the Pacific Ocean. For some time thereafter, map makers gave the Western Hemisphere two narrow isthmuses, like a lady with two slender waists in different latitudes, and evidently Vaca's journey had not shattered the notion that in the north the oceans were close together. In the name of the viceroy, Marcos must take formal possession of all important lands, rivers, or harbors, tell the natives there is a God in heaven whom all must obey, and send back messengers with reports of his reception and of his discoveries. This was a large order for so small an exploring party, and it causes one to wonder whether the written instructions were not greatly modified by word of mouth. The formal draft may have been intended for the eyes of the Emperor.

Early in March, 1539, Fray Marcos left Culiacán on his fateful errand. With him went Brother Onorato, the Negro Stephen, and the Indians freed by the viceroy for the purpose. Besides, there were natives from Petatlán and El Cuchillo, friends of Cabeza de Vaca who had come at Coronado's call and were now escorting the friars to their own country. Apparently everyone went on foot, unaided by horse, mule, or burro, although two greyhounds belonging to the Negro trotted along with the party. In contrast to black Stephen, from whose arms and ankles bells jingled merrily, Fray Marcos, at the request of Coronado, was clad in a sober habit of grey Zaragoza cloth, and in his pack he carried samples of pearls, gold, and precious stones to show the Indians met along the way, as a means of ascertaining what treasures of this sort were known to them. Stephen's baggage, carried by Indian servants, included dishes of various colors, and a gourd rattle decorated with strings of little bells and two feathers, one white and one red. The rattle was one he had acquired while among the Indians of western Texas. He would have been wiser had he left it behind.

The friar's first report to Coronado, written a few days after the party set out, told jubilantly of his initial success. The natives had given him the warmest welcome possible and rendered him every service within their power. The governor forwarded the letter to Mendoza and both made plans to follow Marcos, should news of sufficient import arrive. Expansive ideas were in the air!

Meanwhile the friars trudged northward some sixty leagues to Petatlán—the place of mats—on Sinaloa River. Here, after a rest of three days because Fray Onorato was ill, Marcos left his companion to be carried on a litter back to Culiacán, while he, guided "by the Holy Spirit" and Stephen, continued on his triumphal way. Incidentally, we know that Fray Onorato recovered and returned to Compostela. Farther on, Marcos met some Indians who had come from the coast, part of them being from an island where there were pearls, but they brought none of these jewels with them. At Rio Fuerte, where the natives called him *Sayota*, "Man from Heaven," Fray Marcos learned that a few days beyond, "where the chains of mountains end," there was a level opening *(abra)* with much land and very large settlements of people who wore cotton garments, and had vessels, nose and ear pendants, and sweat scrapers, all made of gold. This was news indeed! The abra thus described was at Mayo River and the people of whom he heard lived in villages along the banks of that stream. Some parts of Marcos' story are hard to check, but they are not vital to our purpose.

Northward the friar continued, and two days before Passion Sunday (March 21) arrived at a large settlement called Vacapa,[1] where he remained until after Easter Sunday. From here messengers were despatched to bring people from the coast to be questioned, and Stephen was sent ahead on the trail "to see whether it was possible to learn of something grand" of the kind they were seeking. Accompanied by Bartolomé, a native lad who had joined the group at Petatlán, Stephen was to go fifty or sixty leagues. If, however, he should learn of a land of great moment he should go no farther, but either return in person or send back Indian couriers. A symbol was agreed upon. If the country heard of was moderately important, the messenger should bring back to Marcos a white cross a palm in length; if of great importance, two palms long; "and if it were something greater and better than New Spain, he should send a large cross." On Passion Sunday, March 23, after the midday meal, Stephen and Bartolomé took their leave of Marcos, and to the settlements on the trail ahead of him the Negro despatched runners with his mystic rattle.

Imagine the friar's surprise when, four days later, messengers arrived at Vacapa bearing a cross as high as a man and urging the friar to hasten forward. Stephen had encountered people who gave him information of the "greatest country in the world," and there were with him Indians who actually had visited that wonderland. One of them, in fact, had come with the couriers to Vacapa. "This person," says Fray Marcos, "told me such great things about the region that I refused to believe them until I should see them later on, or have more certainty regarding the matter. He told me that it was thirty days' travel from the place where Stephen then was to the first city of that country, which is called Cíbola," that city being only one of seven. This appears to be the first time Spaniards heard the name Cíbola applied to the Seven Cities. They had previously

[1] This Vacapa was in Sinaloa, and was not the one in northwestern Sonora visited by Kino much later.

heard of Seven Cities, but not "Seven Cities of Cíbola." In the
old legend they were the "Seven Cities of Antilia."

Fray Marcos' informant, who was probably a Mayo, declared
that in the first province alone there were seven large cities, all
under one ruler and composed of houses of stone and mortar,
the smallest being one storey high. Others were of two, or three,
or even four storeys. "And on the doors of the principal houses
there were many decorations composed of turquoise stones, of
which there was a great abundance in that land." Moreover,
there were other provinces farther on, much greater than Cíbola. "I gave thanks to the Lord," says Marcos, "but because I
had promised the messengers I had sent to the sea that I would
await them, I deferred my departure in pursuit of Estéban . . .
thinking that he would wait for me as we had agreed." He had
a surprise in store.

Experience with natives in the West Indies, Central America,
Peru, and Mexico had taught Fray Marcos to be patient. So,
eager though he must have been to hasten after Stephen, he
remained at Vacapa until the couriers he had sent to the Gulf
arrived on Easter Sunday, bringing with them Indians from the
coast. These people wore shells of a kind which sometimes had
pearls, told of islands whose inhabitants traveled about on rafts,
and presented Fray Marcos with shields made of hides, so large
that they covered a warrior from head to foot, and so tough,
said the friar, "that I do not believe they could be pierced by
a crossbow." This same day Marcos was visited by three tattooed
Indians who lived somewhere in the east or northeast, and who
confirmed Stephen's story of the Seven Cities.

By now other messengers had come from Stephen with a
cross as tall as the first one, and urging the friar to hurry. So,
on April 8, about a month after he had left Culiacán, Marcos
set out eagerly from Vacapa in pursuit of his dark skinned am-
bassador. In three days he reached the pueblo whence Stephen
had first sent news of Cíbola and where he had promised to
wait—but no Stephen! The villagers corroborated the story of
the Seven Cities, and said they had been there to trade for turquoises and cowhides, many of which Marcos now saw in their

possession. They told also of other kingdoms near Cíbola, called Marata, Acus, and Totonteac, names now first heard by Spaniards. Clearly, as far south as Sinaloa, the Seven Cities were well known.

Next day the friar hastened forward to another settlement, where again he found a large cross, a summons to hurry, and word from Stephen that he would be waiting at the end of the first *despoblado,* or uninhabited region, that lay ahead. Fray Marcos was now in the fertile valley of the Mayo River, of whose settlements he had heard when he was near Fuerte River. Here, evidently about at Conicari, in compliance with his instructions, Marcos "erected two crosses and took possession." The friar now understood the Abra to be the opening of Mayo Valley toward the east. "Since this Abra leads away from the coast," he writes, "and my instructions were not to depart from there, I decided to leave it for the return, when it would be possible to see it better." The attractions of the Abra had faded beside the scintillating news of Cíbola. Moreover, Marcos wanted to catch up with the Negro, whose behavior was exasperating.

Stephen was greedy for wealth, and there were women in the case. "It seems that, after the friars and the Negro had started," says Castañeda, "the Negro did not get on well with the friars, because he took the women that were given him, collected turquoises, and accumulated a stock of everything. Besides, the Indians in those places through which they went got along with Stephen better [than with Fray Marcos] because they had seen the Negro before. This was the reason he was sent ahead to open the way and pacify the Indians." The chronicler now charges Stephen with vaulting ambition: "He thought he could get all the reputation and honor himself, and that if he alone should discover those settlements with such famous high houses, he would be considered bold and courageous." But it must be admitted that preparations were made along the road for Marcos, who found everything arranged for his coming, which would hardly have been the case if Stephen had been altogether disloyal.

Going forward, apparently on the Rio Cedros trail, Marcos went through settlements close together, at all of which he was warmly received and where he saw "many turquoises and cowhides" from Cíbola. At the end of five days he was again summoned by Stephen. This time the Negro promised he would wait at Corazones, the place where, on the long hike from Texas, his former master, Dorantes, had received the gift of six hundred hearts of deer. But when, after Fray Marcos passed a *pueblo fresco*—which may have been Nuri, where the people wore turquoise ornaments and talked much of "Seven Cities, Kingdoms, and Provinces," then crossed a desert lasting four days, and reached Corazones, Stephen again had disappeared.

Now comes another puzzle. Fray Marcos tells us: "Here I learned that the coast very suddenly turns west . . . and since this is a matter of importance I wished to know about it. So I went to it and saw clearly that in 35° it does swing west, which caused me no less joy than the good news of the country." Thus, with seven lines, Fray Marcos disposes of what would have been a journey of at least four hundred miles, from the Sonora River at Ures to the head of the Gulf of California and back. And of course he was nowhere near latitude 35°—not above 30° in fact. Scholars have concluded that Fray Marcos did not in person make this side trip, but perhaps reported what was told him by the Indians and misunderstood.

In Valle de Sonora, above the pass at Corazones, Marcos stopped long enough to give a more graphic account of this famous oasis than the one left us by Cabeza de Vaca. The center of the valley, the place to which the name Sonora was then specifically attached, was about at modern Huepac. Turquoises, cotton cloth (*mantas*), and buffalo hides were everywhere in evidence—and all came from Cíbola. As to turquoises, the Beau Brummels here each wore three or four strings, whereas those of Pueblo Fresco were content with only one. "And so," says Marcos, "I traveled through that valley five days. It is so thickly settled with intelligent people, and so well supplied with provisions that it could furnish food for more than three hundred horsemen."

Here everyone knew of Cíbola and told the friar about the place "like persons who had been there many times." When Marcos looked skeptical about the many-storeyed houses, they gave him a visual demonstration. They took earth and ashes, poured water on the mixture, as if making mortar, showed him how they placed the stones, and told him how they ascended to the top of the building. Facetiously, Marcos asked if the Cíbolans could fly. "They laughed and represented the ladder as well as I could have done it myself." Now, for the first time, the friar actually met a citizen of the fabulous country whither he was bound. A fugitive from justice, it is true, this person confirmed all that Marcos previously had heard and gave many additional details, telling, for instance, of the Kingdom of Totonteac, where clothing was made from the wool of animals the size of Stephen's greyhounds. He would gladly guide Marcos to Cíbola if the friar would help him obtain a pardon there.

Now a legendary beast, out of Pliny perhaps, got mixed up in Fray Marcos' mind with what the Sonora people told him. "They brought me a hide half as big again as that of a large cow," he says, "and told me that it was from an animal which has only one horn, on the forehead; and that this horn is bent toward the breast, and that from there a prong comes straight out, and is so tough that nothing however strong can break it. . . . And they say there are many of these animals in that country. The color of the body is like that of a he-goat and the hair as long as one's finger." Was this a buffalo bull of which the natives were telling him? Or was it some legendary monstrosity?

Preparations now were made for the traverse of the Despoblado, the great uninhabited area which, the friar said, began four days from Valle de Sonora, and whose crossing required fifteen days. Here in the upper Sonora Valley, Stephen had been equipped for the arduous journey with more than three hundred companions and carriers, and now messengers arrived saying that willful person was at present traveling across the vast desolate region. No longer as patient as at Vacapa, Marcos urged his Sonora friends to hasten their arrangements for his trek, "because each day seemed to me a year, on account of my desire to see Cíbola." So he set forth, accompanied by thirty or more chiefs and headmen in gala attire, decked out with turquoise necklaces, some of the caciques wearing five or six strings, and by a large train of carriers of supplies for the long march. It was a triumphal procession.

The road to Cíbola, we know from later evidence, led up Sonora River, past the site of Cananea, over the divide near the present international boundary, down San Pedro River perhaps to Benson, then northeasterly across Arivaipa Valley to Eagle Pass, the opening between the Santa Teresa and Pinaleño Mountains. Here apparently stood the ruin known as Chichilticale which became a conspicuous landmark on the road to Cíbola. Thence the trail ran northward to Gila River and across the Colorado Plateau to the vicinity of St. Johns, then northeastward to Zuñi. As far as he traveled Marcos was presumably on this trail. Some writers used to think that he entered Arizona by way of Santa Cruz River and Casa Grande, and they found encouragement in this view from an inscription bearing the name of Fray Marcos which came to light a few years ago in the vicinity of Phoenix. Recently, however, Bartlett and Colton, two Arizona scholars, cleverly proved that the crude scratches on the rock are a clumsy fraud of modern origin.

On the ninth of May, some two months after leaving Culiacán, Fray Marcos and his retinue entered the Despoblado. "On the first day," he writes, "we arrived to eat dinner at a watering place which the Indians had designated for me, and then at another . . . and there were old houses and many vestiges of fire, left by the people who went by this road to Cíbola. In this manner I traveled twelve days, always very well supplied with food—deer, hares, and partridges, of the same color and savor as those of Spain, although . . . a little smaller." From what he said of the distance across the Despoblado, calling it fifteen days, the friar and his caravan would now be three days from Cíbola, whose first pueblo was some twelve miles west of the present-day Zuñi, New Mexico, and near the Arizona-New Mexico line. But there are indications that the friar was not so far north.

Fray Marcos now received what may have been the severest
shock of his adventurous life, for suddenly one of Stephen's
companions came fleeing, with the story that the Negro had met
disaster at Cíbola. With difficulty, Marcos says, he calmed the
fears of his followers. After going forward two days, and when
within one day from Cíbola, they came upon two more fugitives, "all bloody and with many wounds," whereupon everybody, including Fray Marcos, began to weep "from pity and
fear."

Quiet having been restored, the fugitives told their tale.
They said that when Stephen and his companions were at this
same place, the Negro, according to his custom on the long
march, sent messengers ahead carrying his gourd rattle with its
bright feathers, ribbons, and little bells. They were instructed
to tell the Lord of Cíbola that Stephen was coming to make
peace with the Cíbolans and to doctor them, for he was a medicine man who had performed magical cures. But the messengers
were in for a surprise. When they handed the rattle to the
Señor, he, seeing the cascabeles, was very angry. Dashing the
gourds to the ground, he said, "I know these people, because
these cascabeles are not of the same shape as ours. Tell them to
go back at once, otherwise not a man of them will be left alive."

When the couriers returned to Stephen, he boastfully said
that he would have a better reception. Just watch him! "And so,
with all his following . . . he went forward and arrived at the
city of Cíbola just when the sun was about to set." But they did
not permit him to enter the city, lodging him instead outside,
in a large house with good accommodations. "And then they
took from Stephen everything he was carrying, saying that the
Señor so ordered it. And during the whole night they gave us
nothing to eat or drink."

"Next day, when the sun was a lance high," the fugitives
continued, "Stephen came out of the house, and some of the
head men with him. Then many people came outside the city,
and when he saw them he began to flee, and we with him. Then
they gave us these arrow wounds and we fell down and others
fell dead upon us. And thus we remained until night, not daring

to stir. We heard loud shouting in the city and saw on the flat roofs many men and women who were watching. But we did not see Stephen any more, and we think they shot him with arrows, and those who were with him, for no one escaped except ourselves"—three out of more than three hundred!

Such was the tale of the fugitives as recounted by Fray Marcos when he returned to Mexico. He continues his own narrative. His Sonora followers were inconsolable because of the death of their many relatives at Cíbola, and they threatened to kill Marcos as the person responsible for the calamity. To placate them the friar distributed among them the remainder of his baggage and supplies. At the same time, frightened though he was, Marcos resorted to bluff. They would better not carry out their threat because they could not hurt him, for if killed he would go to heaven. On the other hand, Spaniards would come to seek him and "would kill them all." Evidently the bluff worked.

Castañeda, who arrived at Cíbola later with the main army, tells us from hearsay new details regarding the fate of the Negro. He says that when Stephen reached that place the natives lodged him in a house outside the pueblo, and the old men in authority quizzed him as to why he had come. "When they were well informed regarding the matter they held councils for three days. Since the Negro had told them that farther back two white men [Castañeda again assumes that Fray Onorato was with Marcos] sent by a great lord were coming, that they were learnéd in the things of heaven, and were to instruct them in divine matters, the Indians thought he must be a spy or guide of some other nation that wished to come and conquer them. He being black, they thought it was nonsense for him to say the people in the country whence he came were white, and that he had been sent by them. So they went to him, and because after some talk he asked them for turquoises and women, they considered this an insult and decided to kill him. They kept a few boys, but the others, who must have been some sixty persons [from Sonora], they allowed to return to their lands unmolested. As they fled in fright, they chanced to meet the friars in the uninhabited area sixty leagues from Cíbola and told them the sad news. The friars were now seized with such fear that, not trusting these people who had accompanied the Negro, they opened their bags and distributed among them everything they had, keeping only the vestments for saying Mass. From there they turned back without learning any more about the country than what the Indians had told them. On the contrary, they were traveling by "forced marches with their gowns up to their waists."—Graphic, whether true or not! How much of this story Castañeda heard at Cíbola, and how much of it was soldier gossip it is impossible to say. If it is true it sets aside the story that Fray Marcos saw Cíbola, and indicates that he was never within sixty leagues of it—that is, probably not beyond the Gila River. Perhaps more evidence on the matter will sometime be discovered.

According to Cushing, Zuñi legend today still recounts the death of Stephen. "It is to be believed that a long time ago, when roofs lay over the walls of Kyá-ki-me, when smoke hung over the house-tops, then the Black Mexicans came from their abodes in Everlasting Summerland. . . . Then and thus was killed by our ancients, right where the stone stands down by the arroyo of Kyá-ki-me, one of the Black Mexicans, a large man, with chilli lips. . . . Then the rest ran away, chased by our grandfathers, and went back toward their own country in the Land of Everlasting Summer." This is poetic, but Stephen was killed at Háwikuh, not at Kyá-ki-me, as we are told categorically by Jaramillo who was with Coronado in Cíbola. Folklore is not always good history.

In spite of the disaster, so he tells us, Fray Marcos was determined to see Cíbola. Only two Sonora head men would consent to accompany him, and with these, his Indians and interpreters, the friar continued his journey until within sight of the city, "which is situated in a plain at the foot of a round hill. It has the appearance of a pretty pueblo, the best I have seen in these parts. The houses, as the Indians told me, are all built of stone, with their storeys and flat roofs, as it appeared to me from an eminence which I climbed to see it.

"The settlement is larger than the city of Mexico. At times I was tempted to go to it, because I knew that I risked only my life, and this I had offered to God the day I began the expedition. But the fact is that I was afraid, realizing my peril, and that if I should die it would not be possible to have an account of this land, which, in my opinion, is the largest and best of all those discovered." Another Mexico! Another Peru! "When I told the head men with me how good Cíbola appeared to me, they said it was the least of the Seven Cities, and that Totonteac is much larger and better than all the Seven Cities put together, and that it has so many houses and people that it has no end." This Totonteac has been identified with the Hopi pueblos, northwest of Zuñi.

"Having seen the arrangement of the city, it occurred to me to call that land the New Kingdom of San Francisco (*El Nuevo Reino de San Francisco*). And there, with the aid of the Indians, I made a great pile of stones, and on top of it I placed a cross, slender and small, because I lacked equipment for making a larger one. And I said I was erecting that cross in the name of Don Antonio de Mendoza, viceroy and governor of New Spain, for the Emperor our Lord, as a sign of possession, in fulfillment of my instructions; which possession, I said, I was there taking of all the Seven Cities, and of the Kingdoms of Totonteac, of Acus, and of Marata; but that I was not going forward to them, in order that I might report what had been seen and done." How Mendoza must have thrilled when he read of these marvels, all appropriated in his name!

"And so I returned, with much more fear than food," says Fray Marcos, "and traveled with all the speed I could make till I came upon the people I had left." This has the ring of a very human confession of flight for safety. "I overtook them after two days' travel, and with them I came until I had passed the Despoblado," reaching Sonora Valley, "where I was given as warm a reception as at first, and where both the men and the women made a great weeping for their men who were killed at Cíbola. And, because of my fear, I at once said good-bye to the people of that valley and traveled the first day ten leagues; and thus I traveled eight or ten leagues [a day], without halting until I had passed the second despoblado," that is, until he reached the Yaqui River.

One more important stop. When he reached Mayo River, Marcos decided to go to see the Abra, past which Stephen's glowing reports of Cíbola had lured him on his northward trip. He was informed that the Abra was peopled for many days' journey toward the east. "But I did not risk entering it, since it seemed to me that someone must come to settle and rule this other land of the Seven Cities and the kingdoms which I name, at which time the Abra could be better explored, without putting my person in jeopardy and thereby failing to give a report of what I had seen. So I only saw, from the mouth of the Abra, seven fair-sized settlements, and somewhat distant a valley below, very fresh and of very good land, whence came many smokes." This would imply that he had ascended an elevation to obtain a view. "I heard that in it there is much gold, and that the natives of the Abra make it into vessels, and ornaments for the ears, and paletillas with which they scrape themselves to remove the sweat; and that they are people who do not permit those of the other side of the Abra to trade with them. Here . . . I erected two crosses and took possession of all this Abra and valley." This, as he confesses, was a somewhat long-range exploration and a tenuous "possession" of the Abra.

Fray Marcos sums up the remainder of his journey more briefly. "From there I went forward . . . as rapidly as I could until I arrived at Culiacán, where I expected to find Francisco Vázquez de Coronado. . . . But since I did not find him there I continued to the city of Compostela, where I found him. And from there I wrote of my arrival to the Most Illustrious Señor Viceroy of New Spain, and to our Father Fray Antonio de Ciudad-Rodrigo, provincial, asking them to send orders telling me what I should do."

He added, "I do not include here many particulars because they are not important for the present purpose. I merely state what I saw and what they told me of the lands where I traveled

and of which I heard, in order to report it to our Father
Provincial, so that he may show it to all the Fathers of the
Order, as he may think best, or to the Chapter, at whose command I went, and that they may give it to the Most Illustrious
Señor Viceroy of New Spain, at whose request they sent me
on this journey." Such is the story on which the Coronado Expedition was predicated.

Fray Marcos apparently reached Compostela near the end
of June, accompanied from Culiacán by Fray Onorato. Coronado was excited, and he wrote from Compostela on July 15
reporting Marcos' discoveries. Castañeda tells us that when
Don Francisco returned to Compostela from Topira, "he found
there the friars who had just arrived and who told of such
great things about what the Negro Stephen had discovered and
what they had heard from the Indians, and other things they
heard about the South Sea and islands and other riches, that
without stopping the governor set off at once for the City of
Mexico, taking Fray Marcos with him, to tell the viceroy about
it. He made the things seem more important by not revealing
them to anyone except his particular friends, under promise
of the greatest secrecy"—a well-known trick—"until after he
had reached Mexico and seen Don Antonio de Mendoza. Then
he began to announce that they had really discovered the
Seven Cities which Nuño de Guzmán had tried to find."

Notwithstanding his haste to reach the capital, it did not
prevent Coronado, while at Compostela, from attending to a
matter of private business. On July 16, the day after writing
about Fray Marcos' discoveries, Don Francisco took for himself *en depósito,* in the name of his Majesty, several Indian
villages between Compostela and Guadalajara. They included
half of the pueblos of Mixquitlán and Xala, with all their
ranchos and inhabitants; half of the estancias of Mizquitlán,
Guaxacatlán, Cacalotlán, (also called Tepoztlán); half of
Tepuzcuacán, Amaxaque, Amatlán, and Xalancingo; and a
fourth of Atergo, Asán, Talpa, Miztlán, Guachinango, Acatit-
lán, Ocotlán, and Guacatlán, with all their ranchos and inhabitants, as they had been held in encomienda by Alvaro de

Bracamonte, who now renounced them in Coronado's favor, for what in return is not stated. This transaction had a resounding echo.

By August 23, Fray Marcos was in Mexico City, as we know from a letter written by Bishop Zumárraga, who was elated with the news. On September 2, Marcos' *Relación* was authenticated in the "Great City of Temistitán" in the presence of Mendoza, one of the witnesses being Coronado himself. Thus was concluded one of the historic journeys of sixteenth-century North America.

Chapter V

RIVAL CONQUERORS

When Fray Marcos' story became known, a whole galaxy of competitors protested the viceroy's activities, and some of them made plans to beat him to the new El Dorado. Cabeza de Vaca, De Soto, Cortés, Guzmán, and Alvarado all entered the competition.

Hernando de Soto was, in fact, already on his way toward the Land of Promise. Vaca, as we have seen, immediately upon his arrival in Spain petitioned the Emperor for the position of conqueror of Florida, in place of shipwrecked Narváez, and made it appear that he and Dorantes had agreed to join hands in the enterprise. Who would have a better right? But he was too late. In April, 1537, De Soto had been made governor of Cuba and adelantado of La Florida, with the title of marquis of a vast private estate in the country he might conquer. Florida had indefinite extent westward from the Atlantic coast, and might well include Cíbola. De Soto perhaps now imagined himself another Pizarro, from whom, in Peru, he had learned the game of conquistador. News of his appointment did not please Mendoza, for with the notice he received an order from the Queen of Spain not to enter De Soto's preserves. The viceroy kissed the document, placed it over his head, and promised to obey the royal command—but probably at the same time made a wry face and mental reservations.

De Soto was a logical recipient of the honor conferred upon him—insofar as there was any logic in the whole business of grabbing a new continent. He had already made for himself a brilliant career. He had fought in turbulent Nicaragua, whence he went to still more turbulent Peru, served conspicuously with Pizarro, and became one of the wealthiest of the conquerors. He was shrewd as well as lucky. When discord arose between the Almagro and Pizarro factions, he cannily withdrew from the scramble and went to Court in Spain, where his fortune and his personality made him notable and popular. He was very wealthy—*un gran rico!* It is even said that he lent money to the Emperor and that the Florida grant was his reward. Lowery thus characterizes his position: "De Soto was as this time in the flower of his age. . . . He was a skillful horseman, dextrous in all war-like exercises, of strong constitution fitted to endure hardship, and of ripe experience in the conduct of Indian campaigns. He was surrounded by stewards, ushers, equerries, and pages, all the glitter and pageantry of the household of a rich nobleman, displaying the magnificent gifts the Inca Atahualpa had lavished upon him, for his manly and courteous address had endeared him to the royal captive. . . . Small wonder that with the prestige of his wealth and courage, and with all the restless ambition of a young and successful soldier, who chafed under the iron rules of Court etiquette, he should have looked about him for another Perú to conquer and despoil."

In Spain, De Soto met Cabeza de Vaca, as we have seen. Realizing how useful the returned wanderer might be in his new enterprise, Don Hernando invited him to join his expedition, but Vaca did not choose to enlist as a subordinate in the exploitation of a country which he knew better than anybody else. He had said no to Mendoza, and he now said it to De Soto. He had plans of his own. Nevertheless, he greatly assisted De Soto in the raising of his force, by reason of the impression made by his reports of Florida. It was not so much what he said as what he pretended to conceal. He may have been something of a charlatan. The "Gentleman of Elvas," who went with De Soto to Florida, tells us how things worked. Vaca took with him to Spain a written account of his adventures which said in some places, "Here I have seen this; and the rest which I saw I leave to confer with his Majesty." By his mysterious demeanor, Vaca was responsible for the enlistment of some of his own relatives in the Florida enterprise led by his rival. They begged Vaca to advise them whether to go with De Soto or not. He replied that "on account of his oath," given to Dorantes, "he could not divulge what they desired to know. Nevertheless, he would advise them to sell their estates and go." This may have been his way of ditching his relatives. So, instead of accompanying their kinsman to South America, they joined Hernando de Soto in the Florida adventure. Many others like them, influenced by Vaca's mixture of frankness with mystery, turned their assets into cash and enlisted under De Soto's banner. Baltasar de Gallegos, for example, "sold houses, vineyards, a rent of wheat, and ninety geiras of olive field" in order to equip himself for the gamble. His case was typical. So many volunteers assembled at Seville to join the expedition that the ships would not hold them all, "and the cause of this was what Cabeça de Vaca had told the Emperor, and given persons to understand who conversed with him respecting that country."

De Soto's contract, signed on April 20, 1537, just when Mendoza was dickering with Dorantes, well illustrates the current notions of the rights of Europeans in the New World. America was their oyster. The grant covered more than twelve degrees of latitude, and extended from the Atlantic indefinitely westward. All this vast area De Soto was expected to "conquer, pacify, and people." As governor of Cuba, he would have the very best American base for mainland conquest—in fact, the one which had been the springboard for Cortés. He would need laborers, so he was empowered to import a hundred Negro slaves, duty free. Afterward there would be a charge, for the monarch must have his cut of the American melon. Even the dead would be taxed. The Emperor reserved to himself half of all the gold, silver, jewels, pearls, and other objects that might be found in places of burial, Indian temples, or other secret places, and promised De Soto one-sixth of all ransoms of chiefs and caciques, the remainder to be distributed among the soldiers, after reserving the royal fifth. To capture and hold them for ransom would be good business.

De Soto's vast grant might well disturb ambitious Mendoza.

His territory on the shores of the Gulf would hamper the extension of the viceroy's authority toward the northeast. Worse than that, Vaca might have told De Soto about the turquoises and the substantial houses farther west, and consequently Don Hernando might drive straight across the country and beat Mendoza to another Mexico or another Peru. And might not Vaca have divulged to De Soto more about the country than he had told Mendoza?

When De Soto finally assembled his expedition, it was one of the most imposing of all those bound for the Indies. On the sixth of April, 1538, he crossed the bar of San Lucar with ten vessels carrying six hundred or more soldiers, a number of priests and friars, and the families of several of the officers. Permanent colonization was intended. In company with De Soto and under his command went a fleet of twenty merchant vessels bound for Vera Cruz in Mexico. So Mendoza would soon be fully informed of what was going on, or would hear enough gossip to make him still more nervous. In May, 1538, De Soto reached Santiago, in Cuba, of which island he was now governor. Here he collected additional recruits and equipment for his Florida enterprise—Spaniards, Negroes, Indians, horses, cassava bread, swine, salt meat, and whatever else could be obtained. A year afterward the expedition sailed for Florida —May 18, 1539—two months after Fray Marcos left Culiacán for Cíbola. Mendoza had good grounds for misgivings. De Soto was headed toward the same region with large equipment. And according to the map the Atlantic and Pacific oceans were not far apart in that latitude.

Pedro de Alvarado, conqueror of Guatemala, also was a potential rival of Mendoza in the Cíbola field, and soon became one in fact. He had authority from the Crown of Spain to make conquests in the Spice Islands and "to explore by the coast of this New Spain toward the north." Moreover, by grant of the King, he was entitled to a share in whatever discoveries Mendoza might make in that direction. Early in 1539, while Fray Marcos was traveling north, Alvarado, returning from Spain, landed at Puerto Caballos, on the Gulf of Honduras, with three large vessels filled with materials for building a new fleet on the west coast, a large retinue of horsemen, and an army including three hundred arquebusiers, "well armed and accoutered." All this heavy equipment was now carried or dragged by Indians from the Atlantic three or four hundred miles across plain and mountain to the harbor of Iztapa, in Guatemala. There Alvarado built the largest armada then afloat on the Pacific coast of all America, and with it started north, greatly to the disturbance of Mendoza. In the interim the sensational reports of the discoveries made by Fray Marcos, Alvarado's former associate, had doubtless come to the viceroy's ears and increased his eagerness to reach the new El Dorado.

Of all the rivals of Mendoza in the race for northern conquests, Cortés was the most to be feared. He had behind him the longest experience with men and affairs in New Spain, was endowed by nature with the greatest ability, and had enjoyed the highest prestige. In both Spain and America he was known as a man to be reckoned with. By what he had already accomplished in the New World he had made his name immortal and established his fame as one of Spain's ablest sons of any generation. To say nothing of his achievements as conqueror and colonizer on the mainland, and the sending of the first American fleet to the Orient, to him and his brave sailors had been due the first reconnoissance by water of the long western coast extending all the way from Tehuantepec to Fuerte River, a stretch of some fifteen hundred miles. And he had led a short-lived colony to California—the Island of Pearls.

Cortés, it is true, was now on the down-hill road. It was primarily to clip his wings that a viceroy had been appointed. The abandonment of his Santa Cruz colony had been a direct result of Mendoza's arrival in Mexico, and was a symbol of what the Marquis might expect in the future. But Cortés had no intention of quitting. He still claimed, on the basis of contract with the crown of Spain, exclusive right to explore and conquer the unknown north country beyond Sinaloa—Guzmán, Mendoza, or De Soto to the contrary notwithstanding!

After his forced withdrawal from California, Cortés made preparations for further explorations in that direction. In September, 1538, he informed the Council of the Indies that he had nine good vessels ready for a new venture, "lacking only pilots." Next year he protested the sending of Fray Marcos to investigate Vaca's reports, regarding it as an infringement upon his own rights. When he heard the friar's story of Cíbola he declared it was nothing but what he himself had told Marcos before the latter started north, with a view to sending him on the same errand that he undertook, instead, for Mendoza. This claim by the Marquis was flatly denied by the friar and branded as preposterous!

More to the point, Cortés decided to act, and even before Fray Marcos returned he had made arrangements for a sea expedition to the region beyond Fuerte River. Whatever the friar might find he would seize and appropriate to himself. God was in the sky, the King was far away, the west coast was distant from the viceroy's capital, and Mendoza was busy with a multitude of tasks. Many times in his eventful life Don Hernando had triumphed by boldness. It might again succeed.

Nevertheless Cortés suggested coöperation with Mendoza in launching an expedition to the north. This would be a form of insurance in a gamble, for half a loaf would be better than none. His preparations for exploration by sea might soften the viceroy's heart. Writing from Cuernavaca on August 6, 1539, Cortés thanked Mendoza for news from Fray Marcos, and offered to "collaborate in any venture which might be undertaken as a result of these tidings." Then he hurried to Mexico City, where things were happening. Finding Mendoza unresponsive to his suggestion regarding coöperation, the marquis turned for help to Coronado, whom he knew to be in the confidence of the viceroy. But this, too, was without avail. When Coronado reported the proposal, Mendoza rebuked him sharply for even listening to Cortés. "You know very well—for you know me— that I am not going to accept anything from the Marquis. . . . or from anybody else except . . . his Majesty. . . . So I charge you not to speak to me about this again." Thus both Coronado and Cortés were put in their places.

Fray Marcos meanwhile had reached Mexico City after his long odyssey, and Cortés was brazenly claiming credit for the discoveries the friar had reported. In reply, Mendoza had Fray Marcos appear before a notary and declare that when he set out for the north he had received from Cortés no information whatsoever regarding the country he discovered. Marcos shrewdly added that if Cortés had known about Cíbola he would never have despatched his ships to Peru in 1536, but would have sent them north instead. Two days later Cortés began a suit before the Audiencia in support of his claims. Thereupon Mendoza filed in the case the declaration of Fray Marcos, together with Don Hernando's letters of July 26 and August 6. Thus raged the battle of words. The rivalry among the various contestants is illustrated by the legal proceedings now instituted in Spain, where the soreheads registered their grievances after it was too late. Humanly, they all ganged up on the strongest rival. But they accomplished nothing. Mendoza smiled and went ahead with his projects.

Meanwhile the Marquis had despatched his explorers up the coast. The voyage was under the command of Francisco de Ulloa, a relative of Cortés who had been with him on the Island of Pearls. The expedition was equipped at Tehuantepec and Acapulco in the summer of 1539 while Fray Marcos was hastening back to Mexico "with more fear than food." The fleet consisted of three small vessels, the *Santa Agueda,* the *Trinidad,* and the *Santo Tomás,* tiny craft whose average capacity was less than sixty tons. They were three of the many ships which Cortés had built on the western coast of Mexico in the course of seventeen years.

The exact object of Ulloa's voyage when at first it was planned is not known, for we lack the instructions issued by Cortés to its commander. In later statements the Marquis declared that its aim was the discovery of the Seven Cities of Cíbola, and he would have us believe that Mendoza had stolen his thunder. This assertion needs interpretation. At the time when preparations for the Ulloa voyage were begun, Cortés in all probability had never heard the name Cíbola. Guzmán had tried to find Seven Cities, but, so far as we know, the name Cíbola was first brought to Mexico by Fray Marcos, *after* Cortés had begun to organize his expedition. It would therefore seem more nearly correct to say that the Marquis sent Ulloa to take advantage of the reports spread by Cabeza de Vaca of lands in the north—lands which, in the interim, had become known as the Seven Cities of Cíbola. Certainly Ulloa was not despatched "with orders to sail to the head of the Gulf of California," as one writer tells us, for when Ulloa started north nobody knew that any such gulf existed!

Ulloa had a week of smooth sailing; then his troubles began. In a storm the *Santa Agueda* lost her main-mast, without which she sailed to Santiago. Three days after leaving this port a more terrific hurricane was encountered. The *Santo Tomás*, "wracked by wind and waves," sprang a dangerous leak and disappeared. With the two remaining ships Ulloa sailed to Santa Cruz (La Paz) to look for the lost vessel, which had been ordered to meet him there. The *Santo Tomás* was not in sight, so the captain crossed to the mouth of Fuerte River.

From here northward Ulloa was on unexplored coasts, and was the first European known to have seen them. After sailing many days along the mainland he "began to find the water white, like river water." He was approaching the mouth of a mighty stream—the Colorado, previously unknown. Near the eastern shore he found a channel "into which the tides ran every twenty-four hours in their order, flood and ebb, without falling off a jot, with an ebb current so strong that it was marvelous." The captain planned to continue up the channel next morning, but, he tells us, "when the day dawned, it being low tide, we saw the whole sea . . . between one land and the other closed with shoals," where previously there had been only water. The tide was now out. Landing on a sand bar, perhaps Gore Island, the mariner took formal possession in the name of the Marquis. The two ships now turned south, rounded the Peninsula, which formerly had been considered a chain of islands, and sailed up the outer coast to a point near latitude 28°.

In his race to beat the viceroy, Ulloa had performed a great feat of exploration. He had discovered the mouth of the Colorado River. He had put on the map the Sea of Cortés, as the Gulf logically came to be called, and west of it a long peninsula previously unknown. And he had been first to run some two thousand miles of the North American shoreline. How many navigators did more?

CHAPTER VI

A CÍBOLA EXPEDITION IS LAUNCHED

Word that the Seven Cities had been discovered spread like wildfire, and the charge of secrecy was not needed to insure the speedy propagation of so exciting a report. It was like any nineteenth-century gold strike, or a scandal in high society. Fray Marcos and Coronado talked and others multiplied the size and number of the reported wonders. Imagination and gossip were unhampered by knowledge.

Among the first to relay the story in writing was Bishop Zumárraga, the patron who had introduced Fray Marcos to Mendoza when the friar arrived in Mexico nearly two years previously. The bishop had been in on the adventure from the start, and he backed the viceroy against all comers. He now wrote to his nephew that Fray Marcos had found a country much greater than New Spain, beyond the regions opened by Guzmán, and near the California "island" which Cortés had tried to colonize. Many people, he said, were already clamoring to go there. "The Marqués claims the conquest of it belongs to him, but the viceroy is taking it for the Emperor and wishes to send friars ahead without arms, and that the conquest may be Christian and apostolic, and not a butchery." The people of Cíbola, he continued, were more civilized than those of Mexico, "both in their edifices of many storeys built of wood, and in the dress of their persons." The stone houses told of by Fray Marcos had thus easily been transformed into timber. "They have no idols except the Sun and the Moon, which they worship, nor do they have more than one wife, and when one dies they do not marry others." Did the bishop regard this as a virtue or just an interesting fact? "There are unicorns and cows, which they say this father saw; and they say he heard of camels and dromedaries, and of other cities larger than this one of Mexico." Fray Marcos would surely become a bishop!

The news was speedily carried outside of New Spain. By November 12, a number of men who had heard the story in various places before leaving Mexico several weeks earlier, were telling it in Havana under oath. This was bad for Mendoza, for De Soto was now governor of Cuba. Six months previously he had sailed with his army for Florida, and right now he might be conquering Cíbola. In any case, his officials left in Havana would relay the report to him, whereupon he would of course hasten to the new El Dorado!

According to García Navarro, one of the witnesses who testified in Havana, Fray Marcos said that Cíbola "is a land rich in gold, silver and other wealth, and has great cities; the houses are of stone, and terraced like those of Mexico; the people have weights and measures, and are civilized. They marry only once, wear woolen clothes, and ride about on some animals whose name he does not know." Francisco Serrano added to Cíbola's wonders a people who spoke the Aztec tongue, had large walled cities, houses of several storeys, and rulers called kings. Andrés García had heard the news almost from the friar himself—only one telling removed. His son-in-law, who was a barber, had shaved Fray Marcos in Mexico City after he returned from his travels, and the chatty fraile while in the chair told him through the lather on his chin that in Cíbola there were many walled cities guarded by gates. The people were rich. the women even wearing belts made of gold. In the country there were silversmiths, blacksmiths, slaughter houses, baths, sheep, and partridges. Indeed, a certain Bocanegra had told García that a New World had been discovered. Moreover, the viceroy was raising men for Cíbola, and it was proclaimed in the streets that no one should leave Mexico without a license from Mendoza himself. Of course, not all this embroidery of Cíbola can be charged directly to Fray Marcos. The story, like a snowball, grew as it rolled along.

The glowing report by Fray Marcos crystallized the ambitions for northern exploration which Mendoza had been nursing ever since his arrival in Mexico four years earlier. Now, with the marvels of Cíbola in sight, he decided to take a chance. If he succeeded, well and good. If not, he would have to suffer the consequences like any other gambler. So he prepared to send as soon as possible a great expedition up the Pacific Coast by the route already opened, take possession of Cíbola and neighboring kingdoms, win the tremendous riches which the friar advertised so enthusiastically, and add another kingdom to the Spanish Empire. At the same time he took measures to keep the news of the discovery from interlopers. With this object in view, as the barber told García, he promulgated in the streets an order that without his express permission no one should leave New Spain, lest the news leak out and somebody beat him to the Promised Land.

Though prompt to act, the viceroy was likewise cautious. Possibly, too, he recognized the friar's gift for dramatization. Be the reason what it may, at the same time that he made preparations for a great expedition to Cíbola, Mendoza ordered Melchior Díaz, the alcalde mayor of Culiacán who had befriended Cabeza de Vaca, "to take some horsemen and see if the accounts given by . . . Fray Marcos agreed with what he might discover." The task could not have been put in better hands. Díaz was a seasoned frontiersman and a realist, whose findings would carry weight. Since Don Melchior left Culiacán on November 17, 1539, to carry out his commission, Mendoza's order must have been issued soon after Coronado and Fray Marcos reached Mexico City sometime in August, for it took many days for even the swiftest courier to ride the nine hundred miles from the capital to Culiacán. Horses paid their price for official ambition.

The Cíbola expedition was organized in Mexico City, capital of New Spain and metropolis of all North America. It was a new type of conquest, under government control though privately financed. Before many days had passed, a call for enlistments was proclaimed in the streets and plazas with beat of drum, and volunteers responded with enthusiasm, especially since Mendoza publicly announced that he would aid with funds and equipment all needy persons who might join in the adventure. Fray Marcos was now made provincial of the Franciscan Order in New Spain, a move which greatly helped in the propaganda, and promoted the missionary as well as the secular aspects of the Cíbola enterprise. Here again Bishop Zumárraga had intervened. As Castañeda expressed it, the noble viceroy arranged with the Franciscans for the appointment, "as a result of which the pulpits of that Order were filled with such accounts of the marvels and wonders that within a few days more than three hundred Spaniards and about eight hundred natives of New Spain assembled." Fray Marcos' report was headline news, and Cíbola was now the rage. A new El Dorado had been discovered and was awaiting conquistadores. Otro Mexico! Otro Peru! Another Mexico! Another Peru!

A considerable portion of the volunteers were adventurers of patrician blood who had recently arrived in Mexico. Many of them were young blades who had come to the New World with Mendoza, or in his wake. This made it easy to raise an army. On the other hand, the expedition offered a solution of a very real problem of unemployment which was worrying Mendoza. It was a relief measure far antedating the WPA. Mota Padilla sums up the situation: "The viceroy decided to take advantage of the presence of the many noble people who were in Mexico, and who, like a cork floating on the water, went about with nothing to do nor with which to occupy themselves, all importuning the viceroy to grant them favors, and the citizens of Mexico to feed them at their tables. And so it was easy for him to assemble more than three hundred men, most of them on horseback, for already many horses were being bred. He paid them at the rate of thirty pesos, and promised them estates (*repartimientos*) in the country in which they might settle, especially in a place where it was declared there was a mountain of silver and other mines. And because of the good name borne at the time by Francisco Vázquez Coronado, governor of the kingdom of Nueva Galicia, he commissioned him to lead the expedition."

The venture was financed in the main by Mendoza, Coronado, and individual members of the army, for although the enterprise had the royal approval, the Emperor was not disposed to invest the funds necessary to put it through. Should any profit result, the monarch would get his royal fifth, so for him it was "heads I win, tails you lose." Mendoza is said to have contributed sixty thousand ducats toward the cost of the expedition; Coronado put in fifty thousand, raised chiefly by Doña Beatríz, his wealthy wife, her property being mortgaged for the purpose. Some of the well-to-do adventurers provided their own outfits, regarding it as a good investment, among them being Melchior Pérez, son of former Governor Pérez de la Torre, who spent more than four thousand pesos in the expedition and of whom exciting things will be heard in our story. Mendoza advanced the expenses of many who were unable to outfit themselves, besides furnishing most of the provisions for everybody. A person could even join the army by proxy. Thus, "Juan Muñoz was sent with Coronado by Miguel de Santiago, who fell ill as the expedition was about to start and was unable to go. Santiago equipped Muñoz with horses and arms, and paid him sixty pesos per year"—double the sum offered by the viceroy.

Mendoza planned at first to lead the Cíbola venture himself. We are told this explicitly by Tello and Mota Padilla, who wrote with good sources of information, and there is contemporary evidence to the same effect. "The viceroy decided to go in person on this expedition because it seemed to him a matter of importance," says Tello. "But many caballeros and other noble persons of the city of Mexico opposed his going, telling him how much he would be missed throughout the realm, and how necessary were his presence and assistance for the many problems that were arising every day; whereas there were many noble and knightly men in the kingdom to whom the enterprise might be entrusted." That Mendoza intended to go to Cíbola is suggested also by the fact that Coronado was not formally appointed leader of the expedition until it was well on its way to the rendezvous at Compostela.

Don Francisco, however, from the outset took an active part in assembling the army, and eventually he was made its official head. Next to Mendoza he was the logical man for the place. He was popular; he was the son-in-law of wealthy Estrada, and his wife had a large inheritance; he had supervised the sending of Fray Marcos on his northern adventure; he had made a difficult journey into the mountains of Topira; and, as governor of Nueva Galicia he was familiar with affairs on that distant frontier where the expedition was to be given its formal and final organization. In short, as Castañeda wrote, Coronado was put in charge of the expedition because "he had been the author of it all." There was an even more personal reason. Don Antonio made the appointment "because at this time Francisco Vásquez was his closest and most intimate friend, and because he considered him wise, skillful, and intelligent, besides being a gentleman," that is, of noble birth and breeding—three very good reasons.

Mendoza appointed Coronado on his own responsibility without consulting the Emperor, confident that his action would be approved. And he had a legal basis for doing so. He had come to America armed with a royal cédula issued shortly before he sailed, authorizing him, if occasion arose, to name someone to undertake explorations in the north, where Cortés claimed exclusive rights. The occasion had now come—a chance to put Cortés in his place and to forestall De Soto. Coronado's commission, dated January 6, 1540, made him commander of the army that was being assembled, and captain-general of the provinces of Acus, Cíbola, the Seven Cities, the kingdoms of Marata and Totonteac, and of any other lands he might discover, and of all the people now going to or who might be found in those vast regions. These names of the Cíbola provinces came of course from the friar's report. Coronado's salary was that of his governorship of Nueva Galicia, which was now raised from a thousand ducats a year to fifteen hundred. To rule as lieutenant-governor at Compostela during Coronado's absence, the able veteran Cristóbal de Oñate, one of Guzmán's men, and a founder of Culiacán, was named.

As *maestre de campo,* or second in command of the army, Mendoza appointed Lope de Samaniego, a man of ability who at the time was keeper of the royal arsenal in Mexico City. He was assigned to the new office, as Mendoza put it, "because he was a responsible person and a very good Christian, and because he was experienced in matters of this sort." He, too, had been with Guzmán on the Nueva Galicia frontier. Samaniego in fact was friendly with Mendoza, who later was charged with having shown him partiality. But Coronado resented the imputation, declaring that Mendoza was never partial to favorites. On the contrary, even if the pet were his own son "he would not favor him to the detriment of others."

Conspicuous in Coronado's army and destined to be heard of in resounding tones was García López de Cárdenas, a soldier who had already given important service in the New World. Like Coronado, a second son of a Spanish nobleman, he was left without a fortune by the law of primogeniture. He married Doña Ana de Mendoza, daughter of a Spanish count, and a distant relative of the viceroy. Cárdenas came to America, as he tells us, "in the year when his Majesty embarked for Tunis" to fight the Turks, that is, in 1535, the same year when Mendoza came to Mexico with his viceregal court, though by a very different route. He spent about a year in South America and Cuba, and from that island went to Mexico City, where he remained ill another year, *poco más ó menos,* "not undertaking anything whatsoever." Soon thereafter, the viceroy, discovering his ability, sent him to Oaxaca to make a census of the province jointly with Bishop Zárate, and to perform other important tasks. In this work he spent about three years, followed by another year and a half in government service in and near the capital. Some of these periods must have been rather *menos* than *más,* otherwise they add up to more than the five years between 1535 and 1540.

In these ways Don García had demonstrated superior qualities. At the time when Coronado was chosen to head the Cíbola venture, Cárdenas was not in the city of Mexico, being engaged in one of the commissions mentioned. Indeed, when he arrived in the capital he found Coronado about to set forth on his expedition. That Mendoza had a high opinion of Cárdenas is shown by the fact that he now ordered him to go with Coronado and "with his arms, horses, and servants to follow and obey him." Men of mettle and experience would be needed to lead the motley, undisciplined band constituting Coronado's force. Obedient to the viceroy, Don García made hurried preparations and departed from the capital, as an eye-witness tells us, "in the very best order as a *buen caballero*, and admirably equipped with arms and many servants to go forth to serve his Majesty." At a later time Cárdenas said he went unwillingly to Cíbola.

To make ready such an army was no holiday task, but Mendoza was equal to it, for he was thrifty and a competent man of affairs. Moreover, he was almost scandalously rich. So he made liberal provision for the personal equipment of the men enlisted, and for the commissary department of the army, for which he was able to draw upon the immense estates that had gravitated into his hands. "Besides . . . money, horses, arms, and other things," he furnished "a large number of cattle and sheep," in addition to many cattle which the captains and soldiers took on their own account. The vast herd of stock thus assembled kicked up a terrific dust on the trail, and sufficed to supply the expedition from beginning to end.

Coronado tells us that Mendoza gave the men who went on the expedition a great many gold pieces to enable them to provide their necessary outfit for the journey. "To some he gave arms, horses, and money, and to others lances and arms of the country," doing so "in the name of his Majesty for the furtherance of our Holy Catholic Faith and for the increase of the royal patrimony." Most of the equipment furnished by the viceroy was distributed by Agustín Guerrero, Mendoza's majordomo, on orders signed by Coronado. Guerrero issued these funds and supplies "according to the needs he noticed in each one of the soldiers who went in the . . . expedition to serve his Majesty." Thanks to the viceroy's favor and to the wealth of Doña Beatríz, Coronado was able to provide himself with an elaborate personal outfit, including Negro servants, arms, horses, and mules. In his retinue he had a head groom, lesser grooms, and a page. His contribution to the enterprise was fifty thousand pesos, a sum that now would represent perhaps a million dollars.

Several hundred Indians went with the army to serve as scouts, sappers, servants, herdsmen, horse wranglers, camp cooks, or in other occupations. They were enlisted in Mexico City and in the pueblos along the road to Compostela, many of them being from the province of Michoacán. Mendoza gave strict instructions that only volunteer Indians should be taken, but of these there was no dearth. Many more than were needed begged permission to go. Indeed, they told Coronado that if the viceroy would permit them "more than ten thousand" would join the march, for natives as well as Spaniards had taken the Cíbola fever.

Mendoza ordered Coronado to show the Indian allies the greatest consideration, something which had not been done by all conquistadores. They must be dealt with as freemen, and permitted to turn back at any time they might wish, "rich and contented," supplied with provisions for the return march, and, if necessary, with an escort of horsemen for their protection. This promise was carried out to the letter, as will appear in the course of our story. Natives encountered on the way must likewise be treated gently. They were expected to render obedience to his Majesty, "as their sovereign and ours," but they must not be molested, nor their food or other belongings taken from them without compensation. With this in view, many bales of petty merchandise (*rescates*) were carried on the backs of mules as presents for the natives encountered on the way and to barter for provisions. Some of the Indians took their wives and children with them on the long march. Families left behind, Mendoza decreed, must be provided with what was necessary for their sustenance until the husband should return. This order was "well known and public," and there is good evidence that it was carefully observed.

To supervise and facilitate obtaining supplies from the Indians on the way to the rendezvous at Compostela, in each native village through which the expedition passed a Spanish agent was stationed to avoid seizure of provisions from the Indians, "and if they gave any item of food to the Spaniards, they kept an account of it." Coronado tells us that all the Indians who gave service or furnished supplies were well paid, which he knew to be a fact, because, when he went through the country behind some of the soldiers, he made a careful inquiry regarding the matter. Incidentally, his statement throws interesting light on native bookkeeping. When he asked the Indians how they kept track of services rendered or of commodities furnished, they replied that they "painted in their own way, as they are accustomed to do, what they had thus given . . . and that through these paintings and reckonings" they had been paid by order of the viceroy "much to their satisfaction, and that nothing was owed them." Of such native bookkeeping, numerous contemporary examples are still extant.

One of the burning questions of the day was the use of Indians as *támenes,* or burden bearers. Las Casas and Zumárraga were preaching against it, and Charles V was doing his best to stop it. Mendoza at a later time pointed out that because so many horses and pack mules were taken by the Spaniards on the journey to Cíbola, the Indians were spared from transporting the baggage. If they carried any, he said, it must have been their own food, clothing, and other articles, "just as was done by the Spaniards" on the expedition. Coronado confirmed this opinion, declaring that "the Indians were not employed to carry burdens," as he knew from ocular evidence and from an investigation which he made "with ample witnesses."

We get a glimpse of Coronado while he was busy planning for his expedition, and a note regarding an item of his personal equipment for the long march ahead of him. The incident takes us back a few months, and illustrates the intimacy of Don Francisco with the viceroy, as well as Coronado's love of horses, and how some of his mounts in the expedition made history. When Coronado was at Compostela, on his way to the capital with Fray Marcos in the summer of 1539, Cristóbal de Oñate, his friend and lieutenant, demonstrated his affection for the young governor by a handsome gift. Don Cristóbal had two fine mounts in the capital, in the care of Lope de Samaniego, who soon afterward was appointed maestre de campo of the Cíbola expedition. Knowing that Coronado was short of horses, Oñate said he might have these two. *"Son de usted, amigo* (they are yours, my friend)!" Don Francisco protested that he did not need them, otherwise he would gratefully accept them. Further urged, the governor consented and went on his way to Mexico City. Doubtless there were many *abrazos* over both the gift and the leavetaking.

One day in the capital, later on, while Coronado was riding with Mendoza he met Samaniego mounted on a handsome brown horse, one of those Don Cristóbal had put in his charge. Samaniego told Coronado that Oñate had written him of the gift, and he now sent the two animals to Don Francisco's stables. Coronado took the brown steed with him on the journey to Cíbola, but apparently left the other animal in Mexico City. Later, at Compostela, on the way to Cíbola, Coronado said to Oñate, "I have your horse with me. Send for it, for I have brought it back to you because I have plenty of mounts." The governor urged, but Oñate refused to accept the animal, saying he "was sorry only that he did not have a dozen more to give him, since he was going on an expedition in which he would need them." Coronado demurred, but Oñate was insistent, suggesting now that both the governor and Samaniego might use the animal until they came back from Cíbola. So Coronado accepted the brown horse, not as a gift but as a loan, giving Oñate a note (*codicil*) which provided that the animal should be paid for or returned.

Another mount was given to Coronado while on his way to rendezvous at Compostela. When he passed through La Purificación, Juan Hernández de Ijar, alcalde mayor of that frontier place, presented the governor with a "swift horse," chestnut in color. So both steeds went with the general on the long march to Cíbola. The brown died on the way back, but the chestnut made the whole journey, as did many another animal of that hardy Spanish stock.

Coronado's expedition was composed of young men, some of them mere boys, typical of the whole migration from Europe to America at all periods, and especially of the great marches of the conquistadores into the interior of the mainland. Don Francisco himself was only thirty when he set forth at the head of the army bound for Cíbola. His followers were mostly optimistic youths who regarded the jaunt as an adventure and who therefore could endure hardship and privation, since physical endurance is to a large extent conditioned by the spirit. Not having been soured by disappointment, their dreams of wealth and romance were unhampered by discouraging experience.

We have relatively little specific data on the ages of Coronado's soldiers, but such as are available indicate a body of adventurers mostly in the twenties, with many still younger and very few above thirty. In these respects his following was not very different from any army in any period, or from the participants in the Gold Rush to California and others of its kind. War and adventure take the flower of the land. From a single list of seventeen men with Coronado whose ages are given, we learn some very interesting facts. Any other seventeen taken at random would perhaps have told the same story had their ages been asked. When they joined the expedition in 1540, Rodrigo de Frías, Luís de Vargas, Gaspar de Saldaña, and Gerónimo Mercado de Sotomayor were between seventeen and eighteen years old; Francisco Gorbalán and García del Castillo were nineteen; Pedro de Ledesma, Juan de Beteta, Juan Galeras, and Juan de Fíoz were twenty-two; Hernando de Alvarado was twenty-three; Pablos de Melgosa, twenty-four; Hernán Paez, twenty-five; Juan de Vitoria, twenty-six; Diego de Madrid, twenty-eight; Pedro de Navarro, thirty; and Domingo Martín, thirty-seven. Martín no doubt was regarded by the youngsters as just about ready to die of old age. Yet he got through and was still flourishing and telling of his exploits at forty-five. Of the seventeen, only four had passed the age of twenty-five.

Some of the youngest of these seventeen performed a number of the most notable feats of the whole adventure. This, too, is typical of warfare in any period. Twenty-four year old Pablos de Melgosa and twenty-two year old Juan Galeras went with Cárdenas to the discovery of Grand Canyon, and were among the first of all Europeans to descend into that stupendous chasm. Hernando de Alvarado was only twenty-four when he led his historic and rough and tumble expedition into the Buffalo Plains of the Texas Panhandle. On the other hand, Juan Gallego, the most terrific fighter of the whole army, was over fifty when he hewed his way through hostile Sonora and Sinaloa Indians to carry despatches from Coronado in Cíbola to Viceroy Mendoza in Mexico City.

As they set forth, this army, chiefly of new-come adventurers, presented an appearance quite different from that of any group of veterans of ten years in the New World, witness a scene in Guatemala at this very time. The Emperor ordered all land holders there to marry. Next year when Pedro de Alvarado returned from Spain, he brought for the matrimonial market "twenty maidens, well bred, the daughters of gentlemen of good lineage," and expressed confidence that they would not remain long on his hands. But the damsels had their own views of the case. At an entertainment given in Alvarado's honor at which many of the conquistadores were present, these young women, concealed behind a screen, watched the festivities and commented on the appearance of their prospective spouses. "They say," remarked one black-eyed gal to her companion, "that these are to be our husbands." "What! Marry these old fellows," was the reply. "Let those marry them who choose; I will not. The Devil take them! One would think by the way they are cut up that they had just escaped from the infernal regions; for some are lame, some with but one hand, others without ears, others with only one eye, others with half their faces gone, and the best of them have one or two cuts across the forehead." A third innocent took a longer view. "We will not marry them for their good looks, but for the purpose of inheriting their Indians; for they are so old and worn out that they will soon die, and then in place of these old men we can choose young fellows to our tastes, in the same way that an old and broken kettle is exchanged for one that is new and sound."

The *soldadera* as an institution in Mexico did not begin with Pancho Villa in the twentieth century, as some readers may suppose. At least three Amazons were members of Coronado's expedition; namely, Francisca de Hozes, wife of Alonso Sánchez, María Maldonado, wife of Juan de Paradinas, a tailor, and the Señora Caballero, wife of Lope de Caballero. Francisca de Hozes was accompanied by a young son. This lady could speak for herself, and when called upon she gave emphatic opinions regarding certain incidents which occurred in the course of the expedition. She had both a mind and a tongue of her own. María Maldonado, an early Florence Nightingale, nursed sick soldiers, mended their ragged garments, and was generally regarded as an angel of mercy. The Señora Caballero, by the way, was a native Indian woman, perhaps an Aztec. Many of the Indian allies were accompanied by their wives and children.

Chapter VII

RENDEZVOUS AT COMPOSTELA

Most of the recruiting of Spaniards for the Cíbola expedition was done in the capital, but Mendoza thought "it would be rather hard for the friendly Indians in the country if the army should start from Mexico." That is to say, he feared that a large force going through the land in a body might frighten the peaceful natives, and overtax them in furnishing supplies. Perhaps he had in mind the unhappy example of the ruthless march of Guzmán's army to Culiacán just a decade earlier. He therefore ordered the final muster held near the Pacific Ocean, at Compostela, capital of Coronado's province of Nueva Galicia and gateway to the route which already had been opened to the north by way of the West Coast Corridor.

So the men raised for Cíbola, in several contingents, drifted along the beautiful road to the west—La Ruta de Occidente—over a period of two or three months, at the end of 1539 and in the beginning of 1540. Of the march we have only a few details. Jaramillo tells us that the volunteers "set out from Mexico straight for Compostela, the land being inhabited and at peace all the way." These inhabitants were mainly natives, with a small sprinkling of Spaniards at the principal cities and towns. "The route was to the west, and the distance one hundred and twelve leagues," says Castañeda. They were generous leagues, for from Mexico City to Compostela by the most direct road it is more than five hundred miles. From the capital the main trail led much as the highway and railroad run today, across the fertile valley of Mexico, up the steep and winding road to Toluca, perched at an elevation of nearly nine thousand feet, down the western slope, and out into the broad plains of Michoacán to Pátzcuaro. From Jaramillo's statement we infer that most of the

volunteers traveled to the rendezvous by the direct route
through Guadalajara (Tonalá). But both Mendoza and Coronado, who had various errands, went by way of Purificación in
the district at that time called Ávalos, and then turned north to
Compostela.

Coronado remained in the capital, busy assembling, or-
ganizing, and equipping the expedition until or after November 21, 1539. On that date he attended a meeting of the cabildo
of Mexico City, of which he was a member. Soon afterward
he went west to look after the needs of Nueva Galicia, his own
province, and to make final arrangements for his departure for
the north. Early in January, 1540, he was in Guadalajara, which
already had the rank of a city, for, by a recent grant, Emperor
Charles V had declared the place ennobled, and presented it
with a coat of arms. Don Francisco, on January 8, with due formality, assigned *ejidos* or community lands to the city. Next
day, through a public crier, he proclaimed a royal order stating
that, because of the fire hazards of wooden structures, and in
the interest of beauty, no settlers in the city might erect houses
of any materials other than stone, brick, or adobe; "and that
they must build them in the manner of those of Spain, in order
that they might have perpetuity and adorn the sites." City-
planning America did not begin in the twentieth century; the
model was brought directly from Mother Spain.

Mendoza also was soon on the way to the rendezvous. The
viceroy was no tenderfoot, for he already had a good military
record, which he enhanced in America. Having finished arrangements at the capital, he set out for Compostela in person,
to give the adventurers a send-off, and to help them begin their
journey "with everything in good order." We must remember
that Coronado was still only thirty years of age, and an older
head might be useful—at least in the opinion of the older head.
The viceroy made a fine show and was impressive to both Spaniards and Indians. As he traveled westward he was accompanied
by many noble and wealthy men, we are told by Castañeda.
Some of these were royal officials from the capital who went to

assist in the organization of the expedition. Perhaps other grandees went just for the outing, as guests of the noble viceroy, and to see these already famous lands in the Far West. They went *á caballo,* with all the fanfare and gala attire appropriate to the occasion and in keeping with knightly showmanship. And there was a long train of baggage, servants, horses, and pack animals. In short, the journey was both an official promenade and a serious business undertaking. It was a notable jaunt for a gently bred viceroy, a testimonial to his energy and hardihood, and to his zeal for the enterprise in hand.

Mendoza spent New Year's Day, 1540, at Pátzcuaro, then the seat of the bishopric of Michoacán, "and from there he crossed the whole of New Spain, taking much pleasure in . . . the festivals and great receptions which were given him" along the way. One stop after leaving Pátzcuaro was made at Tzin-tzun-tzan, the famous old native capital by the side of Lake Pátzcuaro, still today a notable spot in all North America. Here, on January 6, Mendoza drew up the commission formally appointing Coronado "anew" as governor of Nueva Galicia, and now, in addition, as captain-general of the Cíbola expedition. Apparently, it was here the viceroy finally decided not to lead the army in person to the Seven Cities.

Coronado set out southward from Guadalajara to join Mendoza on the way. He had scarcely started when the citizens of that place were frightened by threat of a native uprising. They were so put to it that they wrote to the young governor, "begging him to find a remedy, and, since he had soldiers with him . . . to send some of them to aid in subjecting the pueblos they held in encomienda." But the general had urgent business ahead and could not turn back. Receiving the letter while on the march, he forwarded it post haste to Mendoza, following at a slower pace.

Having joined the viceroy, Coronado traveled with him "on the road to the west," which led through the province of Ávalos. On the way, he learned that Zacatula was in rebellion, led by a chief called Ximón, who had burned a town and killed some of the inhabitants. So the governor turned aside, had Ximón executed, and thus stamped out the uprising. Rejoining Mendoza, he went north through Purificación, and continued thence through Aguacatlán and Iztlán, pueblos which he then exploited jointly with Alvaro de Bracamonte. To lessen the burden on Indians and Spanish colonists in Nueva Galicia, Mendoza purchased maize in the Ávalos pueblos and took it along to supply Coronado's army. Well-to-do settlers on the route generously entertained Coronado's men as they passed by, and some of them were eaten out of house and home. Alvaro de Bracamonte later wrote that "when the expedition to Cíbola was made I kept a table for everybody in Yztlán and Aguacatlán, and in Compostela for half of the army, which obtained rations at my house, and I was left all the year without a kernel of maize, having to buy it at four and a half reales a fanega in bullion, not to mention many other expenses and a loss in gold mining."

Later it was charged that the march of Coronado's army through the country had caused the Indian revolt known as the Mixton War, which raged while the governor was absent in Cíbola. But Coronado declared this could not be true, because from the pueblos of Ávalos, through which his men passed, to the peñol of Tepetistaque, the one which first resisted, it was more than forty leagues. Coronado was absolved by other testimony. The chiefs of the rebellious Indians in a later inquiry declared the reason for the uprising was that the Devil had appeared in person, telling the natives that before the Spaniards came to Mexico the Indians were happy, and urging them to rise and kill the Christians, "and . . . this and no other was the reason why they had rebelled." Coronado drily remarked that apparently Satan had been pretty busy in that vicinity.

Of what happened on this long march of the army to the rendezvous, says Castañeda, "there is no need to tell"—we emphatically wish he had done so—"but they all finally assembled in Compostela at Shrovetide *(Dia de Carnes Tollendas),*" a time of great merrymaking and feasting. Compostela, it will be remembered, had been moved by the governor about a year previously from the site at Tepic where Guzmán had founded it to the place it still occupies, some twenty miles southeast of the original location. It was then a small affair, with perhaps a score of houses—it had only ten the previous year—for these were pioneer days in Nueva Galicia. But the arrival of the army bound for Cíbola made the place for many days the scene of boisterous activity.

Compostela, still alive today with traditions of Cortés, Guzmán, and Coronado, stands at an elevation of about four hundred feet above sea level, on the main highway from the capital to Guadalajara and the Pacific Coast. With characteristic shyness in Mexico, the Southern Pacific railway station is a long distance from the town, which is scarcely visible from passing trains. The little city now has some twenty-five hundred inhabitants, and on its main plaza stand attractive municipal buildings and an imposing old church whose story reaches back into the distant past. Among all the treasures of the place, none is more cherished than the memory of the imposing review held here of Coronado's caravan on the eve of its departure for Cíbola, land of romance, of which Compostela, because of this colorful event, regards herself as godmother.

Shortly behind the main body of the army, Mendoza arrived with his showy entourage, was warmly welcomed, and found the men "well cared for and lodged" by Cristóbal de Oñate, the veteran who was being left in charge of Nueva Galicia in Coronado's absence. Don Cristóbal was father of Juan de Oñate, the celebrated founder of New Mexico sixty years later, so interwoven with Mexico is all our Southwest. Here at Coronado's capital preparations for the Cíbola adventure were given a final touch, and soon after his arrival Mendoza held a general review of "all the men . . . going to the land newly discovered by the Father Provincial, Fray Marcos de Niza."

The publication by Aiton of the muster roll drawn up on that occasion gives us detailed and accurate information regarding Coronado's force and its equipment at the time the expedition finally set out for the north. The muster was held on February 22—192 years before Washington's birthday. As they passed in review before Mendoza and other high officials, a roster was made of all the men then present, giving names, company affiliation, rank, and equipment, by way of horses, armor, and weapons. This precious record deserves more than passing notice. It was made out with due formality by Juan de Cuevas, chief notary of mines for his Majesty in New Spain, in the presence of Mendoza, the viceroy; Gonzalo de Salazar, factor; Peralmíndez Cherinos, inspector of finance; Cristóbal de Oñate; Licenciado Maldonado, *oidor;* "and many other people." It was a ceremonious occasion.

The list contains the names of 225 mounted men and sixty-two on foot, counting only the members of the expedition in Compostela at the time. In addition, the name of Pablos de Melgosa, captain of infantry, appears on the roll, although, according to the clerk, he was not actually present at the review. He will be heard of again in dramatic circumstances. Besides these men there were the friars and a small escort of soldiers who had gone ahead some time previously, a few belated men who arrived afterward from Mexico, and a number who joined the caravan at Culiacán. Of these stragglers and other contingents, Hammond and Rey have been able to identify forty-eight names not listed in the Compostela muster roll. This gives a total of 336 men in the expedition, besides the wives and children of a few of the soldiers, and several hundred Indians who went as servants, hostlers, or herdsmen. The crews of two ships that sailed up the coast under Alarcón to coöperate with the army are not included in this number.

"Of special interest" in the muster roll, Aiton justly remarks, "is the accurate count of the horses, with a distinction made between horses *(caballos)*, usually stallions in this period, and mares *(yeguas)*. As only two mares are listed, the possibility, biologically considered, that stray horses from Coronado's expedition stocked the western plains with Spanish horses is slight. A solitary specimen of the hybrid mule is to be noted." But there were many mules on the expedition besides those listed in this document—and perhaps other mares, for Mendoza furnished a great deal of equipment apart from that of the individual soldiers. The total number of horses listed in the muster roll here at Compostela is 559, making an average of a little more than two each for the cavalrymen. But they were not evenly distributed. One infantryman had two horses, four had one each, and the rest had none at all. Of the 559 horses, 112 belonged to the thirteen cavalry officers—commander, campmaster, captains, and ensigns. The nabobs, measured in horses, were Coronado with twenty-three, and Samaniego, campmaster, with seventeen. Of the cavalrymen, eighty-four had only one horse each.

From Mendoza we learn that when the army left Culiacán, farther along the trail, there were as many as 250 Spaniards on horseback, and more than a thousand horses and mules for the baggage, arms, provisions, munitions, and other things necessary for the journey. The viceroy does not include here the men who went on foot, who would bring the number close to the total arrived at by Hammond and Rey. Coronado gave a still higher figure for the animals, and his word should have weight, because, later on, he personally "ordered the horses, mules, and stock counted at a certain narrow pass and there were found to be fifteen hundred animals." From these data it would appear that numerous men and animals were added to the caravan at Culiacán. But Castañeda's later estimate of five thousand at Pecos in New Mexico must have been an exaggeration.

"Another striking feature," says Aiton, still commenting on the muster at Compostela, "is the prevalence of native American arms and armor, and the haphazard presence of odd pieces of European armor. Many more buckskin coats *(cueras de anta)* are reported than coats of mail *(cueras de malla)."* The writer of the muster roll notes that "in addition to the arms declared, the horsemen took their lances and swords, and other weapons." The Indian allies doubtless carried their native implements of war, including cotton armor. Just what these weapons were, we are not informed, but it may be surmised that they included bows and arrows, clubs, spears, light javelins, and slings—all of which had been in use by the Aztecs and Tarascans at the time of the Spanish conquest. The bow was probably of a simple type, perhaps five feet long, and strung with animal sinew. The points of the missiles may have been of stone, obsidian, tempered copper, or even bone, and the javelins, it is known, were sometimes equipped with cords so the hurler, having made a throw, could quickly retrieve his weapon. The clubs, which might be so large as to require two hands to wield them, were like flat swords made of wood and given cutting power by flakes of obsidian set along the edges, or they were great maces, the heads and handles bristling with sharp points of obsidian.

A few individual entries in the muster roll illustrate the varied equipment of these treasure-seekers of 1540. Coronado had twenty-three horses and three or four suits of horse armor. The list does not include the commander's famous "gilded suit and helmet with crested plume," which we know he possessed. Campmaster Lope de Samaniego "swore that he took with him sixteen or seventeen horses, two buckskin jackets, a coat of mail and its appurtenances, some cuirasses, and some arms of the country, since the rest that he brought had been burned." There must have been a fire somewhere on the way. Pedro de Tovar, who became famous as the discoverer of the Hopi pueblos, possessed thirteen horses, a coat of mail, other appurtenances, and "arms of the country." Young Hernando de Alvarado, discoverer of Ácoma, Tiguex, Taos, Pecos, and the Buffalo Plains, reported, among other things, four horses and a coat of mail with sleeves. Juan Gallego, fearless express rider and tiger-like fighter, presented at the muster seven horses, coat and breeches of mail, a buckskin jacket, crossbow, and other Castilian arms. Captain Don García López de Cárdenas, discoverer of Grand Canyon, had twelve horses, three sets of Castilian armor, two pairs of cuirasses, and a coat of mail. Best equipped of all with arms and armor was Captain Don Tristán de Luna y Arellano, commander of the main army from Culiacán northward, and later a conqueror in Alabama, for, besides his eight horses, he listed a leather jacket, sleeves and neckpieces of mail, arms of the country, chin-piece, an arquebus, two crossbows, a two-handed sword, three ordinary swords, and other arms for himself and servants. In equipment, Coronado's army was almost medieval.

Besides Spaniards, there were Europeans of other nationalities, including five Portuguese, two Italians, one Frenchman, one Scotchman, and one German, an illustration of the cosmopolitan character of the population at this early date even in the reputedly exclusive Spanish colonies. The Scot was "Tomás Blaque," obviously Blake or Black, who left in Mexico his wife Francisca de Rivera, widow of one of the earliest Spanish settlers there. It has been conjectured that Blake was the first Scotchman to enter what is now the United States. "Firsts" are rather uncertain, but this may be a good guess. Juan Fíoz, a German born in Worms, was bugler of the expedition, and was present "at all the major actions." How his name was spelled in his homeland it would be difficult to say—it may have been Fisch. There were several other persons with non-Spanish names who may or may not have been of non-Spanish birth.

Commander-in-chief of this historic army was Coronado. Lope de Samaniego was campmaster, and second in command. Chief standard bearer or ensign was Pedro de Tovar. The force was divided into six companies of cavalry, one of artillery, and one of infantry. The cavalry captains were García López de Cárdenas, Diego Gutiérrez, Diego López, Rodrigo Maldonado, Tristán de Arellano, and Diego de Guevara, four of whom became conspicuous in the expedition. Hernando de Alvarado was captain of artillery, and Pablos de Melgosa captain of infantry. If, as Aiton says, the men were listed according to their company affiliations, there was great lack of uniformity in the number of soldiers under the different captains. It was something of a personal affair, semi-feudal in character, each officer gathering round him a body of retainers. One company ensign bore the conspicuous name of Torquemada. Other ensigns were Alonso del Moral, Juan de Villareal, Diego Hernández, Alonso Gómez, and Pedro Ramos.

In the muster roll are the names of three chroniclers of the expedition. The Pedro de Nájera in the list is evidently Pedro Castañeda de Nájera, of Culiacán, better known as Pedro de Castañeda, and by all means the most famous of the chroniclers —the Bernal Díaz of the Coronado epic. He was a keen observer and knew how to tell a story, but he was not present at the most dramatic acts in the show. Of similar interest is the name of Juan Jaramillo, whose brief narrative is indispensable, especially for its exact record of distance and for his detailed description of Quivira. Pedro Méndez de Sotomayor was said to have been "chronicler of the army," and to have written a narrative which has not come to light. What a revelation it might make if discovered! And how useless it might render this book! Numerous other names in the muster roll become notable in the adventure as the narrative proceeds. We miss from the list the famed scout Melchior Díaz, one of the most attractive and competent of all the men on the expedition. The explanation is that when the review was held at Compostela, Díaz had not returned from his reconnoissance over the trail of Fray Marcos to check the friar's report. In other words, he was already on the job. For the same reason hardy Captain Juan de Zaldívar does not appear in the muster roll.

As always, there were objectors, sometimes honest, but all too often the victims of frustration. At Compostela, Coronado learned that certain persons hostile to the expedition, or who did not want to be overlooked and therefore made a fuss, had spread the story that many of the men going on the adventure had been coaxed by him to join it, "as a result of which the City of Mexico and New Spain were left deserted." Floaters in the capital had suddenly become indispensable citizens! To scotch this tale, Coronado declared that everybody in the ranks was going of his own free will and that the charge of depopulation was both malicious and absurd. Sure of his ground, he begged the viceroy to investigate the facts, and Mendoza complied. He ordered Oidor Maldonado to make the inquiry at the muster of the troops, in the presence of other royal officials. Maldonado subpœnaed nine witnesses—old residents of New

Spain—to be present at the review and point out any enlisted men they knew to be citizens of Mexico. Anyone in the army unknown to these old-timers could hardly be regarded as indispensable. Of course, anybody who had been there ten years or more was an "oldest inhabitant"—almost a native son.

The report, which, be it noted, was not disclosed until after Coronado's army had gone forward and too late to have any influence, revealed several interesting things besides those already noted. Gonzalo de Salazar, royal factor, declared that the only person in the expedition who possessed a *"repartimiento or estate"* in Mexico was Coronado, the commander. Clearly, the enterprise was not one of rich men. Few of the volunteers were "old residents" of the capital, for Peralmíndez Cherinos, royal *veedor,* or inspector, recognized among the El Dorado seekers only Coronado, Samaniego, Alonso Sánchez, his wife, and Domingo Martín, and he declared that "all the rest . . . were people without settled residences, who had come to the country in search of a living." Moreover, "it seemed to him that it was a very fortunate thing for Mexico that the people who were leaving were about to do so, because they had been injuring the citizens there. For the most part they were young gentlemen who had nothing to do either in the city or in the country. They were going of their own free will . . . and it seemed to him that if the said country [Cíbola] had not been discovered, most of the people would have returned to Castile, or would have gone to Perú or some other place in search of a living." In short, according to the veedor, the Cíbola expedition was a fortunate relief measure, peculiar to the time and place.

In the same vein another witness, long a business man in the capital—not more than twenty years, of course—was "very certain it was a great advantage to Mexico and its citizens to have many of the unmarried men go away, because they had no occupation, were bad characters, and were mainly gentlemen, and persons who did not hold any property or repartimientos of Indians, without income, and lazy, and who would have been obliged to go to Perú or some other region," had

Coronado not given them employment. Here a special definition of "gentlemen" is implied. Oñate, an old-timer of sixteen years in the country, recognized no residents of Mexico City except Coronado, Samaniego, Domingo Martín, and Alonso Sánchez and his wife. No resident of Compostela was in the company bound for Cíbola. Two from Guadalajara were on the muster roll, one a bachelor, the other married to an Indian woman. It seemed to Oñate "that many of the young gentlemen . . . who were going on the . . . expedition would do more good than harm by departing, for they were all idle and without means of support."

Other witnesses gave testimony of the same tenor. Perhaps they said what they were expected to say, for clearly the report was a legal paper intended for effect. And no doubt they protested too much, but, in general, their views are borne out by other evidence. Coronado's army consisted in the main of foot-loose individuals ready to join in any adventure or to gamble on any chance to get rich quickly—the very best material for such an enterprise.

Castañeda, writing several years later, commented on the men who made up the expedition as he remembered them, and he by no means subscribed to the "good riddance" view. They were his old comrades in arms. "There were so many men of high quality among the Spaniards," he says, "that such a noble body was never assembled in the Indies, nor so many men of quality in so small a body." This was an estimate of the personnel of the expedition pronounced by a veteran looking back after the expiration of a quarter-century, when time had cast a glamour on the adventure and softened animosities. Deeds of valor are wont to become increasingly heroic when viewed in the perspective of years. Castañeda now tells us that when Mendoza "saw what a noble company had come together, and the spirit and good will in which they all presented themselves, he was deeply impressed. Knowing the worth of these men he would have been glad to make every one of them the captain of an army." This being impossible, the viceroy had designated a few as officers, on some of whom Castañeda comments in eulogistic terms. Besides these he remembered kindly some of the "other gentlemen" and noted them down for us. He speaks especially of Barrionuevo, "a caballero from Granada," and Melchior Díaz, "who, although he was not a gentleman, well merited the position he held." Among those to whom he gave favorable mention were Manrique de Lara, Urrea, Suárez, Ramírez de Vargas, Juan de Sotomayor, Gorbalán, and Riberos. And there were "other men of high quality" whom he did not recall. "As I say, since then I have forgotten the names of many good fellows, but it would be well if I could remember some of them, so it might be clearly seen what cause I had for saying they had in this expedition the most brilliant company ever assembled in the Indies to go in search of new lands." In retrospect his comrades had all become heroes.

Mendoza regarded the Cíbola expedition as a missionary as well as a business enterprise. We have seen that Bishop Zumárraga, one of the first to report preparations for the *entrada*, wrote that the viceroy wished "to send friars ahead without arms, and that the conquest may be Christian and apostolic and not a butchery." Mendoza had sent Fray Marcos instead of soldiers to make the first reconnoissance over Cabeza de Vaca's trail. Marcos was appointed provincial of the Franciscans primarily to launch the prospectively great missionary venture in Cíbola. Of the friar's discoveries Mendoza wrote that "in our day God our Lord has been pleased to reveal vast lands wherein His Holy Name may be known and adored, and His Holy Faith and the Catholic Church extended." So he was sending with Marcos several other friars of the Franciscan Order, "men of science and conscience, to preach and spread the Holy Evangel, and bring the natives into the fold of the Catholic Church," and soldiers were going to protect these missionaries. So, when Fray Marcos joined the expedition it was not merely as guide. He was head of a band of apostles bound for a new missionary frontier.

From Compostela the friars started several days ahead of the army, accompanied by a military escort. Apparently they went on foot, sandal shod, in true apostolic fashion, and were soon overtaken. Just how many friars went to Cíbola is not clear. The identity of four of them is well established, but other names appear in the records about which there is considerable uncertainty. Fray Marcos is already well known to the reader. He was a noted personage, chosen to give prestige to the enterprise. Next in prominence and more fortunate in the outcome was Fray Juan de Padilla, a "fighting friar," who had been a soldier in his youth. A native of Andalusia, in Spain, he went to Nueva Galicia with Guzmán in 1529, and was the first to administer the sacraments at Tepic. Four years later he was at Tehuantepec with Antonio Ciudad-Rodrigo, who has already entered our story, and the more celebrated Toribio de Motolinía, bound for the Orient in an expedition which Cortés was then trying to organize. But they were unable to sail because the vessels were worm-eaten and unseaworthy. Life on the Isthmus at the time was "just one hell after another," and part of the friars, Padilla and Ciudad-Rodrigo among them, had returned to the capital. By the time Padilla left for Cíbola with Coronado eleven years later, he was already a frontier veteran, having worked among the Indians at Ponzitlán, Tuchpán, and Zapotlán, and having been superior of the monastery of Tulantizingo. Padilla had seen pioneering in the raw, and he had more of it ahead of him.

Fray Antonio de Victoria—identical with Antonio de Castilblanco—functioned as chaplain of the army and took part in the councils of war that were held in the course of the expedition. He was present at the Compostela rendezvous after the other friars had gone ahead, and he played a leading rôle in the impressive ceremony that followed the review. Another whose identity is certain is Fray Luís de Escalona (also called Luís de Ubeda), "a former companion of the Lord Bishop of Mexico," none other than the great Zumárraga. Fray Juan de la Cruz and Fray Daniel figure in the story but their rôles are shadowy. It has been surmised that Fray Daniel stopped on the way and remained at Tuchpán (Tuxpan), but this is not the case, for we find him with the army in Cíbola. With

Padilla there were two Indian oblates named Sebastián and Lucas, from Zapotlán.

After the review was finished, everybody heard Mass, "captains and soldiers together." Then Mendoza, arrayed in his finery, made the men "an eloquent speech," telling them of the loyalty they owed their general, and "showing them clearly the benefits this expedition might afford, through the conversion of those peoples, as well as through the profit for the men who should conquer the territory, the advantage to his Majesty, and the claim which at all times they would have on his favor and aid." How familiar these justifications for conquest became as the decades passed! Souls to save, private gain, profits for the king, and a claim upon his favor! And under the circumstances of time, place, and contemporary outlook upon the world, what better ones could have been offered?

Mendoza's inspiring address greatly moved both officers and men, and we are told by Cuevas, the scribe, that they went in a body to the viceroy and protested their ardent zeal to serve God and the King. Indeed, they begged Mendoza to permit them to take an oath "such as is required in case of expeditions" to help them do their duty. The prayer was granted. Then Coronado swore: "By God all-powerful and by His Holy Mother, and on a cross that was there, and by the words of the Holy Gospels, placing his right hand on a missal book held by the Reverend Father . . . Vitoria . . . that as a good Christian, vassal, and servant of his Majesty, he would exercise said office of captain-general to which his Lordship in the name of his Majesty had appointed him for the said journey and expedition, and would cherish the service of God and of his Majesty, and as a good gentleman and hidalgo would obey and fulfill his commandments and the instructions of the . . . viceroy in his royal name, to the best of his knowledge and understanding."

Following the example thus set, the campmaster, standard bearers, captains, gentlemen, and the rest, each one for himself, "swore in proper form, placing their right hands on the sacred cross and book, that they would be obedient to Francisco

Vázquez de Coronado, the captain-general, and whatever other captain-general his Majesty or the Lord Viceroy in his royal name might appoint, and that they would not desert his captains and subject vassals of his Majesty." This oath—which some of them later forgot—was repeated by the men "in a loud voice" in the presence of many witnesses, and of Cuevas, Chief Notary of Mines for their Majesties. Castañeda, who was not present, tells the same story more briefly. He says that when Mendoza's speech was over, everybody, "captains and soldiers, gave him their oaths upon the Gospels in a Missal, promising to follow their general on this expedition and to obey him in everything he might command them." Castañeda adds, "which they faithfully performed, as will be seen." Next day the army started off with colors flying. The epic march was begun.

Mendoza had made his farewell address to the men. But he wished to view the expedition in actual operation on the trail, and he was loath to see it pass beyond his sight, for he had fondly hoped to lead it. And there were so many things to say to his young protégé. "Be careful about this"; "Don't forget that"; "Be sure to give the Lord of Cíbola my warmest personal regards." Possibly, too, the viceroy had misgivings. Díaz ought to return soon, and perhaps Mendoza hoped to meet him on the way and get his report before turning back. He had heard of the beautiful region just beyond Compostela and longed to see it. So Mendoza delayed his farewell, and rode with Coronado the first two days of the march on the long trail that lay before the captain-general and his followers, probably reaching Tepic. In this stretch of country Coronado was the veteran and Mendoza the tenderfoot, for it was his first visit to the Far West.

From Compostela the route led northwestward down the valley where one now passes a rural school house, banana groves, and villages bright with bougainvillea, canna, and roses. Climbing a high, steep, oak-covered ridge of black volcanic debris, from the crest, if the day was clear, the wayfarers saw in the west, close at hand, the blue Pacific Ocean, with Tres Marías islands in the distance, and in the southwest the deep barrancas which make coastwise travel there extremely difficult.

Not far away in that direction lay famous Valle de Banderas. Coronado's straggling caravan of men and animals, as it climbed steep hills and forded crystal-clear streams, must have been as picturesque as one of the bands of pilgrims now sometimes met on the same stretch of camino, bound for a fiesta at the shrine of the Virgin of Tlapa. Descending the ridge, the travelers entered another beautiful valley, passed pine-crested ranges on the left, and, some twenty miles nearly north of Compostela, reached Jalisco, where the men of Cortés had sought an Amazon queen. On the same stretch of road one now passes cattle, auto-buses, oxcarts loaded with firewood— six or more head to each cart—and admires the modern town with its neat plaza and bright-colored tropical gardens. On opposite sides of Jalisco rise two conspicuous *cerritos,* or peaks, to which, according to tradition, Coronado gave their present names of San Juan and San Juan El Grande. And if this pleasing belief is in error, who shall complain? History deals with things of the imagination as well as of literal fact—otherwise there would be no history of discovery, literature, art, or invention.

Crossing another ridge, captain-general and viceroy descended side by side into the Valley of Tepic, then as now walled in by bare hills at the left, and dotted with other cerritos. The old trail has been cut deep with age-long use by myriad feet. It passes fields of tasseled cane, and, just outside the city of Tepic, runs close to the site of the celebrated cross on the hillside which, according to legend, was miraculously formed of supernatural vegetation. Here still stands the old monastery of Santa Cruz, famous more than two centuries after Coronado's day as the hostelry where Junípero Serra, José de Gálvez, Palóu, Garcés, and many another notable traveler found welcome hospitality on their journeys up and down the coast to and from Sonora, Arizona, and California.

Tepic is now the capital city of the State of Nayarit, with interesting old plazas, tall-spired churches, and thriving industries; but in 1540 it was little more than an Indian village, for the Spanish settlement had just been moved to Compostela. The town was still held in encomienda by Guzmán, its founder who was now securely in jail in Spain, and was administered in his absence by Francisco de Godoy. At Tepic, several mines were in operation. Here Guzmán had planted and Godoy was tending an orchard famous in the region, containing orange, pomegranate, mulberry, and other Spanish fruit trees. Don Nuño's orange trees especially were considered something to see. Were they raised from the eight seeds dropped by Bernal Díaz when he fell asleep near Vera Cruz some twenty years previously? At any rate, in part it was to view them that the viceroy had traveled two days with Coronado.

Díaz did not appear, so Mendoza said a final adieu and faced about on the trail, returning to Compostela. There, when it was too late to do any harm, he read the testimony given at the muster regarding the depopulation of the country by the Cíbola expedition, and on the last day of February he wrote to the Emperor telling of the departure of Coronado with his explorers. From Compostela he set out for Colima, where we shall soon meet him again.

Chapter VIII

FORWARD TO CULIACÁN

Having said farewell to the viceroy, Coronado and his caravan went on their way behind the friars. Most of the men were unused to the hardships of the trail. Many of them, tender sons of well-to-do families, were more accustomed to dallying in drawing rooms than to strenuous outdoor pursuits. The majority were new arrivals from Spain, and wholly unacquainted with the American frontier. Each man had to transport his personal baggage on his own animals. Few of them knew how to fasten the packs, not a simple trick for the uninitiated, and in this matter they had plenty of trouble at first, but they were made of good stuff, and, being young, they quickly learned. Soon they reduced the bulk of their luggage by leaving non-essentials behind, "giving them to anybody who wished them." Other travelers have done likewise. Castañeda philosophically remarks: "In the end necessity, which is all powerful, made them skillful, so that one could see many gentlemen become carriers, and anybody who despised this work was not considered a man."

From Tepic to Rio Santiago, Coronado's trail is closely approximated today by the automobile highway. Threading deep cuts, worn through centuries by the feet of Indians, horses, and mules, by *carreta* wheels, and now by trucks and *camiones,* it descends narrow, wooded valleys walled in by bare ridges, past La Fortuna, El Cuchillo, Espino, and other villages. Twelve miles out from Tepic, one again sees the ocean at the left. At twenty miles, the bottom of the grade is reached at Navarrete, where a side road turns west to San Blas, the harbor which, at a later date, became the base for water communication with Sonora and California. From here, in the flat coast plain—the *tierra caliente*—the road runs through palm groves and dense *monte* toward a small peak straight ahead, which marks the site of Santiago, thirty-three miles from Tepic. Down this now historic route Coronado led his caravan of soldiers, pack animals, Indians, and stock—sheep bleating; cattle bellowing; burros braying; mule drivers, horse wranglers, and herdsmen shouting and cursing; the tenderfoot caballeros frequently dismounting to adjust their unruly packs, or to rest their unaccustomed muscles and relieve their sore spots. After each day's travel, which averaged some ten miles, camp was made by the roadside, supper prepared, blisters nursed, and, we may conjecture, impromptu amusements enjoyed. Card playing was a favorite pastime, and Coronado himself confessed to gambling for moderate stakes. But most precious to the tired young fellows were food and sleep!

Today the highway crosses Santiago River at the town of the same name, where, toward the east, a magnificent view of stream and sierra meets the eye, and where automobiles are ferried over on *pangos,* unless by now a bridge has been completed. Since the friars who had gone ahead were routed through Centispác, it is inferred that Coronado, following their trail, reached the river below the town of Santiago, at the Centispác ford. Here the expedition was delayed three or four days, because it was necessary to take the sheep across the wide river "one by one," on horseback, in the arms of the caballeros. Centispác, then a large Indian town, where Guzmán had once fed his army for many days, and now a small village with an antique plaza, lies in the plain north of Santiago River. We are not told whether Fray Marcos and his band of soutane-clad missionaries had awaited the expedition here or had jogged on ahead, to be overtaken later.

The way to the north by now was fairly well known, and for nearly a thousand miles from Rio Santiago, Coronado's march was not essentially one of pathfinding. As far as the Arizona border he followed a route most of which had been opened by Spaniards who had preceded him—Nuño and Diego Guzmán, Cabeza de Vaca, Friar Marcos, Melchior Díaz, and unnamed frontiersmen who for a decade had explored, prospected for mines, hunted slaves, and lived in Sinaloa. Coronado himself had made at least one journey from Compostela to Culiacán and back. These pioneer Spaniards, in turn, followed trails which had been traveled by Indians since time out of mind. Over slender paths, barefooted or sandal-shod natives had conducted intertribal commerce, some coming north, others going south. For hundreds of years this procession of pack-laden Indians had been jogging over the long, narrow footpaths on the Pacific slope through the regions today called Nayarit, Sinaloa, and Sonora. And now the Spaniards, a step at a time, as they expanded their geographical horizon, used these ancient trails leading up the coast, until they became a continuous highway for Europeans—a *camino real*—to the Pueblo Land of Arizona and New Mexico, where they struck other Indian paths showing them the way to the plains of Texas, Oklahoma, and Kansas. In the task of finding his way around in the New World, the pioneer European owed a heavy debt to Indian guides and to the trails they had already opened.

All the way to Sonora River the main route ran along the coastal plain that lies between the ocean and the foot of the Sierra Madre, that great cordillera which stretches almost the entire length of both North and South America, a natural feature which will provide many of the chief difficulties and the crowning glories of a Pan American highway. So forbidding is this mountain barrier that, although four centuries have passed since Europeans have dwelt upon its eastern and western slopes, there is, between Guadalajara and the United States border, a stretch of nearly a thousand miles of this Sierra Madre which has seldom or never been marked by a wheel track.

From Rio Santiago to middle Sonora, the coast plain is crossed by rivers which emerge from the Sierra Madre and even now in flood season create serious hazards for travelers and pack trains and wash out railroad bridges. In Nayarit and southern Sinaloa the trail ran near the sea, for here the mountains are close at hand. Farther north the plain widens out and the road was more inland, following the best combination of terrain and water. Near the coast many difficulties were created by marshes and lagoons, and here the rivers lacked tributaries spaced to suit the needs of travel from one stream to another. Close to the main sierra, on the other hand, the country is rough and difficult. So the best route was found midway, near the foothills, where a convenient waterline was offered by the affluents of the larger streams. On this line, too, were located Indian settlements which afforded a food supply, though by Coronado's time they had been badly shattered by Guzmán and his ilk. In flood season the large rivers presented real hazards for sheep, hogs, cattle, and horses. The crossing of Rio Santiago, especially, was made perilous to man and beast by wide-mouthed and sharp-toothed alligators, a fact which Coronado learned to his sorrow.

But the chief difficulties of travel for the first three hundred miles from Rio Santiago northward were presented by the *monte,* those jungles of brush and small trees which are so striking a feature of the coast plain of Sinaloa. For long distances this thicket is so dense that it is difficult for a man on horseback to struggle through without the aid of a machete with which to cut away the tangled growth of cactus, *palo blanco,* and other shrubs which everywhere abound. Although there were trails for single horsemen when Coronado made his historic march, it often must have been necessary to use a host of native laborers to widen the road in order that the army and the stock might go forward. This jungle gave perfect coverage for wild animals, and wayfarers were chilled at night by the cry of mountain lions or nerve wracked by the yipping of coyotes. Even now, in broad daylight, a traveler frequently meets these and other wild animals square on the road through the forest.

But the tribulations caused by the *monte* were relieved for nature-lovers by the mad variety of brilliantly colored flowers at certain seasons of the year. Those who traveled the length of Sinaloa in January and February beheld all the ridges bedecked for a stretch of several hundred miles with an almost continuous mass of magenta-hued *amapa,* interspersed with the white and yellow blossoms of other shrubs of the same genus. In season the amapa of Sinaloa offers one of the great flower shows of the world, whose full appreciation only awaits the completion of the Coronado Highway. At every turn of the trail through Sinaloa, flocks of noisy green paroquets and other birds of even gayer plumage were seen, and on the beaches of the lagoons hosts of flamingoes often presented the appearance of a sunset sky.

Coronado again moved forward. At Tuxpan the problem of transit for the stock was raised anew by San Pedro River. Here the travelers saw the sierras closer at hand than at Santiago River—great *baluartes* they are, the majestic ranges rising in an ascending series as they recede in the distance. By them, doubtless, more than one of the wayfarers was made homesick for mountainous Old Spain.

The direct road northward from Tuxpan, which Coronado perhaps took, for he was traveling in the dry season, ran in the coast flat past marshes and lagoons, to Tecuala on Acaponeta River. The main highway today follows a parallel course a few miles farther east, on higher ground, and close to the railroad, which it crosses and recrosses. This latter route is now marked by *higueras,* cotton and tobacco fields, as far as Chilapa. Then, in the more upland country, the soil is thinner, with stretches of sand and gravel, grown with palmettos, sotol, and mesquite, till the town of Rosa Morada—the Brown Rose—is reached. If Coronado passed that way, he missed, because he was born too soon, a costly modern Campo Santo, where people go in splendor to eternal repose. Northward the road continues through mesquite, palm groves, and marsh grass. Round, brown, California-like hills come close on the right, and beyond them rises Sierra de Teponahuastla, bearing on its crest a delicately balanced rock which is the subject of comment by all travelers. We may be sure that Coronado's fellows gave it an appropriate name, as soldiers can. Then, passing San Miguel, cutting through the range at the left, and leaving Resbalón and Las Coloradas behind, in season fertile corn, banana, and maguey fields are reacned at Acaponeta River. On the other bank of this historic stream stands the city of Acaponeta, about a hundred miles from Tepic.

Thus, "with such labor, which they then thought severe, the army reached Chiametla," near the mouth of Rio Chiametla, where it stopped several days to obtain provisions. Here a discouraging event occurred. Lope de Samaniego, army master, led a party of soldiers into the surrounding country to gather supplies, for they were still in pacified country where natives were legally subject to tribute. The Indians were not friendly, and at one of the villages they gave signs of resistance. A soldier who had strayed from his companions was captured by the natives. He shouted for help; Don Lope ran to his rescue and freed him from his peril. Thinking all was safe, when he entered some brush Samaniego raised his visor, and was shot by an arrow that entered an eye, piercing his brain and killing him instantly. This was a serious loss, for, as Mota Padilla says, "Samaniego was one of the most courageous of the captains and was beloved by everybody." He was buried in a brush bower, and later his bones were removed to Compostela. The Indians wounded also five or six of the maestre de campo's companions. It was an interesting coincidence that Chiametla, where the disaster occurred, had been founded by Samaniego himself a few years previously, when he was in Sinaloa with Guzmán.

Diego López, the alderman from Seville, now took command of the foraging party and sent hurried word to Coronado; and when the news was reported in the camp there was great consternation. Sorties were made, a number of natives were captured, and those considered responsible for the ambush were hanged from trees, as previously conquered people who now had rebelled. Samaniego's death was the first major casualty of the expedition, and it cast a gloom over the travelers. It was a grave misfortune, and was so related to the King by Mendoza when he learned the news, for the viceroy greatly prized both the ability and the friendship of the former alcaide of the fortress at Mexico City. To fill Samaniego's place, Coronado named Don García López de Cárdenas, who now became his most conspicuous lieutenant. The appointment was made by Coronado in conference with young Captain Hernando de Alvarado while Cárdenas was absent from camp, punishing the Indians who had slain Samaniego. The promotion was a surprise to Don García, and when he was informed of it he modestly demurred, but, with urging, he accepted the responsibility as a matter of duty, for which he eventually paid an enormous price, as the sequel will show.

At Chiametla, enthusiasm for the adventure was still further dampened by another circumstance. Here the expedition met Melchior Díaz and his way-worn companions returning from their reconnoissance to check the story told by Fray Marcos. Díaz had traveled 220 leagues to Chichilticale, near Gila River, where the Great Despoblado began. Just what part of his report became known to the soldiers does not appear, but the impression gained by the rank and file was that the captain had not found anything important. "Although the bad news was kept as secret as possible," says Castañeda, "things leaked out which did not seem to add luster to the prospect." But Fray Marcos, "noticing that some of the men were feeling disturbed, cleared away the clouds, promising that what they would see should be good, since the army was on the way to a country where their hands would be filled, and in this way he quieted them so that they appeared well satisfied." The friar had a way with him.

We now know more about this historic excursion made by Díaz than was revealed to the soldiers at Chiametla. Under orders from Mendoza the captain had left Culiacán for the north on November 17, with fifteen horsemen and a troop of Indians. The round trip of some fifteen hundred miles lasted nearly four months. Díaz was everywhere well received by the natives, and in his travels he imitated Fray Marcos and Stephen in one important particular. Each day, after fording Sinaloa River, he sent messengers ahead with a cross to the place where he intended to camp, "because this was a symbol the Indians regarded with deep veneration, erecting a house of mats in which to place it. Somewhat apart from this shelter they made a lodging for the Spaniards, drove down stakes to which they could tie the horses, and supplied them with fodder and an abundance of maize wherever they had any." This was not everywhere, for in many places the natives were suffering from hunger because it had been a bad year. After Díaz had ridden a hundred leagues beyond Culiacán it began to be cold; as he got farther north the temperature increased in severity, until he reached a point where some of his Indians died from exposure and two Spaniards were in great danger. Ultimately they arrived at Chichilticale, the Red House south of Gila River at the foot of Pinaleño Mountains. The captain and his party were thus the first horsemen known to have reached the Sonora, San Pedro, and Arivaipa valleys, Fray Marcos and Stephen having gone afoot.

Camp was pitched at Chichilticale, at the beginning of the Great Despoblado, which Díaz could not cross because of snow and cold weather. But he made careful inquiry about Cíbola. A number of his informants, Indians, of course, had been in that famed country "fifteen or twenty years," and knew it well. He quizzed some of them separately and others in groups, and their stories tallied. Beyond this despoblado, they said, there were seven towns, a short day's march from each other, "all of which together are called Cíbola." The houses were of roughly hewn stone and mud. They described the many-storeyed pueblos of Cíbola much as Marcos had reported them; the shields, leather jackets, and weapons of the inhabitants; the turkeys, corn, beans, melons; and some domesticated "hairy animals, like large Spanish hounds. . . . And from the hair they make long, colored wigs like this one I am sending your Lordship," said Díaz. The viceroy could now set a new fashion in wigs. Perhaps his present is still resting in some museum or in some family chest. The men of Cíbola were small; the women were of light complexion, and wore many turquoise ornaments. "The clothing of the men is a cloak, and over this the skin of a cow, like the one which Cabeza de Vaca and Dorantes brought, and which your Excellency saw." Evidently Vaca had taken such a garment to Mexico as a trophy. "They wear caps on their heads; in summer they wear shoes made of painted or colored skin, and high buskins in winter."

The captain's informants were unable to tell of any metal in Cíbola, "nor did they say that they had any. They have turquoises in quantity, although not so many as the father provincial reported. They have some little stone crystals, like this one I am sending . . . and of which your Lordship has seen many . . . in New Spain. They cultivate the ground in the same way as it is done in New Spain, and carry things on their heads as in Mexico. The men spin cotton and weave cloth, and they have salt from a marshy lake two days from the province of Cíbola." This was the famous salt lake south of Zuñi.

Díaz had been told of the Cíbola musicians. The country had many wild fowls and was good for raising corn and beans, but it had no fruit trees and lacked water. The people ate out of flat bowls "like the Mexicans." Of the seven settlements, three were large, the others smaller. Totonteac, seven short days from Cíbola, had twelve towns with "the same sort of houses and people, and they say that cotton grows there." Díaz adds, "I doubt this, because they tell me it is a cold country." By Totonteac he meant the Hopi towns. All this agreed very well with the report Fray Marcos had given.

The scout continued: "The death of Estéban the Negro took place in the way . . . Friar Marcos described it to your Lordship, so I do not recount it here, except to say that the people at Cíbola sent word to those of Chichilticale and its neighborhood, that if any Christians should come they ought not to consider them as anything peculiar, but ought to kill them, because they were mortal—saying they had learned this because they kept the bones of the one who had come there"—this of course was Stephen—"and if they did not dare to do this, they must send word so the people of Cíbola might come and do it." This was hostile talk. "I can very easily believe that all this has occurred, and that there has been some connection between these places, because of the coolness with which they received us and the sour faces they showed us."

The inhabitants along the way to the north, Díaz tells us, did not have any fixed settlements except in Sonora Valley, "which is 150 leagues from Culiacán, is well populated and has houses with flat roofs; and that there are many people . . . but they are not good for anything except to make them Christians." Pious Mendoza remarks, "As if this were of small account." Díaz now joined Coronado's army at Chiametla, and Zaldívar with three companions continued south to carry the report to the viceroy. In this duty he performed one of the heroic feats of the entire expedition.

So the army advanced to Culiacán, with some detours into the country to obtain provisions, for they were still in pacified country. All the way from Tepic to Culiacán, Coronado found that Indian villages were still exploited by the heavy hand of Guzmán although he was now a prisoner in Spain. His agents continued to tax Centispác, near Santiago River; and in the vicinity of Culiacán they collected tribute from the head native village of that name and from two outlying ranches. Farther north, the pueblo of Guachomiles (Guamuchil), still standing to-day on the highway, was under their control.

On the eve of Easter, when he was two leagues from Culiacán, Coronado was met by a delegation of citizens who came out to greet him and to beg him not to enter the town until the day after Easter. They had a show in preparation, and it must not be spoiled, for the governor, who just a year previously had arrived to save the settlement from rebellious Ayapín, must be suitably welcomed. Coronado assented and Culiacán put on a good performance. On the day appointed, the army advanced toward the town. As the visitors approached, the inhabitants came out on an open plain, with foot and horse drawn up in ranks as for combat, with seven bronze cannons in position, "making a show of defending their town." Coronado's army drew up in the same fashion, and a skirmish followed; that is to say, a sham battle was on. After both sides had fired their artillery, the men of Culiacán retreated—for, of course, the governor must win—"just as if the town had been taken by force of arms, which was a pleasant demonstration of welcome," enjoyed by everybody "except the artilleryman who lost a hand by a shot, the order to fire having been given before he had finished withdrawing the ramrod." The unfortunate gunner was Francisco Muñoz.

The town having been "captured" in this delightful fashion, it dispensed its best hospitality. "The army was well lodged and entertained by the citizens, who, as they were all very well-to-do people"—Castañeda, when he wrote, was a citizen of Culiacán and spoke here with local pride—"took the gentlemen and persons of quality . . . into their own dwellings." Some of the townspeople were not ill repaid for this hospitality. Many of the conquerors had started with elaborate wardrobes and accouterments. But since from here forward they had to carry provisions on their horses, or even on their own backs, they were obliged to abandon their fine stuff or risk sending it to the coast to be carried in Alarcón's ships, whose whereabouts at the moment were unknown. So they gave it to their hosts. Perhaps some of these gifts are still treasured by the old families of Culiacán.

While here, Coronado, by order of Mendoza, installed Hernandarios de Saabedra in the office of lieutenant-governor and captain-general in Culiacán. Don Hernandarios was a man of quality, being uncle of the count of Castellar and mayor of Sevilla. His new capital must have seemed crude in contrast with the celebrated metropolis of Andalucía, for as the couplet ran:

> Si no ha visto Sevilla
> No ha visto maravilla.

Coronado remained at Culiacán several days for a very good reason. There was plenty here for man and beast, and new supplies were gathered for the long march ahead. Castañeda tells us that "before his departure a pretty sort of thing happened to the general which I shall relate for what it is worth." A young soldier named Trujillo said that while bathing in the river he had seen a vision. Since it "seemed to be something extraordinary" he reported it to Coronado, "whom he gave to understand that the Devil had told him that if he would kill the general, Trujillo could marry his wife, Doña Beatríz, and would receive great wealth and other very fine things."

One would conclude that Trujillo was rather naïve and Coronado very tolerant. The soldier might have lost his head for what could have been taken as an insult. But from the sequel it appears that Trujillo was just shrewd, and that Coronado was not asleep at the switch. The incident came to the attention of Friar Marcos, who turned it to excellent account. He even preached several sermons on the matter, "laying it all to the fact that the Devil was jealous of the good which must result from this journey, and wished to prevent it in this way." This was too fine a piece of gossip not to spread. The friars with the expedition wrote to their convents about it, and "the pulpits of Mexico proclaimed strange rumors concerning the affair." One would like to see their letters. Coronado appeared indulgent, but he took no risks, and Castañeda concludes his story with this information: "The general ordered Trujillo to remain in that town and not to go on the expedition, which was just what Trujillo was after when he concocted the falsehood."

Here at Culiacán Coronado decided, as a matter of prudence, to go ahead with a small contingent of cavalry and infantry to relieve the main army from unnecessary risk and uncertainty. Díaz had made it clear that the road was long, rough, difficult, and thinly settled by natives, who had few provisions to spare. Nor, according to the scout, was Cíbola everything that Fray Marcos in his zeal had represented it. All things considered, it would be wiser for the general to go ahead to reconnoiter. This he decided to do, and for the purpose he reorganized his forces, selecting an advance guard, headed by himself, with which to make a rapid march to Cíbola. Cárdenas, captain of cavalry went as maestre de campo of the detachment, and Pablos de Melgosa, a youth of twenty-four, was appointed captain of the men going on foot. The main army was left at Culiacán in charge of Arellano to follow at a slower pace. Of Melgosa we shall hear an exciting tale!

Apparently there were about eighty horsemen in the vanguard besides twenty-five or thirty foot soldiers and a large number of Indian allies. In the party went all the friars, "since none of them wished to remain behind with the army." They wanted to be where things were doing. It was their part to deal with the friendly Indians whom they might encounter, and they especially were bearers of the Cross, a symbol which, through Cabeza de Vaca, Fray Marcos, and Díaz, had already come to exert an influence over the natives on the way. The departure of the friars with the advance guard left the main army without a chaplain.

Coronado ordered his men to take rations for eighty days, hoping by the end of that time to be in a land of plenty. The supplies were carried on horseback "at no small labor," each man taking enough for himself and his personal followers, a precaution that was justified by events. Coronado tells us, on the other hand, that, because of previous experience on the road, besides the food "none of us carried any necessary effects weighing more than a pound." They were becoming travelwise.

Before setting out for the north the general ordered Arellano to follow in twenty days with the main army, taking as maestre de campo Velasco de Barrionuevo. They were to proceed as far as Corazones, that place which everybody had so lauded, and there await further instructions. Coronado also left orders that in case Zaldívar, who had gone south to carry Díaz' report to Mendoza, might wish to rejoin the expedition, he should go to Cíbola as captain of a company of men drawn from the other units. Having despatched to the viceroy by courier an account of his doings to date and arranged that provisions should be furnished Alarcón when he arrived at Culiacán with his ships, Coronado fared forth. The start was made on April 22, just two months after leaving Compostela.

Meanwhile Zaldívar and his three fellow horsemen had pushed their mounts from Chiametla to Compostela, thence to Colima. There they found Mendoza, and on March 20 they handed him the messages they bore. The viceroy considered

Díaz' account as far from optimistic. So he hurried Zaldívar back over his long trail with a despatch for Coronado, ordering him to halt with his army at Culiacán and send some captain ahead to Cíbola "to learn what it was like" before continuing his march with the main army. Mendoza was still cautious. With little time to rest, Zaldívar took the back track for the north. "And because the viceroy instructed him to go by sea in order the more quickly to reach Culiacán," he "went to Compostela . . . and embarked in a ship," perhaps at San Blas. Was this the *San Gabriel* which Alarcón later added to his fleet? When, on April 29, Zaldívar arrived at Culiacán he learned that Coronado, just a week previously, had gone ahead with his vanguard. That is to say, on his own initiative the general had proceeded to do just what Mendoza ordered. Zaldívar had made an historic ride.

At Colima the viceroy made plans for sending vessels up the Gulf of California to coöperate with the land forces and continue exploration by water, a matter which had been discussed with Coronado before he started north. Ulloa had discovered the mouth of a great river at the head of the Sea of Cortés, but had not explored it. Perhaps it might offer the best approach to the land of turquoises, or to even more enticing lands in the Mysterious North. There Eldorado might be found. In that direction lay China and the realms of the Gran Khan, of which Cíbola was a part. The enterprise was entrusted to Hernando de Alarcón, whom Bernal Díaz calls "chamberlain to the viceroy." He, like Coronado, was one of Mendoza's protégés, and in all probability the two commanders were well acquainted. Among other objectives of the voyage, Alarcón was expected to carry supplies for Coronado and to seek "the port of Chichilticale."

Before he left Colima, Mendoza contracted a slow fever which lasted four days. Having recovered, he continued his journey to Mexico by way of Jacona where, on April 17, he wrote to Charles V summarizing Díaz' report and telling what he had learned of Coronado's progress since they had separated. When the viceroy reached the capital he had ridden well over a thousand miles. Court life had not made him soft.

Chapter IX

WITH THE VANGUARD

In the advance column went some of the most interesting personalities of the army, chosen for experience, character, and fitness for deeds of daring. Toughness and nerve were at a premium for the task at hand. It was a job for scouts and shock troops; it was also a diplomatic mission, to sound out and make friends with the natives, or to fight them if necessary. If it was a woman who went with her man, she must pay the price demanded by affection, for it was a hard life on which she had embarked.

Fray Marcos of course was in the vanguard, for it was he who had brought the expedition about, and he was the only Spaniard who had been beyond Chichilticale. Among the captains there were Cárdenas, maestre de campo; Diego López, alderman of Seville; and Diego Gutiérrez, commander of the cavalry. Others of note were Pedro de Tovar, who had some dogs which created one of the sensations of the expedition; Francisco de Ovando, whose adventures were more than hair-raising; Hernando de Alvarado, a relative of red-headed Pedro de Alvarado, conqueror of Guatemala; Melchior Díaz, great scout and beloved commander; and Fray Juan de Padilla, who became one of the heroes of the entire Coronado episode. Juan Gallego, matchless hand-to-hand fighter, went in charge of the pack train, which for safety traveled in the rear of the procession and was protected by an escort of armed men, for security of the provisions was a prime consideration. All of these persons distinguished themselves in one way or another and will be heard of as the story unfolds.

Men of lesser note but not of inferior interest were some of Coronado's familiars. Juan de Contreras, an interpreter of the Royal Audiencia of Mexico, and therefore a linguist, "went always with the person of Francisco Vázquez because he was his head groom and ate and slept continuously at the door of his tent." He tells us interesting details about the expedition and probably would have told more had he realized how we would relish personal gossip. Alonso Álvarez was Coronado's page. With the advance guard went also Francisca de Hozes, her young son, and her spouse, Alonso Sánchez. Francisca perhaps rode a mule, according to Spanish custom for women, but from what we learn of her we are sure that she could have managed a spirited stallion it occasion had called for it. The chief distinction of Alonso Sánchez was the fact that he was Francisca's husband and by her was kept well in hand. The famous chronicler, Castañeda, be it noted, was not with this company, he having remained behind with the main army, and therefore missed some of the most exciting scenes of the drama, which he recounted from hearsay.

On the march of the vanguard everything possible was done to carry out Mendoza's strict orders looking to consideration for the natives. Guzmán's methods would no longer be tolerated. The Indians encountered on the way were "regaled and aided" and "treated as if they were Spaniards." In fact, some of the soldiers complained of the excessive tenderness toward the natives, and in this particular they regarded Coronado as a martinet. Whenever he approached a village, the general sent men ahead carrying a cross as a sign of peace, and to assure the natives that no harm would be done them. Guards were placed at the settlements near which the Spaniards camped at night in order that the Indians might not be mistreated by the soldiery. These villages gave the Spaniards a friendly welcome, for the kindness of Cabeza de Vaca and Fray Marcos had done much to obliterate from their memory the harsh deeds of Guzmán and Alcaráz. We are told by Rodrigo de Frías that after leaving Culiacán all the settlements passed before reaching Cíbola rendered obedience to Coronado in the name of his Majesty. How formal this ceremony may have been it is difficult to say, but it must have included much pageantry, often made colorful by bright-hued Indian garb and military fanfare. Generally the natives kept their women and children out of sight until they were fully reassured. When they had provisions to spare, which everywhere south of Valle de Sonora were meager, the Indians offered them to the wayfarers, but if anything was accepted Coronado was careful to give them something in return, as Mendoza ordered.

The natives in their simplicity, or their guile, sometimes all too hospitably invited the soldiers to their settlements and even to their dwellings. But to accept the invitation was forbidden, although it would be rash to say that the order was never violated. Youth has its ways. With this in mind Coronado customarily established his camp in the open country some distance from the villages. To please the Indians he distributed glass beads, knives, and gewgaws which Mendoza had liberally furnished to serve as presents or to exchange for food. Another expressed purpose in doing this was that Arellano's army, which was to follow the vanguard, might be given a friendly reception by the natives.

Coronado ordered his men, some of whom were irresponsible fellows, not to take food or anything else from the natives except under the strictest supervision. If the soldiers failed to obey, the general disciplined them, "imprisoning them and inflicting on them other penalties more severe." Indeed, it was notorious that because a Spaniard had taken some roasting ears, and the Indians complained to Coronado, he ordered the man punished. But the young malefactor will not go down in history with this blot on his record, nor will his descendants have to blush for his youthful misdeed, because Frías, who told the story, did not remember the fellow's name. Another soldier for a similar offense was put in manacles and made to travel thus handicapped and humiliated for three whole days.

The consideration of Coronado for the Indians encountered on the way elicited emphatic comments from men in his army. It was something new. Veteran Cristóbal de Mayorga said that in the many wars and expeditions in this New Spain and in other parts where he had been, he had "never seen any Indians better treated . . . than those where Francisco Vázquez went." Hernando de Alvarado declared that no expedition had been made in the Indies by men "more Christian or more fearful of God." Diego de Madrid "had never seen one so well governed or managed with such moderation." The viceroy's instructions and Coronado's dealings with the Indians made a deep impression.

Mendoza had given strict orders to the effect that Indians must not be used at *támenes,* or carriers. This was humane and laudable, but there was another side to the coin. What the Indians gained by exemption from carrying burdens, the Spaniards paid for in toil and sweat. As a result of this consideration for the natives, the Spaniards—even the general himself—became támenes. Coronado tells us that on the march to Cíbola he saw "soldiers of high rank going on foot because they carried their food and other belongings on their horses," since they were not permitted to use Indians to transport their baggage. Moreover, he had seen soldiers "carrying maize for their own sustenance and to feed their horses." Indeed, the captain-general himself had "many times dismounted so the soldiers who were thus traveling laden," encouraged by the example, "would suffer and withstand the hardships with greater fortitude."

Coronado's orders provided that formal possession should be taken of all regions discovered by him or his men. Presumably this would not apply to areas already claimed in the name of the King by Guzmán, Cortés, and Fray Marcos, although a repetition of the ceremony could do no harm. Be that as it may, we are told that the general, "in all the places and regions where he traveled in the Tierra Nueva, took possession for his Majesty and set up crosses as a sign of sovereignty. And he ordered the captains whom he sent out to explore to do likewise." The formal act involved a long rigmarole set down by a notary in language prescribed by law, but of course, though impressive, it was wholly unintelligible to the gaping natives who looked on.

Of the march of the vanguard to Cíbola we have glimpses of human incidents which occurred on the way and help us to visualize the historic event. Leaving Culiacán, in three or four days Coronado arrived at the pueblo of Sebastián de Evora, so-called because Guzmán had assigned it to a Portuguese of that name. Mocorito today is near the site. Since it was unprofitable, Evora had abandoned the pueblo and left it to the Indians, as it remained when Coronado passed through. The place is mentioned here because some historians, by a careless reading of Tello, have erroneously attributed to Coronado an atrocity perpetrated there at a later time and by another person. So far as Don Francisco is concerned the charge is wholly false.

A little farther along, Father Antonio Victoria broke his leg and was carried back to Culiacán to be cared for. Presumably he was transported in a litter by faithful Indians. The chronicler writes that he "stayed with the [main] army thereafter, which was no slight consolation for all." This comment, which is slightly ambiguous, doubtless should be given its most favorable interpretation. Soon after Father Victoria's accident, Coronado and his men arrived at Sinaloa River, where the Indians were friendly and furnished the travelers a few provisions. Three days later they reached the Fuerte River. They were making good time, for the distance between these places, by the trail, was some fifty miles.

Fray Marcos had told interesting things about the Abra, the opening in the Mayo Valley "where the mountains end." Mendoza had expressed himself as skeptical about its assets, but Coronado's curiosity was piqued, and, in any case, the report of gold and large settlements there called for an investigation. To undertake the inquiry he sent veteran Melchior Díaz ahead from Fuerte River with fifteen men on horseback. They were to go by forced marches to Arroyo de los Cedros, the stream which joins Mayo River at Conicari. From there they were to enter the opening "at the right of the road," described by Fray Marcos, "to see the sierras and what there was behind them." If Díaz needed more time than that specified for the reconnoissance, Coronado was to await him at the Cedros, which was on the direct road to the north. Fray Marcos did not take part in this rapid horseback jaunt, because he always traveled on foot in true apostolic fashion. Once again Díaz brought back a disappointing report. Jaramillo, who was one of the party, tells us: "Thus it was done, but all we found there was some poor Indians settled in a few valleys in the manner of rancherías. The land was sterile. The distance from the [Fuerte] river to this arroyo must be an additional five days' journey." He probably meant five days of ordinary travel, and not forced marches, since from Fuerte River to the Cedros where it joins the Mayo it is only about seventy miles.

Coronado comments pithily on the same matter in a letter written to Mendoza. "Thirty leagues before reaching the place of which the father provincial spoke so favorably in his report, I sent Melchior Díaz forward with fifteen horsemen"—Jaramillo says there were ten—"ordering him to make but one journey out of two, so he might examine everything there before I arrived. He traveled four days through some very rough mountains"—in the Abra, it is to be understood—"but did not find anything to live on, or any people, or any information about anything except . . . two or three poor villages with twenty or thirty huts each. From the natives he learned there was nothing to be found in the country beyond except the mountains, which continued to be very rough and entirely uninhabited, and because this labor was lost I did not wish to send your Lordship an account of it."

Evidently there was muttering in the camp when Díaz' report was made known, for Coronado continues: "The whole company felt disturbed . . . that a thing so much praised, and about which the father had said so much, should be found so very different; and they began to think all the rest would be of the same sort." Fray Marcos must have caught an echo of the disappointment, but Coronado, as a good leader, did his best to cheer his men. "When I noticed this," he wrote to Mendoza, "I tried to encourage them as well as I could, telling them your Lordship had always thought this part of the journey would be a waste of effort; that we ought to devote our attention to the Seven Cities and the other provinces about which we had information; and that these"—and not the Abra—"should be the ob-

jective of our enterprise." This was a diplomatic touch, calculated to raise the viceroy's self-esteem. He could say, "I told you
so!"

From Fuerte River, Coronado and his train followed behind Díaz, past Vacapa, past the famous rock of the Frailes who
still look down upon the old trail, past the site where the
beautiful city of Alamos was later built with wealth from rich
silver mines, and thence to Mayo River, at the mouth of Rio
Cedros. From there he traveled some three days northward to
the Yaqui—Jaramillo calls it the Yaquimí—which was probably
reached near Ónabas. He ascended the stream presumably to
Soyopa, then advanced to a dry arroyo which "extended for
only one league," evidently the Rebeico, and at the end of three
more days came to another arroyo, perhaps at Mátape, where
there was a settlement of Indians with straw huts, and fields
planted with maize, beans, and calabashes. They were now
among the Lower Pimas. Two more days took the explorers to
"the arroyo and pueblo called Corazones, so-named by Dorantes, Cabeza de Vaca, Castillo and the Negro Estebanillo . . . because here they were given, as a customary present, the hearts
of animals and birds."

The hard march over the long stretch from Mayo River
brought forth new complaints against Fray Marcos. The good
roads of which he had told seemed to the soldiers very bad. The
general writes: "We all marched cheerfully along a very difficult way, where it was impossible to travel without making a
new road or repairing the one already there. This troubled the
soldiers not a little because everything which the friar had said
was found to be quite the reverse; for among other things he
had said and declared was that the way would be plain and
good, and there would be only one small hill of about half a
league. But the truth is that there are mountains which, however well the trail might be repaired, could not be crossed without great danger that the horses would fall over the cliffs. Indeed, it was so bad that many of the animals which your
Lordship sent as food for the army were lost on this part of the

route, because of the roughness of the rocks. The lambs and wethers lost their hoofs along the way, and most of those I had brought from Culiacán I left at the river of Lachimi (Yaquimí), because they were unable to travel." Four horsemen remained behind with the poor animals to ease them along at a slower pace, since in their weakened condition they could not keep up with the soldiers. Most of them never reached their destination, but died along the way.

By the time Corazones was reached, heavy toll of man and beast had been taken. Ten or twelve horses had succumbed to bad roads, excessive burdens, and poor pasturage. "Some of our Negroes and some of the Indians also died here, which was no small loss for the rest of the expedition." The shortage of food for the men was another problem. It was as Díaz had reported. Coronado continues: "I reached the Valley of Hearts at last, on the twenty-sixth of May, and rested there a number of days. Between Culiacán and this place I was able to sustain myself only by means of a large supply of corn bread, for I had to leave all the maize behind since it was not yet ripe." He had been traveling in the spring season.

These complaints must not be taken too seriously. Most of Coronado's men were the merest tenderfeet. Fray Marcos, on the other hand, was a veteran on the trail, in Peru, in Central America, and in Mexico. Moreover, he was an enthusiast. What to Coronado's novices looked hard, to him seemed easy. Quite apart from gold, Marcos saw a great harvest all around him—a harvest of souls. What he wrote about treasure was for the encouragement of others. Aside from all this, it is to be remembered that, as he went through the country on his first expedition, Fray Marcos had been treated by the Indians with the greatest care and tenderness.

The Valley of Hearts, or Corazones, near the site of Ures, at the southern end of the gorge of Sonora River, was reached a month and four days out from Culiacán. So the advance guard had averaged about twelve miles a day. The general and his men made interesting comments on the historic settlement which they now entered, confirming in the main what Cabeza de Vaca and Fray Marcos had said of it. "There is an irrigation ditch here, and the climate is warm," Jaramillo remarks. "Their houses consist of huts. After setting up poles in the shape of an oven, although much larger, they cover them with mats. For their food they have maize, beans, and calabashes, in abundance I believe. They clothe themselves in deerskins."

Coronado was well pleased with the place, but he told a rather different story regarding the food supply. "In this Valley of Hearts," he writes, "we found more people than in any part of the country we had left behind, and a large extent of cultivated ground." There was no maize here to spare, but the general learned that some could be obtained in the Valley of Sonora a few leagues beyond. So he sent always reliable Díaz north with trinkets to exchange for maize, in order to supply the needs of the Indian allies who had come in his train, and of certain of the soldiers who had lost their horses on the way and therefore had not been able to transport the provisions with which they had started from Culiacán. Díaz' journey was reasonably successful. "By the favor of the Lord, some little maize was obtained by this barter, which relieved the friendly Indians and some of the Spaniards."

On inquiry the general was told by natives that the Gulf of California was distant five days' travel from Corazones, now the site of Ures. So, while men and horses rested, he sent native messengers down Sonora River to summon Indians from the coast "in order to learn their condition." And there was a much more urgent reason. Mendoza had promised to send Alarcón up the Gulf with ships to coöperate with the land force, and three months should have given the vessels time to be abreast of the vanguard.

Coronado remained at Corazones four days, in the course of which several Indians arrived from the west. They reported seven or eight islands two days' journey from the coast, well populated but poorly supplied with food. In addition they told the general they had seen a ship pass not very far from land—

or so he understood them—and he remarked, "I do not know whether to think it was the one that was sent to explore the country [under Alarcón], or perhaps some Portuguese." This observation illustrates the sensitiveness of Spaniards to the presence of Portuguese in the Pacific at this early date. Don Francisco makes no comment at this point regarding the statement of Fray Marcos that on his former journey he had gone from here to the Gulf, but it must have been talked about in camp. Coronado's silence on the subject is eloquent.

Leaving Corazones, and "passing through a sort of small gateway very close to this arroyo"—Puerta de Oro now, in local parlance—the vanguard ascended the gorge of Sonora River, and at the end of some ten leagues entered the already famous Valley of Sonora. Here the reports of Cabeza de Vaca and Fray Marcos were corroborated. Jaramillo tells us, "It also is irrigated and has more Indians than the others, but the settlements and the food are of the same type. This valley must extend six or seven leagues, more or less." He was speaking of the beautiful and well watered valley reaching north from Babiácora to Senoquipe, and whose central settlement was about at modern Huepac. The general found the Indians friendly like the rest. Jaramillo accurately comments, "They have sierras on both sides that are not very productive." The valley is indeed narrow and closely shut in by mountains.

Men and horses would have enjoyed a longer stay in this fertile spot, but Coronado pushed on. From Valle de Sonora he continued up the river, "crossing its meanderings." The traveler today, like Coronado, has to cross the meanderings many times—in some seasons more than fifty—when ascending the stream. After a day's march through an uninhabited stretch, still little populated today, and threading the deep and narrow canyon of Senoquipe, they arrived at the settlement called Ispa by Jaramillo. This was Arizpe, an ancient culture center then, and now the chief town of this upper valley. "These people are of the same customs as the preceding ones." They were all Ópatas, whose blood still runs in the veins of a large portion of the population of northern Sonora.

Coronado did not linger in this truly enchanting country. Cíbola beckoned. Leaving the settlements of Sonora Valley, perhaps at Bacuache, or at Bacanuchi if he ascended the west fork of Sonora River, he traveled four days over an uninhabited area, including the great plains east of Cananea, and reached a stream which the natives called Nexpa, as the Spaniards understood the word. This was San Pedro River, which rises in Sonora a short distance south of the Arizona border and flows northward to Gila River. The general was now among people of a more primitive culture than that of the Ópates. Here some poverty-stricken natives came out to meet him, bringing presents of little value but nevertheless welcome, "such as roasted maguey leaves and pitahayas." These Indians were perhaps the Pima people called Sobajípuris who were living on the San Pedro in the days of Kino, in the seventeenth century, when they manfully defended Sonora from the raiding Apaches.

"We continued down the arroyo for two days," says Jaramillo. Then, "leaving it," apparently about at Tres Alamos, below Benson, "we went to the right in two days' travel to the foot of the cordillera, where we learned it was called Chichilticalli." The route for the two days after leaving the Nexpa was apparently a little east of north through Galiuro Range and across Arivaipa Valley to the foot of Eagle Pass, the opening between Pinaleño and Santa Teresa mountains. Here was Chichilticale, the Red House, where Díaz and his companions had shivered through part of the previous winter.

Chichilticale was a notable point on the Coronado trail. Castañeda, who saw it later, when he followed with the main army, gives us our fullest eye-witness description of the historic site. The place, he writes, "received its name from the fact that the friars found in this region a house formerly inhabited by people who broke away from Cíbola." He means that this discovery was made during the journey of Fray Marcos and Stephen, forgetting that Fray Onorato had been left by Marcos near Sinaloa River. "The house was built of brown or red earth. It must have been despoiled by the natives of the region, who are the most barbarous people thus far encountered. They live by hunting and in rancherías, without permanent settlements." In another paragraph Castañeda says that Chichilticale was at "the beginning of the despoblado, or uninhabited area, two hundred and twenty leagues from Culiacán." The estimate was sound, and indicates the care taken by the famous chronicler. Jaramillo applied the name also to the gap in the mountain as well as to the ruin. He says: "We called this pass Chichilte-calli, for we had heard from some Indians whom we met farther back that it was known by this name." As a matter of fact, Díaz had reported this name before Coronado started north from Culiacán. From this we see that the designation Chichilticale was given by the chroniclers to the ruin, the mountain range, the pass at whose foot it stood, and the beginning of the despoblado —or rather at the end of the settled region. But the name referred particularly to a building. On 76 Ranch near the foot of Eagle Pass there are extensive pueblo ruins, one of which may well be the remains of the structure which Coronado and his companions called Chichilti-cale, the Red House.[1] *Chichilte* and *calli* are two Yaqui words still in use, and they still mean *red house*. Here the general rested his men and animals two days, and, he says, "there was good reason for staying there longer, because we found that the horses were becoming so tired; but it was not possible to halt longer since the food was giving out."

As Coronado approached the despoblado, shortage of provisions had become a constantly more serious matter, and his anxiety to get in touch with Alarcón had increased, for it was assumed that Don Hernando had sailed with supplies intended for the land force on the march. And at this point Fray Marcos' geography became especially dubious. So the inquiries made at Corazones were repeated at Chichilticale with growing concern. The general wrote to Mendoza, "I set out from Los Corazones and kept near the seacoast as well as I could judge, but in fact I found myself getting continually farther away"—that is to say, the Gulf coast swung westward while he veered toward the east —"so that when I reached Chichilticale I learned that I was fif-

---

[1] Sauer suggests a ruin on Haby's Ranch, a short distance to the northwest of Eagle Pass, as the site of Chichilticale.

teen days' journey from the sea, although the father provincial said that it was only five leagues distant and that he had seen it." From Chichilticale to the Gulf it was in fact well over two hundred miles air line. "We all now became very distrustful, and felt great anxiety and dismay to see that everything was the reverse of what he had told your Lordship! The Indians of Chichilticale say that when they go to the sea for fish, or for anything else they need . . . it takes them ten days; and this information which I have obtained from the Indians appears to me to be correct. The sea turns toward the west for ten or twelve leagues directly opposite Los Corazones, where I learned that sight had been caught of the ships of your Lordship which had gone in search of the port of Chichilticale, on the thirty-fifth parallel the father said. God knows that I have suffered, because I fear they have met some mishap. If they follow the coast, as they said they would, as long as the food lasts which they took with them . . . and if they have not been overtaken by some misfortune, I maintain my trust in God that they already may have discovered something good, for which their delay may be pardoned." It is clear that Coronado was worried, and that Alarcón's whereabouts was a matter of great concern.

Castañeda, on the basis of what he heard later, gives a similar account of Coronado's gradual disillusionment and his growing distrust of the report given by Fray Marcos. "When the general had crossed the settled region and reached Chichilticale, where the despoblado began, and they could not see anything of any account, he could not help feeling some disappointment because, although the reports of what lay ahead were alluring, no one had seen it"—not even Fray Marcos!— "except the Indians who accompanied the Negro, and they had already been caught in several lies. The men were all disgusted on seeing that the famous Chichilticale turned out to be a roofless ruined house." Coronado's quandary at this point is not difficult to understand.

The general now sent Cárdenas a day's march ahead with fifteen horsemen to explore the route, select camp-sites, and give warning of any dangers that might arise. This duty, Coronado wrote to Mendoza, "he performed like the man he is, justifying the confidence which your Lordship placed in him." It was a task similar to the one assigned Díaz when he went to reconnoiter the Abra in Mayo River Valley. Presumably Cárdenas kept Coronado informed of everything by messengers sent back to him daily, or oftener when occasion required it.

The march across the despoblado, from the Red House to the Little Colorado River, where they next met Indians, was a distance of nearly 150 miles, and was one of the hardest stretches of the entire journey. This was due, in part, to the difficult terrain, but even more to the shortage of provisions and the worn-out condition of men and animals. The effects of hardship and hunger were cumulative. Uninhabited then, hence called the *despoblado,* a large part of the region is now a reservation for Apaches, who entered it from the east at a later time. The area contains some of the most beautiful forest and mountain country to be found anywhere in the world. In the nineteenth century it was a land of Apache wars, cattle ranches, rustlers, and "bad men" whose story has been told in lurid fiction by Zane Grey, and more soberly by General Crooke and other soldiers who learned to respect the fighting qualities of these competent Indians. Coronado was traveling now on the trail which in the nineteenth century became known as the Mormon Road to Arizona.

Leaving Chichilticale, the general set forth in the wake of Cárdenas and immediately crossed the Pinaleño Mountains through the gap now called Eagle Pass. Though long, the pass was neither narrow nor difficult, and from the summit it afforded the travelers a spacious view of the valley of Gila River, which they now entered. In their descent to the stream, a distance of some twenty-five miles, they skirted the eastern base of Santa Teresa Mountains and bulky Mount Turnbull which towered above them on the left. At the end of this stretch they arrived at a "deep arroyo and a ravine" where they found water and grass for the horses. The deep arroyo was Gila River, and the ravine was the river valley, which is two or three miles wide where they reached it, at San Gerónimo. The stream was crossed some ten miles farther west, at Bylas, where the old trail ran. The river banks here are low, but, on the north the valley is closed in by a high mesa, beyond which is Gila Range. There is no ground for thinking that Coronado went east from Chichilticale to Clifton, or that he was anywhere near the "Coronado Highway" (No. 666), which runs over White Mountains to St. Johns. The name of that highway should be given to the route we are now following.

Jaramillo is our best guide for the march from the Gila River across the mountains that lay ahead, and his account and that of Coronado harmonize and support each other. Taken together they enable us to identify with certainty the main landmarks in terms of modern geography. Though clearly indicated in the narratives, and sharply marked by natural features, this part of the trail has been badly misinterpreted by most writers on the subject. From the crossing at Bylas, Coronado evidently marched north, ascended the mesa, swung round the west end of Gila Range, marched northeast to Ash Creek, turned north across Natagés Plateau, and on the feast of St. John, having named the stream in that saint's honor, forded Salt River near the mouth of Bonito Creek. Continuing nearly north for some twenty miles, the general came to Rio de las Balsas, so called because the expedition crossed it by means of rafts. This stream was White River, and was reached by Coronado just below the site of Fort Apache. In much of its course White River flows through deep gorges or barrancas, but here, near the old fort, there is a shallow place where it was feasible to use rafts for transporting men and baggage.

Summing up the march from Chichilticale to this point, Coronado says, "To vary our past tribulations we found no grass during the first days, and encountered more dangerous passages than we had previously experienced. The horses were so exhausted they could not endure it, and in this last desert we lost more than previously. The way is very bad for at least thirty leagues or more, through impassable mountains. But when we had covered these thirty leagues we found fresh rivers and grass like that of Castile." The distance by the trail from

Eagle Pass to Fort Apache is about ninety miles, or thirty leagues, and all the way the road is rough and mountainous. But at the site of Fort Apache they reached green, forested, and well-watered country, with "fresh rivers and grass," just as Coronado says.

Beyond Fort Apache it is relatively easy to identify Coronado's route. "From here," Jaramillo records, "we went to another arroyo which we called La Barranca. The distance between them is two short days' travel." They were going slowly now, because men and animals were badly worn. La Barranca is readily identified. On this stretch Coronado was ascending the west bank of the main fork of White River about as highway No. 73 now runs. Some fifteen miles upstream from Fort Apache, and twelve from the town of Whiteriver, a small branch now called Post Office Canyon enters the main stream from the west. It runs through a narrow gorge, with perpendicular walls of solid rock, perhaps two hundred feet deep where it is crossed by the road. This creek, it is plain, is the one which Jaramillo calls La Barranca. The modern highway crosses the canyon on a bridge, but the old trail swung west a short distance and crossed the creek above the gorge. The bend in the old trail is clearly shown on early maps of the region.

Continuing north, says Jaramillo, "we went to another river, which we named Rio Frio, because its water was cold, reaching it in one day's travel." The pace was still slow, and Rio Frio was evidently one of the small streams in the vicinity of McNary, ten miles northward of La Barranca. "Then from here we continued through a pine forest, almost at the end of which we found a spring and a cool little arroyo. This took us about another day's travel." Death now stalked in the camp. "Here at this arroyo a Spaniard named Espinosa and two other persons died from the effects of some plants which they ate because of their great privation." Coronado refers to the same incident, adds to these casualties those of horses and Indian allies, identifies the "other persons" as two Negroes, and assigns the same cause, poisonous plants, for the death of the men. Here, beside the trail, Espinosa and the Negroes were buried, doubtless with Christian rites, for Fray Marcos, Padilla, and other friars were present. The shallow grave in which the bodies of the deceased were deposited, again and with gruesome detail, comes into history later on.

This day's travel through the tall pines and over the divide is likewise easy to follow. McNary, near the camp whence they set forth in the morning, is on the southern edge of the great Mogollón Forest, named for an eighteenth-century governor of New Mexico, and by most Nordics horribly mispronounced "Muggyone"!! On the way, Coronado passed Summit Spring, and perhaps quaffed its icy water. Near the northern edge of the forest, where the Camp of Death was located, there are numerous springs in the vicinity of Vernon. Bannon Springs and the creeks which issue from them would correspond well to the place where Espinosa, the Negroes, and the Indians died. The plant which caused their death may well have been the wild parsnip which abounds in the region, especially in the marshes about McNary, where Coronado had camped the previous night.

Chapter X

CÍBOLA LIES AT HAND!

It was now July. Coronado had been on the road six months since saying goodbye to Doña Beatríz. His men were tired and worn from the hardship and grind of the long rough trail. They were bruised and ragged and footsore. The horses had suffered even more than the men, and not a few of them had died, to have their bones picked by crows and coyotes. Especially trying to the spirit of the caballeros was the endless round of menial tasks, camp duty, caring for their mounts, "loading and unloading like so many muleteers," and even carrying their baggage—things most of them had never done before.

But the chief hardship on the way was not so much the physical toil as the lack of food, for every army travels more on its stomach than on its feet. Coronado had hoped to get supplies from Alarcón's ships, but they had failed to arrive, and by now the men were enduring extreme hunger. Indeed, one witness attributes the demise of Espinosa and the others at the Camp of Death to starvation rather than to eating the poisonous plant. Strangely enough, no mention is made of the utilization of any game in these vast forests; and after leaving Chichilticale the Spaniards apparently did not see a single Indian until they reached the Little Colorado, for this long stretch was the Great Despoblado, which even yet had not been left behind.

Nevertheless, only one Spaniard had been lost in the difficult trek, a tribute to Coronado's leadership and to the mettle of his followers. Most of the men were still in good health, and their morale was all that could be desired, for "there was not a man in the army who would not have done his best in everything if the horses could have done their part." This tribute by an officer speaks well for the soldiers after the gruelling march. The spirit of the adventurers, bedraggled as they were, was now revived by the knowledge that they were nearing the Seven Cities, where, they fondly hoped, they would find food in abundance and fabulous wealth—but first of all food!

As Coronado neared his goal, special precautions were necessary. Therefore, from the Camp of Death at the edge of the Great Forest, he again sent Cárdenas a day ahead with fifteen mounted men to reconnoiter and prepare the way. One of the fifteen was Hernando de Alvarado. In case the natives of Cíbola should resist, the general wished to be prepared and not taken unawares. They had murdered Stephen, and Díaz had been told at Chichilticale that they had threatened vengeance on all Spaniards. So resistance at Cíbola was to be expected.

Emerging from the forest and traveling northeastward down the gently rolling open country, at the end of two days Cárdenas and his men arrived at a stream eight leagues from Cíbola, and "because its water was muddy and red, they called it Rio Bermejo," or Red River. It was the Little Colorado of today, which, with the characteristic tenacity of place names, still bears its original designation by white men. In its murky waters the Spaniards found barbels or mullets "like those of Spain," the chroniclers fondly wrote. The old home, España, now in imagination appeared like heaven to these weary, hungry, and perhaps nervous young fellows—not that any one of them would have turned back, with the goal of their adventure so nearly attained.

The route for these two days from the Camp of Death, over which Cárdenas preceded Coronado, led past Cave Spring to the right of the mesa near Concho, and struck the Little Colorado near its junction with Zuñi River. They evidently crossed the stream about where the old maps show Colorado Bridge, north of the site of St. Johns. It was somewhere along this stretch of the road that, according to Fray Marcos, his companions had come fleeing from Cíbola with the story of the killing of Stephen. But, strangely enough, no allusion to the episode is made in the reports on Coronado's march, nor is Fray

Marcos mentioned anywhere on this part of the trail, although he was with the vanguard.

Cárdenas saw no Indians during his first day's march from the Camp of Death. But Cíbola spies were wide-awake and knew of the approach of the strangers, having been warned perhaps by runners from Sonora Valley or Chichilticale. Next day, at Rio Bermejo, four natives of Cíbola appeared before Cárdenas, making signs of peace, saying through the interpreters that they had been sent to welcome the Spaniards, and that on the morrow all the visitors would be supplied with food—the most joyous news imaginable by the famished soldiers! The Cíbolans had doubtless heard about Spanish horses, otherwise they would have been scared out of their wits and made a scene worth a story, but the subject is not mentioned by the chroniclers. Giving two of the emissaries a cross, Cárdenas instructed them to return to Cíbola and tell their people to remain quietly in their houses, because Coronado was coming in the name of the Emperor to defend and aid them. The two other Cíbolans were held as hostages until the general should arrive, and Cárdenas sent Alvarado back to tell Coronado of the friendly embassy. It was this episode on the Little Colorado that Castañeda had in mind when he wrote years afterward: "Here it was," at Rio Bermejo, "that they saw the first Indians in that land."

From the Camp of Death, Coronado and his hungry men, with tightened belts, followed one day behind Cárdenas. On the way they were met by Alvarado bearing the good news, and were conducted by him to the place where Cárdenas was camped. The soldiers, having visions of the promised food, wished the general would travel faster and expressed their impatience with well-rounded oaths. Coronado dealt gently with the two hostages from Cíbola, giving them "paternosters and some little cloaks," and assuring them they need have no fear. The cloaks perhaps were more appreciated than the paternosters. At the same time, the general sent Cárdenas ahead once more to see if there were any dangerous places where the Cíbolans might ambush the Spaniards, and, if so, to occupy and hold them until he arrived.

Next day, when Coronado was on the road, his scouts saw some Indians near a lake, so he sent Pedro de Tovar and Melchior Díaz, those two reliables, to bring some of them to camp. Accompanied by Mexican Indians bearing a cross as an emblem of peace, Tovar and Díaz went on their errand and succeeded in bringing before the general two or three natives of Cíbola. Through an interpreter from the Valley of Corazones—doubtless one of the many Ópatas who had traded Sonora parrots for Cíbola turquoises—Coronado explained to his guests that he had come in the name of the great Emperor across the water, "to place them under his dominion and afford them a knowledge of God." He told them they ought to become Christians, and that, if they submitted peacefully to the will of his Majesty, they would not be harmed in any way.

With increased caution the army went forward. A direct route from the camp on the Little Colorado would have taken Coronado across the desert plain to the forks of Zuñi River, thence upstream along its northern bank, which offers better footing than the other side. When three or four leagues from Háwikuh, the westernmost Zuñi pueblo, the general was informed that the inhabitants were up in arms, and not disposed to give him a friendly welcome, notwithstanding the message delivered by the Cíbola couriers at Rio Bermejo. He was told also that, a short distance beyond, there was a bad pass in a rocky place where the army might be ambushed. So he sent Cárdenas ahead once more with a small detachment of mounted men to examine the site, "clear it out," spend the night there, and report promptly whatever might happen. The situation reminds one of the approach of Córtes to Tlascala on his celebrated march to Mexico City.

Cárdenas went forward, and we have his account of what occurred. As he neared the Bad Pass, he saw some Indians on the summit of a hill. They had come down Zuñi River from Háwikuh to reconnoiter, and perhaps to check the advance of the strangers. Going ahead of his men toward the assemblage, and making signs of peace, Cárdenas offered the Indians gifts of gewgaws carried for the purpose. Some of the Cíbolans descended the hill and accepted the presents. Wearing his best smile, Cárdenas shook hands with them, gave them a cross, and by signs told them to return home and inform their people that the Spaniards had come on a peaceful errand and desired to be friends—the same message which Coronado had given the two emissaries from Háwuikuh the day before.

Everything seemed to be going smoothly. The Cíbolans departed and Cárdenas made camp, placing a small mounted guard at the near-by pass, while the rest of the men unsaddled their horses with a sense of security. But this feeling was unwarranted. For, at midnight, a large band of Cíbolans attacked the Spaniards, and, says Cárdenas, because of the hullabaloo made by the Indians "and the arrows they shot at them, the horses . . . became frightened and ran away, leaving most of the men on foot. And had it not been for two mounted sentinels the Indians would have killed this witness and the ten companions who were with him guarding the pass." It was a narrow escape for Don Lope.

Castañeda, who was not present at the skirmish, saw in it a little humor, heightened no doubt by his long distance from the danger point. "During the night," he says, "some of the Indians in a safe place yelled so that, although the men were ready for anything, they were so rattled that they put their saddles on hind-side before." But, he charitably adds, "these were the greenhorns, and when the veterans mounted and rode round the camp the Indians fled, and none of them could be caught because they knew the country." The Bad Pass, where this incident occurred, was near Zuñi River and close to the present-day boundary between New Mexico and Arizona. Two or three miles farther east by airline stood Háwikuh, the westernmost and principal Cíbola town.

Immediately after the midnight ambush, Cárdenas sent a courier back on the run to report to Coronado what had happened. The general hurried forward, urged now by a double necessity, a military crisis and the hunger of his men; for, he writes, "we were in such dire need of food that I thought we all should die of starvation if we had to wait another day, especially the Indian allies, since altogether we did not have two bushels of maize." Seeing Coronado approach with a larger force, the Indians sent up smoke signals at various places, and they were answered from a distance, "a method of communication," says the general, "as good as we could have devised ourselves. Thus they both gave warning of our approach and revealed our whereabouts."

Coronado overtook Cárdenas at the Bad Pass and learned more in detail what had happened in the night. The emissaries met at the Little Colorado had encouraged the general, but the attack at the Bad Pass checked his optimism and served as a warning of things to come. On the other hand, by their vigorous demonstration of courage the Cíbolans won Coronado's respect from the start. "According to what I have been told," he wrote to Mendoza, "they attacked like valiant men, although in the end they had to retreat in flight, because our army-master was on the watch and kept his men in good order. The Indians sounded a little trumpet as a signal for retreat, and did no damage to the Spaniards."

As a precaution against another surprise attack, Cárdenas and his men again preceded the main body of troops up the narrow valley of Zuñi River. Hunger now outweighed any fears they might have entertained, and with righted saddles they swung into line like veterans. About a league before reaching Háwikuh the scouting party saw four or five Indians who had come to spy on the strangers and send back the news. Hereupon the Spaniards halted, and Cárdenas went forward alone to talk with them, "making signs and demonstrations of peace," but "they did not wait for him." In other words, they fled. So the march was resumed, with the scouts in the van. The baggage train and the rear guard in command of Juan Gallego followed some distance behind. With this unit went talkative Señora Francisca de Hozes.

Suddenly someone caught a glimpse of Háwikuh! There it was, just beyond. Perhaps, in keeping with Spanish custom, he shouted, "*Albricias! Albricias!* Reward me! Reward me!" At last, Cíbola was in sight! This was the moment to which the Spaniards had looked forward ever since they left Mexico, the time when they should arrive at the portals of the first of the Seven Cities, the very one which Fray Marcos had so lauded. Sore muscles limbered up and bruises were momentarily forgotten.

Then what a shock! For, instead of a great city sparkling with jewels, the weary treasure-seekers saw before them on an eminence a little pueblo "all crumpled together"! And when the soldiers beheld it, and realized what it was, "such were the curses which some of them hurled at Fray Marcos," wrote Castañeda, "that I pray God to protect him from them." From this laconic description of the first of the Seven Cities, it is seen that Coronado paid Mendoza and his home town no great compliment by calling it Granada, "for so it was named in honor of the viceroy, and because some say it resembles the Albaicín," one of the sections of old Granada near the Alhambra.

Chapter XI

CAPTURE OF HÁWIKUH

The natives of Cíbola had been preparing to resist the Spaniards, as is clearly shown by the embassy sent to Río Bermejo and by the midnight attack on Cárdenas at the Bad Pass. And they had planned to combine craft with force. News of the advent of the armored strangers riding armored horses had spread among the pueblos of the province, and from them warriors were sent to join in the defense of Háwikuh, the town which the strangers would first encounter on approaching from the southwest. And before the Spaniards arrived there, the women and children and most of the men over sixty and under twenty had been removed to a place of safety in the cliffs, leaving only the braves to defend the pueblo, together with a few old men to direct them. They had likewise hidden all their movable possessions, including "many turquoises," Coronado tells us. The turquoises may have been an optimistic assumption on his part.

When the Spaniards came in sight of Háwikuh, smoke signals were rising in various places round about. Most of the warriors at this very moment were secreted inside the pueblo, planning a surprise attack at the opportune moment. Part of the defenders, two or three hundred, had gathered on the plain outside the town a crossbow shot from the surrounding walls, to serve as shock troops. Drawn up in squadrons in military formation, armed with bows, arrows, and war clubs, and protected by leather shields, they were blowing a horn, making hostile gestures, and ordering the Spaniards to go back in the direction from which they had come. The Indians were no cowards. Mota Padilla tells us, on the basis of Továr's manuscripts, that the Háwikuh warriors drew lines on the ground and ordered the Spaniards not to cross them. Presumably these lines were made with sacred corn meal, according to a custom still practised by the Pueblo Indians when they wish to exclude strangers from their secret ceremonies.

Coronado had no desire to fight the Cíbolans. Far from it; but they must acknowledge Spanish rule. Halting his men at a suitable distance, he again sent Cárdenas ahead, accompanied by Fray Luís, Fray Daniel, Bermejo the notary, and a small escort of mounted men. Cárdenas was instructed to tell the Cíbolans the Spaniards had come not to injure but to defend them, in the name of the great Emperor who lived beyond the ocean. This message was delivered by Bermejo in the form prescribed by Coronado's instructions and "made intelligible through an interpreter." All this was done "as was the custom in new countries." The formula was doubtless much like the bombastic orations made by Ojeda down on the Spanish Main in the days of Balboa, and as little understood by the natives here as there. Meanwhile, Coronado's hungry followers cared only for quick results, for at the moment nothing counted with them but food.

Cárdenas and his companions spoke gently to the Cíbolans, made signs of peace, laid down their own weapons and by pantomime urged the Indians to do likewise. But the Indians were far from convinced by the notary's ponderous speech. Quite the contrary. "Being a proud people," says Coronado, they paid slight attention to the harangue, because they thought "since we were few in number, they would have no difficulty in killing us." Whatever the Cíbolans may have thought, they now rushed upon Cárdenas and his men, firing arrows right and left. The result of the skirmish was not highly disastrous to the Spaniards. One native shaft cut through the armor of Bermejo and another wounded his horse. Fray Luís, "a former companion of the bishop of Mexico, had the skirt of his cassock pierced by an arrow." This did him no harm, and from the record we learn of the interesting association between Fray Luís and the great Zumárraga.

Coronado, accompanied by a few mounted men, now moved up to the scene of action. Taking some gewgaws for presents, and ordering the army to follow, he joined Cárdenas and his companions. The general in his best armor, with gilded helmet, feather-crested, was a conspicuous figure, and some of the other officers were scarcely less imposing. But the Indians were by no means overawed by all this splendor.

The Cíbolans had twice attacked the Spaniards. The famished soldiers were impatient to get into the city and relieve their hunger. But, while his followers cursed under their breath, Coronado, anxious to avoid an open rupture, once more attempted conciliation, as he explained in a letter to Mendoza. "In obedience to the precepts of your Lordship and of his Majesty, I did not wish them attacked, and although my men were begging me for permission, I enjoined them from doing so, telling them they ought not to molest them; that the enemy was doing us no harm, and that it was not proper to fight so small a number of people. On the other hand, when the Indians saw we did not move they took greater courage, and grew so bold that they came almost to the heels of our horses to shoot their arrows." This was too much for Spanish pride! "On this account I saw the time for hesitation had passed, and, as the priests approved the action, I charged them." So the *Santiago* was given and the soldiers responded with zeal born of hunger. "But there was little to do," says Coronado, "for the Indians suddenly took to flight, some running toward the city, which was near by and well fortified, and others toward the plain, or wherever chance led them. Some of them were killed, and others might have been slain if I had allowed them to be pursued. But I saw that in this there would be little advantage, because the Indians who were outside were few, while those who had retired to the city, added to the many who had remained there in the first place, were numerous." And Coronado was never bloodthirsty.

Cárdenas said the number of Cíbolans killed in this skirmish was "not more than ten or twelve." Even so, it was a bad beginning. Mota Padilla puts the number a little higher. He says: "We attacked them, and after having left more than twenty men dead on the field, they fortified themselves in their quarters." Persistent in his efforts to avoid open war, Coronado again exhorted the natives to submit, but once more in vain.

The crisis brought Fray Marcos to the fore in the narratives almost the first time since the departure from Culiacán. We are told that when the engagement in front of the pueblo was over, "Fray Marcos de Niza . . . came up." He apparently had been in the rear as the Spaniards approached Cíbola—again perhaps because he was not a horseman—and it is noteworthy that it was friars Luís and Daniel who had assisted Cárdenas in his diplomatic efforts with the natives. Coronado now told Marcos what had happened in the course of the skirmish, "and when the . . . friar heard of it and saw that the Indians were fortified he shouted, 'Take your shields and go after them!' " In a pinch he was a fighting man.

This does not mean that Fray Marcos was responsible for events that followed. He merely sanctioned what was inevitable under the circumstances. In the eyes of all the Spaniards the Cíbolans merited punishment for an unprovoked attack. That is to say, unprovoked except that the Spaniards had invaded Cíbola with an army. Coronado had been patient, and several times had attempted to conciliate the Indians, but to no purpose. Spanish arms must be respected. And there was a more urgent consideration than Spanish honor. The soldiers were starving, and within the pueblo there was food, so it is doubtful whether, under the circumstances, Coronado could any longer have restrained his men if he had tried. The Cíbolans had fled inside the pueblo to continue resistance there. "As that was the place where the food was stored, and of which we were in such dire need," said Coronado, "I assembled my whole force, and divided it as seemed best for the attack on the city," for "the hunger we suffered would not permit of delay."

The die was cast! The best account of the fight which now ensued is the one by Coronado himself in a letter written to

Mendoza nearly a month after the event, by which time he had recovered from wounds and bruises received in the fray. His story is conspicuously modest, straightforward, and generous toward everybody concerned. It gives us a good measure of the man.

The capture of the little pueblo was no easy matter. The town was solidly built of stone and adobe, and enclosed by a stone wall. Witnesses reported some two hundred fighting men permanently resident there. At the moment of the Spanish attack there were several times that number inside the pueblo, for most of the warriors of all the Cíbola towns had rallied to the defense of the endangered place. The Háwikuh pueblo was a single structure, in effect a fortified apartment house. It was wide at the base and tapered toward the top, the walls receding in terraces formed by the flat roofs of the dwellings. In the middle it was six storeys high. The roof or azotea of the lower storey was reached by ladders, each made of two poles held together by rungs, in quite modern fashion. These ladders were movable and could be pulled up to a higher level when desired, as in case of attack by an enemy. There were no outer doors to the ground floor apartments, which were used mainly for storage, and were entered by trap doors in the flat roofs forming the lower terrace, "like the scuttles of ships." The apartments in the higher storeys, where the inhabitants lived, were reached by ladders rising from each level to the one next above. On the terraces at strategic points the Cíbolans had assembled a large supply of stones for use as missiles, and the warriors were well equipped with bows and arrows.

The Spaniards at this moment were unfit for battle. Exhausted by the long hard journey and almost starved, "they were more in need of . . . rest than of fighting," and the horses were in even worse condition. Part of the men had spent the previous night on guard and sleepless at the Bad Pass; the rest had made a rapid morning march to overtake Cárdenas at that place, whence the whole force had made two jittery leagues to Háwikuh—for most of these young fellows were not veterans.

Preparatory to storming the pueblo, Coronado deployed

part of his cavalry to surround it, so that no Indian might escape. Before ordering a charge he once more urged the Cíbolans to submit peacefully, assuring them that no harm would be done them. But the answer was another shower of arrows. So the *Santiago* was given and the assault begun. But the arrows came so thick and fast from the terraces that it was impossible for the horsemen to approach the walls, and in the face of this barrage the Spaniards were forced to retreat.

New tactics were necessary. Coronado and some of the horsemen now dismounted, for the purpose of entering the pueblo on foot with part of the infantry. The general ordered crossbowmen and arquebusiers to begin the attack and drive the enemy from the terraces, thus clearing the way for his entrance into the city unhindered by native arrows. Meanwhile he and his chosen companions invested the wall at a place where there was a gate and a scaling ladder. "But," says Coronado, "the crossbowmen soon broke the strings of their crossbows, and the musketeers could accomplish nothing because they had arrived so weak they could scarcely stand on their feet." Consequently the Cíbolans on the terraces conducting the defense were not hindered in the least from spending their whole strength upon Coronado and his little squad.

The general drove forward, but the entrance to the pueblo was narrow, crooked, and skillfully fashioned for protection, and here the Spaniards were roughly handled by the defenders. In short, to the surprise of the invaders, the Cíbolans had the best of it. Coronado with his gilded armor was a shining mark, and he became the central target for the barrage of arrows, stones, and other missiles that rained down in a heavy shower. While trying to reach the first terrace he was twice felled by stones hurled from above, and if he had not been protected by his strong headpiece, and rescued by his men, he most certainly would have been killed. Seeing the general in peril, Cárdenas and Alvarado, like good cavaliers, threw their bodies above the fallen commander and received the blows from the stones. Even so, Coronado had two or three wounds in his face, an arrow in one foot, and many bruises on his arms, legs, and shoulders. In fact, he was put completely *hors de combat* by the Cíbolans, leaving the command to the maestre de campo. By Don García and the soldiers Coronado was carried as dead to a tent where for a long time he lay unconscious; and when he revived he was told the welcome news that the pueblo had been captured and that in it a large supply of provisions had been found.

Coronado was not the only Spaniard roughly handled in the fray, as he himself tells us. "The maestre de campo, Don Pedro de Tovar, Hernando de Alvarado, and Pablos de Melgosa, infantry captain, all sustained bruises, although none of them was wounded." Gómez Suárez and a man named Torres received arm injuries, and two other footmen were wounded slightly by arrows. With Coronado out of the fight, it was to Cárdenas that the pueblo surrendered. The Indians had enough, and they begged him by signs "not to harm them any more, as they wished to leave the pueblo." He told them they might remain if they wished and all would be at peace, "but they desired to leave, so they went away unharmed by the Spaniards." The fight at the pueblo was not long drawn out. The city capitulated in less than an hour after the assault was begun, and the Spaniards promptly moved in. When Francisca de Hozes arrived on her mule with Gallego's rear guard, "the pueblo was captured and peaceful."

If from a military point of view the battle was a draw, to the starving soldiers it was a victory of transcendant importance, for they now had a great feast, highly seasoned by hunger. And how they gorged themselves! On the long march, says one account, "God knows how frugally we had lived, and whether we could have eaten much more than we consumed on the day when his Grace entered the city of Granada. . . . There we found something we prized more than gold or silver; namely, plentiful maize and beans, turkeys larger than those . . . in New Spain, and salt better and whiter than any I have ever seen in my whole life"—doubtless from the famous salt lake some distance south of Háwikuh. For the moment, necessity had changed standards of value.

After the feast a much needed sleep! A few days were spent by the Spaniards nursing their sore spots, filling their stomachs, resting men and horses from their long march, looking around, and wishing the young women would come out of their hiding places and brighten the scene. Meanwhile Coronado made sincere efforts to conciliate the natives and win their confidence. He ordered the Indians who had surrendered at Háwikuh well treated, especially the women and children, and forbade anyone to molest them. When some chiefs came to confer with him, he sent them to invite the others to assemble at Háwikuh to talk things over, promising them good treatment and safety.

In response to the general's message the head men came down from Máçaque, a few miles east of Háwikuh, where they had been in council regarding the crisis which had come to their fair land. Coronado explained to them through an interpreter that they had done wrong in not coming to render obedience peacefully, as he had several times requested them to do, but said he would forgive them if they would comply with the requirement now. If any of them desired to return to live at Háwikuh they would be well treated, their houses and belongings would be undisturbed, and their wounded warriors cared for. These words were effective. The chiefs admitted they had done wrong, and promised to bring the head men of the rest of the pueblos to render obedience.

They were as good as their word. Some days later the chiefs of Máçaque and other towns appeared at Háwikuh, with presents of deer and buffalo skins, "poor blankets" made of "henequén" (probably yucca), some turquoises, and a few bows and arrows. The general was more impressed by the spirit than by the substance of the gifts. He welcomed the ambassadors in the name of his Majesty and told them the purpose of his coming to their distant country, namely, "that they all . . . might become Christians and accept the true God as their Lord, and his Majesty as their King and earthly master." Apparently he said nothing at this juncture about gold and jeweled cities. In return for their tokens he gave his visitors presents, with which they were much pleased. The chiefs now rendered obedience to the King of Spain and said they wished to become Christians. For the moment Coronado was optimistic. The interview over, the embassy withdrew. Then, "suddenly, next day, they packed up their goods and property, their women and children," and, leaving their towns deserted, took refuge in the cliffs.

Undiscouraged, Coronado made another attempt, with better results. A week later, on July 19, when he had recovered somewhat from his wounds, he went to Máçaque, a large pueblo on a cliff toward the east, where the Indians had assembled with a view to resisting the Spaniards. This cliff was the famous mesa of Towayálane, or Corn Mountain. The general found there only a few natives. He told them to have no fear and asked them to send their "lord" to see him at Háwikuh, although, he remarked, "by what I can find out and observe, none of these towns has any lord, for I have not seen any principal house by which any superiority over others might be manifested." Rulers, of course, according to current notions in Europe, must live in style.

The summons was heeded. Soon an old man who said he was the "lord" went to the general, bearing a very modest gift consisting of a portion of a blanket made of many pieces. They had a long and amicable talk, and when the visitor departed he said he would return three days later with the rest of the head men. He kept his word, and at the appointed time he arrived with the chiefs, who brought presents consisting of "some ragged little blankets and some turquoises." Such was the wealth of Cíbola!

An impressive conference followed. Matters of state were discussed, and the Indians promised to become subjects of the King of Spain. Indeed, they said it had been foretold more than fifty years previously that people like Coronado and his men would come from the south and conquer the whole country. Possibly they alluded to the legend of Quetzalcoatl, the Fair God. Or perhaps they had heard rumors of Columbus and his successors, which would not be surprising, for news traveled fast and far among the primitive inhabitants of the Western Hemisphere. The chiefs promised also to become Christians, and to bring their children to be baptized by the friars. Coronado was progressing famously, and he now requested his visitors to have a canvas painted for him, showing all the animals of the country known to them; "and," says the general, "although they are poor artists they quickly painted two for us, one of the animals and the other of the birds and fishes." This treasure was sent to Mendoza, but no one, apparently, has seen it in recent times. It may yet turn up.

Before they departed the chiefs agreed to return to their homes, but Coronado wrote several days later, "they still remain in their stronghold with their wives and all their belongings." Ere many days, however, they came, bringing their families, reassured by the friendly dealings of Coronado and his men. They also brought the general "a present of hares, rabbits, and other game, which he divided among his captains."

After telling Mendoza about the capture of Háwikuh in his letter of August 3, 1540, Coronado describes the place he has conquered. It is our first authentic picture of Háwikuh and its neighbors. It is a classic and deserves to be reported here in full. The general's criticism of Fray Marcos, which had been mildly expressed at several places along the way, now becomes sweeping and emphatic. He wrote: "It now remains for me to tell about the Seven Cities, the kingdom and province of which the father provincial gave your Lordship an account. To make a long story short, I can assure you he has not told the truth in a single thing he has said, for everything is the very opposite of what he related except the name of the cities and the large stone houses. However, although they are not decorated with turquoises, nor made of lime or good bricks, nevertheless they are very good houses, three, four, and five storeys high, and they have very . . . good rooms with corridors, and some quite good apartments underground and paved, which are built for winter and are something like hot-houses." He was here speaking of the kivas, or council chambers, for which the pueblos of the Southwest are famous.

"The Seven Cities are seven little villages, all having the

kind of houses I have described, and all within a space of four leagues. All taken together they are called the Kingdom of Cévola. Each has its own name, and no single one is called Cévola, but collectively they have this designation. This one where I am now lodged and which I have called a city, I have named Granada [Mendoza's birthplace], both because it has some similarity to that place, and in honor of your Lordship. In it there are perhaps two hundred houses, all surrounded by a wall, and it seems to me that, together with the others, which are not so enclosed, there might be a total of five hundred houses. There is another town near by, one of the seven, which is somewhat larger than this, and another of the same size as this one, the other four being somewhat smaller. I am sending to your Lordship a sketch of them all and of the route. The skin on which the painting is made was found here with others." These precious drawings and the map have never come to light, though they may be extant in some archive, museum, or private collection. If they should be discovered, what treasures they would be!

Coronado continues: "The people of these towns are fairly large and seem to me to be quite intelligent, although I do not think they have the judgment and skill necessary to build these houses in the way in which they are made, for most of them"— the men, he means—"are entirely naked except for the covering required for decency. They have colored fabrics like the one I am sending to you. They do not raise cotton, because the country is extremely cold, but they wear mantas, such as you may see by the sample, and it is true that some cotton thread was found in their houses. They wear the hair on their heads like the Mexicans, and are well formed and comely. I think they have many turquoises but removed them with all the rest of their goods except the maize. When I arrived I did not find any women here nor any men under fifteen or over sixty, except two or three old ones who remained in command of the young men and the warriors. Two points of emerald and some little broken stones, rather poor, which approach the color of garnet, were found in a paper under some stone crystals." One wonders what the paper was like. "I gave them to one of my servants to keep until they could be sent to your Lordship, but he lost them, so they tell me." Our censure for this carelessness must remain impersonal, for Coronado does not disclose the identity of the individual thus accused.

"We found fowls here, but only a few." These were turkeys, which the natives had domesticated. "The Indians tell me they do not eat them in any of the seven villages, but keep them merely for the sake of the feathers, but I do not believe this, because the fowls are very good and larger than those of Mexico." The general's skepticism perhaps reflects the psychology of a man who had recently endured a long fast.

"The climate and temperature of this country are almost like those of Mexico, for it is now hot and there are rains." He was writing in August, when it can be either hot or cold in Zuñi. "I have not yet seen it rain, however, except once when there was a little shower with wind, such as often falls in Spain. According to what the natives of the country say, the snow and cold are excessive, and this is very probably true, judging by the nature of the country, the sort of houses the people build, and the skins and other things they have to protect themselves from the cold.

"There are no fruits nor fruit trees here. The country is all level, and is nowhere shut in by high mountains, although there are some hills and rough places. There are not many birds, probably on account of the cold and because there are no mountains near by, nor are there many trees fit for firewood, although they can bring enough for their needs from a grove of very small junipers four leagues distant," toward the east. "Very good grass was found a quarter of a league away, both for pasturage for our horses and for mowing to make hay, of which we had great need, because our horses were so weak and feeble when they arrived." Evidently the Indian allies from Mexico were put to work in the hayfields.

"The food they eat in this country consists of maize, of which they have a great abundance, beans, and game, which they must eat (although they say they do not), for we found here many skins of deer, hares, and rabbits. They make the best tortillas I have ever seen anywhere, and this is what everybody ordinarily eats. They have the very best apparatus and method for grinding that were ever seen, and one of these Indian women will grind as much as four of the Mexicans. They have very good salt in crystals which they bring from a lake a day's journey from here." This was the well-known saline a few miles toward the south. Coronado adds a sentence regarding the religion of the Cíbola people. "So far as I can find out, these Indians worship water, because they say it makes the maize grow and sustains their life, and the only other reason they know is that their ancestors did the same."

"There are many animals here—bears, tigers, lions, porcupines, and some sheep as big as horses, with very large horns and little tails." He apparently referred to elks. "I have seen some of their horns, the size of which was something amazing. There are wild goats, whose heads I have also seen, as well as the paws of bears and the skins of wild boars." These goats were probably mountain sheep, and the wild boars were evidently jabalíes, also called peccaries. "For game they have deer, leopards" —probably wildcats, or perhaps mountain lions—"and very large roebucks. Everyone thinks that some of them are larger than the animal belonging to Juan Meláz with which your Lordship favored me"—a glimpse into hobbies at Mendoza's court.—"The natives here have some very well dressed skins, and according to what they tell me they tan and color them where they kill the cattle"—that is to say, on the eastern plains. He had already heard of the buffalo.

This description of Háwikuh and its environs is one of the precious trophies of Coronado's visit to Cíbola, and will be prized through the ages. The general realized how great a disappointment it would be to Mendoza, who had sent him to gather gold and precious stones.

Were there really seven cities of Cíbola or only six? Did Coronado actually count them, or merely echo tradition, which is always more stubborn than fact? He and his fellow chroniclers repeatedly say there were seven, but mention only two of them by name. They had something more important to do than worrying about inquisitive historians yet unborn. Besides Háwikuh, at the west end of the confederation, they named Máçaque, or Mátsaki, at the east end, which Coronado and Castañeda both called the largest of the "seven." Thanks to the diaries of later explorers, and to the work of archaeologists in recent years, the sites of six of the Cities of Cíbola are well known. "But," says Hodge, the dean of these diggers, "all attempts to identify the seventh pueblo of the early Spanish period have been little more than conjecture." Perhaps they have not done enough digging. More likely the number seven came from the old legend. The six towns whose names are known from sixteenth-century documents and whose sites have been identified are Háwikuh, Kechipáuan, Kwákina, Hálona, Mátsaki, and Kiákima, here named from west to east, the order in which they were first seen by the Spaniards.

The province of Cíbola lay in the valley of Zuñi River, which rises in Zuñi Mountains, runs southwestward from New Mexico into Arizona and joins the Little Colorado, or Río Bermejo, as Castañeda called it. From Háwikuh, the westernmost, to Kiákima, the easternmost of the six identified pueblos, it is some fifteen miles. The Zuñi River Valley is still the home of the descendants of the people seen there by Coronado four centuries ago, for in spite of the shock of European contact they have never left their native land. These descendants are now called Zuñis, and the area where Don Francisco saw and dealt with them in 1540 is now the Zuñi Indian Reservation, which forms a moccasin-shaped patch on the map of New Mexico, some fifty miles south of Gallup, on the main highway (U.S. No. 66) from Albuquerque to Grand Canyon. All the descendants of the people seen by Coronado now live in one pueblo called Zuñi, which stands almost on the site of Hálona of Coronado's day. Its population of a little over two thousand is probably about a third of the total of all the inhabitants of Cíbola when the Spaniards arrived.

Chapter XII

HOPIS AND GRAND CANYON

Coronado meanwhile had lost no opportunity to make friendly inquiries regarding regions and peoples beyond the confines of Cíbola. He encouraged the natives to tell their neighbors about his arrival, and to invite them in his name to come and see him. They must inform their acquaintances that he, as representative of His Majesty, Carlos V, desired nothing but their friendship, and to learn of good lands wherein the Spaniards might settle. The Cíbolans complied with the gently phrased request and sent the general's message by runners to tribes with whom they had trade and other relations. What else they may have reported we cannot say, although we might venture a guess.

Some of the things Coronado heard as a result of these inquiries were far from encouraging. He was told that the Kingdom of Totonteac, "which the father provincial had praised so highly, saying it was something marvelous," was "nothing but a hot lake," on whose shores there were five or six houses. The Indians had never even heard of Marata, another imaginary creation of the friar or of his informants, said Coronado. Acus, or Ácoma, the Cíbolans assured him, was only "a single small city," although in Fray Marcos's narrative it had been magnified into still another "kingdom." Certain of these discrepancies, of course, can be charged to misunderstanding, for much of the conversation of the Spaniards with the natives was conducted by signs.

More promising than any of these regions, though not excessively alluring, was Tusayán, another province of Seven Cities said by the Indians to be at a considerable distance northwest. Here again was the mystic number seven. They were the villages now known as the Hopi towns. These pueblos, said Coronado's informants, greatly resembled those of Cíbola, except that the houses were smaller and built of mud instead of stone. The first pueblo was called Tuçano, as Coronado understood it, hence the name Tusayán, which came to be applied to the whole group of Hopi towns. Coronado was skeptical. "They could not tell me much about the others," he says, "nor do I believe they are telling me the truth, because they think that in any case I shall soon have to depart from among them and return home. But here is where they will soon discover they are mistaken." In this sentence Coronado comes nearer to braggadocio than anywhere else in all his known writings, for he was a modest and temperate man, though by no means timid.

To follow up this report of Tusayán, Coronado sent Captain Pedro de Tovar at the head of a troop of seventeen mounted Spaniards and three or four on foot. Don Pedro was the captain of cavalry whom Coronado had appointed chief ensign of the expedition. One of the best equipped men in the whole army, in the muster at Compostela he was able to report "thirteen horses, a coat of mail, some cuirasses, and some native accouterments and weapons." As already noted, he had some dogs that come prominently into our story. Fame now attended him.

In the historic band went Fray Juan Padilla, the zealous Franciscan friar "who in his youth had been a warrior," and who had been with Cortés in Tehuantepec. He knew his way around. Although Cíbola and Tusayán were not always on the best of terms, Coronado seems to have had no difficulty in finding guides and interpreters for the expedition. Thus equipped, on July 15, only a week after the capture of Háwikuh, Tovar set forth on his reconnoissance, which, it was expected, would require thirty days or more. His speed would be limited by the foot soldiers and the pack train, for the Indian guides could outtravel the horses.

When Coronado wrote to Mendoza nearly three weeks later, Tovar was still absent and nothing had been heard of his doings. "If I thought I could have any news from him within twelve or fifteen days," he writes, "I would not send this package to your Lordship before learning what he had found there. However, since he will be gone at least thirty days, and believing this information will be of little importance, and that the cold weather and the rains are approaching"—they would interfere with the travel of the couriers to Mexico—"I ought to do as your Lordship commanded me in your instructions, namely, that as soon as I arrived here I should advise you thereof, and this I will do by sending you the plain story of what I have seen, which is bad enough, as you may perceive." It was the story set forth in the preceding chapter.

Meanwhile Tovar went on his way to Tusayán, or Hopi Land, now one of the famous places in all the Southwest, and visited annually by thousands of globe trotters, tourists, artists, and scientists. He was led by Zuñi guides who presumably took him over the accustomed route by which the Hopis periodically came to the famous Zuñi salt lakes to supply their needs. The old trail led northwest past well known water holes, skirting the now famous "stone trees" of the Petrified Forest, through country today included in the Navajo Reservation. This route lies westward of the present highway to Hopi Land through Gallup, but converges with it near the ruins of the first town visited by Tovar.

The Hopis lived on four high and relatively inaccessible mesas, or plateaus, from which they descended to cultivate their fields and to obtain water, which the women carried on their heads in pottery jugs up the steep and dizzy cliffs. The seven Hopi towns inhabited at the time of Tovar's visit, named in order from east to west, were Kawaíokuh and Awátobi on Jeddito Mesa; Sikyátki and Kuchóptuleva (old Walpi) on a second mesa; old Shungópovi and old Mishóngnovi on a third mesa, and Oraibe on a fourth. The social organization, town building, and daily life of the Hopis were similar to those of the Cíbola pueblos, with numerous distinguishing features and cultural traits, notable among them being the weird Snake Dance. Tovar and his men first reached Hopi Land at the easternmost pueblo, much as does the modern highway from Gallup.

"When they arrived there," says Castañeda, "they entered the land so secretly that they were not noticed by a single person, the reason for this being that between the two provinces there are neither towns nor country houses, nor do the people go outside of their pueblos any farther than to their fields." Especially was this true at this time, when they heard that Cíbola had been conquered by ferocious men, "who were riding about on animals that devoured people." The Spaniards arrived at the first Hopi town after nightfall, and were able to conceal themselves below the high cliff on which the pueblo was perched, and to remain there listening to the natives talking in their houses. But in the morning they were discovered, so they prepared for battle in the plain below the mesa on whose precipitous edge the town was situated. Though taken by surprise, the plucky little natives, armed with bows, arrows, clubs, and shields, sallied forth in battle array to attack the visitors and the strange beasts they rode.

Tovar's interpreters now stepped forward to talk with the chiefs of the Hopi army, "because they were people of good intelligence," and Don Pedro made the customary requirement of obedience to God and the King. Unconvinced and undaunted, the chiefs ordered the Spaniards to depart at once, drew a line on the ground with sacred corn meal, and warned Tovar that he and his men would cross it at their peril! Thus at the outset the Hopis showed the stubbornness and independence for which they still are famous. Notwithstanding this bold challenge, in an effort toward appeasement some of the visitors crossed the line and tried to converse with the villagers, but all in vain. "Finally it came to such a pass," says Castañeda, that a native was so impudent that he struck one of the horses over the head with a club.

This was too much for Fray Juan, the fighting friar. Thinking that time was being wasted, he said to Captain Tovar, "To tell the truth, I don't know what we came for!" Thereupon the war cry was given. *"Santiago y á ellos!* St. James and at them!" The Spaniards made a sudden rush, felled several of the natives, and routed the rest, who fled into the town, "though some of them were not given this opportunity," which would seem to mean they were either killed or captured. The Indians were convinced, "and such was the promptness with which they came forth from the pueblo with presents to sue for peace" that Tovar called off his men. The Hopis evidently considered discretion the better part of valor.

Dismounting in the plain below the mesa, Tovar now held a conference with the native head men, who had come out bearing presents. They said they came to render obedience in the name of the whole province; they wished to be friends with the Spaniards, and brought the gifts as a token of their sincerity. The presents consisted of some cotton cloth, "although not much," a few tanned skins of animals, some native birds, turkeys perhaps, and a plentiful supply of maize, flour, and piñon nuts. "Afterward they gave us some turquoises, but only a few." The news quickly spread, and before the day was over natives from other Hopi pueblos farther west came to render obedience, at the same time offering the freedom of their towns, and inviting the Spaniards to visit them to "buy, sell or barter." We are not specifically told whether or not Tovar accepted the invitation and made a tour of all the pueblos, but it is inferred that he did so.

Since Don Pedro had no authority to go beyond the confines of the province of Tusayán, he returned to Háwikuh and reported not only what he had seen, but what he had heard as well. He said the Hopi pueblos were ruled, like those of Cíbola, by a Council of Ancients. "They have their governors and captains ranged in the order of seniority." But of all the things Tovar told Coronado, the most interesting was that while he was in Tusayán "notice was had of a great river, and that downstream several days there were some very tall people with large bodies."

Tovar arrived at Háwikuh on his return about the middle of August. If he toured the entire Hopi province his round trip would cover a distance of some two hundred and fifty miles. There are still seven Hopi towns on the mesas where the natives lived at the time of Tovar's visit, but not all of them are on the old sites. The Hopis are now best known to the tourist for their pottery and for their weird and picturesque Snake Dance, but they have many other cultural assets.

The news of a river in the west had to be investigated, for might not this be the very stream that Ulloa had discovered the previous year in the service of Cortés, and that Alarcón had been sent by Mendoza to explore? Coronado therefore immediately equipped another expedition, placing it under command of Cárdenas, his right-hand man and a hard-fisted soldier who so often had demonstrated superior ability in Mexico. Perhaps it was the report of giants in the west that determined the choice of a leader. Hitherto our main reliance for the story of this Cárdenas expedition has been Castañeda's narrative and another called the *Relación del Suceso*. We now have a declaration made by Cárdenas himself which adds new information.

With twenty-five horsemen (Castañeda erroneously says twelve) the captain set forth on his errand on August 25, 1540. In his absence Francisco de Ovando, a most attractive captain of whom later we shall have a hair-raising story, filled the post of maestre de campo at Háwikuh. Cárdenas was instructed to take the same route which Tovar had followed, "for the purpose of going west beyond . . . Tuzán" to look for the stream whose shores were inhabited by giants, and was allowed eighty days for the round trip—that is, until November 14. Presumably he had the usual accompaniment of servants and guides, but he explicitly states that "he did not take any interpreter because he did not need one," since the Spaniards were well versed in the sign language of the Indians. By now they were veterans. In the party was young Pedro de Sotomayor, official historian of the Coronado expedition.

Retracing Tovar's trail to Tusayán, Cárdenas was well received there by the natives, given lodgings, furnished guides for the journey to the Great River, and liberally provided with supplies, "because they had to travel over uninhabited country before coming to the settlements, which the Indians said were at a distance of more than twenty days." The settlements re-

ferred to were apparently those of the Havasupais, who lived
west of the Hopis and down Colorado River.

Thus equipped, Cárdenas went forward on the new leg of his
journey, traveled twenty days, and arrived at a place fifty leagues
from Tusayán and eighty from Cíbola. Here, says Castañeda,
they came to the gorge of a river, "from whose brink it looked
as if to the opposite side it must be more than three or four
leagues by air line." Cárdenas and his men had discovered one
of the most impressive scenic wonders in all nature—the Grand
Canyon of Colorado River! The approximate region where the
gorge was first reached by the explorers can be conjectured
from the description given by Castañeda. The evidence indicates that it was in the vicinity of Grand View. The country was
high, dry, "open to the north," and covered with low and
twisted pines. It is at Grand View that vision sweeps north as
far as Vermillion Cliffs and Lee's Ferry, some fifty miles away.
The travelers from a southern clime found the temperature
at the Canyon extremely severe at night, "so that although it
was the warm season, no one could live on this barranca because
of the cold." Modern equipment has overcome this drawback, as
is evidenced by the fine settlement at Grand Canyon National
Park.

Castañeda's next paragraph is one of the most precious passages in all the writings ever put on paper with respect to discovery in North America, for it records the first attempt of
Europeans to descend into the most stupendous gash in the
earth's surface anywhere in the world, and rivaled for depth
only by Urique Canyon in western Mexico. Every reader who
has seen Grand Canyon will wish to know the exact words of
the chronicler; and everyone who has made his way on foot or
on horseback from the brink to the bottom of the incomparable
chasm will recognize the faithfulness of the all-too-brief account
given by Cárdenas and his men.

"They spent three days trying to find a way down to the
river, which from above appeared to be only a fathom wide, although, according to what the Indians said, it must be half a
league across." They apparently meant it was that far from preci-

pice to precipice. "The descent was found to be impossible, for at the end of these three days Captain Melgosa, with Juan Galeras and another companion, they being the lightest and most agile, undertook to clamber down at a place that appeared to them the least difficult. They kept descending in sight of the men left above until they were lost to view. . . . At four o'clock in the afternoon they returned, without having been able to reach the bottom because of the great obstacles they encountered, for what from above had appeared to be easy, proved to be, on the contrary, rough and difficult. They said they had been only a third of the way down, but from the place they reached, the river looked very large; indeed, judging from what they saw, it must be as wide as the Indians had said. The men who remained above estimated that some small rocks jutting out from the wall of the canyon must be about as high as a man; but those who went down swore that when they reached them they were found to be taller than the highest tower of Seville." Now, to observers standing on the brink of the "divine abyss," a group of modern houses less than half-way down Bright Angel Trail appear to be about the size of beehives.

To our regret, but little is known of the personal history of these lithe daredevils who, first among Europeans, descended into the bowels of the earth at Grand Canyon. We do know that Juan Galeras was a native of Almendralejo, a Spanish town with an Arabic name. At the Compostela muster he had appeared with three horses, coat of mail, beaver, and native weapons. As we have seen, Captain Pablos de Melgosa, a native of Burgos, was not present at the Compostela rendezvous, not yet having arrived from Mexico, so he must have overtaken the caravan somewhere on the trail, for at Culiacán he was made captain of the infantry and went with Coronado in the Advance Guard. After returning to Mexico, Melgosa recrossed the Atlantic to his home in Spain, and was in Flanders when he gave testimony regarding the Coronado expedition. No doubt he could have told a marvelous tale of the gash in the earth into which he had descended, but he said nothing about it in his statement, which concerned other matters than scenery. He was helping to get Cárdenas out of trouble. The third hero of this historic adventure remains nameless. It would be appropriate to erect a group statue in memory of all three at a suitable place on the brink of the stupendous and now famous gorge which they so gallantly pioneered.

Cárdenas and his men did not travel close to the canyon of the river any farther because they were in desperate need of water. Indeed, "as far as this place they had turned aside each day in the afternoon, going a league or two inland," that is, toward the south, away from the canyon, "to look for water." Thus, leaving the river at a distance, they continued westward from the place where Captain Melgosa led the descent into the mighty chasm. But they soon turned back, and with very good reason. For, "when they had traveled about four more days," writes Castañeda, "the guides said it was impossible to go any farther, because there was no water ahead in three days nor in four." To make this news emphatic the guides told Cárdenas that when the Hopis traveled through this region they brought women carrying water in gourds which they buried along the route for use on the return. Moreover, they said the Indians on foot went twice as fast as the Spaniards on horseback, for "the distance traveled by our men in two days they covered in one." Manifestly the explorers were not going rapidly, and did not get very far west. They may have reached the brink of Havasupai Canyon, whose depth and roughness would furnish a real impediment to further advance. If they had crossed it they surely would have recorded the difficult feat, as will be attested by all who have descended into it by the hair-raising old trail to the Havasupai village at the bottom.

So Cárdenas and his men turned about, little realizing that because of this jaunt they were destined to lasting fame. On the way back they saw a waterfall pouring over a rock, and from the guides they learned that "some clusters which hung like fine crystals" were salt. "They went thither and gathered large quantities of it" and distributed it among the men when they returned to Háwikuh. Dr. Katharine Bartlett, who has made a careful study of the old trails in all this region, locates the salt deposit northwest of Cameron near the mouth of the Little Colorado River where it joins the larger stream. At Háwikuh, Cárdenas gave Coronado a written report of what they had seen, "since . . . Pedro de Sotomayor, who was chronicler of the army, had accompanied Don García López." As has been stated, Sotomayor's narrative, which would be priceless, unfortunately has never been found, but it may yet come to light. Here is a challenge to some young historian!

Cárdenas in a recently unearthed manuscript tells us that on this expedition he and his men went "almost a hundred leagues inland, without finding in all that distance any Indian settlements other than those which had already been discovered," that is, the Hopis. "They endured much thirst and hunger . . . and returned to Cíbola, where they found Francisco Vázquez." On the wonders of the Grand Canyon Cárdenas makes no comment. In fact, at the time he made his declaration he was in jail in Spain, and was feeling sour about the whole matter of conquest in America. Castañeda concludes his precious account of the discovery of Tusayán, which he personally did not see, by laconically saying "the pueblos of that province were left in peace, for they never again visited them, nor did they learn of or make attempts to find other settlements in that direction." They were looking for gold, not scenery, and the east now beckoned.

Chapter XIII

SCENES SHIFT

Couriers were about to set out from Háwikuh with messages and presents for the viceroy who was waiting anxiously in Mexico City. In his letter written on August 3, Coronado told of the hard march to Cíbola, the capture of the town, what he had seen and heard of the people and the country, and the sending of still absent Tovar to Tusayán. He was sorely disappointed with what he had learned, and by no means optimistic with regard to the future. "So far as I can judge, it does not appear to me there is any hope of finding either gold or silver, but I trust in God that if there is any to be had we shall get our share of it, and it shall not escape us through any lack of diligence in the search." Then a slight contradiction, in an effort to be strictly accurate. "Some gold and silver has been found in this place, and those who know about minerals say it is not bad, but I have not been able to learn from these people where they got it." The mystery was solved at a later time, when it was learned that the small quantity of gold in question had been brought from Mexico by one of the Spaniards.

Coronado asked Mendoza for new supplies. "We have great need of provisions, and you should know that among all of us here there is not one pound of raisins, nor any sugar, nor oil, nor wine, except barely a pint saved for saying Mass, for everything has been consumed, some of it having been lost on the way. You may provide us whatever seems best, but if you are planning to send us cattle you should know they will have to spend a year on the road, because they cannot come in any other way nor any quicker." A whole year on the road from Mexico to Cíbola!

Point was given to this admonition by experience with the sheep on the journey north. It will be remembered that because they had lost their hoofs along the way, some of these woolly wayfarers had been left by the advance guard at the Yaqui River to travel more slowly. In fact, "four horsemen who remained with them have just arrived," says Coronado. "They brought only twenty-four lambs and four wethers; the rest of them died from the hardship, although they did not travel more than two leagues a day." The poor animals and their shepherds had been nearly four months on the trail from Culiacán. The main drove of cattle, sheep, and swine was coming still farther behind, with Arellano's army.

Of course Mendoza would be interested in native products and curiosities from Cíbola. So Coronado wrote: "I would like to send to you with this dispatch many samples of the things they have in this country, but the journey is so long and rough that it is difficult for me to do so." It would require more horses and men than could be spared. "However, I am sending you twelve small mantas such as the people of this country ordinarily wear, a fabric which seems to me to be very well made. I selected them because I do not think anyone else has ever seen any needle work in these Indies, unless it was done since the Spaniards settled here."

Then the pictures. "I am sending also two canvases showing the animals they have in this country, although, as I have said, the painting is poorly done, because the artist did not spend more than a day in executing it." These were the drawings the chiefs of Cíbola had made hurriedly at Coronado's request. "I have seen other pictures on the walls of the houses with better proportions and much better done." He had been looking around. Some of the remarkable old kiva paintings by the Pueblo Indians fortunately have survived to this day and are a sight worth seeing.

Into the packages made up for the viceroy the general put an interesting assortment, but one quite in contrast with the fabulous treasure sent from Vera Cruz by Cortés to Charles V twenty years before. Cíbola was by no means *Ótro México.* Coronado's gift included: "A cowhide, some turquoises, two earrings of the same, fifteen Indian combs, some panels decorated with these turquoises, and two wicker baskets," which were plentiful in Cíbola. "I send also," wrote Coronado, "two pads such as the women ordinarily wear on their heads when they carry water from the spring, just as they do in Spain. One of these women, with such a pad on her head, will carry a jar of water up a ladder without touching it with her hands." At Zuñi today their descendants can still be seen performing the same skillful feat and using the same sort of pads. "And, lastly, I send you samples of the weapons used by the natives of this country in battle—a shield, a mallet, and a bow with some arrows, among them two with bone points, the like of which have never before been seen, according to what these conquistadores say." As to the efficacy of these weapons Coronado, remembering the battle at Háwikuh, could give personal testimony, with exhibits from his own body.

Regretfully Don Francisco wrote, "I am unable to give your Lordship any reliable information about the dress of the women, because the Indians keep them so carefully hidden that I have not seen any except two old ones." Nevertheless, old as they were, he seems to have taken attentive note of their garb, and he described it to the best of his masculine ability. "They wore two long robes reaching down to their feet, with a girdle, and fastened with some cotton strings. Since the Indians were not willing to let me see the women, I asked them to give me a sample of what they wear to send to you. So they brought me two mantas, the ones I am sending, painted almost all over." Before many days had passed the natives returned to Háwikuh, and Coronado's curiosity about the costumes of the women was then doubtless satisfied.

The general did not hide his disappointment about gold and turquoises, a matter so much publicized by Fray Marcos, and so close to Mendoza's heart. "God knows I wish I had better news to write to your Lordship, but I must tell you the truth, and, as I wrote you from Culiacán, I must inform you of the bad as well as the good. But you may be assured that if all the wealth and treasures in the world had been found, I could not have done more in his Majesty's service . . . than I have performed in coming here, where your Lordship sent me, all my companions and myself carrying our provisions on our backs for three hundred leagues, and traveling on foot many days, making our way over hills and rough mountains, not to mention other hardships that I refrain from recounting. Nor shall I think of ceasing my efforts until death overtakes me, if it serves his Majesty or your Lordship to have it so."

The past was past. *Hecho hecho!* Now as to the future. "I have decided to send men throughout all the surrounding regions in order to find out if there is anything worth while; to suffer every hardship rather than abandon this enterprise; and to serve his Majesty if I can find any way to do so. And I shall not be lacking in diligence while waiting for your Grace to order me what I ought to do." We may be sure that Coronado at the same time wrote a long and tender letter to Doña Beatríz, which some day may be found in the family archives of her descendants. What a treasure it would be!

New details regarding the fortunes of Stephen had been learned by the Spaniards at Cíbola. "The death of the Negro is perfectly certain," Coronado wrote, "because many of the things he wore have been found; and the Indians say they killed him here because the people of Chichilticale said he was a bad man, and not like the Christians . . . and because he assaulted their women, whom the Indians love better than themselves"—even to hiding them from Coronado's soldiers. "So they decided to put him to death, but they did not do it in the way reported, for they did not kill any of the people who came with him"—about three hundred, Fray Marcos had said—"nor did they wound the lad from the province of Petatlán who was with him, but captured him and kept him in safe custody until now." He refers to young Bartolomé, who had accompanied Fray Marcos to Cíbola. When Coronado tried to obtain this boy the Cíbolans made excuses, saying now that he was dead, and again that the Indians of Ácoma had carried him away.

Finally, after this had gone on for two or three days, and Coronado told them if they did not deliver Bartolomé he would be angry, they complied. "He is an interpreter," the general wrote, "and although he cannot speak much he understands very well." More specifically, according to Juan Troyano, one of Coronado's soldiers, Bartolomé knew Aztec, and through an additional interpreter—perhaps one of the Indian allies from Mexico—who understood that language and Spanish, the Cíbola tongue could be communicated to Coronado and his men. In fact, a good many Aztec words were found in use among the Indians of the New Mexico Pueblos.

The letters finished and the curiosities safely packed into bundles, Juan Gallego, one of the boldest spirits and toughest fighters in the whole army, was despatched with a small guard to Mexico to deliver them to Mendoza, together with some verbal messages which the general apparently preferred not to put in writing. If perhaps these word-of-mouth communications cast reflections on someone, Coronado's charitable method has been justified, for we do not know what the criticisms were nor upon whom they may have fallen. Time often justifies such self-restraint, but we humanly confess we would keenly relish the gossip, if such it was. Gallego was charged, likewise, to return to Cíbola as quickly as possible with a pack train loaded with supplies for Coronado's army, for the general saw that unless prospects improved he could not hope to live off the country. It was a man's job that Gallego was undertaking— another horseback journey of more than three thousand miles! Included in Gallego's escort was the standard bearer, Juan de Villareal, who, after he completed his duty as courier, accompanied Viceroy Mendoza to the Nueva Galicia frontier and served under him in the famous Mixton War.

Gallego was accompanied also by veteran Melchior Díaz, who bore orders for Arellano. It will be remembered that when Coronado left Culiacán he ordered Don Tristán to advance to Corazones, Vaca's "Town of Hearts," and there await further instructions. He now commanded him to move forward

to Cíbola with the major portion of his army—but not all of it.
Plans had been somewhat upset. Coronado tells us that "upon
reaching Cíbola and seeing it was not what had been claimed,"
he decided to found a settlement on Sonora River, for it was
now plain that Cíbola could not support all the people coming
with Arellano, and that a half-way base was needed to keep
open the line of communication with Mexico. So he now sent
Díaz back to the Valley of Corazones to take charge there, "and
try to bring the natives to obedience to his Majesty and to the
knowledge of God our Lord." The settlement was to consist
of a detachment from Arellano's army, and of it Díaz was commissioned alcalde mayor. There was another urgent matter.
No news had come from Alarcón. So Díaz was ordered to take
some of Arellano's horsemen and go to the coast in search of
the food-laden ships with which Alarcón presumably had sailed
up the Gulf, and which had caused Coronado so much anxiety.
For these hard jobs the general picked a man who had proved
his mettle.

With Gallego and Díaz went Fray Marcos de Niza, who was
now returning to the capital, with his back turned forever on
the Seven Cities whose fame he had done more than anyone else
to spread. Fray Daniel and one or two other friars may have gone
with him, for they are not again encountered in the New Land
—*Tierra Nueva*, as Coronado's discoveries were now generally
called. Just what were the father provincial's reasons for departure we cannot say, for lack of first-hand evidence. Castañeda, writing years later, says it was because the friar "did
not consider it safe to remain at Cíbola, since his report had
proved false in every particular. For they had not found the
kingdoms he had told about, neither populous cities, nor the
wealth of gold and precious stones that had been proclaimed,
nor brocades, nor other things that had been told of from the
pulpits." Castañeda had not reached Cíbola when Fray Marcos
set forth for Mexico, but he met the friar and Gallego on the
way, and from them doubtless heard the disappointing story
of the Seven Cities, and whatever gossip may have been current, whether vicious or harmless. Others more charitably at-

tribute the departure of Fray Marcos to his illness. Finally, it was with Díaz, apparently, that thirty Indians from Mexico returned to their homeland, in keeping with Mendoza's promise to the native allies that they were free to go back whenever they might wish.

Díaz must have been more than a little surprised to encounter the army a good forty miles north of Corazones, where Arellano had been ordered to await further instructions. Don Tristán had remained at Culiacán several days after Coronado set forth from that place with the Vanguard. On the one hand, there were many preparations to be made, and on the other hand, Culiacán had abundant food for man and beast, besides being a pleasant spot in which to linger, as it still is today. Castañeda tells us "the inhabitants had gathered a good supply of provisions that year, and each one very gladly shared his harvest with his guests from our army. They not only had an abundance to eat while there, but also plenty to take with them, so when the departure came they started off with more than six hundred loaded animals, besides the friendly Indians and the servants—more than a thousand persons." Most of the stock, several thousand head of horses, mules, cattle, sheep, goats, and hogs, also went with Arellano's division of the army. It was an imposing caravan in the wilderness.

Don Tristán de Luna y Arellano, like Coronado a younger son, had been forced by the law of primogeniture to seek his fortune in the New World. Of an old Castilian family, he was a cousin of Mendoza himself. As a shipmate of Cortés, who was returning from Court with recently bestowed honors, Don Tristán in 1530 had made a voyage to Mexico but later returned to his homeland and there joined the retinue of Mendoza when he came to New Spain as Viceroy. He was an obvious choice for the important position of commander of the main army to which the general had appointed him.

Two weeks behind Coronado, that is to say, early in May, 1540, Arellano and his men set out from Culiacán to follow the general's trail, "with lances on their shoulders, and all on foot," in order that their horses might be used as pack animals.

Castañeda, the garrulous chronicler, was one of these hikers, and it is from him we learn the greater part of what we know of the details of their journey to Cíbola. We only wish there had been other chatty writers like him. Juan de Zaldívar also sheds light on the events of the long hard trek. Having missed Coronado's vanguard at Culiacán by a week, he too came with Arellano, as we have seen, and he tells us about relations with the Indians on the way. Many of the chiefs no doubt recognized him, for he was now passing over the road to the north for the third time, a real veteran on the historic highway.

Like Coronado, Don Tristan met a friendly welcome as he traveled. From villages the natives came out to greet the caravan, and gave obedience to Arellano in the name of his Majesty. Nothing was asked of the natives, and all the captains "went with great vigilance, in order that nobody might take provisions or other things from them." One slight echo of discord with the natives is heard in the story of this long march. At Valle de Señora, Arellano punished a Spaniard "because he said the Indians had stolen some hampers, and this on the word of Don Tristán's Negroes."

Traveling through mountains and valleys on the already well-known trail, the army crossed Sinaloa and Fuerte rivers, ascended the Cedros and the Yaqui, and traversed barren Mátape desert. And thus "with no little toil, one day's march after another," they finally arrived at Corazones, where Arellano halted to await further orders, as his instructions required. Meanwhile, in the scorching heat and drenching rains of July and August, 1540, he established his followers in a villa, or town, which he named San Gerónimo de los Corazones (St. Jerome of the Hearts). The site of this short-lived Spanish settlement was near the present city of Ures, at the mouth of the historic canyon of Sonora River, a spot already made famous by Cabeza de Vaca.

From Corazones, Don Rodrigo de Maldonado was sent with a party of soldiers down Sonora River to the Gulf of California to look for a harbor and scan the horizon for the ships of Alarcón. He got no news of the fleet, but when he returned to camp he had an exhibit that caused his comrades to stare their eyes almost out of their heads. For, says Castañeda, who was present at the time, "he brought with him an Indian so big and so tall that the biggest and tallest man in camp did not come up to his nipples. And it was said that on the coast there were other Indians even taller than he." Maldonado had been among the giant Seris who then inhabited and ever since that time have dwelt in the vicinity of Tiburón Island, haunt of huge turtles and terrifying sharks as well as of native giants.

Arellano and his army of some two hundred Spaniards, with a host of Indian allies, remained at Corazones till the rainy season was over. The food problem meanwhile became critical, from which it may be inferred that the natives were not as friendly as Vaca and Coronado had found them, or that they had little to spare. Seeing that his town could not sustain itself there, without awaiting orders from Coronado, Arellano moved it upstream through the gorge to the valley called Señora. And, says Castañeda, "since the Spaniards called it Señora, I shall henceforth refer to it by that name." This word, it will be remembered, was a Spanish corruption of the native name Sonora, which today is applied to the river, to the valley, and to the large State in northwestern Mexico. In the place-name, Ópata has prevailed over Castilian.

Following Sauer, this settlement of San Gerónimo at its second site is here referred to for convenience by the name of San Gerónimo II. The town was situated in fertile Valle de Sonora, which begins at the north end of Ures Canyon and extends upstream to the deep and narrow gorge of Senoquipe, a stretch of some twenty miles. The new site was about forty miles by the river above Corazones, and close to or identical with the location of the modern town of Huépac. The name Sonora adhered specifically to this spot and was frequently used to designate it all through the seventeenth century, but meanwhile it came to be applied to the whole river valley and finally to the large State in the Republic of Mexico. Arellano's men learned at the new site, much to their sorrow, the villainous nature of a poisonous plant used by the natives. "Judging from what we saw of it and its effects," says Jaramillo, "it is the worst that could be found. From what we have learned, it was obtained from the sap of a small tree like the lentisk, which grows among broken shale and in sterile soil." [1]

It was about the middle of September, soon after Arellano had moved from Corazones to San Gerónimo II, when Díaz and his fellow travelers arrived there with the disheartening news from Cíbola. Fray Marcos and Gallego, with their slender escort, continued on their way to Mexico City, passing through country where the natives were becoming every day more hostile. Announcement was immediately made at San Gerónimo that eighty men, with Díaz as commander, were to remain at the new settlement, while Arellano and the rest of the army marched forward to join the vanguard at Cíbola. The selection of personnel having been made, provisions were packed, and once again Captain Arellano and his men set forth toward the north. Adventures unimagined rode with them.

[1] "The arrow poison of the Indians of Sonora encountered by Coronado in 1540 has never, with certainty, been identified. The Opata arrow poison (yerba de la flecha) called 'mago' or 'magot' was probably the sap of the tree *Sebastiana Bilocularis*. This tree is held in dread by the natives of northern Mexico among whom is a belief that birds who perch in its branches fall dead, or men who sleep in its shelter never awaken, but die in their slumber. See Standley, *Trees and Shrubs of Mexico*. For this note I am grateful to Dr. Robert F. Heizer.

Chapter XIV

ALARCÓN ON COLORADO RIVER

Meanwhile Alarcón was making history. His little squadron at first consisted of two ships, which, besides keeping in touch with Coronado as they sailed northward, were to stop at Culiacán and pick up the baggage and supplies left behind by the army. The vessels were equipped at Acapulco, that jewel among West Coast harbors. The flagship *San Pedro* was commanded by Alarcón, and her companion, the *Santa Catalina*, by Marcos Ruíz. With the expedition went Domingo Castillo, who as map maker had ascended the Gulf with Ulloa in 1539.

Captain Alarcón was a personality—a humorist, a braggart, and something of a dandy, with a well supplied wardrobe of which he was vain. His beard was magnificent, and was especially admired by the natives he encountered, who marveled when he combed it. He had a dog like the one taken to Cíbola by Stephen, and his table service on board included metal dishes, possibly of silver. In his crew there were a drummer and a fifer, and he took with him an interpreter who knew Yuman speech. Perhaps he had been picked up in the Gulf region, taken to Mexico, and there learned Spanish. The sailors were equipped with swords, shields, and muskets, and presumably with helmets. Besides provisions for his men Alarcón had a supply of petty merchandise for barter, and as gifts for the Indians he carried beads, silken cords of various hues, bright-colored cloth, and "other trifles." Among the articles of food on board were beans, wheat and other grains, and Spanish cocks and hens. Thus we learn something about contemporary life on ship-board.

The expedition did not leave Acapulco until May 9. This was more than two months after Coronado said goodbye to

Compostela, seventeen days after he left Culiacán with his advance guard, and about the same time that Arellano started north from there with the rest of the army. So the vessels were far behind the land forces. Soon after sailing, the crew of the *Santa Catalina* became "unduly frightened" in a storm, and threw overboard nine cannons, two anchors, a cable, and many other "indispensable things." At Santiago, near Manzanillo Bay, Alarcón repaired the damage, took on new supplies and additional men, and sailed for the port of Culiacán. Here he found at anchor and added to his fleet the *San Gabriel*, already loaded with provisions for Coronado.

With his squadron thus increased, Alarcón continued north. White sails were becoming a familiar sight to natives on these coasts, up which Cortés had already sent a number of vessels and where the Marquis himself had sailed. Keeping close to the mainland shore, Alarcón looked for "markers" erected by Coronado, and for Indians who might give word of the land party bound for Cíbola. But he sought in vain for news, which seems a little strange; for at the time when Alarcón passed up the Sonora coast, Arellano was founding San Gerónimo on Sonora River, whence he sent Maldonado to the Gulf to look for the ships. On his way north, Alarcón tells us, he discovered some harbors which Ulloa had not mentioned, but what ones they were he does not specify in the *Narrative* that has come down to us. The voyage was slow, and it was August 26 when the little fleet reached the shallow waters near the head of the Gulf, where Ulloa had turned back . From here forward Alarcón was a discoverer.

These murky shoals, which extended several miles into the Gulf, were Alarcón's first major hazard. They were "so dangerous and forbidding that it was temerity to venture over them even with small boats." Pilots and sailors wanted to turn back, as Ulloa had done. "But," says jaunty Alarcón, "since your Lordship had commanded me to report on the secrets of that Gulf, I was determined, even at the risk of losing the ships, not to fail, under any pretext, to reach its end." He wanted to go beyond the place reached by Ulloa. This would help to classify both Ulloa and himself, and since Ulloa was Cortés' man, Mendoza would be especially pleased. So Alarcón ordered chief pilot Zamorano to take a launch, and, with sounding lead in hand, to enter the shoals and seek a channel for the ships. The captain attempted to follow with the fleet, but soon all three vessels were grounded and helpless.

But the day of miracles was not past. "We were in such danger," says Alarcón, "that many times the deck of the flagship was under water. And had it not been for the miraculous rise of the tide, which had raised the craft, and, as it were, given us a chance to breathe again, all of us would have been drowned." And who will deny that the rising and falling of the tide is a twice-daily miracle of Nature? The smaller vessels had a somewhat less difficult time, and soon all three were afloat once more. Then, by dint of much twisting and turning, sounding and tacking, the miles of shoals were passed and the head of the Gulf was reached. Alarcón had gone beyond the mark set by Ulloa.

"Here we found a mighty river with so furious a current that we could scarcely sail against it." But the reward for the struggle was adequate. Alarcón was the first explorer to enter the mouth of the Colorado River of the West. He named the stream the Buena Guía, or Unfailing Guide, from a part of the motto on the coat of arms of Viceroy Mendoza, his chief. And God willing, the river would guide him to the Promised Land of Cíbola or even to greater kingdoms! For Alarcón was sent by the viceroy not merely to support Coronado, but also to take a hand in piercing the Northern Mystery. If he should win the prize, all honor to him—and so much the worse for Coronado.

Two successes had been scored. But what was ahead? Now, leaving the ships at anchor in the river mouth, Alarcón took two launches and prepared to ascend the turbulent stream, in the hope that he might effect a junction with Coronado in the interior and with his cargo of supplies relieve the army's needs, for this was his primary mission. But he would explore as he went, see new sights, tread unknown lands and meet strange peoples. Only explorers know this thrill of discovery, in whatsoever realm. With the captain in the first launch went Rodrigo Maldonado, treasurer of the fleet, not to be confused with any of the four Maldonados—the "Smiths"—in Coronado's army. In this boat also went Gaspar de Castillejo, accountant, a quota of sailors, and a few pieces of artillery.

This day, Thursday, August 26, witnessed another triumph, for then Europeans first navigated the great Colorado River, a furious stream which from the beginning to the present has had a romantic history, but which at last has been tamed and made a slave to puny man—not by any means wholly a gain, for Nature deserves a little respect, and punishes Man when he violates it. Alarcón had been helped over the shoals by the rising tide, only to meet the backwash of the receding water which with deafening roar added its terrific force to that of the river. This clash of the tidewater with the current of the Colorado, the "bore," a phenomenon duplicated on so grand a scale in only a few places in the entire world, was now first braved by Europeans. And Alarcón had arrived at the very worst season, just before the September equinox. In spite of this serious impediment, before night the adventurers "by pulling on the ropes" had covered six leagues. That is to say, some of the men walked on shore and towed the launches to help out the rowers and the sails.

The lower Colorado in Alarcón's day was not just what it is now. Before the twentieth century, in times of spring flood its waters swept through various secondary channels (Alamo River, Paredones River, Pescadero River) westward toward Cócopa Range, along whose base they formed the streams known in modern times as New River and Hardy's Colorado. By the former the flood waters ran north into the vast depression called Salton Sink, where Salton Sea was formed; and by the latter they roared southward, entering the main Colorado near its mouth. The Salton Sea through the ages has several times evaporated on the subsidence of the waters. In 1906, in the course of a flood, the entire volume of the great river ran for a time into Salton Sink, leaving the old bed of the Colorado dry, and thereafter the main stream ran in a new channel. Other revolutionary changes have resulted from the building of titanic Boulder Dam and the development of irrigation along the lower reaches of the stream, causing the desert to bloom.

Thus began the historic first voyage by Europeans up the Colorado River among the tall Yuman peoples who lived along its banks on either side. What garrulous Alarcón tells us of the natives in a somewhat confused but highly interesting manner, becomes clear to anyone who knows the terrain and when considered in the light of reports made by later visitors.

Next day was likewise memorable, for then the first Indians were seen at a village on shore—which side is not stated, whether in Arizona or in Lower California. The natives were as excited as the Spaniards at the meeting. All shouted, some scurried to hide their belongings in the brush, others ran to the shore and with threatening gestures and vociferous harangues importuned the strangers to go back. "To reassure the Indians," and himself perhaps, Alarcón swung his launch into midstream, rode at anchor, and ordered his men to make no sound, sign, nor motion. Soon about 250 natives, at least they looked that many, had assembled on the bank, in warlike mood, with bows and arrows, "and some banners like those of New Spain," that is, banners similar to those carried into battle by the Indians of Mexico.

The boats again approached the shore and a conference was held in pantomime well worthy of a camera. Standing in the stern of his launch, Alarcón, through his interpreter, addressed the assembled Indians, "but they did not understand him nor he them." The natives shouted, gesticulated, motioned the visitors away, and placed logs in the water to prevent them from landing. It was not a warm reception. The mob increased. "The longer I lingered," says Alarcón, "the larger was the number of Indians in evidence." This made him all the stronger for appeasement. "Looking at them," he writes, "I began to make signs of peace. Taking my sword and shield, I threw them on the deck of the launch . . . trying to make them understand by this and other signs that I did not want to fight them, and that they should do likewise. I seized a flag, lowered it, and told my men to sit down. Then, taking some of the things I carried for barter I called to the natives and offered them as presents. But no one approached to accept them."

The Indians now went into a huddle on shore and held a noisy confab. Should it be peace or war? They decided on peace. Suddenly a chief emerged from the crowd bearing a staff decorated with inlaid shells. Boldly entering the water, he climbed on board the launch and presented the emblem to Alarcón. The captain embraced him, and gave him some beads and other trinkets, with which he returned to land. The mob on shore caught the point—the white strangers brought gifts. The natives now lowered their banners, laid down their weapons, boarded the launch, and were given presents in their turn.

Two leagues farther upstream Alarcón was invited ashore at a newly made arbor, but fearing an ambush he declined the invitation. When "more than a thousand Indians" armed with bows and arrows emerged from the arbor, he steered for midstream. The estimate of the number was doubtless generous, with perhaps an extra cipher for good measure. However, the Indians were not intending to fight, for the Spaniards were followed to the river by women and children, who in case of battle would presumably have been concealed.

The captain here gives us our first description of the tall Cócopas whose land he had invaded. "These Indians were adorned in different ways. Some had streaks almost entirely covering their faces, each one being painted according to his own fancy. Others had their faces half covered with black soot, and still others wore masks of the same color. On their heads each one had a deerskin two spans high, worn like a helmet, and on it a crest made of feathers. Their weapons were bows and arrows and two or three kinds of mallets made of wood hardened by fire.

"These people were large and well formed, without being corpulent." They are still noted for their superb physique.

"Some have their noses pierced, and from them hang pendants, while others wear shells. They also have their ears pierced with many holes, in which they place shells and beads. All of them, big and little, wear a multi-colored sash about the waist; and, tied in the middle, a round bundle of feathers hanging down behind like a tail. Likewise, on their biceps they wear a narrow band, wound around so many times that it has the width of a hand. They carry small blades of deer bones tied around one arm, with which they scrape off sweat, and from the other arm reed canes are hung. They have also a kind of sack a span long tied to the left arm, using it as an armbag for the bow; and it is filled with seeds from which they make a sort of beverage. Their bodies are branded by fire; their hair is banged in front, but in the back it hangs to the waist." So much for the men. The women had less, or perhaps more, to talk about. "They go about naked, except that, tied in front and behind, they wear large bunches of feathers, colored and glued. They wear their hair like the men."

Leaving the Village of a Thousand next morning early, for the summer heat was intense, Alarcón proceeded upstream, oars and sails now supplemented by men pulling at the ropes—*cordeling*, as the French trappers at a later date and in a different area would call it. From now forward most of the motive power was furnished in this way by friendly natives.

Having inquired by signs about their religion, Alarcón concluded that these Indians were Sun worshippers. From this he took his cue and posed as Son of the Sun. His racket worked. "They stared at me from head to foot, and showed me greater respect than before." He had established himself as a supernatural being, or at least a great medicine man—so he imagined. "From then on, whenever they brought me anything they first cast some of it toward the sun, then turned to me and gave me the rest. So I was more respected and better served by them, both in pulling at the ropes and in being supplied with food. They . . . wanted to carry me bodily in their arms to their homes, and did not refuse anything I asked of them. . . . They took to the ropes so willingly and in such a spirit of rivalry with

one another that it was not necessary even to request it of them."
Alarcón had no more labor troubles.

In his pagan rôle of Son of the Sun, Don Hernando was in
danger of going to unseemly limits, since a primary obligation
as conquistador was to spread the Christian Faith. So he made
little crosses of sticks and paper and distributed them among
the natives, telling them by signs they were symbols of heaven.
The Indians venerated the tokens and were rewarded with
presents, but here again Don Hernando found himself in
trouble. The fashion spread so rapidly that he could not manu-
facture enough crosses nor provide an adequate supply of gifts.

Thus Alarcón traveled upstream six days, till Tuesday, August 31, meeting mobs of Indians at every turn, for the news had
spread among them. That afternoon he saw at a village on shore
a native who understood the interpreter. This Indian was
called Old Man, a name which the Yuman tribes still give their
chiefs. Alarcón interrogated him, but the tables were soon
turned, and the Indian assumed the rôle of quiz-master. He
asked who the visitors were, where they came from, whether they
had sprung from the water, or the earth, or had descended from
the sky. When Don Hernando replied that he was the Son of
the Sun, Old Man plied him with a number of posers. How
could the Sun send the captain when it was so high in the
heavens, and never stopped in its voyage through the sky? Why
had Alarcón not come sooner to put an end to intertribal wars?
Why should a child of the Sun need an interpreter? To these
and other queries the captain gave what to him seemed clever
answers, worthy at least of being reported to Mendoza. Old
Man was duly edified, and passed the explanations on to the
crowd of listening natives, whereupon Alarcón's prestige waxed
greater. "Come here, then, and be our lord," said Old Man.
"Since you do so much good and do not wish to engage us in
wars, and since you are a child of the Sun, we wish to serve you
always, so we pray you not to go away and leave us."

The head man of one village was called Naguachato, a
word suspiciously like *Naguatate*, a Nahua term for interpreter

which came into frequent use far north of Aztec land. Here Alarcón went ashore and again exercised his missionary function. He had the Indians bring him a log, fashioned it into a large cross, and knelt before it with all his crew to pray, after which the natives set it up on shore. The captain exhorted the people to carefully guard the treasure and kneel before it every morning at sunrise. When they asked him how they should put their hands together and how kneel before the cross, he instructed them with all the zeal of a friar. This done, Alarcón took Naguachato on board and continued upstream.

The chief described the settlements for his distinguished visitor. He said there were twenty-three along the river, besides others far away. Some of the people lived in villages, others in scattered houses, each group having its recognized territory. There were frequent petty wars, he said, over equally petty causes. Some people who lived at a distance planted crops along the river in summer and after harvest went to live near some mountains, apparently in the west. Naguachato said the river people were monogamous, cremated their dead, were afflicted with tuberculosis (emitted blood through the mouth), and were doctored by medicine men who healed "with words and by blowing on the sick." The natives carried hollow reeds with which to perfume themselves, "in the same manner as the people of New Spain use tobacco"—that is, they smoked. They raised maize, melons, and squashes, ate fish from the river, had *metates* for grinding their food and earthen pots in which to cook it. When Alarcón inquired about native marriage customs, Naguachato replied in effect, "I have a marriageable daughter. I go among the people and ask if anybody wants her. If so, the groom's father brings presents, and they are then considered as man and wife." It was as simple as that, and father paid the bill.

After passing through an uninhabited region Alarcón was welcomed at another village of equally friendly people. "Behold the Master," said one of the elders. "Let us give him what meat we have, for he is doing good, and has traveled among many discourteous people in order to visit us." These new people were Quícamas, who came here only during the summer to gather the harvest of their planted fields. They had cotton, but took little interest in cultivating it, because there was no one among them who knew how to weave.

Speaking of their weapons, a Quícama chief told Alarcón that some of them carried large shields more than two fingers thick, made from the hide of an animal "resembling a cow" but much larger, "with broad feet and forelegs as thick as a man's thigh, the head seven spans long and the forehead three spans wide, eyes as big as fists, and horns the length of a man's shin, with sharp points a span long. Its legs were more than seven spans long; and it had a short but heavy tail. Raising his arms above his head, he said it was still taller than that." Perhaps the Indian was describing the buffalo, or more likely just spinning a yarn for the benefit of his visitor. He told also of a remarkable Old Woman who lived on the seacoast, perhaps the one who appears in the legends of the Island of California. Alarcón was warned that the natives farther upstream were "bad people," and when he went forward he took an escort of twenty warriors. Soon he found Quícama sentries "watching at the border of their country," from which we conclude that here a definite tribal boundary was recognized. The "bad people" were the Coanos, next above.

As he proceeded upstream Alarcón continued to make inquiry about Cíbola. On September 1, an Indian told him he had not only heard of that place but had been there himself. It was a month's travel across country, or by following the river one could reach it in forty days. Of Cíbola he gave a circumstantial account, somewhat misunderstood one suspects, but well calculated to whet Alarcón's interest and cause him to hasten forward. The Lord of Cíbola had a dog like Alarcón's, and dishes like those in use on the launch, except that the ones he saw in Cíbola were green. The plates and the dog had been obtained from a bearded Negro—an allusion to Stephen.

Farther upstream, still in Quícama territory, another Old Man said he likewise had been in Cíbola and "that it was something great." In that country there was metal of the same color as some bells he saw on board the launch, and the Negro wore on his feet and arms some things which jingled. These were Stephen's cascabeles. The Cíbolans had killed the Negro, and torn him in pieces "which were distributed among many chieftains so they might know he was dead." The evidence must have been conclusive. Still farther north, among the Coanos (September 6) Alarcón heard later news of Cíbola, telling of the arrival of Coronado there. The report had reached the natives on the Colorado and was causing a commotion among them. On shore an Indian shouted that in Cíbola there were bearded men, and that Alarcón and his followers ought to be killed lest the others come from Cíbola to join them and harm the river people. But the Old Man came to Alarcón's defense. Pointing to the captain, he said, "This man is the Son of the Sun, and is our lord. He is doing good; he does not enter our houses even when we invite him; he does not take anything away from us; and he does not molest our women."

Alarcón was now eager to send messengers to Coronado, but when he consulted his men no one would risk going, although he offered liberal rewards. "Only a Moorish slave," another Stephen, volunteered to make the journey. Don Hernando now decided to go in person to Cíbola, and he sent a native messenger downstream to the ships to inform the Spaniards there of his plan. Meanwhile he conferred with his companions and again called for volunteers. But he "found the same opposition as before." His own men having failed him, he turned once more to the Indians. Sending for the local chief he begged him to furnish braves to accompany him to Cíbola and provisions for the journey. But the chief likewise demurred and gave his reason. He was afraid of the Cumanas, native enemies upstream, whom he now asked the captain to punish. Says Alarcón, "We argued so long over this matter that we became angry, and the Old Man would have left the boat in a rage, but I restrained and placated him with kind words, because it was very important to retain his friendship. But no matter how attentive I was to him, I was unable to change his mind."

Thus Alarcón was forced to alter his plan because the Coano chief was afraid of hostile Cumanas upstream. Moreover, some of his men were ill. So he recalled the messenger sent to the ships and decided to descend to them himself, leave the sick men there, get provisions and able-bodied soldiers, and make a new attempt to reach Coronado. Telling the Indians he would come back, he turned his prow downstream. As a guarantee that he would keep his word he left one of his Spaniards at a Coano village near the place where he turned back. The Indians were certain that Alarcón was leaving through fear. If so, the unnamed Spaniard who remained as hostage, and whom we shall call Fulano de Tal, deserved the captain's gratitude and our admiration. Alarcón had traveled upstream only a short distance since September 6, but had spent some three additional days discussing with sailors and natives the proposed march to Cíbola.

The voyage downstream was rapid and easy. The distance which had cost him fifteen hard days to sail, push and pull his boats up the river, he covered on the return trip in two and a half days, "so great and swift was the current." He had left the ships on August 26, so he must have turned back from the Coano country about September 10 and reached the vessels about the twelfth or thirteenth. The natives along the river were sorry to see the jolly captain depart, and on the way downstream he was hailed by crowds on the shore who came to ask him: "Why are you leaving us, Señor? What displeasure have you experienced? Did you not say you would remain among us always, and be our master? Go back, and if anybody up the river does you any harm we will accompany you with our warriors and kill him."

When Alarcón reached the ships he found his men all in good health, but much worried over their captain's long absence. The moored vessels had suffered some damage in the interim. Four cables had been broken by the swift current of the river, and two anchors had been lost, but were recovered. Alarcón now removed all the camp to a more sheltered place, ordered the necessary repairs made and the *San Pedro* careened. When he announced his intention to return upstream in an attempt to join Coronado the men demurred, but he went ahead with his plans. All the small boats that could be spared were made ready, one of them being loaded with "trading goods, wheat, and other grains, and also Spanish cocks and hens." He left orders with his subordinates that in a place called La Cruz they should build a shrine or chapel and christen it Our Lady of La Buena Guía. Having made these preparations, which consumed two days, he took on board chief pilot Nicoláas Zamorano to observe latitudes, and two musicians to relieve the crew from boredom. Then, on September 14 he once more started up the great river.

Next day Alarcón arrived at the first houses of the Indians. When they saw the Spaniards they rushed to obstruct his passage, thinking they were some other people, says Alarcón, "because we were taking along a fifer and a drummer, and I was dressed differently than when they saw me the first time." From this we learn that the captain had more than one uniform. When the natives recognized him they desisted from their charge. Alarcón now gave the villagers some of the seeds he carried, and showed them how to plant them. "However," he says, "I could not induce them to become good friends." Something had happened since his last visit. Perhaps these Indians near the river mouth had heard disturbing news from Cíbola.

In due time Alarcón reached Coano, where Fulano de Tal had been left as a hostage. "Seeing me in different clothes they did not recognize me," says the captain. "But the moment the Old Man here saw who I was, he entered the water, saying, 'Señor, here is the man you left with me.' " Don Fulano appeared very happy. He told Alarcón of the many attentions the people had showered upon him, and how they had vied with each other to take him to their homes. Pleased with the report, Alarcón distributed seeds among the Coanos and thanked them for their good treatment of the Spaniard. They in turn begged Alarcón to leave the hostage there till the end of his voyage. The request was granted "and he remained among them very willingly." Plainly, Don Fulano was having a good time, but the nature of his diversions is not disclosed.

Alarcón continued up the river, taking along the Coano chief. This Indian told the captain that in the latter's absence two Indians from Cumana, upstream, had come to Coano to inquire about the Christians. Old Man told them he did not know any Christians, but was acquainted with a stranger called Child of the Sun. The distinction was important; the Christians were the people who had conquered Cíbola. Old Man added that emissaries from upstream had urged him to unite with the Cumanas and massacre Alarcón and his men. The captain called the bluff. He asked Old Man for two Coano braves by whom to send word ahead to the Cumanas that he was coming to see them, and desired their friendship, but if they wanted war he "would give it to them in a way they would not like."

Nor did Alarcón turn back because of the threatening rumor. As they went along Old Man told of other peoples whom he knew or had heard of. Being invited to spend the night on board the launch, he declined, because Alarcón "would tire him out with questions about so many things." The captain was too inquisitive. Alarcón replied that he would not ask another thing of him "except that he mark on a piece of paper what he knew of the river, and what people lived on each of its banks. He complied with pleasure. Then he asked me to describe my country in the same way as he had described his. To please him I ordered pictures of a few things drawn." It was a fair exchange of courtesies. These Spanish drawings and Old Man's map, if we had them, would be more precious than all the turquoises Coronado found in Cíbola! They may be discovered someday in Mexico or Spain. Who will have the thrill of finding them?

Next day Alarcón "came to some very high mountains through which the river flowed in a narrow canyon, where the boats passed with difficulty because there was no one to pull them." The captain was now apparently at Yuma, where the Colorado River runs for a mile, more or less, through a narrow channel, with high, cliff-like banks on either side. Here he had an interesting encounter. "At this place some Indians came to tell me they were from Cumana, and that among them there was a wizard who wanted to know which way we were going. Upon being told I was coming by the river, he placed some reeds clear across the stream," evidently thinking they would have some sort of magic power. "But we passed over them without suffering any of the harm he thought he would cause us."

"Thus we traveled until I came to the house of the Old Man who came with me," therefore still in Coano territory. "I had a very tall cross erected here, and on it I carved some letters to indicate that I had come to this place. I did this in order that if people from the general should arrive here they would know about me."

Alarcón now gave up his efforts to reach Coronado and Cíbola. "At last," he says, "seeing that I could not learn anything I wanted to know, I decided to return to the ships." As he was about to leave, two Indians arrived, saying they had come at his call. "They said they were from Cumana; that their chieftain could not come because his country was so far away, but that I might send him any message I wished." In reply Alarcón sent word to the Cumana chief that he must endeavor to maintain peace at all times; that he had been on his way to visit him, but now found it necessary to return downstream. However, he would come on some future day. With the messengers he sent their chief a cross with some feathers on it. "Then, on the following day," says Alarcón, "I sailed down the river."

Apparently Alarcón's farthest north was in Coano territory just above the Gila-Colorado junction. We have his clear-cut statement that he turned back at the place where he erected the cross, and where he parted with the messengers from Cumana, whose settlements he did not reach. "Next day," he says, "I arrived at the place where I had left the Spaniard," namely at the Coano village. So his farthest north was only one day's downstream travel above Coano. "I talked with the Spaniard [Fulano de Tal] and told him things had turned out well for me, and that on this and my previous voyage I had gone more than thirty leagues inland." Counting the twists and turns of the tortuous stream, this is about the distance from the mouth of the Colorado to the Yuma junction. The Indians at Coano asked him why he was leaving, and when he would return. He replied that he would be back soon. "Thus I reached my ships."

A final incident in the voyage is of human if trifling interest. As they were sailing along, a woman waded into the water, shouting and begging Alarcón to take her on board. When he halted she climbed into the boat and crawled under a bench, a refuge from which the crew could not extract her, try as hard as they might. "I learned that she did this," says Alarcón, "because her husband had another wife. . . . She said she did not want to stay with him any longer since he had another woman. She and an Indian came with me of their own accord." Perhaps this latter Indian gives us a clue to the cause of the lady's troubles.

Domingo Castillo, who had been with both Ulloa and Alarcón, in 1541 made a map showing Cíbola and the lower reaches of the Buena Guía or Colorado River. Incidentally it may be remarked that Alarcón at Yuma touched California on its eastern border a year or more before it was "discovered" by Cabrillo on the western shore. It is noteworthy also that these sturdy Yuman tribes still live in essentially the same region where Alarcón found them more than four hundred years ago. They have been a most stable group.

From the data afforded us by the Díaz expedition, as narrated in the next chapter, it would appear that Alarcón's launches were left fifteen leagues from the head of the Gulf. Counting the bends in the river this would be perhaps nearly halfway upstream to Yuma junction.

Chapter XV

DÍAZ SEEKS ALARCÓN

While Alarcón's little craft were moving up and down Colorado River, Díaz, in compliance with orders given him at Cíbola, took up his duties as alcalde mayor of San Gerónimo in Sonora Valley. His most urgent task was to go in search of Alarcón and his food-laden ships, for the Spaniards at Cíbola were needy, and Coronado was anxious for the safety of the voyagers, of whom nothing had been heard since the expedition left Compostela. To rule at San Gerónimo in his absence Díaz left Diego de Alcaráz, the villain who had given Cabeza de Vaca that brutal reception in Sinaloa some five years previously. It was too bad that Díaz was not free to make a better choice, for he well knew the qualities of the man he was leaving in command. The appointment was made by a "higher up."

Having seen Arellano and the army on their way to Cíbola behind Coronado, Díaz without delay organized a force of twenty-five Spaniards and a contingent of Indian allies, valiant Ópatas no doubt. The Spaniards were mounted on horses, the allies presumably going on foot. To supply food on the way, sheep were driven along by native servants. In the company went guides and interpreters, and a greyhound which might prove to be useful in case of need. The dog was destined to leave his mark on history.

Thus equipped, late in September Díaz set forth northwest to fulfill his important commission. His route lay through the Pima and Pápago country which later was made so famous by Kino, Garcés, and Anza. Apparently he went over the Camino del Diablo—the Devil's Highway—that terrible desert trail through Sonóita which became well known for its perils, and on which even today inexperienced travelers die of thirst and hardship. The first band of the European procession across this difficult but enchanting stretch of country was now being led by dauntless Melchior Díaz, to be followed later by Sonora gold seekers in the California rush and whose mònument is the historic mining town of Sonora.

Details of the journey are lacking, for no diary has come to light; but, thanks to Castañeda, we have an outline of the story, with many circumstantial passages. Having traveled 150 leagues, according to the estimate, the captain and his followers reached the Colorado River thirty leagues above its mouth, and near its junction with the Gila. Here they found themselves in "a province inhabited by people like giants, exceedingly tall and muscular." They were one of the Yuman tribes Alarcón had visited shortly before. Díaz' coming must have disturbed the natives, and if Naguachato saw him, some questions doubtless arose in the garrulous chief's mind. Alarcón had come by launch; these new visitors arrived on horseback, like those who had captured Háwikuh. Were they Christians, like the conquerors of Cíbola, or Children of the Sun, like Alarcón and his men? Why were they accompanied by Ópata warriors and a greyhound? And did they have in their packs plentiful gifts such as Alarcón had so freely dispensed?

Díaz' expedition to the Colorado gives us new glimpses of these river people, who to this day have never failed to command attention. "They went . . . naked, and lived in huts made of long straw, built underground like caves, with only the straw rising above the ground." They entered these dwellings at one end, without stooping, and came out at the opposite end. More than a hundred persons, large and small, slept in one house. There may have been a post-war housing shortage.

The amazing strength of the Yuman giants especially caused remark. "When transporting burdens they carried on their heads more than three or four hundreds pounds. It once happened that when our men wished to bring a log for the fire and six of them were unable to carry it, one of the Indians picked it up in his arms, put it on his head all by himself, and carried it with great ease." In more recent years some of the descendants of these prim-

itive athletes have become famous wrestlers and football stars, by
virtue of the same qualities observed in them by these first European visitors. Mota Padilla tells us Díaz was so impressed with
these Arizona giants that he wanted to send one of them to Mexico in order that Viceroy Mendoza might behold his magnificent
physique. Seeing a youth who would fill the bill, Díaz tried to
capture him, "but he made such resistance that four Spaniards
were unable to bind him, and he yelled so lustily they had to let
him go, in order not to indispose the minds of the rest." The
young fellow had not forgotten his childhood technique of yell-
ing when in trouble.

One of the native customs here especially caught the attention
of Díaz and his men. "Because of the intense cold"—and this at
Yuma!—"when they travel about from place to place they carry
a firebrand with which they warm their hands and body, changing
it from one hand to the other from time to time as they travel
along. For this reason the large river which flows through that
country is called Rio del Tizón." Thus Alarcón's Buena Guía
River became known and for a long time afterward was called
the River of the Firebrand. "It is a mighty stream," said Castañeda, "more than two leagues wide at its mouth, and at this
place," where Díaz first arrived at its banks, "it was half a league
wide." This was probably an exaggeration, but it represents the
impression made by the great river upon Díaz and his followers.
Castañeda himself never saw it but repeated the stories he had
heard. Sedelmayr at a later date reports the same custom regarding the use of firebrands. "Their blanket in cold weather is a
burning brand, with which, applying it to the mouth of the stomach, they go about in the morning, and when about eight o'clock
the sun gets warm they throw the brand away, with the result
that, because of the great number they have cast along the roads,
they would serve as a guide for travelers. Thus all these rivers
might be called Ríos del Tizón, a name which some maps give
to one only." And the unfair discrimination has continued in
spite of Sedelmayr's protest—so helpless is fact when it comes in
conflict with tradition.

Díaz learned from the natives that Alarcón had been with his launches at a site farther downstream. Here was a clue and hope-fully he followed it, each moment filled with suspense. Descend-ing the river for three days he "reached the place to which the ships had come, which was more than fifteen leagues up the river from the head of the bay," or about half way from the Gulf to Yuma, a statement confirmed by Castillo's map. Alarcón was not there, but Díaz found carved on a tree an arresting message:

ALARCÓN CAME THIS FAR. THERE ARE LETTERS AT THE FOOT OF THIS TREE.

Díaz, in great eagerness we may well imagine, unearthed the let-ters, and from them learned how long the ships had waited for news of the army, and that Alarcón had returned to Mexico with the vessels because he could not proceed any farther, "for that sea was a gulf extending toward the Island of the Marquis [Cortés] which is called California. They reported that California was not an island, but a point of the mainland on the other side of the gulf"—that is to say, a peninsula, now called Lower California. Since there is no evidence that any of Díaz' party reached the Gulf, we may assume that the distance of the carved tree from the mouth of the Colorado was an estimate based on conversa-tion with the natives or that this information was contained in the letters Díaz unearthed.

Because of the news conveyed by Alarcón's report, Díaz now turned north, without having seen the Gulf, and traveled up-stream to look for a place where he might ford the river, with a view to continuing his explorations on the other side. After marching five or six days to the vicinity of Yuma, he decided to cross the stream on rafts such as the natives used, and he called on the Indians for help in building them.

Nothing could have suited the tall natives better than Díaz' proposal, for they had been planning an attack on the bearded strangers and were only awaiting a good opportunity. Here it was, made to order! When Díaz disclosed his wish they hastened to make the rafts, at which they were expert, hoping to catch the Spaniards in midstream and drown them, or to attack them at some moment when their forces were divided and unable to make a united stand. But their scheme miscarried. While the rafts were being constructed, Díaz learned what the Indians were up to. A soldier while foraging outside the camp saw a large band of natives going through the brush and, as he thought, intending to cross the river by stealth. When this was reported to Díaz, says Castañeda, he had an Indian "captured and locked up secretly in order to question him and learn the truth." The captive was stubborn, but under torture "he revealed the whole plan the Indians were preparing to execute the moment the Spaniards should undertake to cross the stream." This implies that Díaz had good interpreters. The stratagem of the Indians did not lack cleverness. When some of the Spaniards had crossed the river, others being in midstream on the rafts, and the rest waiting on the east bank for the rafts to return for them, the natives would strike the blow, drowning in the yellow waters the men on the rafts, and at the same time attacking those on both banks. "If they had possessed discretion and courage in proportion to their power and strength they would have succeeded in their plot," says Castañeda.

Having thus learned what was on foot, Díaz caused the captive informant to be killed. His body, heavily weighted, was thrown that night into the river, in order that the natives might not know their plot had been discovered. But all this secrecy was of no avail. The Indians, seeing that their plans had miscarried, decided to act before it was too late. Early next morning they attacked the strangers with a shower of arrows, and a battle was on. While the Spanish horsemen ran some of the natives down and pierced them through with lances, the arquebusiers fired well-placed shots into the midst of the mob of warriors, forcing them to abandon the field and take to the woods "until not a man was to be seen." This, of course, is the Spanish side of the story. The other side has not been told, except perhaps in native folklore. Nor do we learn what part in the affray, if any, was played by the Ópata allies of the Spaniards, nor by the greyhound, nor what was happening meanwhile to the sore-footed sheep.

Díaz now returned to the river and crossed it on the very conveyances the natives had built for themselves, the Spaniards and allies going over in groups on the rafts, "the horses swimming alongside." Presumably the sheep and the greyhound rode across with the men. Here is another scene for the artist, quite in contrast with Kino's peaceful transit in a basket near the same place a century and a half later. Having safely effected the crossing, Díaz went to look for the "other coast, which in that region turned south or southeast," says Castañeda. This would mean that Díaz intended to reach the western shore of the Gulf by swinging south.

The travelers soon had another bizarre adventure; another story to tell to their friends back home and to intrigue future historians. "While they were traveling in this direction they came upon some beds of burning lava. No one could cross them, for it would be like going into the sea to drown. The ground on which the Spaniards walked resounded like a kettle-drum, as if there were lakes underneath. It was amazing to see the cinders boil in some places, for it looked like something infernal. They turned away from this place because it seemed to be dangerous, and also because of the lack of water." When Díaz and his men saw this phenomenon they may have been in the neighborhood of black Volcano Peak, which rises above the plain in Lower California near Cócopa Mountains, and in whose vicinity, especially near Salton Sea, there still are hot springs or mud volcanoes into which an incautious traveler is in danger of falling, as I myself once did when following Anza's trail.

The Spaniards traveled beyond the crossing some five or six days, apparently having swung south, and then the expedition suddenly ended in tragedy. One day the greyhound amused himself by chasing some of the sheep brought along for food. Seeing the fracas, Díaz started in pursuit, throwing his lance at the dog as he galloped. It was a disastrous thrust. The weapon, missing the animal, stuck upright in the ground, and the captain, not being able to stop his horse, ran upon the shaft of the lance in such a way that it pierced his groin and ruptured his bladder. The soldiers ran to the captain's aid, thinking him dead. "But he was a man of spirit, and he came to," says Tello, a later chronicler. "Seeing there was no one who dared to doctor him, he doctored himself. With a desire to live, he said with great effort, 'If I only had a silver tube I could get along.'" Such a man would grace the pages of Homer. Díaz was made of the same stuff as Ojeda, who near Panama amputated his own leg, and to stop its bleeding seared the raw flesh with a red-hot ax.

Díaz' misfortune, which occurred near the last days of December, 1540, put an end to exploration, and the soldiers, sick at heart, turned back toward San Gerónimo carrying their gallant captain on a litter. In addition to this burden they had to fight daily skirmishes with Indians who beset their path as they retreated. Díaz lived twenty days after the accident, his soldiers meanwhile enduring hardships and dangers in their vain effort to get him back alive. But death won the race. Tello writes: "Although they traveled rapidly with the desire to reach the settlement in time for him to be confessed, for there was a priest there, he died on January 18 [1541], and the soldiers with great sorrow buried him on a little hill and there erected a cross, covering him with a large mound of earth and stones." We are reminded here of the burial of Sir John Moore at Coruña, as narrated by the poet Wolfe: "Not a drum was heard, not a funeral note, as his corse to the rampart we hurried."

Just where Díaz was buried is unknown, but his remains lie somewhere in the desert between the Colorado River and Sonora Valley—perhaps beside the Camino del Diablo. Who will discover and identify them? In spite of Indian hostility and other hazards, the men reached San Gerónimo without losing another man. Among all the brave and competent adventurers who participated in the Coronado expedition in an effort to lift the veil from the Northern Mystery, there was none who played a more gallant part than Melchior Díaz. He deserves a monument to his memory, erected in Sonora Valley, or beside the old channel of the Colorado, or on the Camino del Diablo!

When the soldiers arrived at San Gerónimo, Alcaráz despatched messengers to Coronado telling the story of Don Melchior's death, and perhaps from this account Castañeda obtained his information regarding the calamity. The names of two members of Díaz' party are known. They were Hernano de Orduña, a native of Burgos, who went with Arellano to San Gerónimo; and Pedro de Castro, who had gone to Háwikuh with the vanguard and, apparently, from there accompanied Díaz, Fray Marcos, and Juan Gallego on their journey south. Orduña tells us that after they returned "from the discovery of the Mar del Sur with the men who went on that errand," they went "to where . . . Coronado was"; that is, to Cíbola. By the same messengers Alcaráz informed Coronado that in Díaz' absence seditious soldiers at San Gerónimo had caused several mutinies. He had sentenced two of the men to the gallows, but they had escaped from prison and fled. The episode formed another chapter in the stormy career of Alcaráz.

Alarcón, meanwhile, having left the Colorado River about the middle of October, 1540, sailed for Colima, directing his course along the mainland of Sonora and Sinaloa. He landed frequently and went inland in an effort to get news of Coronado, but without avail. As he sailed southward he laid formal claim for Spain to numerous places along the shore, and set down the record in wordy legal documents. "I bring with me many acts of possession of all that coast," he wrote to Mendoza.

Early in November, with the little ships that had made the historic voyage to Colorado River, Alarcón entered the port of Colima. Pedro de Alvarado, conqueror of Guatemala, who then chanced to be in the same harbor with his fleet, ordered Alarcón to lower his sails, for Tonatíuh himself had ambitions regarding northern explorations. But, says Alarcón, "as it seemed unusual, and not knowing what the situation was in New Spain, I prepared to disobey him and to defend myself." At this juncture Castillo reminded Alarcón that discretion was the better part of valor, so he sailed out of the harbor in the night to avoid a battle, confining his defense to the words in his report. Before leaving he delivered to Castillo an account of his voyage which he had written to send to Mendoza as soon as he might land in New Spain. He adds, "If your Excellency will grant me permission to come and kiss your hands, I shall give you a long and complete report."

It was apparently the one we have used for our story. If he wrote a longer narration of his voyage it has never come to light.

Soon after Alarcón reached Colima a new sea expedition to coöperate with Coronado was planned. Mendoza was worried; Coronado must have supplies, and help if he needed it. On May 31, 1541, the viceroy issued to Alarcón instructions for the voyage. Its purpose was primarily to support Coronado, and secondarily to seek Díaz, of whose death the viceroy had not heard, and to make a settlement on Buena Guía river among the Quícamas and Coanas. These tribes had registered in the official mind.

Alarcón was ordered to take a ship that was in the harbor at Navidad, and a large sea-going sloop, built especially for this voyage, equip them with provisions, arms, and munitions, and man them with sailors and artillerymen. This gave the enterprise a warlike aspect. Alarcón was to be accompanied by two friars who had been in the Gulf with Ulloa, and Indians were to be taken along as interpreters. The first business was to try to get in touch with both Coronado and Díaz by inquiry at Culiacán or farther north on the mainland coast. Failing in this Alarcón must proceed to Buena Guía River—that is, the Colorado—find Coronado, and deliver despatches to him. "For I am writing to him," says Mendoza, "that since you were the discoverer of that river, and since its people liked you, and you have served his Majesty by exploring that region, he should place you in charge of it, and since you have information of the country beyond, he shall, if necessary, furnish you more men with whom to go farther up that river."

In other words, Alarcón was to establish a post on the Colorado and himself command it, under Coronado. There must be no swearing by Alarcón's men, and he must set a good example as a Christian. "You should see to it that the chiefs of Quícama and Coana are not annoyed or injured in the least, for they welcomed you graciously." Now a mild word of censure by Mendoza for his ebullient favorite: "Try to be discreet in your dealings and conversation with the Indians, for it would seem to be necessary to be more circumspect with them than you were the last time." The viceroy probably alluded to Alarcón's pagan parade among the natives as Son of the Sun. This bordered on heresy! And, Mendoza wrote, "you are to take . . . certain articles which Doña Beatríz . . . is sending to the captain-general, her husband. You must order that good care be taken of these and of other things which you may take along for some of the soldiers from their friends and relatives." The men on the distant frontier were not forgotten by the people back home.

The vessels were equipped for this new voyage looking to the permanent settlement of Colorado River, but the expedition was never made. For when the ships were on the point of weighing anchor the Mixton War was raging, all Nueva Galicia was endangered, and Alarcón was sent to defend the town of Autlán against the native warriors. Mendoza's soldiers could not be in two places at the same time. Thus may the history of one spot be changed by events at another spot far remote.

Chapter XVI

ALVARADO AND THE GOLDEN BRACELET

When he wrote to Mendoza on August 3, 1540, Coronado told of places round about Cíbola that he had heard of. One of them was Acus, which Fray Marcos had called a kingdom, carefully distinguishing it from Áhacus, or Háwikuh. He was speaking of the famous pueblo of Ácoma. Coronado took a fling at both Marcos' geography and his etymology. Acus, said the general, is "a single small city called Ácucu where they raise cotton. I say this is a town, because Acus with or without aspiration"—here he paraphrases the friar—"is not a word of this region; and because it seems to me that Ácucu may be derived from Acus, I conclude that it is this town which has been converted into the Kingdom of Acus." The course of his philologic reasoning is not altogether clear, but his guess proved to be correct. "They tell me there are some other small kingdoms not far from this settlement and situated on a river that I have not seen but of which the Indians have told me." The stream was the famous one now known as Rio Grande.

On the heels of these rumors more interesting news came from the same direction. A small band of natives arrived at Háwikuh from a pueblo named Cicúique or Cicúye, some seventy leagues to the east and beyond Rio Grande. It was the one now called Pecos. At the head of the delegation were two chiefs whom Coronado called Bigotes and Cacique (governor). By signs and through such interpreters as were available they told Coronado they had learned that "strange people, bold men," had come to make their acquaintance. Coronado's message had been carried abroad and these chiefs had come in response to his invitation, and no doubt to satisfy their curiosity.

The principal spokesman for these picturesque visitors was Bigotes, so dubbed by the Spaniards because he wore a long moustache. This Indian was a striking personality and he became a key figure in our story. "He was a tall young man, well built, and robust in appearance. He told the general they had come to serve him in response to the request that they should offer themselves as friends, and that if the Spaniards planned to go to his land they would be welcomed." The visitors gave Coronado a generous present of dressed skins, shields, and headpieces, specimens of their finest handiwork, all of which were accepted "with much affection." In return the general provided the strangers with lodgings and gave them glassware, pearl beads, and little bells, which they prized very highly "as something they had never seen before." It is quite likely, however, that they had heard of the tinkling bells worn by Estevanico, the gay blade from the south who had preceded the Spanish soldiery to Cíbola, and had paid for his spree with his life.

From handsome Bigotes and his companions, Coronado learned more than the Cíbolans had reported about the settled regions in the east and the country still beyond. Among other things they "told of the cattle. They were made out to be cattle by the picture one of the Indians had painted on his body"—tattooed, perhaps—"although this could not be determined by the hides, because the hair was so woolly and tangled that one could not tell what the animals were." The picture was more revealing than the sample itself, and by the soldiers its bearer was dubbed Vaquito, the Calf.

So Cabeza de Vaca and Stephen had told the truth about the cattle on the eastern plains. This Cicúique must be an important place; and several others had been mentioned as lying along the route, among them Ácoma, a fortress city build on top of a lofty and inaccessible cliff. The general's mind was quickly made up. He told the visitors he wished to send Captain Hernando de Alvarado to inform the natives in the east of his arrival at Cíbola, to explain why his Majesty in Spain had sent him to these regions, "and to explore what was beyond." Bigotes and Cacique, with dignity characteristic of their race, expressed themselves as well pleased. They invited Captain Alvarado and his men to go east by way of their pueblo, offered to guide them thither, and to bespeak for them a friendly reception by the settlements along the way. At Cicúique the Spaniards would be furnished with provisions and guides to "the country of the cows."

Here was a rare opportunity, and Alvarado was just the man to take advantage of it—the same Don Hernando who with Cárdenas so gallantly in the rough and tumble fight at Háwikuh had caught the blows aimed at the general's shining helmet and thereby saved his life. So Coronada equipped Alvarado with twenty-odd Spaniards and gave him a commission for eighty days —the same time he had set for Cárdenas—after which he was to come back and report what he had found. With him went Father Juan Padilla, the fighting friar, fresh from his adventure in Hopi Land with Tovar. A new experience was in prospect for this already seasoned pioneer. Two other members of the company were Juan de Troyano and Melchior Pérez, both conspicuous personalities, as hardy as they come, and whose exploits in our story have never before been told. Most of the men were mounted on horses, but four were crossbowmen who went on foot, and thus determined the speed of travel for the party.

Saddle girths were cinched and pack animals loaded. Guided by Bigotes and his companions, Don Hernando set out from Háwikuh toward the east on Sunday, August 29, 1540, "Feast of the beheaded St. John." This was just four days after Cárdenas left Cíbola to see the Great River in the west, and three days after Alarcón entered the mouth of that stream. New lines were being drawn simultaneously on the map, and one by one the secrets of the Northern Mystery were being disclosed. On their historic jaunt Don Hernando and his men were the first Europeans to traverse a stretch of some seven hundred miles of Tierra Nueva, as they called their new discoveries. They deserve a monument at some appropriate spot.

The first segment of Alvarado's trail, though doubtless well known to the natives, was apparently not much traveled by them because of its extreme difficulty. Instead of ascending Zuñi Valley, past the great cliff where the Cíbolans had taken refuge, Don

Hernando took a more direct eastward route through Ojo Caliente Valley. Within some four or five leagues after leaving Háwikuh he saw, just south of the Cíbola towns, five ruins then already long abandoned, and little known today. His record is an archaeological gem and should be an incentive to much enthusiastic digging. Two leagues from Háwikuh, says Alvarado, "we came to an old edifice resembling a fortress; a league farther on we found another one, and a little farther on still another. Beyond these we came to an ancient city, quite large but all in ruins, although a considerable portion of the wall, which must have been six estados high," some thirty-three feet, "was still standing. The wall was built of finely cut stone, with gates and gutters like a Castilian city. Half a league beyond . . . we found the ruins of yet another city. Its wall must have been very good, being built about an estado high of large granite rocks, and above this of very fine blocks of hewn stone." It is plain that time or native foes had wrought much destruction among these pueblos before the Spaniards arrived. Alvarado was now some fifteen miles east of Háwikuh, and not far from the cliff of Towayálane, where the Cíbolans had taken refuge after the battle of Granada.

"Two roads branch out from here," says the narrator, "one leading to Chía, the other to Coco." By Chía he meant Zía and by Coco he referred to Ácomo, both now famous in Pueblo Land. The road to Zía ran northeast to that distant pueblo near the Rio Grande; the other continued eastward through a rough and difficult *malpaís,* or badland, thickly strewn with volcanic lava that is murderous to the feet of horses. Even today it is one of the horrors of travel in that vicinty, and the lava now is just as black as then. Alvarado followed the latter trail and reached the pueblo of Ácoma some seventy-five miles east of Háwikuh. It had been tough going. Dr. Hodge, who has an intimate acquaintance with the region and the people, writes that "no Zuñi Indian of the present time is known to have taken this trail through to Ácoma." If Alvarado had ascended Zuñi Valley, by the easier but longer way, he would have passed near Inscription Rock, but he evidently went south of that imposing monument, which has become a famous "historical album." Perhaps he chose the more difficult route to avoid disturbing the nervous Cíbolans by going with soldiers up Zuñi Valley.

The pueblo of Ácoma, writes Alvarado, "was one of the strongest ever seen, because the city is built on a very high rock. The ascent was so difficult that we repented climbing to the top. The houses are three and four storeys high. The people are of the same type as those in the province of Cíbola, and they have abundant supplies of maize, beans, and turkeys like those of New Spain." Another member of the party called Ácoma "the greatest stronghold ever seen in the world. The natives . . . came down to meet us peacefully, although they might have spared themselves the trouble and remained on their rock, for we would not have been able to disturb them in the least." But the people were friendly, and gave the Spaniards cotton cloth, skins of buffalo and deer, turquoises, turkeys, and some of their other kinds of food, "which were the same as those at Cíbola."

Leaving the Sky City on its lofty perch, the adventurers went a few miles northeast to a pretty lagoon, where there were trees "like those of Castile." The lake, fed by the stream now called Rio San José, was the one where the pueblo of Laguna was later built and still occupies the site. Three days and twenty leagues beyond Ácoma the explorers came to a river which they named Nuestra Señora, because they arrived at its banks on September 7, eve of the Feast of Our Lady. The stream was the now famous Rio Grande, which they apparently reached in the vicinity of Isleta, where the old trail from the west cut across the angle between Rio San José and Rio Grande. Farther north, above the site of present Albuquerque, founded a century and a half later, they made camp near the southern border of the group of towns called by the Spaniards the Province of Tiguex.

From here, says Alvarado, "we sent the cross by a guide"—our handsome young chief Bigotes—"to the pueblos beyond"; that is, up stream. Next day, "from twelve pueblos came chieftains and people in good order, those of one pueblo after the other." The whole province had turned out to welcome the strangers, but presumably the reception committee included no women and children, for this was man's business. It must have been a colorful procession, with the natives in their holiday regalia, which even yet charms all beholders. "They marched around our tent, playing a flute, and with an old man for spokesman. In this manner they came inside the tent and presented me with food, cotton cloth, and skins which they had." In return Alvarado distributed little gifts among the delegation, whereupon they went away. Tiguex had shown the strangers its best hospitality, quite in contrast with the reception given Coronado at Háwikuh and Tovar in Hopi Land.

In his report to Coronado, Alvarado gives us our first view of the Rio Grande Valley above Albuquerque, that region which has had so eventful and so dramatic a history. "This river of Nuestra Señora," he tells us, "flows through a broad valley planted with fields of maize and dotted with cottonwood groves. There are twelve pueblos, whose houses are built of mud and are two storeys high." These towns comprised the province of Tiguex, so-called by the Spaniards from the Tigua Indians who lived in the vicinity of present-day Bernalillo. "The natives seem to be good people, more devoted to agriculture than to war," says Alvarado; but he had yet to learn how well they could fight. "They have a food supply of maize, beans, melons, and turkeys in great abundance. They clothe themselves in cotton, the skins of cattle, and coats made of turkey feathers, and they wear their hair short." There was no Youth Movement here, and nothing like jitterbugs, for, says our chronicler, "the old men are the ones who have the most authority among them. We thought these elders must be wizards, because they said they could ascend to heaven, and other things of that sort," which the Spaniards probably misunderstood.

To Tiguex, says Alvarado, "the Indians from the surrounding provinces came to offer me peace. These provinces are the ones your Lordship will note in the report, in which will be found eighty pueblos of the kind I have described." Another witness gives the number of pueblos as seventy, "a few more or less, counting large and small. They are of the same type as those of Cíbola, except that they are nearly all of well built mud walls," whereas the Cíbola pueblos were mainly of stone. "Their food is exactly the same. The natives grow cotton—I mean those living near the river, for the others do not. And there was plenty of maize here. These people have no markets." The writer was perhaps thinking of the famous trading marts in Aztec Mexico, from which he had just come.

Don Hernando repaid the visits of these friendly embassies by making a tour of the pueblos far up the river, still guided by staunch chief Bigotes. As they traveled along, Alvarado and Padilla did not forget their missionary function. "In places where we erected crosses we taught the natives to worship them,"—just as Alarcón was doing with more fanfare and histrionics at the same time on Colorado River—"and they offered their powders and feathers, even the cotton garments they wore. They showed such eagerness that some of them climbed on the backs of others to reach the arms of the crosses to decorate them with plumes and roses. They brought ladders, and while some held them others climbed up to tie the strings in order to fasten the roses with the feathers." Clearly these crosses were far from diminutive.

Alvarado was told the settlements extended more than fifty leagues along the river, some of the pueblos being fifteen or twenty leagues apart. So he continued upstream to the northernmost town, which he called Braba. It was the now famous pueblo of Taos, near which an artist's colony has grown up in recent times. Here as elsewhere Bigotes caused the natives to come out in peace. They welcomed the visitors and offered them lodgings within the pueblo, "but the Spaniards, having entered, returned outside, in order not to offend them or cause disturbance." Perhaps they felt safer there, and undoubtedly the outdoor air was better. The pueblo as described consisted of three storeys of mud or adobe, each storey wider than the one above it, and having on each level an outdoor terrace running clear around the edifice. Above the highest adobe storey there were two or three others built of wood and without terraces. The town comprised eighteen or twenty wards or sections, with passages between them, and a small patio inside each ward. Braba, remarks one witness, "has more inhabitants than any other pueblo in that land"—a population estimated by Alvarado at fifteen thousand persons and by Melchior

Pérez at twice that number, probably an exaggeration in each case. Outside the pueblo there were earthen burial mounds. The chroniclers of Alvarado's journey reported that the country at Braba, "being in the sierras," was very cold, and that the natives raised neither turkeys nor cotton, their clothing being made of deerskins and buffalo hides. Strangely enough these first eye-witness writers describe Braba as consisting of only one pueblo, but a few months later another contingent of Coronado's army visited the site and described two pueblos on opposite sides of the river, thus making identification with Taos certain.

Don Hernando now returned downstream, and from Tiguex, with his report and a map, he sent Coronado a rare present from some of the Indians he had thus far visited—"the head of a cow and several loads of clothing and tanned skins." Both Alvarado and Padilla proclaimed to Coronado the superiority of Tiguex over Cíbola, and advised him to send the rest of the army there for winter quarters. They had painted an attractive and gener-ally accurate picture of the upper Rio Grande Valley as first seen by Europeans. Coronado, when he heard the news, "was highly pleased to learn that the country was improving." It may be remarked that Alvarado's precious map has not been discovered.

Alvarado was now ready to continue on his way to the Buf-falo Plains to see the strange beasts of which the Indians had told. Bigotes offered to lead him first to other settlements—perhaps southward down the Rio Grande, or west to Xia and Xémez. But Don Hernando insisted that he must obey his instructions and go east. So Bigotes led him to Cicúique, his own home town. To reach that place Alvarado traveled five days from Tiguex, cover-ing a distance of some seventy-five miles. He presumably followed the route determined by geography, the main trail between the two places in historic times and one doubtless long in use before the arrival of Spaniards. From Tiguex the road led up the Rio Grande to a point north of Manzano Mountains, then swung eastward into the country of the Tano Indians, and ascended Galisteo River. On the way Alvarado would pass the mines at Los Cerrillos, whence had come the turquoises that Vaca and Fray

Marcos saw in Sonora Valley. Continuing northeastward, about as the Santa Fe Railway now runs, past Galisteo and other Tano pueblos, some of them then already in ruins, he would enter the mountains by Lamy Canyon, thread Glorieta Pass, and swing southeast a short distance to Cicúique, then a town four storeys high and the strongest of all the pueblos. The inhabitants sallied forth to welcome their young war-chief with demonstrations of joy, conducting him inside with drums and flageolets, similar to fifes, of which they had many. They presented the Spaniards with quantities of clothing and likewise of turquoises. Bigotes had fulfilled his promise to Coronado.

We have an eyewitness account of this place by a member of Alvarado's party. After describing the Tiguex pueblos he tells us: "There is one called Cicúique that is larger than any of the others and very strong. Its houses are four and five storeys high, some of them being very fine. It has eight large patios, each with its corridor. These people neither plant cotton nor raise turkeys, because it is fifteen leagues east of the river [Rio Grande], and close to the plains where the cattle roam."

The ruins of Cicúique are still to be seen at the site where Alvarado visited it, close by the modern town of Pecos. This is one of the most historic spots in the Southwest, for in every era since it was first seen by Alvarado as the guest of Bigotes, it has occupied a distinctive position in all the major developments of the region. It was the gateway for Pueblo Indians when they went buffalo hunting on the Plains; a two-way pass for barter and war between Pueblos and Plains tribes; a portal through the mountains for Spanish explorers, traders, and buffalo hunters; for the St. Louis caravan traders with Santa Fe; for pioneer Anglo-American settlers; for Spanish and Saxon Indian fighters; for Civil War armies; and for a transcontinental railroad passing through the Southwest. Pecos deserves an historian.

At Cicúique, Alvarado and his men rested a few days, replenished their wardrobes, and enjoyed the generous hospitality of the kindly natives, except that the young women were carefully guarded from the soldiers. Here Alvarado found two characters who became central figures in this drama of Pueblos and Plains which was now unfolding. They were captive Indians from the northeastern prairies where there were large native settlements, and they exemplified the lively trade in slaves maintained by the Plains tribes with the Pueblos of the upper Rio Grande from earliest times to the nineteenth century. The younger of these slaves, called Ysopete, or Sopete for short, was from Quivira, in the region we now call Kansas. The other, called the Turk, "because he looked like one," was from Harahey, a region beyond Quivira. The Turk and Sopete had been captured on the eastern border by manful Bigotes and Cacique themselves, and were now their slaves. Though small in stature, the Pueblo Indians were none the less good fighters, and apparently Bigotes was not always as polite as he was represented by Alvarado.

When early in October Don Hernando was ready to go forward, Bigotes asked to be excused from joining the party, saying he was tired, because he had already traveled with the Spaniards forty or fifty days since departing from Cíbola. That is to say, Alvarado had already spent more than half of his allotted eighty days. So, leaving Bigotes behind, Don Hernando set forth with the Turk and Sopete as guides. Both he and the anonymous author of the *Relación del Suceso* give us eyewitness accounts of the first great buffalo hunt by Europeans in North America. Their narratives can now be supplemented by those of Juan Troyano and Melchior Pérez, who also participated in and recorded the exciting adventure.

Alvarado journeyed eastward, and at the beginning of the plains he found a small river flowing in the same general direction. Evidently he had descended Pecos River some distance and then swung eastward down the stream now called the Canadian. "Within four days he came upon the cattle, which are the most monstrous beasts ever seen or read about. We availed ourselves of them, although with danger to the horses at first, until we had gained experience. There are such multitudes of them that I do not know what to compare them with unless it be the fish in the sea . . . because the plains were covered with them. Their meat is as good as that of the cattle of Castile, and some said it was even better. The bulls are large and fierce, although they do not attack very often. But they have wicked horns and they charge and thrust savagely. They killed several of our horses and wounded many others. We found that the best weapon for dispatching them was a spear for hurling at them [when they are running] and the arquebus when they are standing still."

One day as Alvarado and his men were traveling along the river the Turk created a sensation. He said "by signs and in the Mexican tongue of which he knew a little," that he did not know the region toward the east, and that Alvarado ought to turn northeast, because in that direction there was a country called Quivira, "with gold, silver and fabrics," and "abundant and fruitful in everything." He added that Bigotes was acquainted with Quivira and possessed a gold bracelet from there. The Turk said he had brought it to Cicúique, but it had been taken from him by his captors, who were none other than Bigotes and Cacique.

This incident evidently occurred at the place where the trail to Quivira swung northeast from Canadian River, the stream which Alvarado had been following. It becomes a pivotal spot in later developments. The Turk hoped by his story to get back home and thus escape from captivity. But Alvarado insisted that he had been ordered to go east, not northeast, and besides, his time was up. More to the point, he wanted to get his hands on that golden bracelet. So he faced about and led his party back to Ciqúique. Alvarado says he had followed the river a hundred leagues and Pérez says eighty, both evidently exaggerations. Castañeda, who next year went over the same ground with Don Hernando, confirms this opinion. He says that on the first expedition the Turk "told so many and such whopping lies about the wealth of gold and silver to be found in his country that the Spaniards did not care to look for the cattle, and as soon as they saw a few they turned back to report the great news to the general." As later will be evident, Alvarado had descended the waters of Canadian River nearly to the Texas Panhandle where the trail to Quivira swung northeast. Don Hernando, Padilla, Pérez, Troyano, and their companions had made a significant expedition and one that had a dramatic sequel.

The Turk's story of the bracelet proved to be bad luck for both Bigotes and Cacique. Excited by the tale, Alvarado with his companions hurried back to Pecos to see the golden ornament, his head filled with visions of wealth in Quivira, whither he would have Coronado lead his army without loss of time. On the way the Turk whispered to Don Hernando that he must not repeat to Bigotes the story about the bracelet for fear the natives of Pecos would kill him, for a reason that will appear.

Arrived at Pecos, Alvarado was given a friendly welcome and furnished new supplies, but when, ignoring the Turk's wish, he asked Bigotes and Cacique about the bracelet, they showed wide-eyed surprise, and "denied in all possible ways that they had any such ornament. In fact, the Turk was lying." To learn who was the liar—or rather, the whereabouts of the bracelet—was Alvarado's next task. When he was ready to resume his return march to Tiguex he asked Bigotes and Cacique to accompany him, in order that Coronado might quiz them, but they emphatically declined the invitation. Alvarado argued and he coaxed; then it became rough and tumble. Seeing "no other recourse, he managed to get Captain Bigotes and the governor to come to his tent," where he put them in chains, hoping to force them to confess, but in vain. At the same time, the Turk was taken in custody, for he would be the star witness in the case. Resenting this high-handed procedure, the warriors of the pueblo came out to fight, "shooting arrows and berating . . . Alvarado, and saying he had broken his word and violated friendship."

El Turco was not eager to be quizzed, and in a day or two he escaped. Thinking Bigotes and Cacique were responsible for his flight, Alvarado declared he would not set them free until the fugitive was recovered. A bargain was struck, the old governor and one or two others were released, went to find the Turk, and brought him back. Hereupon the chiefs were again put in collars and chains—not a nice way to reward them for recovering the Turk. Angered at Alvarado for his ingratitude, the Indians of the pueblo expressed their minds. They told him that "since they had been his friends and given him a generous welcome, supplying the Spaniards with whatever they had, he ought to deliver Bigotes to them." But this Don Hernando refused to do. He must get his hands on the bracelet!

Now a strange diversion occurred. Alvarado turned aside from his main task to help Pecos fight a hostile province called Nanapagua—perhaps the enemies told of by Bigotes when he had visited Coronado at Cíbola. Momentarily the bracelet fell into the background and the chiefs were relieved of their shackles. Pecos assembled three hundred warriors for the campaign, with whom went Bigotes, Cacique, the Turk, and Sopete, as well as Alvarado, Father Padilla, and all of Alvarado's men. But the Turk soon again took the center of the stage. The "comrades" having marched two days toward Nanapagua, the Turk again disappeared, and Sopete with him. Alvarado now sent Bigotes and Cacique to find the fugitives, and when they failed to bring them into camp, Don Hernando once more put the chiefs in irons, "saying he would keep them thus until the Turk should appear." The threat was effective, and soon both the Turk and Sopete were returned.

At this juncture the campaign against Nanapagua was suddenly abandoned, the Cicúique *bravos* were sent home, and Don Hernando, Padilla, and the soldiers resumed their way westward to Tiguex, taking Bigotes, Cacique, the Turk, and Sopete in collars and chains. Alvarado had made a notable exploration, but he had prepared the way for infinite trouble.

Chapter XVII

WINTER QUARTERS ON RIO GRANDE

Thus, in the autumn of 1540, six months after Coronado left Compostela, several fragments of his little army were widely scattered throughout the interior, engaged in an effort to uncover the secrets of the north. The general, Tovar, and Cárdenas were still at Cíbola with the major portion of the advance guard, perhaps seventy-five or eighty men, whom Coronado had led from Culiacán. Alvarado was exploring the upper Rio Grande Valley, eastern New Mexico, and the Buffalo Plains. Díaz with a handful of men was on his way to the lower Colorado seeking Alarcón, who at the time was about to leave that river and return to Acapulco. Part of the army were stationed at San Gerónimo in Valle de Sonora. The expedition had already executed an immense reconnoissance in *Tierra Nueva;* "Cíbola" was too narrow a designation.

In the meantime Coronado was preparing to move forward. Arellano by now should be on his way from Sonora with the main army, and better quarters would soon be necessary. The plan had been to winter at Cíbola, but circumstances had changed, for the discovery of Tiguex had given Coronado a new outlook. Cíbola was a small and poor community, but the Río Grande was more promising. Alvarado on his way east had reported to Coronado the friendliness of the natives there and forwarded to him their generous gifts of tanned skins, cotton cloth, and other useful things. Tiguex could supply the army with food and clothing. The valley of Our Lady—La Señora— had bountiful crops, and there were pleasant groves of cottonwood trees, that unfailing sign of water and fertility in a desert country. Both up and down the river there were numerous other pueblos.

Clearly, then, opportunity lay in the east. This was recognized by both Captain Alvarado and Fray Juan de Padilla. Before leaving for Cicúique and the Buffalo Plains, Alvarado wrote from Tiguex to the general, "asking him to come and spend the winter in that land." Fray Juan reinforced the suggestion, telling Coronado that on the banks of the great river there were fine pastures, and that it seemed to him winter quarters ought to be established in Tiguex. The general acted on this advice, for it coincided with his own views. Soon after Cárdenas returned from his excursion to Grand Canyon, Coronado ordered him to go to the Rio Grande and establish a rendezvous for the whole army "at the place indicated by Fray Juan," taking for this purpose thirteen or fourteen horsemen, with Indian allies from Mexico and some natives from Cíbola —for the Cíbolans had come out of their hiding places and were now coöperative, and glad perhaps to speed the departure of their uninvited guests.

Cárdenas set forth promptly to execute his commission, thus helping to deepen the old Indian trail past Ácoma into a Spanish *camino*. He found the Indians of Tiguex friendly, and began to prepare lodgings for the Spaniards outside the pueblos, in order not to cause the natives unnecessary hardship. But when cold weather came on, accompanied by snow, his men from the tropics were in distress. So he asked the Indians to vacate one of the twelve pueblos—six on each side of the river—in order that his soldiers might be quartered in it, requesting the displaced natives to find homes for the time being in the other towns. The Indians complied without resistance—though not without resentment—vacating the pueblo of Alcanfor, or Coofor as it was also called. It was the southernmost of the Tiguex group, and stood on the west bank of the river near the site of present-day Bernalillo. Thereupon Cárdenas and his shivering soldiers moved into the town and began to prepare housing in it for the entire army which, when all assembled, would number some three hundred men, not counting Indian allies and servants. Soon after Cárdenas took over Alcanfor, Alvarado arrived there from his expedition to the Buffalo Plains, bringing the Turk, Sopete, Bigotes, and Cacique. It was not necessary now for Don Hernando to continue west to Cíbola, and with his prisoners he was lodged in the pueblo to await the coming of the general.

Meanwhile Arellano was conducting the main army slowly north over Coronado's trail. Leaving part of his men at San Gerónimo in Sonora Valley, as we have seen, he went on his way to Cíbola shortly before Díaz set out westward toward the coast to look for Alarcón. The men left at San Gerónimo were the dregs of the army—"all those who had but one horse and those who were the least dependable." This was not highly propitious for the settlement, and it helps to explain what happened there soon afterward.

On the way north Arellano found the natives "everywhere cheerful, submissive, and without fear," says Castañeda, who was with the army. This speaks well for the impression left upon the Indians by Coronado as he had passed through the same country a few months previously. The most serious trouble of Arellano's followers now came from unsatisfactory food, the difficulty which Coronado's vanguard had experienced in a much higher degree on the same stretch of the trail, for most of the cattle had been left behind to travel at a slower gait. At a place called Vacapan—apparently this was Arivaipa—they obtained from the Indians a supply of food made of tunas, or prickly pears. The natives "brought much of this preserve as a present, but when the people of the army ate of it they all became drowsy, with headache and fever, so that the Indians could have done them great harm if they had wished to do so. This illness lasted intermittently for twenty-four hours." Castañeda evidently was one of the sufferers, and vividly remembered the symptoms when he wrote many years afterward. "Then, marching from there they reached Chichilticale." It is this last statement that gives rise to the comment about Arivaipa, which is the name of the valley they had crossed just before arriving at the "Red House." *Vacapan* is apparently a scribe's corruption of *Arivaipa*. In any case, both places, if they were distinct, were in the same vicinity and near Chichilticale. Plainly, Vacapan could not have been, as one writer has assumed, the Vacapa told of by Cabeza de Vaca near Fuerte River, several hundred miles south of San Gerónimo, through which Arellano had passed many weeks earlier on his journey to Sonora.

Going forward once more, Arellano now entered the Great Despoblado, where a welcome diversion soon arose to help the men forget their recent headaches caused by tuna preserves. One day's march beyond Chichilticale, about when they must have been threading the pass between Pinaleño and Santa Teresa Mountains (Eagle Pass it is now called), the advance guard of the army saw a flock of mountain sheep. This was enough to stir the blood of any young adventurer. Some of the men gave chase, Castañeda among them, and as a result he wrote for us what apparently is the earliest mention of these interesting Arizona animals by an eyewitness. "I saw them and followed them," he says. "They were large of body, had abundant long wool, and very thick horns. When they run they raise their heads and rest their horns on their backs. They are fleet in rough country, so we could not overtake them, and had to let them go."

Two or three days after the mountain sheep episode the travelers learned another bit of natural history. They found on the bank of a stream running in a deep barranca—it was evidently Gila River—a horn which Coronado had left on the trail to guide Arellano's men. So the army was traveling square on Coronado's route. The horn was a large one, if Castañeda does not exaggerate, which of course is asking too much of him, for big game works wonders with eyesight. "It was a fathom long"—six feet!—"and as thick at the base as a man's thigh. From its shape it looked more like the horn of a he-goat than of any other animal. It was worth seeing!" Castañeda was writing, some twenty-five years after the event, what he doubtless had

told in conversation a hundred times, for he was a second-gen-
eration Bernal Díaz. In that period, with the retelling, the horn
may well have grown.

And so they marched northward, their packs of food getting
lighter, their feet heavier, their faces and bodies thinner. They
crossed Salt River and its tributaries that ran in deep gorges,
and entered the Great Forest. Tello relates that on this stretch
of the trail some of the Indian allies found themselves unable to
keep up with the army. "And since they did not now carry anything to eat, God furnished them a worn-out horse which also
had fallen behind." Not being able to kill the animal "because
they had no knife or anything else," they tied it to a tree by all
four feet; "then, carrying firewood to the horse, they set it on
fire, burning it alive, and eating it singed and half-roasted."
Farther on, when the army passed the Camp of Death where
the advance guard had buried Espinosa, the place offered a
gruesome spectacle, for they found that coyotes and foxes had
dug him up and gnawed his bones. Emerging now from the
Great Forest, they entered the desert country, crossed the Little
Colorado, the stream whose waters were muddy and red, and
ascended Zuñi River. When they neared Cíbola they had been
on the road some two months since leaving Valle de Sonora, and
November was well on its course. They were not making more
than seven or eight miles a day, for they were driving with them
the main herd of stock.

The day before the wayfarers finally reached Cíbola was
one of the hardest. Everybody was weary. A bitterly cold wind
arose in the afternoon, followed by a heavy snowstorm, such as
the poet Villagrá survived in the Zuñi country sixty years later,
and such as modern residents of the region sometimes experience to their extreme discomfort. The thinly-clad Indian allies
suffered most, and they won Arellano's compassion. To save
them from freezing to death he kept them on the move well into
the night, when by good fortune he came to some rocky caves
that afforded a slight shelter from the storm. Perhaps the caves
can be identified. "Great fear was felt for the allies," says Castañeda, "for, since they were from New Spain and most of

them from warm regions, they suffered excessively from the cold that day; so much, indeed, that next day there was plenty to do taking care of them and carrying them on horseback while the others went on foot." Such is the picture made by the little army when it marched into Háwikuh. But Coronado was awaiting them there with food and lodgings prepared. To the wayfarers Cíbola was a welcome refuge, as it had been also to Coronado's starving advance guard.

The general had anxiously awaited Arellano. for he was eager to be on his way to Tiguex and the River of Our Lady, of which Alvarado and Padilla had written so favorably. Before departing from Cíbola he ordered Don Tristán to recuperate his weary men there for twenty days and then march with them to winter quarters at Tiguex. All this being arranged, Coronado took thirty of "the most rested men," and late in November he set forth eastward. Presumably the majority of his followers were those who had been longest with him in camp at Háwikuh. But there were others—choice spirits who had just arrived with Arellano. Juan de Zaldívar, who had reached Culiacán too late to come with Coronado, now caught up with him and joined the vanguard. Rodrigo de Maldonado and Father Castilblanco were likewise transferred from Arellano's division to that of the general. Apparently there were others.

Coronado's march from Cíbola to winter quarters was attended by memorable incidents. The weather was severe and water scarce. From the time when they left camp one morning until noon of the third day, when they came in sight of snow-covered Zuñi Mountains, neither men, horses, nor pack mules had partaken of a single drop of the precious fluid. Farther on Coronado with part of the army deviated from the trail followed by Alvarado and Cárdenas. Having heard of Tutahaco, a province of eight pueblos south of Tiguex, he decided to go and see them, apparently descending San José River instead of cutting across more directly to Tiguex. After a hard journey lasting a week from Háwikuh he arrived at Tutahaco, near the Rio Grande. Here the white chief with the golden helmet was welcomed by people living in terraced houses much like those in the districts already discovered. Leaving Captain Ovando to make further explorations, apparently among the Piros pueblos downstream, the general swung northward and visited other towns on the way up the River of Our Lady. Eventually he reached Tiguex, where he found Cárdenas with lodgings prepared in the pueblo of Alcanfor. Most of the colony at last had reached the heart of the Pueblo Land.

Arresting news greeted Coronado at Tiguex. The first night after his arrival he was visited in his quarters by Alvarado and El Turco, who had recently returned from their boisterous jaunt in the east; what they told him quickened his pulse and called forth new visions. Don Hernando gave the general a full account of his expedition to the Plains, where he had seen myriad buffaloes and experienced thrilling adventures. More exciting was what the Indian told Coronado, for El Turco's gift for vivid narration had been in no way impaired by the uncomfortable iron collar he had worn from Cicúique to Tiguex in Alvarado's train. He now reported with added detail and artistic embellishment what he had told Alvarado when among the buffaloes on Canadian River. Especially he painted in glowing colors the wonders of the far northeast. The Turk declared that in a country called Quivira, near his homeland, "there was a river flowing in the Plains, with fish as big as horses, and a vast number of very large canoes with sails, and carrying more than twenty oarsmen on each side." The nobles, he said, "rode in the stern, seated under canopies, and at the prow there was a great golden eagle." The lord of that land, the powerful Tatarrax, took his siesta under a tree from which hung numerous golden bells that amused him as they played in the breeze. Still more wonderful, "the common table service of everybody was generally of wrought silver, and the pitchers, dishes, and bowls were made of gold." He called gold *acochis*. The Turk was believed, "because of his straightforward manner in telling the story, and also because, when they showed him ornaments made of tin, he smelled them and said they were not gold, for he knew gold and silver very well, and cared little for other metals." The general now walked on air. He had something exciting to write to Doña Beatríz and Mendoza!

Among other things he told Coronado, the Turk repeated the tale of the golden bracelet, that bewitched jewelry which already had raised such a furor at Pecos. As evidence of his entire veracity, he declared that if the general would permit him to return to Cicúique *without Bigotes,* he would go and bring the precious ornament. But Bigotes he simply could not endure. Alvarado advised against the proposal, saying he feared that if the wily Turk went back to Cicúique he might cause the country to rise in revolt, for he had left the people there in very bad humor. And besides, the Turk might abscond and leave the wonders of Quivira forever hidden from the Spaniards! God forbid!

The story told by the Turk was exciting indeed. But could it be taken at face value, or was it all a lie? Most immediate was the question of the golden bracelet. If that trinket could be obtained and proved to be genuine gold, it would be a promise of greater things in Quivira. The tale must be investigated. Coronado consulted Padilla about the matter. Fray Juan agreed it was "very important to the service of his Majesty that the truth about the rich country should be ascertained," and he suggested that it might be learned from Bigotes, who was said to have been in Quivira and actually to possess the bracelet. Why not question the chief, since he was right on hand? The general concurred in this opinion. It was a fine idea. But Father Padilla had been with Alvarado, had traveled and talked with Bigotes, and could understand him. Would Fray Juan "take hold of him" and learn the truth? Padilla, also modest, replied that Alvarado was the person who best understood Bigotes, and should have the honor. However, if Coronado wished, said the friar, he and Don Hernando together might make the inquiry, especially about the bracelet. The plan was acted upon, and Padilla soon afterward reported to Coronado that when Bigotes was quizzed "he denied everything." Of course, the fellow must be lying!

More vigorous measures were now taken. It is impossible to say just what happened, but from bulky evidence recently acquired, it appears that with Coronado's knowledge Bigotes was taken by Alvarado to a field outside the pueblo of Alcanfor. Here a dog, or dogs, belonging to Captain Tovar, were set upon the chief to force him to reveal the whereabouts of the bracelet, but he persisted in his denial. Bigotes was bitten on an arm or a leg, or both, and the wounds were bandaged. The victim was not seriously injured, but his scars were visible several days after the occurrence. Dogs were set upon aged Cacique also, but there is no indication that he was injured. Stoical Bigotes and Cacique were not terrorized into confessing anything. They declared the Turk's tale of the golden bracelet was a barefaced lie, and so they consistently branded it. Lest we be too greatly horrified by this dog-baiting, it may be remarked that it was so common a practice among our ancestors in sixteenth-century Europe that most people took it as a matter of course.

Cárdenas seems to have had no part in "dogging" the chiefs, but all four of the captives—Bigotes, Cacique, the Turk, and Sopete—were delivered to him for safe-keeping. The first three were kept in chains throughout the winter. Cacique also remained in Tiguex, but apparently he was not shackled, as were the others, because he was old and considered relatively harmless.

Chapter XVIII

BATTLE OF ARENAL

Alvarado and Padilla had found the Tiguex Indians friendly, and generous with provisions. They were hospitable to Cárdenas when he went to establish quarters for the army among them, although they felt misgivings when they learned the Spaniards were to spend the winter there. For some time, Cárdenas tells us, they remained outwardly peaceful, mingling with the strangers and trading supplies for petty Spanish merchandise of the kind with which Coronado had come so well provided. But there was smouldering dissatisfaction, for long-term house guests may become as irksome to red men as to white. Tempers get shorter as time grows longer, and ultimately issues are bound to arise.

Cárdenas himself, having only a small force of men—some fourteen Spaniards and a greater number of Mexican allies— felt by no means secure in the midst of so large an Indian population. Some of the actions of the natives were ominous. While his camp was still in the open, the Indians were in the habit of coming to the quarters of the soldiers, to "wrestle with them and try their strength"—to see if the Blancos were *muy hombre* —and they hung around the tents of the Spaniards at night to learn whether they were on their guard. By these and other signs Cárdenas "knew from the moment he arrived that they wanted to rebel, and all the Spaniards had the same suspicion," so they were on the *qui vive*, wishing the rest of the army would hurry up. Fifteen Spaniards in the midst of a dozen hostile pueblos were none too safe. Of course, a part of this foresight later claimed by Cárdenas may have been hindsight, with which all of us are so richly endowed.

The undercurrent of distrust felt by the natives was aggravated by a number of specific incidents. One outspoken complaint had been made before Coronado arrived. Two or three Indians went to Cárdenas one day to report a grievance. By signs the excited visitors appeared to say that "an unruly Spaniard" had gone to the pueblo of Arenal, two leagues upstream, and molested an Indian woman. Since they told their story chiefly in pantomime, Cárdenas was not sure whether the accused Spaniard was trying to steal the woman's blanket or had a more personal intent. So Don García looked into the matter. He assembled all his soldiers in a room, and there the injured husband attempted to identify the offender, but was unable to do so. Cárdenas declared that he would certainly have disciplined the culprit if he had been identified, for "he had punished less serious offenses."

Castañeda tells this story of the woman affair with a more Boccaccio-like touch. He had not yet arrived at Tiguex when the incident occurred, but this was a tale which inevitably spread, and his hearsay version was probably that of the camp gossips, who doubtless knew even more about the matter than would reach the ears of the commander. In the words of the chronicler, "an outstanding person, whose name I shall omit, to spare his honor, left the pueblo where the camp was located and went to another a league distant, and, seeing a beautiful woman"—much more beautiful in retrospect, no doubt, when he told the story twenty years later—"he called her husband down below and asked him to hold his horse by the bridle while he went up, and, as the pueblo was entered from the top, the Indian thought the Spaniard was going to some other place. While the native remained there holding the horse a commotion occurred, after which the man came back, took his mount, and rode away." It was as simple as that. But when the Indian returned to his house and heard a shocking story he hastened to report it to Cárdenas.

Accompanied by prominent men of the pueblo, he went to the captain to complain, saying a Spaniard had outraged his wife, and told how it had happened. Cárdenas ordered all the soldiers to appear before him, but the Indian could not identify the offender, either because he had changed his garb, or for some other reason. But he was sure he would recognize the man's horse, because he had held it by the reins. So he was led through the stables, and when he came to a dappled animal covered with a blanket he said the owner of that mount was the guilty person. But the owner denied it, adding that since the plaintiff had not recognized the man, it was not strange that he was mistaken also in the horse. In the end the Indian went away without getting any redress.

Castañeda, *muy caballero,* in telling the story refrained from naming the Spaniard charged with the misdeed, but his identity came out. Juan de Contreras, Coronado's chief equerry, testified many months afterward that the guilty person was none other than Juan de Villegas, brother of a high official in Mexico, "for which reason he was not punished." He had influence at Court. At a later time Coronado was asked about this incident, although Cárdenas categorically says it occurred before the general arrived. He replied that he did not hear of the outrage, but if he had known of it he would have punished the offender "in keeping with an order he had issued." In fact, with the *esprit de corps* of comrades, the affair was purposely kept from the general.

Then came the dog-baiting episode. "This," says Castañeda, "was the beginning of the distrust with which the Indians from then forward regarded the pledge which had been given them." The observation was essentially correct, insofar as we can judge from the available evidence. And it was the opinion of the majority of eyewitnesses who later testified as to the cause of the trouble which soon followed. The conduct of Villegas toward the Indian woman did not produce resistance in force. The natives were patient when Alvarado arrived from the east with another contingent of uninvited guests. But the effect was cumulative. The imprisonment and rough treatment of Bigotes, Cacique, the Turk, and Sopete were followed by Indian conferences looking toward rebellion. Messengers now ran from Tiguex to Cicúique and other neighbors to talk of resistance to the white men, who not only had entered their country without asking permission but had openly violated a solemn promise of peace for Tiguex. The natives had heard of events in Cíbola and Hopi Land, and they feared what the coming of the Spaniards presaged for themselves. But still there was no open warfare.

Unrest in Tiguex was enhanced by harsh methods employed in the collection of clothing and provisions for the soldiers, who, having come from the far south, suffered grievously from the severe winter weather of the high plateau, and who welcomed in their monotonous diet the turkeys, maize, beans, calabashes, and other articles of food with which Tiguex was endowed. To arrange for needed clothing, Coronado, soon after his arrival, sent for a friendly chief whom the soldiers dubbed Juan Alemán, because he resembled a resident in Mexico known by this name—"Juan the German." Juan the Indian, who was a chief of the pueblo of Moho, five leagues north of Arenal, looked to the soldiers like an old friend in Mexico, hence his nickname. Coronado asked Chief Juan to arrange to obtain from the pueblos three hundred or more articles of clothing needed for the shivering soldiers. Juan replied that he could not do this. The request must be made of each pueblo individually. Only the headmen of the towns could handle such a matter, and each of them would have to discuss the question with his own people, for their government was highly democratic.

Acting on this advice, Coronado sent commissioners through the province to undertake the negotiation. "As there were twelve pueblos, some went on one side of the river and some on the other." But if we may believe Castañeda, who reported what he heard after his arrival, the men sent on the errand made a bad job of it. The request being so unexpected, the natives had no time to discuss the matter. As soon as a Spaniard came to a pueblo he demanded the supplies at once, and the Indians had to give them promptly, because the commissioner said he must hurry on to the next town. "Under the circumstances there was nothing the natives could do but take off their own cloaks and hand them over, until the number requested by the Spaniards was obtained." It was even worse when insult was added to injury. Soldiers accompanied the collectors, and were provided by them with mantas and skins. But if they did not consider them satisfactory, or if one of them saw an Indian with a better one, he forcibly exchanged with him "without any consideration or respect, and without inquiring about the importance of the person despoiled." Such treatment—perhaps overdrawn by Castañeda—was, of course, deeply resented by these dignified people.

This levy was not confined to clothing. The soldiers obtained from the Indians also "turkeys, maize, and other necessary provisions." It must not be assumed that these articles were always taken by the Spaniards without remuneration, for Coronado had a large supply of petty merchandise, furnished by Viceroy Mendoza to enable the army to make purchases from the natives, and he was under strict orders not to take anything from the Indians without compensation. It was the inconsiderate manners of some of the soldiers that chiefly offended the Tiguex people. Moreover, with winter coming on, they had little to spare.

Castañeda evidently presented the darker side of the clothing levy. Hernando de la Cadena, one of the collectors, tells how he and his companions did their work and, in one instance at least, how tolerant Cárdenas was toward the natives, even to softness. Together with Alonso de Saavedra and other Spaniards, Cadena went from pueblo to pueblo begging garments "for the love of God." On one occasion Saavedra approached a native house where four chiefs were chatting, and asked for clothing with which to cover his nakedness, but they bluntly refused. After many rebuffs Saavedra stooped to pick up an old garment that was lying on the ground. Thereupon the chiefs seized him, beat him with hoes, thrust him inside the house, and lectured him on the subject. This was too much for a Spaniard to stand from an Indian. Witnessing the scene, Cadena and his companions ran to Saavedra's rescue, carried him away on a horse, and took the chiefs before Cárdenas that he might do with them whatever he saw fit. But Cárdenas let the soldiers down. After listening to the story he said to the Spaniards: "What do you expect, Señores? Why don't you do as the captain-general has ordered, namely, that if an Indian gives a Spaniard a blow in the face he must turn the other cheek?" And in this way "he dissembled with the Indians and let them go free to their houses." In all probablity the case was hardly typical of the clothing levy as a whole. Perhaps Cárdenas was trying to be humorous.

Out of these circumstances a crisis eventually arose. The temper of the natives at last reached the boiling point. One morning a Mexican who had been guarding the horse herd ran into camp at Alcanfor, "bleeding and wounded," and shocked his hearers with his story. The natives of Tiguex had killed one of his companions and were now driving the horses of the Spaniards to their pueblos! Rebellion! As usual, it was Cárdenas who took the situation in hand, for that was his business as maestre de campo. With the approval of Coronado, he went with seven or eight mounted men to the scene of the disturbance. When he arrived at a pueblo about a quarter of a league from Alcanfor, apparently the one called Alameda, he found it abandoned. A little farther on he discovered the carcasses of two or three horses killed by Indian arrows. Clearly, the natives were in open resistance. The center of the trouble was the pueblo of Arenal, presumably so-called by the Spaniards because it occupied a sandy site. It was the town where the affair of the Indian woman had occurred, and was two leagues from Alcanfor, the southern-most pueblo, with Alameda between them.

Following some horse tracks, Cárdenas was led across the Rio Grande at a place where the Indians had forded the stream "with all the horses they could round up in the fields." In the open country and in the pueblos on both banks of the river he found twenty-five or more dead mounts, among them being seven mules belonging to Cárdenas. It was now to him a personal matter as well as one of concern to his Majesty. The occurrence was ominous, especially since the number of Spaniards at Tiguex was still small, for Arellano had not yet arrived with the main army. Rounding up all the live horses he could find, Cárdenas drove them to camp at Alcanfor. On the way, as he passed by the towns, the Indians were insolent, shouting derisively at him and his men. He found the pueblo of Arenal enclosed by palisades, and "heard a great hullabaloo inside, with horses running around as in a bullring and the natives shooting arrows at them."

Cárdenas stopped to talk with the Indians, chiefly through signs. He told them he would forgive them for killing the horses, since the Spaniards had plenty of these animals; and he urged them to be friendly, promising that if they submitted they should not be punished for what they had done. But the Indians were stubborn and gave Cárdenas no satisfaction. They evidently regarded Spanish conciliation as weakness, as perhaps it was. Indeed, Castañeda, who had not yet arrived, intimates that the gentle words of the maestre de campo were in some part due to necessity rather than to inclination. "The natives were all up in arms," he writes. "Cárdenas could do nothing because the Indians refused to come out into the open, and as the pueblos were strong they could not be harmed." When Don García returned to Alcanfor and reported what he had seen and heard, Coronado sent him back to talk peace with the natives once more, but it was a thankless errand, and he had no better success than before. Arenal had decided to try its strength with the handful of Spaniards. Let them come!

Coronado now called a council of war, in keeping with the democratic spirit of Spanish armies at this period. The membership of the conference included not only the general, the maestre de campo, and all the captains, but also Fathers Padilla and Castilblanco. Coronado stated the case to his counselors; there was a discussion, apparently with little disagreement, and at the end opinion was unanimous. Less bellicose than when at the Hopi towns with Tovar, "Fray Juan Padilla said it was not permissible for them to kill anyone, but he would approve and consider appropriate whatever the general might do." Fray Antonio gave a like answer. In short, all agreed that war should be waged against the rebellious Indians.

Cárdenas now went to the pueblo of Arenal to notify it of the decision, and to "tell the natives of all the evil they had done."

If they had rebelled because of some abuse committted by any of the soldiers they should say so, and he would punish the offenders in the presence of the aggrieved Indians; and if they would render obedience to his Majesty he would pardon them. But while Cárdenas exhorted the natives to submit, they climbed to the balconies of their houses, "shouted their war cries to heaven and waved as banners the tails of the Spanish horses they had killed." On the same errand Coronado sent Don Rodrigo Maldonado several leagues north to the pueblo of Moho, which, like Arenal, had been fortified with a palisade in preparation for war. Juan Alemán, head chief there, was likewise defiant. "At both places the Indians tried to kill the Spaniards through trickery."

Having done his best to maintain peace, Coronado now carried out his threat to punish the mutinous natives by proceeding first to attack Arenal. Moho's turn would come later. He explained this step in simple terms. He was planning to go east in continuation of his explorations. If he left the Indians in revolt behind his back, "it would be dangerous to go forward," so he attacked them, "with great risk to the army." This bold decision Coronado made in spite of the fact that his force was small, for Arellano had not yet arrived with the main army.

The assault on Arenal was led by hard-fisted Cárdenas, who was ordered to take a detachment of men and discipline the stubborn town. Before attacking the place he must again offer the inhabitants a chance for peaceful submission, but if they refused he was to "do them all the damage he could." In fulfillment of his commission Cárdenas marched from Alcanfor with some sixty horsemen, a number of infantry, and a contingent of Mexican allies. Among the captains with him were some of the flower of the army—Juan de Zaldívar, Rodrigo Maldonado, Diego López, Pablos de Melgosa, Diego de Guevara, and Velasco de Barrionuevo, all men who had proved their mettle. According to Castañeda, Coronado also went with the soldiery, but from the evidence it is clear that the general remained in camp at Alcanfor while Cárdenas directed the attack.

Before reaching Arenal, Cárdenas ordered his men to halt while he went ahead with a few of the captains to make another attempt at conciliation. Don García tells us, in fact, that for full two hours he exhorted the natives to submit peacefully. But he again was greeted with jeers and threats. The native warriors, some inside the fortification and others perched on the terraces of the pueblo, showed no fear of the helmet-crested Spaniards, nor of their horses, swords, lances, crossbows, and arquebuses. This account of the arrival of the army at Arenal, as given by Cárdenas, who was a chief participant, is quite at variance with that of Castañeda, who says, "They caught the Indians so unawares that they soon took possession of the terraces." But it must be remembered that Castañeda had not yet reached Tiguex, and that he was telling the story twenty years after the event.

Cárdenas had done his full duty, and patience was no longer a virtue. So he "waged war," as his orders required. Profiting by experience at Háwikuh, he first surrounded the pueblo with horsemen, to cut off escape from within and aid from without. Then, giving the "Santiago," he ordered the attack. The soldiers responded with a will, the natives fought with valor, and the battle was furious and bloody. It lasted several hours before the Spaniards gained the terraces, and by the time this had been accomplished a number of Mexican allies had been killed and thirteen or fourteen Spaniards were badly wounded by arrows and other missiles. How many of the defenders of the pueblo succumbed in this assault we do not know.

Nerves were on edge that night. Through all the long dark hours the Spaniards remained alert on the terraces, while the Indians watched from the inside, anxious but by no means cowed. When daylight came at last, Cárdenas again exhorted the defenders to submit, but once more they refused, and the battle was renewed. It was a fierce encounter, with deeds of personal valor such as we read of in Homer. The Indians wounded numerous Spaniards with arrows fired from inside the houses, and in return the Spaniards placed "many good shots with crossbows and arquebuses." Cárdenas was in the thick of the fight from start to finish, hurrying hither and yon to give the necessary orders. The native war chiefs were no less alert.

Up to this point the battle was a draw—or perhaps the Indians had the best of it. Whether or not the pueblo could be taken without too great cost was an open question. So Cárdenas sent to Coronado at Alcanfor a report of what had been done, and asked for further orders. The messenger was accompanied by wounded Spaniards and Indian allies who had been put *hors de combat*. The pueblo had been entered by the Spaniards, said Cárdenas, but inside some of the houses there were Indians alive and still resisting. Should he try to drive them out, or go forward and wage war on the other rebellious pueblos? In reply Coronado sent Pedro de Ledesma double-quick with orders not to raise the siege until Arenal should be "completely subjugated," and he informed Cárdenas that he was coming to look into the situation himself.

But Cárdenas was unable to await commands. Things were moving too fast, and before Ledesma arrived he had renewed the battle. The Indians must be driven from the rooms where they had barricaded themselves. But it would be a tough job for the Spaniards, for "the houses were solid and there would have been great risk" if they had tried to go in, "especially since every one of the apartments was narrow and the entrances small." Finding himself unable to dislodge the Indians by force of arms, Cárdenas decided to smoke them out. So he ordered the horsemen and native allies outside the pueblo to break through the walls of the lower storey and build some "heavy smudge fires."

The plan was all too effective. A breach in the walls was made by battering rams, and fires were lighted. Suffocated by the smoke, the Indians rushed from their hiding places, and as they emerged many of them were killed by the soldiers. Some escaped from the buildings, only to be run down and slain by horsemen who had surrounded the pueblo. Others were captured and taken as prisoners to a near-by tent. Still others were carried outside the pueblo, tied to stakes and burned to death.

When those imprisoned in the tent saw what was happening they made desperate efforts to escape but were lanced by the guards and cast into the raging fire. It was a frightful holocaust. The Indians were defeated and the survivors fled. Among the Spaniards wounded in the battle was the hard-riding courier, Juan de Zaldívar. When he entered a room of the pueblo to aid Don Lope de Urrea and other soldiers whom the Indians had surrounded, he received three wounds, one in the nose and two in the head. So badly was he injured that after the battle he spent a month convalescing.

Castañeda, who arrived with Arellano at Tiguex just after the battle was over, many years later gave this lurid account of the burning of the Indians: "Down on the ground the mounted men, together with many Indian allies from New Spain, built some heavy smudge fires in the basements, into which they had broken holes, so that the Indians were forced to sue for peace. Pablos de Melgosa and Diego López, the alderman from Seville, happened to be in that place and they answered their signs for peace by similar ones, which consisted of making a cross. The natives soon laid down their arms and surrendered at their mercy. They were taken to the tent of Don García, who, as was affirmed, did not know of the truce and thought they were surrendering of their own accord, as defeated men. As the general had ordered them not to take any one alive, in order to impose a punishment that would intimidate the others, Don García at once ordered that two hundred stakes be driven into the ground to burn them alive. There was no one who could tell him of the truce which had been agreed upon, as the soldiers did not know about it, and those who had arranged the terms of peace kept silent, believing it was none of their business. Thus when the enemies saw that their comrades were being tied and that the Spaniards had started to burn them, about one hundred who were in the tent began to offer resistance and defend themselves with whatever they found about them and with stakes which they rushed out to seize. Our footmen stormed the tent on all sides with sword thrusts that forced the natives to abandon it, and then the mounted men fell upon them; as the ground was level, none escaped alive except a few who had remained concealed in the pueblo and who fled that night."

The Arenal episode was given another sinister touch. During all these days, ever since Alvarado had brought them in chains from Cicúique, luckless Bigotes, the Turk, and Sopete had been in duress at Alcanfor, held as hostages for use later on. They were in the custody of Cárdenas, but when he went forth to the attack on Arenal he left them in the care of a servant named Cervantes, or Cerbates. Cacique, the old governor of Cicúique, also was held as a hostage, but he was considered as in a different category from the Turk, Sopete, and Bigotes. After the pueblo of Arenal had been set on fire, Cárdenas sent a messenger to Coronado informing him that he had captured some of the rebels, and asking for instructions. In reply Coronado sent Juan de Contreras, his head groom, with orders not to punish the captives until he might send the Turk and Sopete to "witness the penalty inflicted upon them in order that they might spread the news among their people in their new land," that is, in Quivira. Thereupon Coronado sent to Arenal all four of the hostages in charge of García del Castillo, Francisco Gorbalán, and Melchior de Robles, to see how rebels were treated. This was a bitter dose for Bigotes and his companions to take.

Later on the same day, Coronado despatched a courier to Cárdenas instructing him to go forward from Arenal to discipline other pueblos which were in rebellion. Cárdenas replied "that what had been done was enough; that the men in his company were tired out and used up, and that since a heavy snow was falling," for the present it was better to return to headquarters. This he did, and when he reached the pueblo of Alameda, about a quarter of a league from Alcanfor, he was met by Coronado who "approved what Don García had done," and gave him hearty embraces.

Judgment of Cárdenas for his part in the battle of Arenal must rest on fundamental assumptions which few of his contemporaries would question. Coronado, his superior officer, had been sent as the King's representative to explore, spread the Faith, and establish royal authority in the interior of New Spain, wherever he might go. Whether or not the Spanish army had any right to be in Tiguex is another question, which could be raised in many other cases of empire building, such, for example, as the Anglo-American Westward Movement into the Indian country between the Atlantic and the Pacific. The Indians of Arenal had killed horses belonging to the royal army, for such it had been constituted by act of the viceroy. They had insulted Cárdenas, a royal officer, and jeered at him as he passed by in the performance of his duties. Then, in a council of war it was decided to exact obedience from the rebellious pueblo, and Cárdenas was sent as the King's representative to carry the decision into effect. If the Indians again refused obedience, as they did, he must make war upon them. This is an explanation—not a justification.

Meanwhile, his men having recuperated at Cíbola, Arellano followed Coronado to Tiguex, according to his orders. The record of his march gives us new glimpses of the native settlements and new echoes of the adventures of the wayfarers. With Arellano's departure Cíbola was left to the natives, who no doubt breathed deep sighs of relief. The backs of the intruders were a welcome sight. The opinion which has been expressed, that Arellano left a garrison at Cíbola, does not appear to be warranted by the available sources. But some cannons were left behind and later recovered.

Setting forth in early December from Háwikuh, Arellano marched up the valley of Zuñi River, and on the first day out he camped at Mátsaki, "the largest and most beautiful pueblo in all that province." As we have seen, it stood near the northwestern base of Towayálane, or Corn Mountain, about fifteen miles from Háwikuh, and was therefore a short distance eastward of present-day Zuñi. Castañeda, who was with Arellano and now had his first view of the New Land beyond Háwikuh, tells us that "this pueblo alone is seven storeys high. There are special houses that serve as fortresses in the pueblo. They are higher than the others, and rise like towers at the top, being provided with embrasures and loopholes for defending the roofs, for as the pueblos have no streets, and the roofs are of the same height and common to all, the terraces have to be conquered first, and these larger houses are their protection."

When the army reached Mátsaki it began to snow, and the soldiers sought shelter under the eaves of the pueblo, which projected "like balconies," supported by wooden pillars. "These balconies," says Castañeda, "are often reached by climbing up to them by ladders, for there are no doors in the lower storey." This was true of most of the pueblos. In the ten days while the army remained at Mátsaki it snowed every afternoon and nearly every night. Since the soldiers camped under the eaves of the pueblo, we infer that the natives were inside, otherwise the Spaniards would have moved in to escape the snow and cold.

When the storm abated the army went on its way, but the snow was so deep that "nearly every night wherever they camped they had to clear away a cubit of it"—about eighteen inches— "in order to prepare a camping place. Moreover, there was no road visible, but the guides, knowing the country, led us by their sense of direction. Throughout the land there are junipers and pines, with which we built big fires, succeeding, with the heat and smoke, in clearing a yard or two of the ground around the fire. The snow that was falling was a dry one, for even if three feet of it fell it did not wet the baggage, and by shaking it the snow dropped off and the bundles remained clear. As the snow continued to fall in the night, it covered the baggage and the soldiers in their beds, so that if someone had come suddenly upon the camp he would have seen nothing but mounds of snow and the horses. Even if the snow were half a yard deep one could endure it, and in fact it rather warmed those who were under it." Many persons have experienced this phenomenon. The snowstorm told of here was evidently the same one that occurred at Arenal at the time of the battle.

From Mátsaki the Spaniards apparently traveled past the site of the present summer village of Pescado to El Morro or Inscription Rock, where later explorers carved their names, across pine-clad Zuñi Mountains, through Guadalupe Pass, to El Gallo, where the town of San Rafael now stands, and where the first Fort Wingate was long afterward established, thence past the site of McCarthy to Ácoma.

Arellano stopped a short time at the Sky City, and Castañeda gives us another first-hand account of it to supplement the one by Alvarado. "As it was at peace, the people entertained us well, giving us vegetables and fowls, although, as I have said, the people there are few. Many soldiers climbed to the top to see the pueblo, finding it very difficult to clamber up the steps in the rock, not being used to them. The natives, on the other hand, go up and down so easily that they carry loads of provisions, and the women carry water, apparently without touching the walls with their hands, whereas our men had to pass their weapons up to one another when they tried to make the ascent." The nimble-footed natives doubtless laughed at the clumsy visitors, just as their descendants laugh at tourists now. Recently most of the natives have moved down from the cliff to the fields below.

From Acoma the army continued without incident to Tiguex, where they were welcomed with rousing cheers, and lodged at headquarters in the pueblo of Alcanfor. "There they learned the good news [of Quivira] told by the Turk, which brought no little rejoicing, as it helped to lighten our hardships, although when the army arrived there we found the country up in arms, for causes that were sufficient and not at all slight. . . . Our men had already burned a pueblo the day before we arrived, and were returning to their quarters." The burned pueblo, of course, was ill-fated Arenal. Now, for the first time since leaving Culiacán, Coronado's entire force was together, with the exception of the lone garrison in Sonora Valley.

The charge, to which Castañeda subscribes and magnifies, that Cárdenas, by the sign of the Cross had pledged amnesty to the Háwikuh warriors if they would surrender, and then broke his promise, is reserved for consideration for a later time, in the light of new evidence now available.

Chapter XIX

SIEGE OF MOHO

The Tiguex War was by no means over. But just when they had conquered Arenal, says Castañeda, now an eye-witness, "it began to snow in that land, and it snowed so much for two months that the Spaniards could do nothing but go over the trails and tell the natives to come peacefully and they would be pardoned, giving them all sorts of assurances. To this the Indians replied that they would not trust people who did not know how to keep their promised word, and reminded the Spaniards that they were still holding Bigotes a prisoner."

The new evidence indicates more strenuous relations than Castañeda implies. With Arellano's force now at hand the general felt more confident. Arenal was captured near the end of December, 1540. Five or six days after that lurid event Coronado sent Cárdenas out with a party to demand the submission of the rest of the Tiguex pueblos, and to make war upon them if they refused. Don García left Alcanfor with some forty cavalrymen and a contingent of foot soldiers. Crossing the Rio Grande to the east bank, he visited the towns on that side of the stream, but found them abandoned, because all the Indians, seeing the Spaniards approach, precipitately fled. At the last pueblo, presumably the northernmost of the Tiguex group on that bank, which was likewise the smallest, he found seven or eight dead horses in the plaza, so he set fire to the town, "in order to teach the Indians not to kill any more Spaniards or their mounts." Some of the houses were burned, but others were left standing. Not wishing to linger in the pueblos or to do them any harm, Cárdenas returned to Alcanfor and reported to the general.

The destruction of Arenal had so frightened the Indians

that most of them left their homes, although it was mid-winter and the removal entailed excessive hardships. But they had not lost their spirit of resistance to the intruders from the south. A few days after the return of Cárdenas from his excursion across the river, Coronado learned that the people of several of the deserted towns were assembling in and fortifying Moho, said to be the largest pueblo in the province and situated on the west side of the river three or four leagues north of Alcanfor, on an elevation and near a spring, data which may enable someone to identify the exact site. Castañeda called this pueblo Tiguex, which was the name used by the Spaniards for the entire province. Moho was apparently a sort of capital, temporarily at least. Head man of this now composite settlement was our well-known Juan Alemán.

With a view to bringing the stubborn place to submission, Coronado now sent Don Rodrigo de Maldonado to Moho with a small detachment of men to inform Alemán and his fellow chieftains that if they would render due obedience he would pardon them for their misdeeds, otherwise he would wage relentless war upon them, as the Emperor required—the same message he had sent by Cárdenas to Arenal before it was attacked. But all efforts to soften Moho were unavailing. The Indians tried to spring a trap on Don Rodrigo, but being warned in time by Diego de Madrid, the captain escaped and returned with his men to Alcanfor. Two or three days later Coronado sent Cárdenas to undertake the task which Maldonado had failed to accomplish.

So Don García was again on the move. With thirty horsemen he rode forth on his mission, passing on the way the charred and deserted ruins of Arenal. Moho he found fortified and prepared for war, as had been reported. Going ahead of his army, the captain approached the pueblo on horseback with a bodyguard of three mounted soldiers, stoically watched the while by the natives on the terraces. When within speaking distance he told them "by signs and a few words which they already understood" that they must be friendly and mingle on good terms with the Spaniards, who would treat them kindly.

Juan Alemán now appeared on one of the terraces and made himself spokesman for the natives. With soft eloquence such as one may still hear at the New Mexico pueblos, the chieftain said he was pleased with the visit of the Spaniards, and he invited Cárdenas to approach so they might embrace each other and "seal their friendship." Cárdenas consented to the plan. Alemán then stipulated that Don García should dismount, order his soldiers to withdraw to a safe distance, and come to the meeting unarmed, the chief promising that he likewise would be unattended. With this understanding Cárdenas left his horse, sword, and lance in care of a young Spaniard, and with friendly gestures approached Alemán, who by now had come outside the palisade.

In spite of all these polite words, neither of the principal actors trusted the other, and, contrary to the agreement, as they neared the meeting-place the personal guard of each was kept close at hand. The Spaniard's caution was justified, for Alemán had a trick up his sleeve. With smiling countenance he embraced Don García, binding his arms thereby. At the same instant several Indians sprang forward, and with mallets they had concealed behind their backs they stunned Cárdenas with blows rained upon his helmet. Other Indians now rushed forth, seized Don García, carried him off "suspended in mid-air," and would have taken him a prisoner inside the pueblo if the opening in the palisade had not been so narrow that he was able to brace himself against the walls and thus resist until some of his men galloped to the fray and rescued him. Meanwhile a shower of stones and arrows rained down from the terraces. In the scrimmage several Spaniards were injured and a horse was pierced through the nose. Among the casualties was Cárdenas himself, wounded by an arrow in one of his legs.

But Don García had not been put out of commission. Far from it! Leaving part of his men at Moho, he continued his reconnoissance. Half a league "farther on," presumably northward, there was another pueblo, not named, but which for identification we shall designate as X, because it again comes into the story. Here, as at Moho, Indians from the uprooted towns were assembled for defense, for, after the destruction of Arenal, most of the people of the twelve pueblos had taken refuge in these two places. But Cárdenas had no better luck than before, and the inhabitants paid no attention to his demands for peace. "On the contrary, they shot arrows from the terraces" accompanied by loud and ribald shouting.

Cárdenas now rejoined the men he had left at Moho, where another adventure was awaiting him. Here he was assailed by Alemán's warriors, but it was now the Spaniards' turn to pull a trick. When the natives came out to give battle, "our men," says Castañeda, "pretended they were running away, and thus drew the enemy into the plain, then turned upon them in such a way that they struck down some of the most prominent among them." The rest of the natives took refuge on the highest terraces of the pueblo, and Don García returned to quarters at Alcanfor.

When he heard the report brought back by Cárdenas, the general decided to discipline the two stubborn pueblos, beginning with Moho, and to lead the assault himself. It was about time Chief Alemán should learn to respect the authority of the Emperor's representatives, otherwise no Spaniard would be safe in this remote corner of Spain's dominions. Coronado proceeded to make good his threat, and soon after the Alemán episode he set out from Alcanfor with his entire force "in good array." Profiting by experience at Háwikuh and Arenal, he went equipped with ladders for scaling the pueblo walls to reach the terraces. Having arrived at Moho, he established his camp near a spring beside the pueblo and again went through the oft-repeated formula. He enjoined the inhabitants to submit to Spanish authority, in which case he would do them no harm; but he was rewarded only by jeers and obscene gestures. So the army surrounded the town and prepared for war. Next day Coronado again demanded submission, and again without success, whereupon he gave the "Santiago." Another fierce struggle was on, man to man. During the combat there were many valorous deeds on both sides, about which veterans, both

Spaniards and Indians, no doubt continued to reminisce for many years afterward, the flavor of the tale improving with age.

The Spaniards first attempted to open a breach in the pueblo wall. Having broken through the outside coat of mortar, they discovered that the palisade was made of the trunks of trees firmly planted in the ground and interwoven with poles and willows, and so strong that it withstood all the blows they gave it with crowbars, logs, or anything else available. Meanwhile ladders were placed against the walls, and some fifty Spaniards, in the face of desperate resistance, and fighting their way every inch, managed to clamber up to the terraces. The Indians, preparing for just such an emergency, had assembled a large supply of stones, which they now hurled at the invaders so effectively that they "stretched many Spaniards on the ground." The difficulty of reaching the terraces was greatly increased by the fact that "the Indians craftily had many rooms open to the sky in order that they might not communicate"—that is, leaving open gaps, so the assailants could not walk on one terrace to reach the one next above, whence the Indians were sending down their deadly volleys.

More devastating than the barrage of stones was the shower of arrows shot by the natives from towers provided with portholes, and so well aimed that they wrought havoc among the Spaniards, driving them from the terraces and ending the battle for that day. The damage from the arrows was all the more serious because they were poisoned. The venom was thought by the Spaniards to have come from rattlesnakes, "for it was learned that . . . the Indians shut vipers in willow vessels and poked them with arrows so they would bite the points and make them poisonous." Castañeda estimated that in this engagement nearly a hundred Spaniards were wounded by arrows, "of whom some died later because of the inefficient care of an incompetent surgeon," whose name he charitably concealed. But from another source we learn that it was Ramos. Mota Padilla gives the number wounded as "more than sixty." Dr. Ramos probably did his best to cure the injured, but the arrow wounds festered, some of the patients died, and others were left with disfiguring scars.[1]

Of five or six Spaniards killed outright or fatally wounded in this battle, four were accounted for by name and written in the roster of Spanish heroes. Francisco Pobares met instant death from a well-aimed shot. When he "was trying to plug up with mud a porthole from which great damage was being done, an arrow pierced his eye, causing him to fall dead." Juan Paniagua, "a very good Christian and a noble person," was more lucky than his buddy, for, being wounded by an arrow in one of his eyebrows, he escaped death from poison, "and spread the report that he owed his life to his devotion to the rosary, which he was always saying." Edified by the story, his comrades experienced a temporary wave of increased piety.

Two others who died from arrow wounds in this battle on the banks of the Rio Grande were a Spaniard named Benítez and "a certain Carbajal," brother of Hernando Trejo who afterward was lieutenant-governor for Francisco de Ibarra in Chiametla. Mota Padilla says a Basque named Alonso de Castañeda also died of wounds received at Moho, but it is known that he later turned up at Guadalajara. The same writer cynically remarks, "and it was all their own fault, for, since they had few firearms with which to attack, they might have set fire to the walls, for they were made of large tree trunks and palisades plastered only with mud." Here speaks the armchair strategist from a safe distance in space and time, for he wrote just two hundred years after the event. And now, two centuries still later, we are quoting him. Printed words, whether wise or foolish, are wont to be long-lived.

Having failed in these attempts to take the pueblo by storm, Coronado sat down to besiege it, hopeful that the imprisoned

[1] Dr. Robert F. Heizer writes: "A common western arrow poison extracted from a deer's liver which has been struck by a rattlesnake is not, so far as ascertainable, attested for the Puebloan peoples of the Rio Grande river except in the accounts of the Coronado expedition. There is no reason to doubt the reference, however, since it is explicit, and men are said to have died from its effect. Arrow poison made from rattlesnake venom impregnated deer's liver has been recorded from the White Mountain Apache, Mohave, and Seri, and on distributional grounds its occurrence on the Rio Grande seems perfectly plausible."

natives would soon be forced to yield for lack of water, though not for shortage of food, for through some channel he learned that Moho had storerooms well stocked with maize. Soon the Indians were hard pressed by thirst, as the general had anticipated, and to relieve their need they dug a deep well inside the pueblo but failed to reach water. Instead, the walls caved in while they were digging and killed thirty persons, but in spite of this disaster the natives held out much longer than Coronado had expected. Nature took their part. "For, just when he thought they must be soon forced to yield, a snowfall began and continued for several weeks, enabling the Indians to supply themselves during all that time by melting the snow."

So the siege dragged on interminably, as it seemed to the people both inside and outside the pueblo walls. Meanwhile several new attacks were made "without doing the Indians any harm." Each day Coronado went through the formula of "summoning" the Indians to peace. Finally, says Cárdenas, "seeing that they would not surrender, that the winter was severe, and that the Spaniards could not endure it any longer, the general ordered that they be attacked." This was about February 20, 1541.

The assault was made. In the red-hot, hand-to-hand battle that ensued, Captain Francisco de Ovando, in a daring attempt to get at the enemy, started to crawl on hands and knees through a narrow opening, but scarcely had he shown his head to the vigilant Indians when they seized him, dragged him inside, and put him to death, in spite of all the efforts of his comrades to save him. Cárdenas declared that the natives perpetrated great barbarities upon the captain, "cutting him into pieces." But this statement is flatly contradicted by Castañeda, who wrote that forty days later, when Moho was finally captured, the Spaniards found Ovando's body "intact among the native dead, with no other injury than the wound from which he died. He was as white as snow, and had no bad odor."

Ovando seems to have been a favorite in the army, and his death was deeply regretted by his comrades, for, as Castañeda asserts, "he was a distinguished person, and likewise very honorable, gracious, and unusually popular." He was well equipped, for the muster roll shows that he left Compostela with five horses, a coat of mail, head armor, and native weapons. That Don Francisco was esteemed by his commander also is evidenced by the fact that while Cárdenas was absent from Háwikuh on his expedition to Grand Canyon, Captain Ovando was appointed in his place as maestre de campo, and by the added fact that he had headed an exploring expedition shortly before Coronado arrived at Tiguex, going down the Rio Grande among the Piros towns.

For numerous tedious days the siege was continued. During all this time, says Mota Padilla, the Spaniards "attempted many foolish things," in vain efforts to dislodge the defenders of Moho from their fortification. "One of these was to make of timbers some engines which they called *vaivenes,* the name for the ancient rams used for battering down fortresses in times before powder was known. But they did not work." Later on, for lack of artillery "they tried to make some cannons of timber, well bound with ropes." These were likewise useless. "But," repeats the persistent armchair strategist, "they never tried bringing fuel to the walls and setting them on fire." This, of course, would have turned the trick! Unfortunately, as in the case previously cited, Mota Padilla's wise suggestion, written in 1742, was somewhat late.

With the approach of spring the season of snowfall ended, and water again became scarce inside the walls of Moho, to the dire distress of the imprisoned inhabitants. Then, one day, about the middle of March, when the suffering from thirst was becoming unbearable, the besieged Indians asked for a parley. Perhaps it was Juan Alemán himself who made the request. When the chiefs were asked what was on their minds, they replied that, having been told that Spaniards did not harm women and children—a significant testimonial under the circumstances —they had decided to surrender their wives and their progeny, because they contributed to the shortage of water. The urgency must have become extreme indeed to bring the Indians to such a pass.

A bargain was struck, the terms of which are not revealed, but presumably the unfortunate persons most concerned were to become servants or slaves of the Spaniards, for such was the custom. Be the case as it may, the Indians proceeded to deliver to Coronado about a hundred women and children. No more than these would consent to leave the pueblo, the rest preferring death from thirst with their own people. Taking advantage of the brief armistice, Coronado again endeavored to persuade the warriors of Moho to surrender under a promise of amnesty. But, says Castañeda, "we were unable to induce them to make peace, for they insisted that we would not keep our word."

The chiefs now proceeded to hand over the women and children, a dramatic scene in which one of the caballeros played a gallant part, for which he got into print back home. "While they delivered the captives, our men remained on their horses in formation before the pueblo," says Castañeda. In the center of the picture was Don Lope de Urrea, a young caballero from Aragón who had been prominent in the battle at Arenal. Now, on horseback, without a helmet, he was "receiving boys and girls in his arms," and turning them over to the care of other Spaniards or their servants. When the full quota had been thus transferred, Don Lope, speaking for Coronado, again urged the natives to submit, "offering them all sorts of pledges of security. But they warned him to withdraw, and the more he urged the angrier they became." Finally, "an Indian came out armed with bow and arrow and threatened to kill him, saying that if he did not go away he would shoot."

Urrea's comrades were anxious for his safety, but he was cool. "However much the other Spaniards shouted for Don Lope to put on his head armor, he refused, saying the natives would not harm him." One suspects of Don Lope a little bravado. When the pugnacious Indian saw that Urrea would not depart, he shot an arrow which landed at the foot of Don Lope's horse—just to scare the Spaniard perhaps, for he could hardly have been as bad a marksman as that. Fitting another arrow to his bow, he once more ordered him to leave, saying this time he would shoot to kill.

But Don Lope still was nonchalant. When finally the spirit moved him, the caballero deliberately put on his helmet and slowly rejoined the other horsemen, unharmed by the Indians. But as soon as they saw he was beyond their reach they began to shoot and howl, and to send after him a shower of arrows. On the other hand, the insolence of the Indians was resented by the soldiery, and they were eager to get at them. But, says Castañeda, "the general did not wish to fight them that day, because he wished to see if he could find a way to make peace with them—to which they never consented." Don Lope's coolness and chivalry were long remembered.

Relations with Tiguex having been so sadly disrupted, with no improvement in sight, Coronado found himself forced to turn elsewhere for provisions, and even for aid in the war. He was in a difficult position, and the sky looked dark. It was a hard winter, and both Spaniards and Indian allies complained to the general that they were "naked and dying from cold," at the same time requesting that he order clothing gathered from pueblos outside of the province of Tiguex.

Recognizing the needs of the thinly clad men from the south, Coronado did his best to relieve their suffering and to keep his army in condition for combat. He turned first to Sia, a large pueblo a few miles west of the Rio Grande and inhabited by people who spoke the Keresan tongue, which was quite distinct from the language of Tiguex. The general himself being fully occupied in the siege of stubborn Moho, and part of the time being ill, he sent Cárdenas on the urgent mission. With a small force of men and some petty merchandise, Don García went to Sia and obtained "a certain number of *mantas*, skins and quilts," though not as many as the shivering soldiers needed. Probably the Indians furnished Cárdenas all the clothing they could spare, for they too were suffering from the severe winter. On the other hand, recent experience in Tiguex tempered any disposition to use force which Cárdenas may have felt. When Don García returned to headquarters he was given a warm welcome by the soldiers, and the clothing which he brought was apportioned "among the people most in need." Aid from Sia did not end with this expedition by Cárdenas, for soon afterward a delegation of natives from that pueblo arrived at camp, bringing turkeys and other provisions. They had a conference with Coronado and "offered to aid him"—presumably in the Tiguex War.

Plucky Moho would not surrender to the invaders, even though they came with horses, cannons, crossbows, and lances, but it was finally conquered by shortage of water. Coronado's strategy had succeeded. Moreover, spring was at hand, and crops must be planted somewhere, lest families should starve next winter. When the water supply had completely given out, and there was no longer any hope of relief, the Indians decided to make a break for freedom rather than trust to any bargain with invaders in whom they had no confidence. So, two weeks after the Urrea episode, and "after having been besieged for what must have been eighty days," near the end of March the natives of Moho fled, driven more by thirst than by Spanish arms.

The plunge was taken one night in the drowsy fourth watch, just before dawn, when forty mounted Spaniards were on guard —enough, one would think, to have made such a happening impossible. Placing their remaining women and children (more precious now) between the warriors, to give them protection on all sides, the Indians slipped from the pueblo and made a bold dash for liberty. But fate was against them. The fugitives had scarcely passed outside the pueblo walls when they encountered Coronado's sentinels, two of whom they disposed of in a running battle. One disappeared and was never again seen by his comrades—carried off perhaps as an object of long contemplated vengeance; the other was found dead with his heart pierced by an arrow. When his body was recovered by the Spaniards they placed it beside the campfire to await a decent burial. But even in death the nameless Spaniard was destined to another adventure. On the return of a party of soldiers who had pursued some fugitives, one Spaniard, when dismounting from his horse, to his horror stepped with heavy tread square on the mouth of the corpse! "Holy Mary!" This ghastly event was thought by the dead man's comrades to have symbolic significance, "and his tragic death was attributed to his having been a backslider and a blasphemer." He was punished in the very member which had most offended.

Meanwhile alarm was sounded in the barracks of Captain Maldonado and his company turned out; but the fugitives in their desperation fell upon them, killed one Spaniard and a horse, and wounded others. In return the soldiers rallied and slew many of the natives as they emerged from the pueblo. Finding themselves overpowered, the surviving Indians fled to the near-by Rio Grande, which at this season was icy cold and boisterous with the spring flood then rushing from the snow-covered peaks of Sierra de Sangre de Cristo. The Spaniards, close on the heels of the fugitives, ran them down with horses and slashed right and left with their weapons. Some of the Indians escaped across the river, others were captured.

Mota Padilla, our armchair historian, saw divine justice in this heroic flight of the Indians, which had cheated the Spaniards out of victory and left them deeply mortified as well; for in his opinion the cruelty with which Coronado and his men had killed 130 braves "made them unworthy of triumph. And so, one night the besieged people sallied forth and fled, leaving our men ridiculous and without a thing of value from the spoils in the plaza, whereas the Indians succeeded in their valorous exploit."

Next morning, when daylight enabled them to follow up their victory, Spaniards crossed the stream and found on the other bank numerous Indians who in their flight had collapsed from wounds, exhaustion, the intense cold, or all three combined. The soldiers took back to camp those still alive, to care for their wounds and to keep them as servants, the prize of war. At the time of the escape from Moho a number of Indians, refusing or too frightened to flee, barricaded themselves in an interior section of the pueblo, where they continued to resist, but in a few days they also were overcome. "This siege was over by the end of March," 1541, says Castañeda.

When the Spaniards at last entered the pueblo they had so long beleaguered, they found it still supplied with food, but lacking water, for the well which the Indians with such toil had dug in vain was bone dry and contained only the bodies of the victims of the "cave-in." Scattered about and contributing to a melancholy characteristic of deserted houses, there were a few discarded garments.

All this time Bigotes, the Turk, Cacique, and Sopete had remained in duress. And now, just as when Arenal was captured, they were sent to Moho "to see how the pueblo was conquered." They also saw it burned, at least in part, for, by command of Coronado, the soldiers set fire to some of the houses. "Then the army and these Indians returned to Alcanfor." Either during the siege of Moho or after its fall there was another dog-chasing episode, apparently accidental. Coronado stated that after the taking of the pueblo, he learned "that while he was ill in his tent some Indians who had been captured during the war were set free, and that a dog chased and bit them, but no one died." So far as Coronado was aware, no one had set dogs on the Indians, but Alonso Sánchez several years later testified "that one of those who committed these cruelties . . . was a soldier called Martín de Estepa." Be that as it may, when the Indians were brought back to camp the general ordered them released, "so they might go where they pleased." But where could they go?

Meanwhile "the other large pueblo," the one we have labeled X, which, like Moho, had flouted Cárdenas, was conquered in a siege directed by captains Guevara and Zaldívar, who by this time apparently had recovered from his wounds received in the battle of Arenal. While the pueblo was under siege "certain warriors" were in the habit of coming out every morning to make a display in an effort to frighten the Spaniards. One day when a Spanish force went from camp to ambush these impudent fellows, the scouts saw that the Indians were leaving X and going to the country. News of this flight was spread, and some of the men in the army now sacked the pueblo and apprehended all the people found there, comprising about a hundred women and children.

Yet another scene was enacted on the Tiguex stage that spring of 1541. Soon after the fall of Moho, but while the army was still there, Coronado was informed that some of the Indians had returned and were fortifying the pueblos they had deserted. Thereupon he sent Captain Maldonado with soldiers to "destroy and level" the defensive works that were being built. Just how much destruction Maldonado wrought does not appear. But he seems to have carried out his assignment more thoroughly than the general had intended, for it was reported that "these men who had gone to raze the fortifications" did not stop there but also "set fire to some of the pueblos."

Coronado at a later time declared that he did not order any of these pueblos burned. But he remembered that one day when he was in camp he saw smoke above the horizon, and upon inquiry was told that one of the towns had been set on fire; and he thought that because of the cold weather, the remoteness of firewood, and being camped in the open, the soldiers must have burned the timbers of the abandoned pueblos to keep from freezing. Moreover, he personally sent Maldonado to one of them, "said to be the strongest," to confiscate all the provisions he might find in it. But if he ordered Maldonado to burn or destroy the place, it was only "to prevent the Indians . . . from returning and fortifying themselves there." He added the information that the pueblos destroyed were half a league, and one, two, or three leagues from Alcanfor, and ranged on both sides of the river. So the whole Tiguex War was fought in a small theater extending not more than eight or ten miles above Bernalillo. The area should be a fertile field for archaeologists.

In viewing the scenes which occurred in the course of the Tiguex War, one's sympathies are likely to be altogether in favor of the Indians, whose country had been invaded, and which they tried manfully to defend. But there is another consideration that cannot be wholly overlooked by the historian, who must judge events, not by absolute standards, but in the light of ideas and accepted practices of time and place. And we cannot forget other Indian wars in the West.

Various and conflicting estimates were made of the number of persons killed, wounded, or captured during the Tiguex War. On the Spanish side no deaths were reported in the fight at Arenal, but Coronado stated that in the engagement the natives wounded more than fifty Spaniards and Indian allies. Zaldívar increases the number to seventy. At Moho, according to Castañeda, Spanish casualties were heavier than at Arenal. In the first attack on that pueblo the natives wounded "close to a hundred men with arrows, some of whom later died."

As to Indian losses, Castañeda tells us that many natives in the fight at Arenal surrendered under promise of amnesty and were taken to the tent of Cárdenas. One infers that a hundred surrendered, since that many stakes were prepared for burning them. About a hundred of those in the tent, it was said, resisted and were driven out, whereupon the horsemen fell upon them and "none escaped except a few who had remained concealed in the pueblo and fled that night." The implication is that all of the one hundred who fled from the tent were burned. But Cárdenas was officially charged with burning only thirty Indians in the Arenal fire, and the testimony of those who were with the expedition indicates that this number is essentially correct. According to the same witnesses, eighty or more Indians were killed in the uprising in the tent. Indian casualties at Moho were greater than at Arenal. Castañeda estimated that "of the besieged, two hundred men died in the various attacks." This figure seems rather high, but we have no way to check it. Besides the Indians killed and wounded we have to count the captives. During the siege about a hundred women and children were surrendered to Urrea as prisoners, and as we have seen, a number of persons, apparently men, women, and children, were captured after they had fled across the Rio Grande. Finally, when the Indians deserted Pueblo X, the soldiers "apprehended . . . about a hundred women and children."

The Tiguex War was a deplorable episode in Spanish empire building, but lest we make invidious comparisons we must not forget analogous chapters in the epic story of our own "Westward Movement," which we regard as so heroic.

CHAPTER XX

HO FOR THE LAND OF THE TURK!

Through the long, cold, winter months while the army was encamped on the banks of the Rio Grande, the captive Turk continued to talk about the wonders of Quivira, teasing the imagination of the Spaniards with new revelations nicely spaced, and stimulating their manifest desire to see the country farther on— *mas allá!* He told them so many fabulous tales "that he caused them to marvel," for he said "there was so much gold there they could load not only horses with it but wagons." Since the Turk in all likelihood had never seen or even heard of a wagon, we may assume this vivid touch was the gratuitous contribution made by the chronicler in recounting the tale.

In Quivira, said the oily-tongued Indian, there was a lake on which sailed canoes, and . . . those of the ruler had golden oarlocks." What at first was a river had now become a lake. To test the Turk's knowledge of the metals of which he so glibly talked they showed him a piece of silver, and he said, "No," the oarlocks were not like that, "but like a gold ring which he saw," perhaps on the finger of some Spaniard. The lord of Quivira was a grand and powerful monarch. His subjects carried him to war on a litter, and when he wished, terror that he was, he unmuzzled greyhounds who tore his enemies in pieces—a touch suggested perhaps by the dog-baiting of Bigotes, which the Turk had witnessed. The lord of Quivira had a very large house where everybody went to serve him, and in its furnishing there were cotton fabrics. He must be another Montezuma! The things told by the Turk "were amazing indeed in regard to both gold and the ways of obtaining it, to edifices, the trade and customs of the inhabitants, and many other things which I omit as too prolix. All this

. . . moved us to go in search of that country, as the opinion of the friars and all those who offered advice," said Jaramillo.

In this way the Turk tantalized Coronado's men, and they would have given him full credence if they had not observed him doing strange and mysterious things. Indeed, some of the Spaniards regarded the Turk as a magician or a witch doctor. Cervantes, jailer of the prisoner during the siege, swore under oath that he had seen him talk to the Devil in a jug filled with water; and that although he was kept under lock and key, and unable to communicate with anyone, the Turk had asked him what Christians had been killed at Moho by the people of Tiguex. He would like to know their names. With a straight face, Cervantes replied that the Indians had not killed any Spaniards. "You are lying," the Turk retorted, "for they have killed five Christians, including a captain." His numbers were nearly correct. The slain captain of course was the favorite Ovando, whose fate we have recounted. Seeing that the prisoner was telling the truth, Cervantes admitted it, in order to find out who had told the prisoner what had happened. The Turk replied "that he knew it already and needed no one to tell him. For this reason Cervantes spied upon him and found him talking to the Devil in the jug."

The Turk told of another country richer than Quivira, and farther inland. This was Harahey (Harale, Arahe, Arae). It was, in fact, sometimes said to be the home of both the Turk and Sopete, now fellow-prisoners. And beyond Harahey there was Guaes, also a marvel of wealth. In Quivira, said the Turk, "gold and silver would be found, but not as much as at Arahe and Los Guaes." What he said of Harahey, "had it been true, would have led to the richest prize in the Indies." Montezuma's treasure and the gold of Atahualpa would be mere pocket money in comparison. Here lived King Tatarrax, "bearded, grey-haired, and rich, who was girdled with *bracamarte* and who prayed from a book of hours, worshiping a woman, queen of heaven." The Turk appeared to be talking of a country of Christians, which "greatly cheered and encouraged the army, although some took it to be false, and a stratagem of the friars." But false or true, "they determined to go there, with the intention of wintering in a land reported to be so rich." What the Turk said had a basis in fact, for Harahey has been regarded by scholars as a region in Nebraska, inhabited by the Pawnee tribe, and the Guaes people were the Kaws or Kansas, who lived west of the great bend of the Missouri River.

So, while the siege of Moho was still in progress, Coronado made preparations to lead his army to Quivira as soon as the war should be over and winter past. The situation demanded such a move, for after the disappointments in Cíbola and Hopi Land, the trouble in Tiguex, the failure to effect a junction with Alarcón, and the lack of news from Díaz, it was all-important to discover some new El Dorado. Otherwise how could Coronado expect to retain the backing of Mendoza and the King? How could he maintain discipline with his camp-weary followers? How could he write convincing letters to Doña Beatríz, or to his cronies in Spain? Moreover, it was his duty to investigate any promising report of wealth in the interior that might come to his notice—and the Turk promised much.

As a first step in his new plans the general set about restoring friendly relations with provinces adjacent to Tiguex, for it would be dangerous to leave powerful enemies behind his back, athwart the road to Mexico, and able to cut off communication or retreat. He began with Cicúique, the strongest of all the pueblos, and one which stood on the road to Quivira. As can be easily understood, this town was deeply offended by Alvarado's high-handed arrest of their chiefs, Bigotes and Cacique, and by the abduction of their slaves, the Turk and Sopete. The wound was deepened by the dog-baiting of Bigotes, and they had suffered another indignity. A delegation of Cicúique Indians had gone to Coronado and begged for the liberation of Bigotes, Cacique, the Turk, and Sopete, complaining that he had shabbily repaid the good treatment their people had accorded the Spaniards. Instead of releasing the prisoners, it was charged, the soldiers set dogs on the messengers, much as had been done with Bigotes.

But now that arrangements were being made to go to Quivira the situation changed, since, for the success of this undertaking, the friendship of powerful Cicúique would be vital. Sensing this, Bigotes and Cacique plotted to go home, thinking that with Coronado so hard pressed it could perhaps he managed. So the prisoners suggested that if the general were to offer one of the Tiguex pueblos as a prize, help in the war might be forthcoming from Cicúique. Thus, as a part of his policy of conciliation and to make arrangements for this bargain, Don Francisco decided to visit the pueblo on Pecos River.

The scheme of the captives was but partially successful, for Coronado took with him on the journey only Cacique, so Bigotes was still playing in hard luck. Left in shackles at Alcanfor, he was to be the final pawn in the game. Upon their arrival at the Pecos pueblo, the general, Don Lope de Urrea and Fray Juan de Padilla entered the town with the old chief, who was welcomed home with much affection and rejoicing. Coronado presented the plan conceived by Bigotes and Cacique and promised that after the war had been won with aid from Cicúique, and when the Spanish army was on its way to Quivira, Bigotes likewise would be returned to his home. The people of Cicúique were not enthusiastic, and excused themselves by saying they were busy with their crops, but if the general insisted they would abandon everything they were doing, and go to his aid. Since they did not volunteer to go willingly, Coronado refrained from urging them. "On the contrary, he told them he was grateful to them and if he needed them he would let them know." He had met a rebuff, but he had to be polite.

Likewise in the interest of conciliation Coronado sent one of his captains with soldiers to Zia, which already had furnished him much-needed supplies and offered him aid against his Tiguex enemies. The Spaniards found the natives still friendly, and left at Zia for safekeeping four bronze cannons brought from Cíbola by Troyano while the war was in progress. Another detachment of six soldiers went on a similar diplomatic errand to Quirix (Queres, or Keres), a province of Keresan pueblos ranged along the Rio Grande north of the Tiguex towns. At the first of these pueblos the people ran away, frightened by the visitors, whose doings in Tiguex they had watched with misgivings during the siege. But the soldiers pursued them and took them back home, "fully protected" and reassured. While at Quirix the captain sent friendly messages to the rest of the Keresan pueblos, "and thus the whole region was gradually restored." But all efforts to conciliate the conquered towns were without avail, and, says Castañeda, "the twelve pueblos of Tiguex were never reoccupied as long as the army remained in that region, in spite of all the assurances given them." In other words, an entire tribal group had been displaced by the intrusion of Coronado's little army.

The general was advised by some of his leading associates not to mobilize all his men for the Quivira adventure, but first to send some captain ahead to verify the Turk's report. "But he would not do this; on the contrary, he decided to take the whole army." He wanted to be personally in at the discovery, and to have enough men to do the job. King Tatarrax might indeed be a formidable potentate, and his land another Mexico.

What was in Coronado's mind on the eve of his departure for Quivira is revealed by the letter he wrote to the King on October 20, 1541. He reviewed the expedition to date, told about the country and the people he had seen, and set forth his reasons for going northeast. "While I was engaged in the conquest and pacification of this province, some natives of other provinces farther on told me that in their lands there were much larger pueblos and better houses than those in this country, that they had lords who governed them, and that they used gold vessels, together with other magnificent things. . . . However, since these accounts were given by Indians, and, furthermore, had been obtained by signs, I refrained from giving them credence until I might verify them with my own eyes. Since to me the information seemed important, and it was befitting the service of your Majesty that it should be investigated, I decided to go with the men I have here to see it for myself." This was his duty.

There was a hitch in the program. Just when Coronado was about ready to start for Quivira he heard news from Sonora Valley that greatly disturbed him, and caused a reduction of the force available for his expedition to the east—a serious matter in the light of the Turk's report of the awful might and military prowess of the Lord of Quivira. Díaz' men had returned from the Colorado River to San Gerónimo early in 1541 and reported the accidental death of their heroic commander. Thereupon Alcaráz, who had been left in charge at San Gerónimo, dispatched messengers with the sad tidings to Coronado. The report of discoveries made by Alarcón perhaps was cheering in spite of his failure to reach Cíbola by way of the River of the Firebrands, but the death of Melchior Díaz was a hard blow, for he was one of Coronado's ablest lieutenants and a most attractive personality. Alcaráz gave other unpleasant news. A number of the soldiers at San Gerónimo, becoming "restless," had caused trouble. He had sentenced two of them to be hanged, but they had escaped. The precise nature of their urge does not appear, but for Coronado it was another reason for worry.

Some of the returned Díaz men, among them Hernando de Orduña and Pedro de Castro, now came from San Gerónimo to Tiguex to join Coronado's army, and apparently it was they who carried to the general the message sent by Alcaráz. They arrived at Tiguex just after the siege of Moho had ended, and when the soldiers were dismantling the abandoned pueblos for firewood. The letters found at the foot of the tree where they were buried by Alarcón on Colorado River had been taken by Orduña's party to San Gerónimo, and we may assume they were forwarded by the same messengers to the general at Tiguex. But they have not yet come to light.

On receipt of these distressing reports Coronado sent competent Pedro de Tovar, chief ensign of the expedition, and famed discoverer of the Hopi pueblos, to restore order in Sonora. This accomplished, he was to bring to Tiguex part of the soldiers stationed there, and with them as soon as possible to follow the army to Quivira. When he went southwest on his errand with members of his own company, Tovar escorted as far as San Gerónimo the couriers whom Coronado was sending to Viceroy Mendoza with reports of what had happened in Tiguex. The messengers carried also a letter written by Coronado to the King on April 20, 1541. These couriers had a dangerous mission to perform, for the natives along the trail to Mexico were now hostile; and with the task only the toughest men could be entrusted.

After Tovar had departed for Sonora, and just when Coronado was holding a final review of the army preparatory to starting for Quivira, Indians arrived from Cíbola to see the general. It is inferred that their visit was occasioned by something which Tovar had learned on his way to San Gerónimo. Coronado charged the Cíbolans to treat kindly any Spaniards who might accompany Don Pedro on his return to Tiguex. By the same messengers Coronado sent Tovar instructions for overtaking the army on the way to Quivira, telling him that on the route he would find letters under crosses that Coronado would set up on the way. Alvarado, and those who had been with him on the treeless plains, might well have asked the general, "What are you going to use for wood to make the crosses?"

The couriers whom Tovar escorted from Tiguex arrived in Mexico City about July 20, where they delivered Coronado's dispatches to Mendoza. It is not clear whether the viceroy was more elated by the exciting account of Quivira, or worried by reports of the Tiguex War and troubles in Sonora. He was mysterious about the news, and kept it from his officials. One of these, Perarmíldez, wrote from Mexico on July 28 to Secretary Juan de Sámano in Spain, that "from the Tierra Nueva, to which . . . Coronado went, letters arrived about eight or ten days ago, but the viceroy has not told anybody what he has heard, except to say that all are well, and that they have found the country thickly settled. But he has wished that his Majesty and members of his Council should learn all the rest through himself. I am sure he will write, especially to your Grace, giving you a report of everything, but until the ships depart [for Spain] he will not divulge anything relating to Tierra Nueva." In this mysterious way Mendoza piqued the curiosity of everybody and set tongues a'wagging. Had Coronado discovered another Mexico? Another Perú? Or had he met some disaster?

Chapter XXI

MARCH TO THE PLAINS

Some three weeks after the capture of Moho—on April 23, 1541, to be exact—Coronado set forth from Tiguex with all the Spaniards still in the Pueblo country. Castañeda tells us the departure was arranged to take place while the ice was yet thick on the Rio Grande, making it possible to cross over on horseback. This would be much easier than getting people and animals through what would soon be a raging flood. Remembering that shortly before this, fugitives from Moho had been drowned in the stream, one must assume that there had been a subsequent freeze, or that this statement was just a literary flourish on the part of our chronicler.

Coronado's retinue when he left Tiguex included, according to the same writer, a thousand horses, five hundred cattle, some five thousand sheep, and more than fifteen hundred persons, counting Mexican allies and recently acquired Tiguex captives. Among the latter was a woman who entered permanently into history, as will appear. Three wives of Spanish soldiers, with their children, rode forth on the historic adventure, to supplement their arduous horseback trip from Mexico to Pueblo Land. These were sharp-tongued Señora Sánchez; Señora Paradinas, known as the Angel of Mercy for her ministrations to the sick; and Señora Caballero, who acquired no special fame except to be listed among these pioneer women in the Southwest. With so unwieldy a caravan, progress was necessarily slow, and the march must have been attended by a constant bedlam of shouting and cursing by herdsmen and horse wranglers, mingled with the bellowing and bleating of the animals. At what he heard, Father Padilla, veteran though he was, perhaps crossed himself many times and said silent prayers. The Turk and Sopete were taken along as guides and interpreters, and Bigotes to be restored at last to his own people at Pecos. The number of persons and animals reported by Casteñeda in Coronado's train is an obvious exaggeration.

Before starting Coronado had equipped himself with provisions for thirty days, some of them obtained at Zia, and some perhaps from the towns north of Tiguex which he had recently conciliated. The Turk asked why they loaded the horses so heavily with supplies, saying they would become tired out "and unable to bring back all the gold and silver they would find." Moreover, it was unnecessary, he said, since plentiful food would be found at Ayas, a large settlement on the way. To measure the distance traveled in the long march ahead, an unnamed hero was assigned the task of counting the steps or paces in each day's march. Surely this human pedometer must have had assistants to relieve him of the fatigue and monotony of such a trek, and to help him keep the record, which we know was carefully and accurately done.

A new adventure had begun. The first stage of the march, covered in four days, was the stretch from Tiguex to Cicúique, over a trail already familiar to both Coronado and Alvarado, north up the Rio Grande, around the end of Sandía Mountains, and eastward through Galisteo Valley, passing the famous turquoise mines. On the way they noted several towns similar to those of Tiguex, some of whose ruins are still to be seen today. The first pueblo, reached after one day's travel, had about thirty inhabited houses. Coronado stopped here in passing, embraced the chief, and instructed the people to tell their neighbors to remain quiet in their homes, "without fear that any charge whatever would be made against them for what had taken place." The implication is that these people had joined in the Tiguex rebellion but were now forgiven.

Farther east they saw a town called Los Silos, because of its many granaries or silos for storing maize. The place was almost deserted, only one section being inhabited. Castañeda says: "This pueblo must have been large, to judge by its remains, and it seems to have been destroyed recently," by Indians of the plains we infer. A third settlement, a small but strong pueblo "between Cicúye and the province of Quirix" was called by the Spaniards Ximena. It has been identified with the Tano pueblo of Galisteo, now in ruins. All the occupied towns seen on this stretch except the first one "maintained themselves fortified," not even permitting the Spaniards to talk with them. They were probably frightened. Beyond Ximena there was another large town, completely destroyed and leveled to the ground, the patios being covered with stone balls as large as jugs holding an arroba, or about four gallons. "It looked as if the stones had been shot from catapults or cannons with which an enemy had destroyed the town." The query arises whether the missiles had not been assembled at the place for defense, instead of having been hurled upon it by an enemy. It would not be surprising if the stones were still there today, a clue to the identity of the spot.

From the stone-battered pueblo Coronado continued northeast over Alvarado's trail, presumably through Lamy Canyon and Glorieta Pass, or perhaps more directly over the mountains, to Cicúique, or Pecos, twenty-five leagues from Alcanfor. According to his promise the general now restored Bigotes to his own people, at which they were greatly rejoiced, showing their gratitude by a liberal gift of supplies for the expedition. They also gave Coronado a captive boy named Zabe, or Xabe, a native of Quivira, "so that from him he might obtain information about that country." Being quizzed, Zabe said it was true there was gold and silver in Quivira, but not in the quantities reported by the Turk. But this did not shake the testimony of the latter, who reaffirmed with new emphasis what he had previously said. He was ready to talk down all comers.

Cicúique, or Cicúye, was a large pueblo situated on the eastern bank of a creek between nearby mountains. The remains of Pecos, Cicúique's lineal descendant, still mark the site. It then contained about fifty houses, with terraces like those of Cíbola, the walls being of adobe. The inhabitants had abundant maize, beans, calabashes, "and some turkeys." Castañeda gave a graphic description of this important place, the strongest and the easternmost of all the pueblos, standing sentinel on the frontier of roving tribes of the Buffalo Plains. What is now a saddening ruin was then a hive of vigorous, self-reliant people. Castañeda, who now first saw it, described it as an eyewitness:

"Cicúye is a pueblo containing about five hundred warriors, and is feared throughout that land. It is square, perched on a rock in the center of a vast patio or plaza, with its *estufas* (kivas). The houses are all alike, four storeys high. One can walk on the roofs over the whole pueblo, there being no streets to prevent it. The second terrace is surrounded by parapets, enabling one to encircle the entire town. These parapets are like overhanging balconies, under which shelter may be found. The inhabitants use movable ladders to ascend to the corridors that are on the inner side of the pueblo" and surround the patio. "They enter them that way, since the doors of the houses open into the corridors on this terrace, which are used as streets. The houses facing the open country are back to back with those facing the patio, and in time of war they are entered through the interior dwellings. The pueblo is surrounded by a low stone wall, and inside there is a spring of water that can be diverted to the houses. The people of this pueblo pride themselves on the fact that no one has been able to subjugate them, while they dominate any pueblos they wish. The inhabitants are of the same type and have the same customs as those in the other pueblos. The maidens here, as in the others, go about naked until they take a husband, for they say that in this way if they do anything wrong it will soon be noticed, and so they refrain from misconduct. Nor need they feel ashamed that they go about as they were born." The chronicler seems to have been quite modern—or quite ancient—in his views.

Castañeda tells us the army departed from Cicúique, "leaving the pueblo at peace, to all appearances pleased, and under obligation to maintain their loyalty, since the Spaniards had returned their governor and their captain." But appearances were deceitful. Though outwardly friendly, the natives regarded the departure of the Spaniards as good riddance. Moreover, while here the Turk had a secret confab with the chiefs, the ominous nature of which was not revealed till a later time.

Coronado now traveled "in the direction of the plains, which are on the other side of the mountain range," that is, the range just east of Pecos River, which here reaches an elevation of nearly eight thousand feet, and is therefore a serious obstacle to travel directly eastward. But Coronado was headed southeast, paralleling the range. "After four days' march they came to a deep river carrying a large volume of water flowing from the direction of Cicúye," so "the general thus named it." It was the Pecos River, on whose banks they had traveled all these four days. "They stopped here in order to build a bridge for crossing it. This was completed in four days with all diligence and despatch, and when it was finished the entire army and the livestock crossed over."

The above is what an eyewitness had to say of the historic march to the bridge. In terms of modern geography and of what the traveler today may see, Coronado had left Pecos pueblo, situated on an arroyo tributary to Pecos River, and descended the valley by a route which for a few miles approximated the present-day highway to Las Vegas. On his right, close at hand, was the range now called Glorieta Mesa. On his left was Pecos River, and beyond it the higher range mentioned. His road took him through the site of present-day Rowe to that of San José, where the highway to Las Vegas crosses Pecos River. Continuing downstream, he passed the site of Ribera (meaning River Bank) to that of San Miguel, the town so famous three centuries later as a station on the Santa Fe trail. Across the river he saw impressive Starvation Peak, now the subject of many legends in the lore of red men and white. Farther downstream he passed the sites of Pueblo and Villanueva. All these charming little present-day towns are peopled by Spaniards, some of whom are descendants and bear the names of colonists brought by Oñate at the beginning of the seventeenth century to the Nuevo México which Coronado was now making known to the world. From San Miguel southward the valley becomes narrow and the modern route zigzags from one side of the stream to the other. At Villanueva the river enters a gorge, and here the road, as did the old trail, climbs up a steep long grade to the western mesa, then swings for a short distance through rough country eastward, and even northeastward, as Jaramillo says, to the river at Antón Chico. In this vicinity Coronado built a bridge and crossed Cicúique River—that is, the Pecos.

One who sees this stream at low water may wonder why Coronado found it necessary to build a bridge. But it must be remembered that the winter of 1540–41 was one of heavy snowfall, and in late April, or early May, with the melting of the snow on towering Sierra de Sangre de Cristo, the Pecos must have been a raging torrent, quite different from what it becomes in midsummer and fall. Moreover, the general had a large caravan of people, livestock, and baggage to get across the river, and sheep with watersoaked wool are very poor swimmers.

Leaving at his back the historic bridge, Coronado and his caravan marched leisurely eastward across a wide plateau broken by boldly scarped mesas sprinkled with scrub juniper, cactus, and other desert plants. Speed was limited by the slow-moving cattle and sheep, which grazed as they went, making at best only a few leagues a day. For a hundred miles or more they traveled along the southern drainage of Canadian River, until they approached the area now comprised in the Texas Panhandle. Putting it in modern terms, their route after leaving the bridge was north of but converged with the line of the Rock Island Railroad and of Highway 54-66 and with the route Alvarado had taken to the Buffalo Plains. The expedition skirted Cerro Cuervo, and probably entered the basin of Pajarito Creek in the vicinity of present Newkirk. Toward the east they could see the imposing line of rampart-like cliffs which gave the vast level expanse ahead of them the name of Llano Estacado (Stockaded or Palisaded Plain), later mis-translated by Anglo-Americans into "Staked Plains," which completely misses the point of the Spanish designation. They were called Stockaded Plains from the rim-rock which at a distance looks like a stone fortification. The usual explanation, about driving down stakes to avoid getting lost, is an engaging folk tale. Soon they beheld, looming above the northeastern horizon, conspicuous Tucumcári Peak, a guide to all travelers in that area.

Coronado and his men were first among Europeans, after Cabeza de Vaca and Alvarado, to see and describe that wonder of the animal kingdom, the buffalo herd; and that other prodigy of Nature, the Llano Estacado, where the buffalo was seen at its best. Scarcely less amazing to the Old World observers were the native hunters who lived with and off these hump-backed animals, and the trains of dogs that transported the belongings of the itinerant people who followed the herd. These four marvels, the buffalo, the great plains, the buffalo hunters, and their dog trains were described by the chroniclers of the expedition as more or less inseparables.

The incidents of this notable trek from Pecos River to the plains are best narrated by the participants themselves. They saw no buffaloes for some four or five days after leaving the bridge, and then began to encounter large numbers of bulls separated from the main herd. These divorced creatures intrigued loquacious Castañeda, who was a keen observer and pushed a facile pen. "I want to tell you . . . about the appearance of the buffalo bulls, for it is remarkable," he writes. "At first there was not a horse that did not run away on seeing them. . . . Their faces are short and narrow between the eyes, the forehead two spans wide. Their eyes bulge out on the side, so that when they run they can see anyone who follows them. They are bearded like large goats, and when they run they carry their heads low, their beards touching the ground. From the middle of the body toward the rear they are covered with very fine woolly hair like that of choice sheep, and from the belly forward they have thick hair like the mane of a wild lion. They have a hump larger than that of a camel, and their horns, which barely show through the hair, are short and thick. During May they shed the hair on the rear half of the body, and then they look exactly like lions. To remove the hair they lean against small trees found in some of the gorges and rub against them until they shed the wool, as a snake sheds its skin. They have a short tail with a small bunch of hair at the end, and when they run they carry it erect like a scorpion. One peculiar thing is that when they are calves they are reddish like ours, but in time, as they become older, they change in color and appearance. Furthermore, all the bulls slaughtered had their left ears slit, although when they are calves they are whole." What would an old-time buffalo hunter say to this? "Excellent garments could be made from their wool, but not bright colored ones, because the wool itself is dark red. Another remarkable thing observed was that the bulls roam apart from the cows in such large herds that there was no one who could count them. They range so far away from the cows that from the place where we began to see the bulls to where the cows were encountered it was more than forty leagues." Our writer remarked that Marco Polo "says he has seen these same cows, with the same humps." Perhaps Coronado was in Asia!

Continuing in the same general direction, when eight or ten days beyond Pecos River, the Spaniards came to the edge of "an immense herd of cows, calves, and bulls, all together." Here, says Coronado, "I came upon some plains so vast that in my travels I did not reach their end, although I marched over them for more than three hundred leagues," or nearly a thousand miles. On them I found so many cattle . . . that it would be impossible to estimate their number, for . . . there was not a single day until my return that I lost sight of them."

Soon after reaching the great herd of buffaloes, some of Coronado's men noticed marks on the ground such as would be made by dragging lances. Led by curiosity, they followed the tracks and came upon a ranchería or temporary village of some fifty Indians, where they learned that the scratches were caused by the dragging of poles with which the natives built tall and beautiful tents. Thus they first encountered the interesting people who, with their families and all their belongings, gypsy-like, followed the buffaloes for a living. It was now about the tenth of May, and the travelers, having passed Tucumcári Peak, were nearing Canadian River and the New Mexico-Texas line. To here, Alvarado, Padilla, Troyano, Pérez, and the rest of Alvarado's former band of explorers, were going over familiar ground. To the others it was a new adventure.

The life of these nomads, who were apparently a branch of the great Apache people so conspicuous in the same region at a later date, was graphically pictured by members of the expedition. These wandering natives, whose physique Coronado described as "the best . . . of any I have seen in the Indies," were Querechos, a name by which they were known to the pueblo dwellers of Tiguex and vicinity. In fact, it has been suggested that they were called Querechos because of their trade with the Queres or Keres pueblos of New Mexico. They lived with and off the buffalo, and by this animal their whole life was regulated. "These Indians subsist . . . entirely on cattle, for they neither plant nor harvest maize. With the skins they build their houses; with the skins they clothe and shoe themselves; from the skins they make ropes and also obtain wool. From the sinews they make thread, with which they sew their clothing and likewise their tents. From the bones they shape awls, and the dung they use for firewood, since there is no other fuel in all that land. The bladders serve as jugs and drinking vessels. They sustain themselves on the flesh of the animals, eating it slightly roasted . . . and sometimes uncooked. Taking it in their teeth, they pull with one hand; with the other they hold a large flint knife and cut off mouthfuls, swallowing it half chewed, like birds. They eat raw fat without warming it, and drink the blood just as it comes from the cattle. . . . They have no other food."

In spite of their primitive habits, Castañeda spoke well of the Querechos. "They are a gentle people, not cruel, faithful in their friendship, and skilled in the use of signs. They dry their meat in the sun, cutting it into thin slices, and when it is dry they grind it, like flour, for storage and for making mash to eat. They cook it in a pot, which they always manage to have with them. When they put a handful in the pot, the mash soon fills it, since it swells to great size." The dried and powdered meat here described was the food which among more northern tribes was familiarly known as pemmican. It contained much nutriment in small space, and was therefore highly useful for long journeys. That the Querechos were far from squeamish is shown by two of their beverages reported by Castañeda. "When these Indians kill a cow"—that is, a buffalo cow—"they clean a large intestine, fill it with blood, and hang it around their necks, to drink when they are thirsty. Cutting open the belly of the animal they squeeze out the chewed grass and drink the juice, saying it contains the substance of the stomach," including pepsin.

The same observer remarks on the skill of the Querechos in skinning a buffalo. "They cut open the cow at the back and pull off the hide at the joints, using a flint the size of a finger, tied to a small stick, doing this as handily as if they used a fine large knife. They sharpen the flints on their own teeth, and it is remarkable to see how quickly they do it." Experts in the tanning of buffalo hides and deerskins, the Querechos not only put them to a multitude of uses in their own daily life, but profited by them as a marketable commodity, "dressing skins to take to the pueblos to sell . . . , since they go to spend the winter there." These skins, and likewise dried buffalo meat, they traded for maize and cloth with the towns on the upper Rio Grande, where also they obtained their pottery.

Comment on the tents of the Querechos was made by both Coronado and Jaramillo. "They fasten . . . poles at the top and spread them apart at the base," covering the whole structure with tanned and greased buffalo hides. The equipment necessary for erecting these dwellings, as well as other belongings, was transported by dogs similar to those of Mexico, except that they were somewhat larger. "They load the dogs like beasts of burden and make light pack-saddles for them like ours, cinching them with leather straps." When the load slipped to one side the little beasts howled for someone to come and straighten it. "The dogs go about with sores on their backs like pack animals. When the Indians go hunting they load them with provisions, and when they move—for they have no permanent residence anywhere, since they follow the cattle to obtain food—these dogs transport their houses for them. In addition to what they carry on their backs, they transport the poles for the tents, dragging them fastened to their saddles. The load may be from thirty to fifty pounds, depending on the dog." Farther north, and at a later date, by the French pioneers these dog trains were called *travois*.

Here on the edge of the Llano Estacado, Coronado had a conference with these "Bedouins." The Turk, as guide and interpreter, went ahead with the advance guard and talked with the

Querechos before Coronado arrived. The parley was in the marvelous sign language, for the Indians "were so skillful in the use of signs that it seemed as if they were speaking. They made everything so clear that an interpreter was not necessary." Communication between different tribes by means of signs was indeed surprisingly effective. It was found by Coronado in use as far west as Zuñi, but it was most highly developed among the Indians of the Plains, and the records of the expedition give us one of our earliest references to the practice. This gesture system for all ordinary purposes "hardly fell short of a spoken language." And it is still in use. Signs are made almost entirely with the hands, one or both. Minor tribal differences exist, but even with these slight dissimilarities, at a later date a Sioux or a Blackfoot from Missouri "had no difficulty in communicating with a visiting Kiowa or Apache from the Texas border on any subject from the negotiating of a treaty to the recital of a mythic story or the telling of a hunting incident." Among the most expert in the use of the sign language were the Kiowas, who in the nineteenth century frequented the Canadian River, and to this tribe the Querechos met by Coronado may have belonged. Mooney, a great authority on the subject, writes that "in fluent grace of movement, a conversation between a Cheyenne and a Kiowa is the very poetry of motion."

Chapter XXII

"NOTHING BUT CATTLE AND SKY"

Castañeda was surprised, and doubtless Coronado also, that the Querechos did not take fright at the approach of the Spanish caravan, a sight to them so unfamiliar, for "although they saw our army they did not move away nor disturb themselves in the least. On the contrary, they came out of their tents and scrutinized us. Then they spoke with the advance guard," who were led by the Turk, "and asked what the army was." When Coronado came up, he, too, conversed with the Indians, inquiring about the country farther on.

What the Querechos told the general was cause for another surprise, for the expedition at this point was approaching the place just west of the New Mexico-Texas line where the trail to Quivira crossed Canadian River, the stream whose tributaries they had been following. It was in this vicinity that the Turk, wishing to go home, had tried to induce Alvarado the previous year to turn northeast to Quivira, as a bait telling him the story of the golden bracelet. It was near here that Alvarado had turned back to report the exciting news of Quivira and to get his hand on the coveted jewelry. Now, however, the Querechos gave Coronado to understand that the land he was seeking lay toward the east. "They said that by going down toward the sunrise there was a very large river, along whose banks the army could travel through continuous settlements for ninety days . . . and that the first settlement was Haxa," which apparently was the Ayas of which the Turk had told. Later it was learned that the Turk, going ahead of Coronado, had coached the Querechos for his own purposes.

The day after the caravan arrived at the Querecho camp these Indians pulled down their tents, loaded their dogs with tent-poles and baggage, and moved away. Simultaneously the Spaniards went forward and traveled "along the waters found in the cattle country," that is, along the Canadian River and across its tributaries. Two days later, when the army was going in the same direction, "which was between north and east, or rather toward the north," they arrived at another ranchería of Querechos. Here were seen "such large numbers of cattle that it now seems incredible."

The location of this second Querecho village was pivotal in the whole story of Coronado's march to Quivira and back. In fact, its significance becomes spectacular. Just west of the Texas line, where Coronado was at this time, there are stretches of the Canadian River which run northeast, or for shorter distances even nearly north, as Coronado says. Moreover, since the compass here points several degrees to the east of true north, and did then, as we shall see, the direction of their travel seemed to the explorers even more northerly than it was in fact, for they probably did not know the direction or the amount of the compass declination. It was near here, where Coronado saw the second Querecho camp, that the trail to Quivira left the Canadian River. This was what Alvarado had been informed by the Turk on his former journey to the Plains a few months previously, and was what Coronado had understood. At a later point in our story this conclusion is confirmed beyond dispute. But now the Turk told another tale, greatly to the confusion of the Spaniards he was guiding.

The general talked with the Querechos at the second village, and like those at the first, they gave "lavish reports of settlements, all of them east of our present location!" Moreover, the Turk said that Haxa was only one or two days distant. News indeed, and welcome, though puzzling as it must have been, especially to Alvarado, Troyano, and Pérez, who had been here the previous autumn; for at that time the Turk had pointed northeast, and told of Quivira and its wonders. Sopete, the junior guide, himself a Quiviran, now protested that they were being misled, but no one paid any attention to him. The Turk had the floor.

Every day furnished more than one incident. Here at the second Querecho village some soldiers went out to kill buffaloes. One of the men strayed from his companions, thinking he would return to camp by another route, but he failed to put in an appearance. "When he found himself alone, like a bark without a rudder, he must have started to run, and the farther he traveled the farther he went astray. Seeing what had happened, the soldiers lighted some bundles of dry grass so that he might see them. Others rode out on horseback blowing trumpets. But the poor fellow was never seen again." Castañeda tells us that here Cárdenas broke an arm; just how, he does not explain. It was an injury from which he never recovered, perhaps through lack of proper surgical attention. Diego López now took his place as second in command. Don Diego it will be remembered, was the alderman from Seville. One of the best equipped of all the men in the army, when he passed muster at Compostela he had seven horses, a coat of mail "with its trappings," a beaver, and native weapons. In modern parlance, he was a "brass hat."

To investigate the story of Haxa, Coronado sent his new maestre de campo eastward down the Canadian with a few companions, traveling light. In the stretch ahead of them the affluents on both sides of the stream are short and enter the river more or less at right angles, giving the map the appearance of a caterpillar; and, traveling in the valley, below the cliffs at their right, the explorers would not get far from the main channel of the stream. López was instructed to go down the river "with all speed for two days to find Haxa and then rejoin the army promptly." Captain López had a big adventure in prospect. Assuming that the Turk was telling the truth, he might have the good luck to be the discoverer of great things! Setting forth next day, and journeying "toward the rising sun by means of a sea-compass, López and his men came upon many cattle, and "those who went in the advance guard found a large number of bulls in front of them blocking the way." The soldiers rode on, enjoying the sport. As the animals were running and jostling one another, they came to a barranca, and so many buffaloes tumbled into it that they filled the gorge and the rest of the herd crossed over on their backs. It was a wild scramble. The men on horseback who were giving chase fell head over heels upon the floundering animals, not knowing what had happened, so sudden was it all. Three horses disappeared, with their saddles and bridles, among the cattle and were never recovered, although their riders apparently came out with nothing worse than bruises, a good scare, and a yarn to spin for the rest of their lives. This adventure occurred not far east of the Texas line. Perhaps some modern cowboy has picked up and wondered at the metal work of bridles and saddles lost that day, just as other Spanish relics have been found in the vicinity.

When the time agreed upon had expired—probably four days at least—the explorers had not returned from their adventure. So Coronado, thinking that López should be back, sent six men up a small creek and an equal number down it "to look for signs of his horses at the source and mouth of the stream." This passage is significant. If in a brief space of time the searching party could reconnoiter the whole length of the creek from source to mouth, it must have been a short one. Coronado was obviously still close to Canadian River, most of whose branches here are short, run north and south, and would thus cut across the path of López returning from the east.

The men went forth on their search. "No tracks could be found in the meadows because the grass rises up again after being trampled upon," says the chronicler. However, "they found by chance some hoof prints showing which direction the party had taken. Some Indians from the army who had gone out in search of fruit, a league from the place where the tracks were found, on their way back discovered López and his men," whose return had been delayed by the loss of the three horses, and "they marched down the stream to the camp." They had enjoyed an exciting experience, but had no news of Haxa to report. They told the general that in the twenty leagues they had traveled—perhaps as far east as Vega—"they saw nothing but cattle and sky." Coronado now was still more puzzled and his men shook their heads, but the brazen Turk offered new assurance.

After the return of López to Coronado's camp, the expedition, following the Querechos, wandered eastward among the buffalo herds. "For five days," Coronado wrote, "I went wherever they led me until we reached some plains as bare of landmarks as if we were surrounded by the sea." This would mean that for the first five days the terrain was of a character different from that which followed, the inference being that this time was spent in the valley of Canadian River, after which the Spaniards ascended to the plains. Highway 66 does the same here, climbing from the Canadian drainage to a vast flat, west of Vega, whose very name is significant. López in his scouting trip apparently had reached the same place. The name "La Vega" was intuitive, as natural as "Las Tetas" or "Les Trois Tetons" for cone-shaped peaks. And when other Spaniards saw the place in the seventeenth or eighteenth century they again called it La Vega, for that is what it is—a vast flat, and the name has endured.

Coronado now swung southward, leaving the Canadian River at his back, whereupon Sopete again tried to make himself heard, protesting that the Turk was misleading them and had enlisted the collusion of the Querechos. Quivira was northeast and not south, he insisted. But still nobody would believe him. The Turk was the official guide and the Turk they followed. By now the Querechos had parted company with the Spaniards, and left them helpless in the vast expanse of earth and sky. "Here the guides lost their bearings," says Castañeda, "because there is nowhere a stone, a hill, a tree, or a bush, or anything of the sort. But there are many excellent pastures with fine grass."

The general and his caravan were now on the great plains of the Texas Panhandle, the Llano Estacado, at which the chroniclers of the expedition marveled even more than at the numberless buffaloes. Their own words cannot be improved upon. "The country where these animals roamed was so level and bare that whenever one looked at them one could see the sky between their legs, so that at a distance they looked like trimmed pine tree trunks with the foliage joining at the top. When a bull stood alone he resembled four such pines. And however close to them one might be, when looking across their backs one could not see the ground on the other side," but only sky. "This was because the earth was so round, for, wherever a man stood, it seemed as if he were on the top, and saw the sky around him within a crossbow shot. No matter how small an object was placed in front of him, it cut off his view of the ground. . . . There are no trees except along the streams found in some barrancas, which are so concealed that one does not see them until he is at their very edge. They are of sand and gravel (*tierra muerta*), with trails made by the cattle in order to reach the water, which flows quite deep." Coronado's men were getting an impressive geography lesson.

The region where Don Francisco was now traveling is not difficult to identify. His general direction now was southeastward, and by this route he would cross numerous branches of **Palo Duro** and **Tule** creeks. In early historic times cottonwoods and willows grew along the courses of these streams, and still do in some cases. In its wanderings the expedition traveled over "plains with no more landmarks than if we had been swallowed up by the sea, because there was not a stone, not a bit of rising ground." This is true at Vega; and farther south in Castro, Hale, and Swisher counties there is amazingly flat country such as is here described. According to Castañeda, "several lakes were found at intervals; they were round like plates, a stone's throw or more across." In the spring season this area, before it was opened to farming, was always sprinkled with fresh water rain pools, which quickly became foul buffalo wallows, as Castañeda described them. The salt water lakes seen by Coronado's men were encountered farther south and west, and at a later time, as we shall see. "The grass grows very tall near the lakes, but away from them it is very short, a span more or less." This was the famous buffalo grass, for which the Texas Panhandle is noted. "Traveling in these plains is like voyaging at sea," says another witness, "for there are no roads other than cattle trails. Since the land is so level, without a mountain or a hill, it was dangerous to travel alone or become separated from the army, for on losing sight of it one disappeared. Thus we lost one man, and others while out hunting were lost for three or four days."

Castañeda, in Part III of his chronicle, remarks that "It was not without some mystery that in the Second Part of this book, chapter seven, which tells of the plains, I suppressed or concealed the things that I shall relate in this special chapter." Just why he had omitted them and what was the mystery is not clear. "Here they will be brought together, for they were extraordinary things, not seen anywhere else. I dare to record them now because I am writing at a time when many of the men who saw them all are still living [c. 1565] and will vouch for my story." Otherwise, he feared, he might be discredited for telling such whoppers. Perhaps, on the other hand, there were men whose deaths he had awaited before finishing his book. This has been done by more than one writer.

"Who could believe that although a thousand horses, five hundred of our own cattle, more than five thousand rams and ewes, and more than fifteen hundred persons, counting allies and servants, marched over those plains"—here again one questions these numbers—"they left no more trace when they got through than as if no one had passed over them, so that it became necessary to stack up piles of bones and buffalo chips at various distances in order that the rear guard might follow the army and not get lost." These were now substituted for the crosses Coronado had promised to set up for Tovar, who, as will be remembered, was under instructions to follow after the caravan upon his return from San Gerónimo. "Although the grass was short, after it was trampled upon it stood up again as clean and straight as before."

"In these plains there are many wolves, with white hair, which follow the cattle; the deer are white spotted and have long hair. When they are killed the skin while warm can be pulled off easily by hand; then they look like skinned pigs. Hares, which are very plentiful, run about so stupidly that mounted men kill them with their lances. This is because the

hares are so used to running among the cattle. But they flee
from men on foot." This passage suggests a picture, with caballeros in the center having a good time chasing jack-rabbits.

Thus led by the Turk, notwithstanding the continued pro-
tests of Sopete and a growing distrust by the soldiers, Coronado
and his company wandered for many days over the trackless
plains, going generally southeastward, and at right angles from
a direct route to Quivira, with a final swing well to the eastward. Then, after nearly three weeks had passed since leaving
the valley of the Canadian, and when food supplies were almost
exhausted, Don Rodrigo Maldonado made a discovery. Captain
Maldonado was one of the conspicuous soldiers of the expedition. An aristocrat, brother-in-law of the Duque del Infantado,
and an intimate friend of Coronado, he had left Compostela
with five horses, a coat of mail, "with trappings and breeches,"
a beaver and sallet, besides ordinary weapons. It was he who, on
the way north to Cíbola, went from Corazones to the Gulf of
California to look for Alarcón's ships and took back to camp
the giant Seri Chief to whose nipples only the tallest Spaniard
reached. He will be remembered also as one whose followers
were in the thick of events that night when the Tiguex Indians
made their bold break and fled from Moho at the end of the
siege.

And now Don Rodrigo had another experience to tell about
the rest of his life. One day while he and his company were out
hunting buffaloes they happened upon some Indians who were
engaged in the same occupation. These people were called
Teyas, and were enemies of the Querechos at whose rancherías
in the Canadian River valley Coronado had stopped. Maldonado and his men now accompanied the native hunters, and
when they were four days of travel ahead of the main army
they came to a great barranca, or canyon, "like those of Colima,"
at the bottom of which they found a large camp of the Teyas
people. A clue to the general location of the canyon is given by
the *Relación del Suceso,* which tells us that the expedition had
traveled since leaving Tiguex "150 leagues,—one hundred to
the east and fifty to the south"—measured for us by the man

who so monotonously and so faithfully had counted his steps. This barranca, as we shall see, was Tule Canyon, which cuts a deep gash in the eastern escarpment of the Llano Estacado, and was reached east of Tulia near the line between Swisher and Briscoe counties, Texas. The estimate of the eastward march was remarkably accurate, but for the southward distance it was a little too high, which should be no cause for surprise or censure. Our identification of the historic canyon rests upon topographical data, combined with the distances recorded, and upon contributory items as the story goes forward, that make the conclusion certain.

In the barranca the natives presented Captain Maldonado with a heap of tanned skins, "and a tent as big and as high as a house. He ordered the skins left untouched until the army should arrive, and sent some men back to guide the army there so it would not get lost, although they had already been placing markers of bones and cow dung, and by these means the army was already following the advance guard." It was a far cry from Don Rodrigo's life at the royal court to his present occupation. What a tale he would have to tell fastidious cronies when he returned to Madrid! Some of them would hold their noses at the same time that they envied the red-blooded adventurer.

Coronado arrived soon with the army, whereupon there followed a scene which at this distance in time might appear ludicrous, but not so to the participants. On seeing the heap of skins the general proceeded to distribute them among the Spaniards, thinking they were a present from the Indians. A lively scrimmage ensued. Observing, says Castañeda, what they regarded as favoritism by Coronado in dividing the treasure among his men, the overlooked soldiers, "angered at the unjust distribution, laid hands on the hides, and in less than a quarter of an hour there was nothing left but bare ground. The natives, likewise, when they saw what was going on, lent a hand to the job. The women and even some of the men wept, because they had thought the army would not take anything, but would merely say a blessing over the goods, as Cabeza de Vaca and

Dorantes had done when they passed that way." It was a clear case of misunderstanding on both sides. But the bad manners of the Spaniards do not seem to have alienated the Teyas, rudely though they were disillusioned.

Jaramillo clarifies his fellow-chronicler's reference to Cabeza de Vaca and recalls an earlier romance of this romantic "Llano Estacado." Among these Teyas in the barranca, he says, "there was an old Indian, blind and bearded, who gave us to understand by signs that, many days before, he had met four others of our people near there but closer to New Spain," that is farther south. "Thus we understood and assumed them to be Dorantes, Cabeza de Vaca, and the others I have mentioned," namely, Castillo and the Negro, Stephen. Jaramillo's inference has caused a raising of academic eyebrows, but what more natural assumption, when we remember it was the story told by Vaca in Mexico that started the chain of events which had brought about the Coronado expedition? Our skepticisms are often more irrational than our credulities, and more a sign of timidity than of superior wisdom. No doubt the exploits of this wanderer and his companions many times had been a subject of conversation by Coronado's men on the long march from Mexico and out into the plains where he had traveled. Moreover, there are very good reasons for thinking that Jaramillo's conjecture was well founded.

Only six years before Coronado talked with the blind old man in the barranca, Vaca and his three companions were creating a great sensation in this very region. They were on everybody's tongue. After several years of slavery on the Texas coast they had managed to escape their captors, and the summer of 1535 found them ascending the upper Colorado River. Thanks to Hallenbeck, one place in the area through which they are believed to have passed was Big Spring, which is not far southeast of the very barranca where Coronado saw the blind Indian. It is safe to say that in many a day the natives of the vicinity had not experienced a more exciting event nor one more talked about than the visit of these four strangers, who might have dropped out of the sky. Through this country Vaca's journey was a triumphal march. He had become a famous healer, even an object of worship, and for his miraculous deeds his advent was heralded far in advance. As he traveled westward he blessed the sick, touching them with his hands and making over them the sign of the Cross. In return the natives gave him liberally of such food as they possessed, including meal made of the mesquite bean. "Now, of this meal," says Vaca in his *Narrative,* "the Indians made a great feast in our behalf, and danced and celebrated all the time we were there. And at night six Indians to each one of us kept watch at the entrance to the lodge we slept in, not allowing anybody to enter before sunrise." The strangers must be emissaries from heaven!

Farther west Cabeza de Vaca and his party reached a village of a hundred lodges, and, says the wanderer, "as we approached, the people came out to welcome us. . . . So great was their excitement and their eagerness to touch us that everyone wanted to be first; they nearly squeezed us to death, and without suffering our feet to touch the ground they carried us to their abode. So many crowded down upon us that we took refuge in the lodges they had prepared for our accommodation. . . . The whole night long they spent in celebration and dancing, and next morning they brought every living soul of that village to be touched by us and to have the Cross made over them, as with the others," farther back. "On the whole journey," westward from here, "we were much worried by the number of people following us. We could not escape them even if we tried, because they were so anxious to touch us, and so obtrusive that in three hours we could not get through with them. Next day they brought us all the people of that village; most of them had one eye clouded [with cataract perhaps], while others were totally blind from the same cause, at which we were amazed." Such an incident was certain to be heralded far and wide by the natives. And it seems highly probable that the old man met by Coronado in the barranca was himself one of those blind unfortunates seen by Vaca farther south, six years before. Stranger things than this have happened.

Castañeda adds another item of human interest regarding experiences at the barranca. "At this place we saw an Indian woman who was as white as if she were from Castile, except that her chin was tattooed like that of a Barbary Moorish woman. In general they all adorn themselves in that fashion there and decorate their eyes." Was she an albino Indian, or a half-breed of European ancestry on one side? Someone may have a better guess!

Coronado himself makes no reference to the white woman, but he does comment upon the Teyas people as a whole. "They tattoo their bodies and faces, and are large people of very fine appearance. They, too, eat raw meat like the Querechos, live like them, and like them follow the cattle. From them I obtained information concerning the land where the guides were leading me," a determining factor in subsequent movements. Writers have assumed that these Teyas met by Coronado in the Texas Panhandle were of the same tribe as the Tejas, several hundred miles distant in eastern Texas, amongst whom De Soto's men traveled a few months later. But there is no good reason for this view, for the well-known Tejas were already a sedentary agricultural people when De Soto's men visited them at almost this very time, and they had cultural traits markedly different from those of the followers of the buffalo. For one thing, they made pottery and the Teyas did not. Indeed, one may conjecture that these Teyas seen by Coronado were members of the group later known in western Texas and eastern New Mexico as Jumanos.

Chapter XXIII

FACING ABOUT

When Coronado reached the barranca "like those of Colima" he had suddenly come to a distinct change in conditions of travel, and it shocked him into attention. He had arrived near the great escarpment which forms the eastern rim of the Llano Estacado, across whose wide prairies he had been moving. On the plains the going had been smooth and easy. Just ahead of him the cliffs were especially high, steep and rough, the drop from the upper to the lower level in some places being several hundred or even a thousand feet. If he had continued eastward he would have descended this declivity to the eroded plain below, where the terrain is marked by "bad lands," often very difficult to traverse.

Sopete now comes down stage. The Turk had been under a growing suspicion, which at this juncture was emphatically confirmed through information given to Coronado by the Teyas, combined with the sudden change of terrain. It is surprising only that the climax had not come sooner. Led by the crafty advertiser of Quivira, the expedition had wandered for many days southeastward over the endless Llano Estacado, far away from the route so often described by him before leaving Tiguex. From the time when the caravan left the second Querecho village on Canadian River, Sopete had done his best to convince the Spaniards that the Turk was leading them astray, but they refused to believe him. El Turco had a way with him, and he seems to have exercised an almost hypnotic influence over Coronado. Indeed, some of his men complained *sotto voce* about the general's partiality for the Indian and his continued reliance on the rascal's word. Sopete declared that the Turk had primed the Querechos before they told Coronado

about Haxa, and before he led the Spaniards southward from
La Vega into the plains, but he was not believed. Castañeda
testifies in behalf of the junior guide; "this Indian persisted in
saying the Turk was lying, but nobody paid any attention to
him." As they wandered farther and farther astray, Sopete became more and more insistent, and finally at the barranca he
went into a tantrum over the matter. In desperation he "threw
himself on the ground and indicated by signs that he would
rather have his head cut off than go that way because it was
not the correct route to Quivira!"

What Coronado was told by the Teyas Indians confirmed
Sopete's protest, and at last he was ready to listen. Now, he
tells us, from the Teyas "I obtained information concerning the
country to which the guides were leading me"—that is, Quivira,
—"and their reports did not agree with those which had been
given me, for these Indians described the houses there as being
of grass and hides, and not of stone and several storeys high, as
painted by my guides." Furthermore, according to the Teyas,
Quivira was poor in maize. "This information caused me no
little worry," says Coronado, "and I also suffered greatly from
lack of water on finding myself on these endless plains, for many
times I drank [from buffalo wallows] what was so bad that it
tasted more like slime than water." So the general now questioned the Turk, Sopete, and Xabe, the boy captive from
Quivira who had been given to Coronado at Pecos on the way
to the plains. He would have a showdown. There, in the barranca at the Teyas settlement, the Turk confessed that he had
misled the Spaniards. Moreover, he had lied about the grandeur
of the houses of Quivira, which, he now admitted, were only of
grass.

From the barranca Coronado sent explorers northward, for
at last he realized that he had strayed far south of his goal and
must regain lost latitude. In the course of four days the scouts
passed through a large Teyas settlement whose rancherías of
tall white skin tents extended for three days of travel, and when
viewed from a distance they reminded one Spaniard of Alixares.
Did he mean the settlement looked like a sycamore grove—

alisales—or like the suburb of Granada on the mountainside above the Alhambra? Probably it was the former. The country produced abundant frijoles, grapes, and plums like those of Castile. In all likelihood the frijoles were the fruit of some wild plant such as the mesquite, for the Teyas practiced no agriculture. The rancherías were evidently along arroyos running into the main Tule Canyon, which forms a great network of gorges as it cuts its way to the escarpment. Presumably the settlements were temporary villages of native hunters, for at this very time the plains in that vicinity were covered with buffaloes, and the killing season was in full swing. The name Cona, which the Indians gave to the country of these villages, appears to have applied to the region from the barranca northward. Might there be some distant connection between this name and that of the famous chief for whom at a much later date the nearby town of Quanah was christened?

While the army was resting here, an event occurred which was not merely an exciting experience, but was also a decisive episode in Coronado's long trek—as decisive as the former lies of the Turk or his confession now. The tale, as told by Castañeda, should not be spoiled by departing from the chronicler's own language, for it is a model for all hailstone stories. "One afternoon"—another witness even tells us it was at three o'clock —"a great cyclone began with a furious wind and hail. And in a short time there fell such a quantity of hailstones, as big as bowls and even bigger and as thick as raindrops, that in places they covered the ground to a depth of two or three spans and even more." It is to be noted that the size of these bowls is not specified. "One man abandoned his horse—or rather there was not a horse that did not get loose, except two or three that were held by Negroes and covered with helmets and shields. All the rest were swept away until they ran up the cliff, some of them climbing to places whence they were brought down with great difficulty. If the storm which caught them in the canyon had found them on the level plain, the army would have been in great danger of losing its mounts, for many of them would never have been recovered. The hailstones destroyed many tents and dented numerous helmets. Many horses were bruised, and all the pottery and gourds of the army were broken. This was a great misfortune, because pottery is not made in that region, nor are any gourds found there. These people neither cultivate maize, nor do they eat bread, but live on meat and fruits, either raw or badly cooked."

The terrifying hailstorm, the unfavorable reports of Quivira given by the Teyas, the shortage of food, the bad water of the buffalo wallows, the confession of the Turk, and the sudden change of terrain brought matters to a head. Something must be done about the situation. So here at the Teyas village, says Jaramillo, "the general, seeing our troubles, called a meeting of the captains and other persons whose advice he was accustomed to seek, in order that we might compare our opinions with his. We all agreed that to save itself the main army should return to its point of departure [Tiguex] in search of food, and that thirty picked and mounted men should go to look for the place El Indio [the Turk] had told about." Mota Padilla, following an unknown source, presumably authentic since the item is so circumstantial, tells us that this decision was made on the Feast of the Ascension of Our Lord [May 26], 1541, a date which is confirmed by other evidence at our command. To encourage volunteers for the journey to Quivira, Coronado said he wished to be the first of the thirty. Apropos of this show of spirit by the commander, the historian Herrera remarks, "and I am glad to say here that the captains of the Indies were like those of Rome, who ate, dressed, worked, and fought just like a private soldier, without any distinction." This is but another testimonial to the democratic tone of the Spanish army in the sixteenth century. The choice of the thirty picked men was left for another day, at another place.

To select a campsite suitable for making preparations necessary to carry out his new plans, Coronado set out with the army on the trail of the explorers who had discovered Cona. The caravan was accompanied by a mob of Teyas Indians, with their women and children, who, doubtless, were enjoying the show afforded by the armored horsemen and the large retinue of Indian allies from Mexico, the cattle, and the pack animals. We may assume that as he went along Father Padilla did a little missionary work among the Teyas, and perhaps Coronado distributed small presents from his meager store.

These friendly Indians won Castañeda's admiration. "During this journey," he says, "we saw a Teyas shoot an arrow through both shoulders of a bull, which would be a good feat for an arquebus. These natives are an intelligent people. Their women are well treated, and through modesty they cover their whole bodies. They have shoes and buskins of tanned hides, and wear blankets over their short underskirts, made of skins tied at the shoulders, and a sort of short tunic (sanbenito) . . . with small fringes reaching to the middle of the thighs." This description of feminine gear was written by one man, and now four centuries later is translated by another man, and it may not be altogether adequate. We should have called upon some woman for help. The escort of Teyas people stopped when they reached their last village; but before they said goodbye they furnished guides to set Coronado on his way to Quivira. The general did not permit the new guides to communicate with the Turk, lest they be contaminated by him. They again said that Quivira was toward the north—not to the southeast, whither the Turk had been misleading them. "After this," says Castañeda, the Spaniards "began to believe Ysopete." It was about time!

The scouts now rejoined the army, and, according to Jaramillo, after leaving the Teyas, "all marched together for one day [May 29] to a stream flowing between some high cliffs where there were good meadows. Here we were to select the men who were to go ahead, and send the rest of the army back" to Tiguex. This passage suggests a special reason for going to the Second Barranca to make final arrangements for sending the two contingents forth on their respective errands. It was perhaps the lack of water and pasturage at the First Barranca. Or, possibly it was to get away from the mob of too-friendly Teyas. The exploring party had learned of and reported this second canyon to the general as an excellent camping place, suitable for making preparations for what has been miscalled a "dash" north to seek Quivira.

"Thus," says Castañeda, "the army arrived at the last barranca," a deep one, "which extended a league from bank to bank. A little river flowed at the bottom, and there was a small valley covered with trees, and with plenty of grapes, mulberries, and rose bushes. This"—the mulberry—"is a fruit found in France and used to make verjuice. In this barranca we found it ripe." It is interesting to note that one of the mouths of the Palo Duro is today called Mulberry Canyon. "There were nuts, and also turkeys of the variety found in New Spain, and great quantities of plums like those of Castile."

To reach this Deep Barranca, which became an historic spot in the story of Coronado, and a turning point in the expedition, "they had traveled from Tiguex thirty-seven days of six or seven leagues each." And this was no guess, as we know, for a man had been detailed to make calculations and even to count the steps. "They said the distance . . . was 250 leagues," or some 650 miles, which was a remarkably sound estimate. According to Castañeda's figures, they arrived at the Deep Barranca on May 29, 1541, a date which is confirmed by other circumstances.

Clearly, we must look for the two barrancas in the eastern edge of the Llano Estacado. Here are found the headwaters of the Red, Brazos, and Colorado rivers, which by erosion have formed great gorges. East of the escarpment there are no such canyons. A member of the Coronado party called the second canyon "La Barranca de los Llanos"—the Canyon of the Plains. From the evidence it is clear that the First Barranca, where the blind Indian was seen, the hailstorm occurred, and the first council was held, was Tule Canyon, as we have stated, and that the Deep Barranca was Palo Duro Canyon, the tremendous gorge cut in the Llano Estacado by the Prairie Dog Fork of Red River. Palo Duro Canyon, now a State Park, was and is *par excellence*, the "Barranca of the Plains." It is not without interest to know that this great abyss, first made famous by Coro-

nado, was in the nineteenth century made still more famous by
Charles Goodnight, celebrated ranchman, who, besides raising
vast herds, here cross-bred domestic cows and buffalo bulls, pro-
ducing the animal called *cattalo,* long before the experiment
was tried by ranchmen of western Canada, who by *Time* magazine were recently called the pioneers in this enterprise!

Palo Duro Canyon and the adjacent region are graphically
described by Haley, the brilliant Texas historian and successful
cattleman, who knows the area from long and intimate experience. There, he writes, "the Staked Plains reared their high and
colorful abutments, those escarpments that broke away from
the plateau in flashing reds and dull yellows, in sober browns
and subdued purples. Out of that country of shimmering hori-
zons, a land that has 'the vastness without the malignancy of the
sea,' gashed the rugged cañons of the Palo Duro, with their clays
and sandstones swept into turrets, battlements, totems, and effi-
gies by the everlasting winds of the West. There, and in the
[Tule and the] Quitaque to the south, and on to Las Lenguas,
and Casas Amarillas, and the Double Mountain Fork, was
rough land into which Indians might sweep from bloody forays
on the Texas border. To the north were the breaks of the Salt
Fork and the North Fork, and the long valley of the Canadian,
and to the east the refuge of the narrow granitic mountains of
the Wichita . . .

"The Palo Duro, the Prairie Dog Town Fork or headwaters
of Red River, received the drainage of the northern portion of
the Staked Plains, and cut a colorful system of cañons nearly
sixty miles long. Nearly a thousand feet in depth, and varying
from a few hundred yards in width to extensive bad lands fifteen miles across, it furnished shelter from the northers of the
bleak Plains, and water and grass sufficient for many thousands
of cattle. Its cottonwood, wild china, hackberry, and cedars had
been fuel and shade for Comanche camps from time long past,
and a *comanchero* [New Mexico trader with the Comanches]
told Goodnight that he had once seen twelve thousand Indian
horses grazing therein. It was an unexcelled winter range, with
the high bluffs of the Cañon, the cap-rock, more effectively

fencing the animals in than posts and wire." (J. Evetts Haley, *Charles Goodnight*, Boston, 1936.)

Here in the Deep Barranca, Coronado made final plans for sending the army back to Tiguex and for his own march north, holding another council of captains and ensigns to put into effect the decision previously made. It was now definitely arranged that Coronado with thirty mounted men and half a dozen footmen should go rapidly north in search of Quivira, and that Arellano should lead the rest of the army back to Tiguex, establish camp there, and seek among the pueblos provisions for the coming winter. In a report to the King at a later time, Coronado sums up in the simplest terms his reasons for sending the army back and himself making a forced march to Quivira with a handful of men, a step which we must admit was a bold venture. "In view of the conflict of opinion among the Indians," with regard to Quivira, "and also because many of the people, including women and children who accompanied me, had not eaten anything except meat for several days, I decided to go ahead with thirty horsemen and reach that country, examine it, and give you a reliable report of what was there. And although it was more than forty days' travel from the place where I met the Teyas to the land where the guides were leading me, and although I realized the hardships and dangers I should encounter on the journey due to lack of water and maize, I considered it best to go, in order to serve your Majesty." So he went.

The Turk was now deposed from his high office as guide for the Quivira expedition, and Sopete installed in his place. He could now laugh at the Turk, and probably did. The new guide was "asked to tell the truth and lead us to the land we were seeking," writes Castañeda. "He said he would do so," and he reiterated his assertion "that the truth was not as the Turk had told us." As a reward for guiding Coronado to Quivira, Sopete requested that he be left in that country, since it was his homeland, and that the Turk should not be allowed to accompany the party, because he was quarrelsome and annoyed Sopete whenever he tried to do anything in the Spaniards' behalf. This was of course ingratiating, and Coronado "granted all of it insofar as it was to our advantage," says Jaramillo, an arrangement which to some persons might appear to be one-sided. And in spite of Sopete's protest, the Turk was taken along for whatever purpose he might serve. In captivity he might still be useful, but if turned loose he might raise more hell than he had already caused.

The selection of the thirty having been made, the unlucky ones, those not chosen, "knowing now the decision reached, begged the general not to leave them behind, but to take them along, for they all preferred to die with him rather than go back." This appeal, touching as it may have been, was of no avail. However, not to close unalterably the door of hope to the loyal petitioners, Coronado promised that within a week after starting north he would send back messengers to let them know whether it was advisable for them to follow after him. Something might turn up. These arrangements made, the general and his Chosen Thirty climbed out of the Deep Barranca and started north on or about June 1, 1541. Sopete, as official guide, was assisted for a short distance by the Teyas. The Turk, poor devil, was assigned to the rear guard and taken along in chains. Among places where a Coronado monument or an annual Coronado celebration would be appropriate, Canyon City, Texas, stands high in the list.

Coronado had his troubles from the start. On the first day out the Teyas guides absconded, sick of their bargain. Thereupon Captain López returned to the camp in the Deep Barranca to get other Indians to show the way, and with further orders for Arellano. With new guides, furnished voluntarily by the Teyas, López rode north once more to overtake Coronado. The army still entertained some slight hope that the general might change his mind and send for them. To encourage him in such a decision they drew up a touching petition and sent it after the Chosen Thirty by two couriers traveling light and provided with remounts. But the request was without avail. Coronado had other problems to think of, and the couriers returned to the Deep Barranca to rejoin the army and to participate in new adventures no less diverting than those already experienced.

Chapter XXIV

THE ARMY RETURNS TO TIGUEX
AND A RIVAL APPROACHES

Meantime, while awaiting the return of the messengers to Coronado, the soldiers spent fifteen days in the vicinity of the Great Barranca preparing a supply of jerked buffalo meat for the return journey to Pueblo Land. This gave the women and children a much needed rest. Someone estimated that in the course of the two weeks the hunters killed five hundred bulls. "It was incredible that there should be so many of them there without cows." Not so incredible after all—it was because at this season they were not wanted around by the feminine members of the herd. Domesticated cows in the calving season entertain similar notions. With all these carcasses lying about the plains we may be sure that buzzards, crows, and coyotes took their toll, and made day and night a veritable bedlam with their screeches and howling.

The work in hand provided plenty of excitement, well spiced with danger for the hunters. The bulls had sharp horns and under provocation they viciously charged biped enemies and their quadruped mounts. Many of the horsemen who went out hunting got lost and sometimes were unable to find their way back to camp for two or three days, "even though they could hardly miss the lower and upper ends of the barranca in which the camp was located. Every night, on checking up to ascertain whether anyone was missing, the soldiers fired their muskets, blew their horns, beat their drums and lighted great bonfires. Some of the hunters were so distant and had gone so far astray that all these devices put together profited them little," but apparently nobody was permanently lost. "The best method by which to find their way was to go back to the place where they had slaughtered the cattle and march first in one direction and then in another until they came to the barranca, or until they met someone who could direct them." Even this was a pure gamble. "It must be remembered," says Castañeda, that "since the land is so level, when they had wandered aimlessly until noon following the game, they had to remain by the kill without straying until the sun began to go down, in order to learn which direction they must take to get back to their starting point. But this could be done only by experienced men; those not experienced," helpless tenderfeet, "had to put themselves under the guidance of others." Greenhorns are always a nuisance when there's a man's job to be done, but they have to be given a chance to learn. Castañeda tells of another interesting occurrence while the expedition was in this vicinity. "During this journey a tattooed woman ran away from Juan de Zaldívar. When she recognized the country she fled down the barrancas, for she had been a slave at Tiguex, where they had obtained her." We shall hear of the lass again under significant circumstances.

The messengers sent north to overtake Coronado returned at the end of two weeks, "and as they brought no other word than what [López] the alderman of Seville had reported, the army was soon on its way from the barranca to the Teyas." That is to say, they went back southward to Tule Canyon, the First Barranca, which was on the best route to Tiguex. Here they sought Teyas guides, who were willingly furnished, to lead them to Pueblo Land over a more direct trail than the tortuous one by which they had come. Young Xabe remained with the army, but as he was from Quivira he probably could give no aid on the return journey. With Captain Arellano also went all the friars but Father Padilla, the Spanish women and children, the Indian allies from Mexico, and the captive Pueblo Indians, except the gal who had escaped from crippled Cárdenas at the Barrancas.

The Teyas being people "who travel continuously in that land," says Castañeda, "they are very familiar with it." Their method of guiding the army was as follows: "Early in the morning they watched where the sun rose, then they would shoot an arrow in the direction they wished to take, and before coming to it they would shoot another over it. In this manner they traveled the whole day long, until they reached some water where they were to stop for the night. By this route, what had taken them thirty-seven days to go, they now covered on their return in twenty-five, hunting cattle on the way." The gain was perhaps not so much in distance as in speed, through less loitering and wandering about lost. From the above we conclude that Arellano left the Deep Barranca about June 15, and reached Tiguex about July 9.

On their way back, by crossing them in a different region, the Spaniards saw new wonders of the plains. Castañeda was with the army, and he gives us an eyewitness account of the return. "Along this route they found many salt lakes, for salt abounds there. One could see salt slabs on the water larger than tables and five fingers thick. Two or three spans under the water there was granulated salt more palatable than that of the slabs, which was somewhat bitter. It was crystalline salt." These salt lakes were part of a chain extending west and still conspicuous along the Santa Fe Railroad all the way to the Rio Grande. Since Castañeda is the only one of the chroniclers who returned with the army, and likewise is the only one who anywhere mentions salt lakes, it is inferred that none had been seen on the march to the barrancas, a conclusion already expressed. In fact there are none on that route.

On the south side of one of these lakes there was "a heap of bones a crossbow shot in length or very close to it. In places it was nearly twice as high as a man and three or more fathoms wide. The bones were found at a place where there are no people who could have gathered them." From this the Spaniards concluded that the bones had been piled up in the lake by the waves caused by the high north winds. "They must have been the bones of cattle that died in the lake, not being able to get out because of being old and feeble. The astonishing thing was the number of cattle that must have been required to account for all those bones." Such deposits of buffalo bones have been visible in relatively recent times in some of the old lake beds in the vicinity described. On this route there were large numbers of animals resembling squirrels, and many of their burrows. These, of course, were the multitudinous prairie dogs so characteristic of the region, and so interesting for their community life.

On the way the army "endured great hardships, because most of the men had no food but meat, and it made many of them ill." Every day it was necessary to hunt buffaloes to supplement the rations provided before starting west. "Enormous numbers of both cows and bulls were killed, and there were days when sixty or seventy head were brought into camp. As a result of this hard work and of not eating any maize during all this time, the horses fared very badly." What shambles the camp-sites must have been!

Arellano's return route from Tule Canyon across the Llano Estacado was almost due west over the vast treeless plain past the northernmost salt lakes, and after reaching the present New Mexico boundary it approximated the line of the Santa Fe Railroad, from whose trains one now sees the very lakes so graphically described by Casteñeda. Starting west from Tule Canyon, Arellano would find fresh water in South Tule River for twelve or fifteen miles beyond the present town of Tulia. Farther west his animals could drink at Running Water Draw, in the Upper Blanco Canyon, and in the North Fork of Yellowhouse Canyon as far upstream as Abernethy. Now, ascending the North Fork of the Yellowhouse, he would find water at Sodhouse Spring north of Littlefield, at Spring Lake north of Amherst, and in Blackwater Draw at Muleshoe. From here running water would be found all the year as far as the New Mexico line and for some distance beyond. Farther west there is a spring at Portales and another south of Melrose. Descending the western escarpment of the Llano Estacado and entering the valley of Taibán Creek, Arellano would find Taibán Spring, near the town of Taibán, and only fifteen miles from Pecos River, which he reached "more than thirty leagues . . . below the bridge that had been built on the outward journey"—that is, some seventy-five miles below Antón Chico, and in the vicinity of old Fort Sumner, where in the nineteenth century Kit Carson imprisoned his Navajo captives. For help in tracing this stretch of Arellano's trail I am greatly indebted to Dr. Hammond with whom I went over the route and to Professor W. C. Holden, of Texas Technological College at Lubbock, Texas, who knows the country as well as he knows his own dooryard. The Llano Estacado extends far south of the region where Arellano crossed it, but below this latitude the escarpment is not nearly so bold as farther north.

The guides said the River of Cicúique joined the River of Tiguex more than twenty days below the place where they reached it, after which it flowed east. This was essentially correct. The Pecos River enters the Rio Grande about 375 miles airline from the place mentioned. By the crooks and turns the distance is, of course, much greater. Now turning up the Pecos River, the travelers marched along its bank and rejoined their outgoing trail at Coronado's bridge, near Antón Chico. Almost everywhere along the river there were "bushes with fruit which tastes like muscatel grapes and grows on slender stalks as high as a man, and with leaves resembling parsley. There were unripe grapes . . . and marjoram." As the army marched north they had the cliffs of the Llano Estacado on their right, and rising higher as they advanced.

Castañeda concludes: "Thus, as I have said, the army went up the river until it reached the pueblo of Cicúye. They found it unfriendly, for the inhabitants would not come out peacefully nor furnish any aid in the way of provisions," demeanor quite in contrast with that shown when Coronado started east. The special reason for this coolness, apart from old scores, came to light at a later time, as will appear. From here the Spaniards continued westward over the former trail, finding the people on the way also hostile. Mota Padilla says they managed to pass by the pueblos of Ximena and Silos, "whose people behaved as before," barricading themselves within their pueblos. During the absence of the Spaniards some natives had reoccupied Tiguex, but when they learned that the army was returning they fled. Arellano found all the Tiguex pueblos deserted, so he lodged his men "in the same pueblo . . . of Coofert [Alcanfor] where they had been before."

Viceroy Mendoza meanwhile was worrying over De Soto, of whose doings many echoes reached Mexico by way of Havana and Veracruz. And well he might be anxious, for since leaving Cuba, Don Hernando had explored and plundered a vast area and crossed the Mississippi River. As Coronado traveled eastward, De Soto moved westward, toward the same area, each doubtless wondering where the other might be. Compared with De Soto's swashbuckling raid, in the matter of human relations Coronado's expedition to Quivira was a Sunday school picnic. With several hundred followers Don Hernando landed at Tampa Bay in May, 1539, about when Fray Marcos, on the other side of the continent, turned back from his quest of Cíbola and fled toward Mexico . Leaving at Tampa Bay a garrison of fifty footmen with thirty horses, on August 1 Don Hernando started northward by land. His equipment was far superior to that of Coronado. In his train he had some five hundred lancers, crossbowmen, and arquebusiers, several priests and friars and about two hundred horses. There were a ship's carpenter, caulkers, a cooper for boat building on inland waters, and armorers and smiths with their forges and tools, since "mail shirts must be mended, sabers tempered, and iron slave collars kept in repair." For food he took a large drove of hogs on the hoof, the ancestors, some say, of the old-time razorbacks of the Southeast.

Marching expectantly up the Florida peninsula, De Soto heard of Cale, where Narváez had sought natives who wore "golden hats like casques," but when he reached the place it was found to be only a huddle of mud and palmetto huts on Suwanee River. Confident of better luck farther on, De Soto pushed forward to Caliquen, on the way capturing Indians to serve as guides and carry the baggage. When Don Hernando seized the chief of Caliquen, the Indians attempted to rescue him, and a pitched battle ensued. In the fray some thirty or forty Indians were killed; others jumped into near-by lakes,

only to be captured and put in chains. Thirty miles farther on
De Soto went into winter quarters [1539–1540] at an Indian
town called Apalache, in the vicinity of modern Tallahassee.
While here he sent ships with despatches to Tampa Bay, and
organized an exploring party that went west and discovered
Pensacola Bay.

Winter passed. Early in March, 1540, just after Coronado
left Compostela, De Soto broke camp, traveled northward
across Georgia, and at the end of April reached the Savannah
River at Silver Bluff. On the other bank was the town of
Cufitachique, whose "Queen," draped in furs and feathers,
and with strings of pearls round her neck, crossed the river in
a canoe to welcome the dazzling conqueror. With the "Queen's"
consent Don Hernando opened burial mounds in deserted towns
near by and obtained 350 pounds of pearls. Prospects were improving.

Being told of a rich country farther on, De Soto pushed
northwest up Savannah River, taking his hostess a captive in his
train. Entering the country of the powerful Cherokees, he
visited a large town called Xualla in North Carolina (May 21),
and then crossed the mountains to Guaxala in eastern Tennessee. Meanwhile, the Queen of Cufitachique, having changed
her mind, escaped, and another romance was ended. De Soto
now turned southward, visited Chiaha in Tennessee, and continued to Coosa in central Alabama, where "men and beasts
waxed fat on the abundance of the land." Here, too, a number
of young Spaniards found life partners among the handsome
Alabama women, and took them along on the march. They
were heard of in after years—a link between Mexico and the
Gulf Coast.

Leaving this Lotus Land, and continuing down the basin
of Alabama River, in October, 1540, De Soto reached Mavila,
a large walled town near Choctaw Bluff. The name of the
place is preserved in that of Mobile, city, river, and bay. Here
was fought one of the hardest battles of De Soto's entire march,
shortly before Coronado engaged in the Tiguex War. In both

east and west the natives were manfully resisting the invaders. Quite unlike the friendly people of Coosa, the hardy Mobilians attacked the Spaniards, drove them outside the city walls, captured baggage and provisions, scattered the "pearls of Cufitachique," and released the Indian captives whom the strangers had brought in chains. Then the tide turned. De Soto and his armored warriors assaulted the stockade and set fire to the town. In the mêlée the Indians were slaughtered almost to a man. Eighteen Spaniards and twelve horses were killed, and one hundred and fifty Spaniards and seventy horses were wounded. It was a costly battle, in contrast with which Coronado's fight at Zuñi seems a minor affair. Among those seriously injured was Don Hernando himself. By now more than a hundred of De Soto's men had been lost on the hard march, and the rest were in rags and tatters. Many of the hogs the Spaniards were driving along were killed in the fire. Such was the "romance" of gold hunting and adventure in the New World.

Undaunted by his losses at Mavila, De Soto tightened his belt, went to Mass, swore a mouthful of oaths, and with his ear to the ground pushed forward to conquer Fortune. Pacaha, another El Dorado, loomed above the horizon. So, on November 17, he turned sharply northwest, ascended the valley of Tombigbee River, and a month later, when Coronado's men were alternately freezing and fighting at Tiguex, went into winter quarters (1540–1541) at a settlement of Chickasaw Indians in northern Mississippi. Here again proximity of Spaniards and Indians led to war—"inevitably," the white man always says. Some of the natives, convicted of theft, were put to death; another, his hands having first been severed, was sent to his chief as a warning. Four Spaniards who pillaged some Indian houses barely escaped an equally hard fate, for De Soto, stern with friend and foe alike, ordered two of them executed. Deaf to all pleas, he would have carried the sentence through "but for the subtlety of Ortíz, the interpreter, who mistranslated the complaints of the Indians into prayers for pardon." Ortíz had been a captive among the Florida natives, probably had progeny among them, and had come to know their admirable qualities. For his linguistic fraud we trust he has been forgiven.

When in March De Soto was ready to take a new start for Pacaha he made his usual demand for men as baggage carriers and women for various services. Considering this an insult, the Chickasaws fell upon the Spaniards, set the town afire, and before the strangers knew of it half the houses were in flames. Blinded by the smoke, and unable to find their weapons or saddle their horses, the Spaniards were at the mercy of the native bowmen. The horses broke loose and stampeded or were burned to death in their stalls. It would have been a complete victory for the Indians—and the end of the expedition—if they had not mistakenly believed the thunder of hoofs meant that the cavalry was gathering to fall upon them. In the battle eleven Spaniards and fifty horses perished, a heavy loss for so small an army.

Near the end of April, 1541, about when Coronado left Tiguex for Quivira, De Soto went forward, and early in May, near Sunflower Landing, he stood on the east bank of the Mississippi River, of which he had been hearing much as he traveled northwest. In the history of exploration this was a breathless moment. Other Spaniards, sailing on the Gulf of Mexico, from the torrent of water pouring out of the mainland had learned of the existence of the great river, but none had ever seen it. In the truest sense De Soto was the discoverer of the Father of Waters.

Pitching camp on the bank of the mighty stream, Don Hernando cut down trees and built a fleet of boats in which to cross over, for Pacaha was on the other side and farther north. While thus engaged he was visited by the chief of Aquixo from west of the river. The name Aquixo, by the way, is still preserved in that of Arkansas, state and river. The chief's followers "were fine looking men, very large and well formed, and what with the awnings, the pennons, and the number of people in the fleet, it appeared like a famous armada of galleys." The chief brought gifts of furs, buffalo robes, dried fruits, and fish, but refused to land, perhaps fearing men in such strange armor. Regarding this conduct as unfriendly, De Soto fired upon his visitors, killing half a dozen in cold blood. He had made a bad start with the tall Arkansans. A month was spent by De Soto in building his barges. Then, one morning in June, before sunrise, with all his men and horses he crossed over to the west bank of the Mississippi, to the surprise of the natives there.

Don Hernando now hurried north toward Pacaha, his next objective, for gold was said to be there in plenty. On the way he found numerous towns deserted, the inhabitants having fled, but from their hiding places behind trees and brush they showered the strangers with arrows. Passing Aquixo, south of present-day Modoc, on June 19, six days later De Soto entered a town named Casqui, on Crowley's Ridge, where he set up a cross on the village mound. No gold was found at Casqui, but, taking the Indians off their guard, the Spaniards seized all the buffalo robes and furs in the town, and many of the men and women as well. The white man came like a scourge. On June 29 De Soto at last reached Pacaha, near the mouth of St. Francis River. It was a substantial palisaded town, but boasted of no gold. Casqui and Pacaha were on bad terms, so De Soto turned diplomat, reconciled the chiefs, and entertained them both at dinner, "whereupon the chief of Casqui gave De Soto his daughter to wife;" and the chief of Pacaha, by an equally simple marriage ceremony, gave him two of his sisters, Macanoche and Mochila. Of the Pacaha ladies, says the Gentleman of Elvas, who was with De Soto, "they were symmetrical, tall, and full; Macanoche bore a pleasant expression; in her manners and features she appeared the lady; the other was robust." De Soto now had more wives than he knew what to do with.

No gold at Pacaha! But there was some at Coluça, *mas allá!* So eighty men were sent north to see the place and find a road to Chisca, "where there was gold in plenty and a copper foundry." And it was hoped also that they might find Indians who could give information regarding the Pacific Ocean, which could not be far away! After a week's journey into northeastern Arkansas the explorers found Coluça near the site of present Wheatley, between St. Francis and White rivers. When they returned they could report no gold, and they had learned nothing about the Western Sea. But they had news of the great buffalo herds in the prairies beyond, many of whose skins they had already seen among the Indians. Biedma tells us that the Coluça people lived in "huts covered with rushes sewed together. When the owner of one moves away, he will roll up and carry off the entire covering, the wife taking the frame of poles over which it is stretched; these they take down and put up so readily that though they should move anew every hour they conveniently enough carry their house on their backs." The Querecho women of Texas, with their dog trains, were better equipped for moving, as Coronado had learned.

This journey to Coluça, in northeastern Arkansas, was De Soto's farthest north in the trans-Mississippi country. He now turned south, down the course of White River, and near the mouth of the Arkansas, on August 5, he entered Quiguate, the largest Indian town he had seen since landing at Tampa Bay. It was situated in the delta between the White and Arkansas rivers, at the famous Menard mounds near Arkansas Post, later an historic spot. After living off the natives here for three weeks, Don Hernando turned northwest up the Arkansas in search of Coligua in a mountainous country said to have precious metals. Reaching the place on September 7, he saw no gold or silver, but found there an abundance of provisions, plentiful salt, and a few buffaloes from the prairies.

Coligua, in the vicinity of Little Rock, was the highest point reached by De Soto on Arkansas River. Now by a sinuous route he went westward, visited an excellent salt spring at Calpista on the upper waters of Saline River, passed near Hot Springs, and reached Tula on the upper Ouachita. Here he was attacked by natives who, besides ordinary weapons, had "long poles like lances, the ends hardened by fire." One of the chroniclers calls these Indians "the best fighting people met by the Christians." Tule, at Caddo Gap, was the westernmost point reached by

De Soto. He now descended Ouachita River and at Utiangue (Autiamque) near Camden or Calion, went into winter quarters (1541–1542). There we shall leave him for the present. The opinion of recent students is that De Soto touched neither Missouri nor Oklahoma. While De Soto entered the Arkansas River Valley from the east, Coronado approached it from the west and marched toward his rival. It was a drama staged in the vast Mississippi Valley.

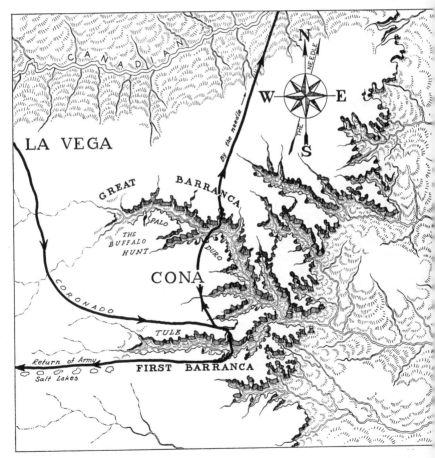

THE BARRANCAS

Chapter XXV

QUIVIRA

Meanwhile Coronado was on his way northward from Palo Duro Canyon with his detachment of thirty horsemen, half a dozen foot soldiers, the *remuda* or extra mounts, pack animals, wranglers, and servants, a total of some forty men. They traveled with light baggage and lived mainly off the country for their sustenance, killing buffaloes on the way. The horses at that season had some of the finest pastures in all North America.

For the Chosen Thirty Coronado selected, as he tells us, the men "who seemed most dependable and had the best horses." His reliance was on human stamina and sound horseflesh, the surest guarantee of success in such a task as the one he was about to undertake. We have recently learned the names of most of the members of this famous band, the first Europeans to traverse the eastern edge of the High Plains from the Deep Barranca to the Arkansas River, and the first to behold the lush beauty of the middle valley of that noble stream. They deserve to be enrolled on a monument at an appropriate site, and no doubt will be so honored now they have been identified.

Coronado, of course, was at the head of the little detachment. Closest to the general was Juan de Contreras, chief groom, who cared for his horses, watched over his person, and carried his confidential messages. If occasion had called for it he probably could have told more than anyone else about Coronado's doings. How we wish he had gossiped! Second in command was Diego López, alderman of Seville, and he played a leading rôle in the events of the bold march into an unexplored land. Conspicuous among all the company was Fray Juan de Padilla, the fighting friar who with Tovar had taken part in the discovery of the Hopi pueblos, had accompanied Alvarado to the buffalo country, and later was to acquire in Quivira his most enduring fame.

In the party went Juan de Zaldívar, the gallant horseman who had made the long, hard ride with Melchior Díaz from Culiacán to Chichilticale to check Fray Marcos' story of Cíbola, had carried Díaz' report to Viceroy Mendoza at Colima, and then had ridden north again, caught up with Coronado at Cíbola, and fought manfully at Arenal, sealing his pledge of loyalty with his own blood. There was dashing Alvarado, discoverer of Ácoma, the Rio Grande, Tiguex, Taos, Cicúique, Pecos River, Canadian River, the Buffalo Plains, and the Querecho Indians. Likewise Juan de Troyano and Melchior Pérez, companions of Alvarado in that boisterous exploration, and authors of significant and hitherto unknown accounts of the episode. Prominent also were Rodrigo Maldonado, who had performed spectacular feats in the Tiguex War, and Juan Jaramillo, who wrote one of the best narratives of the long peregrination to Quivira which he now was making. A person of importance to the historian was the anonymous author of the *Relación del Suceso*. It is a cause for regret that he has not been identified by name, although one surmises that he was swashbuckling Alvarado.

Others who did their part in the exciting anabasis were Gaspár de Saldaña, Gómez Suárez, Juan de Torquemada, Rodrigo Ximón (or Simón), Juan Galeras, Diego de Madrid, Luís de Vargas, Pedro de Ledesma, Francisco Gorbalán, Domingo Martín, Rodrigo de Frías, Hernando del Valle, Juan Ruíz, Froilán Vermúdez, and Juan Pastor. Two at least of the company were crossbowmen. They were Francisco Martín and Juan Bermejo, who were equipped with crossbow, sword, dagger, and native weapons. For these crossbowmen no horses are mentioned. Indeed, their impedimenta would not fit well into a saddle.

Besides the men listed by name there were a number of servants. Not to be overlooked were the Turk, the discredited guide, and young Sopete, his successor and all-out enemy. The Turk, safely manacled, was now in deep disgrace, but he might still be useful, so he was taken along, although he presented a problem in human relations. Jaramillo tells us that on the march "we always . . . kept him concealed among our rear guard, and whenever we came to a camping place we managed it in such a way that he would not be noticed by . . . Isopete. This was done to give Isopete the satisfaction he had asked for"—that is, the satisfaction of seeing his mortal enemy humiliated.

Twenty-one of these men had left Compostela with a total of ninety-two horses. Some of the mounts by now had been lost, and we cannot assume that on this long jaunt the men took from the Barranca Grande all they still possessed. One horse, a large and powerful animal belonging to Alvarado, left his special mark on the Quivira story, as we shall see. The outfit of Fray Juan de Padilla is not described. He probably went apostolically on foot, but had with him one or more servants. It is not stated whether or not he had the equipment necessary for saying Mass, but presumably he had, since when the expedition left Tiguex it moved forward with bag and baggage, bound for a new El Dorado.

On or about June 1, 1541, just when De Soto was building barges in which to cross the Mississippi River into the eastern basin of Arkansas River, Coronado set forth on his spectacular march from the Deep Barranca, bound for the middle course of the same stream. To what extent each was conscious of the approach of the other we do not know, but we may be sure that neither one was oblivious to possibilities, for when Coronado left Mexico City, De Soto was his most feared rival.

Traveling "by the needle," that is, going generally ten or twelve degrees east of true north, as we shall see, Coronado kept on the High Plains and west of the escarpment, which, by an interesting coincidence, for a long distance runs in approximately the direction indicated by the compass in the area he was now traversing. Thus the great escarpment had become both an obstacle to travel east of the Teyas settlements, and a directive for the march to Quivira. On the high plains the terrain was smooth and travel relatively easy, whereas east of the "breaks" it was rough and difficult. Another factor pointed in the same direction. Coronado was following the buffalo trails, and these for the same topographical reasons ran parallel to the escarpment.

Brower and others rightly concluded that Coronado on his way to Quivira crossed the Arkansas at Ford, Kansas, a short distance east of Dodge City, but on antiquated and wholly inconclusive data they assumed that the declination of the compass needle in 1541 in the area of Coronado's march was about two degrees west of true north. Then starting at Ford they drew a line bearing two degrees east of true south. This put the Great Barranca on Brazos River far east and south of its true position.

Using topographical data, I and my collaborators have unmistakably identified the Barranca Grande with Palo Duro Canyon. This gives us two fixed points of Coronado's northward march, Palo Duro Canyon and the ford of Arkansas River. A direct line between these two points bears about eleven degrees east of true north. I was much interested to learn that this is approximately the average declination of the compass needle in that area for the century between 1830 and 1925, for which period we have scientific records, and to learn, moreover, that this area is one of pronounced magnetic stability. The inference is that in Coronado's day the declination was approximately the same. So Coronado furnished data regarding terrestrial magnetism of great value. Apparently his primitive compass worked pretty well. When a mere historian solves a problem of science which scientists more than once have fumbled, he may be forgiven for feeling a modest degree of satisfaction. My predecessors who have wrestled with this question, instead of looking for the canyons, which are still there, have speculated about the declination of the compass needle in Coronado's day, and on the basis of these guesses have come out with routes for Coronado's march so many and so varied that when put together on a composite map it resembles a cat's cradle covering the whole Southwest.

So we may conclude that, in terms of the modern map, Coronado and his Chosen Thirty, after parting from the army, traveled until June 29 on and near the edge of the High Plains by a route some ten degrees east of north, ascended the Texas Panhandle, crossed the Oklahoma Panhandle west of the 100th meridian, thus avoiding the breaks of Cimarron River, and continued with a slight eastward swing through southern Kansas to the Arkansas River. The low speed made by Coronado is noticeable. The distance from Palo Duro Canyon, the second barranca, was about 240 miles, and the rate of advance therefore only

Table showing compass variation along *longitude 100° between latitudes 34° and 38°*, or, along the eastern boundary of the Texas Panhandle and north to the vicinity of Dodge City, Kansas, for the period 1830–1925. From Daniel Hazard, *Magnetic Declination in the United States in 1925* (Washington, 1926), p. 16.

Longitude Latitude	100° 34	100° 36	100° 38
	° ′	° ′	° ′
1830	10 57 E	11 42 E	12 10 E
1840	11 09	11 54	12 22
1850	11 13	11 58	12 25
1860	11 12	11 56	12 22
1870	11 05	11 48	12 13
1880	10 45	11 27	11 50
1890	10 16	10 57	11 19
1900	10 06	10 46	11 06
1905	10 16	10 54	11 13
1910	10 30	11 07	11 25
1915	10 43	11 19	11 35
1920	10 50	11 23	11 37
1925	10 50 E	11 20 E	11 30 E

some eight miles a day air line, or perhaps ten miles of actual travel counting the twists and turns of the trail. Clearly there is little propriety in calling this march Coronado's "dash" to Quivira.

Near this historic trail of 1541, on one side or the other, and participating in the tradition and romance of Coronado's spectacular march "by the Needle," today stand many cities, towns and hamlets, for whose history Coronado raised the curtain. To name only a few, in Texas there are Canyon City, Pullman,

Amarillo, Royal, Granada, Horace, Bugbee, Adobe Wells, Jeffrey, McKibben, Fritch, Borger, Hanford, Spearman, Mulock, Morse, Gruever, and Hitchland; in Oklahoma are Panhandle, Hardesty, Adams, Tyrone, and Stone; in Kansas are Liberal, State Line, Milner, Hayne, Archer, Arkalon, Kismet, Plains, Collano, Meade, Fowler, Advance, Minneola, Bloom, Kingsdown, then Ford at the historic crossing. Residents living today in these and other places along Coronado's trail to Quivira have indeed interesting traditions of the historic event.

We have several glimpses of Coronado's band on its historic jaunt to the valley of the Arkansas River. "Guiding always toward the north," Jaramillo writes, "we continued on our way for more than thirty days, or about thirty days of actual travel, although the marches were not long. We never lacked water in all these days, and we were always among the cattle, on some days seeing more of them than on others, depending upon the watering places we came to," for here the buffaloes were likely to be assembled. At this season of the year the herds were moving slowly north to their summer pastures, and their fresh trails served as road and guide for the Spaniards.

Coronado wrote to Emperor Charles V, whom as a courtier in Spain he must have known personally, that during the whole journey they lived on only the flesh of the cows they killed, "at the cost of some of the horses slain by the cattle, for, as I told your Majesty, these animals are very wild and ferocious." Coming from a Spaniard accustomed to jousts and gory bull fights, this comment may reflect the general's regret for the loss of precious mounts rather than compassion for the gutted horses. He knew, too, that this red-blooded tale of hunting buffalo bulls would catch the interest of the Emperor, who was a lusty sportsman himself, and no doubt would have been glad to participate in such an adventure, for boredom at Court is a part of the awful price usually paid for royal glory—so they say. Coronado adds: "We went without water for many days, and had to cook our food with cow dung"—here the Emperor might hold his fastidious nose—"because there is no other fuel in all

these plains, except along the arroyos, of which there are few."
Jaramillo, much later, told a more cheerful story with respect
to the water supply. Apparently Coronado's memory of hardships, being fresher, was more vivid.

"Thus," says Jaramillo, "on the Feast of San Pedro y San
Pablo," June 29, 1541, "we came to a river which we found
there below Quivira," that is, at a lower latitude, though higher
upstream. They named it in honor of these two saints, and also
called it the River of Quivira. Upon reaching the stream Sopete
recognized it and said it was the one he had been telling about,
and that the Quivira settlements were toward the northeast. This
perhaps explained why no royal barge was in sight—an imposing
show which the Turk had promised. The river was the Arkansas, and was reached by Coronado near the site of the present
town of Ford, Kansas, which got its name, several centuries later,
from the famous crossing there. Reasons for this conclusion as
to the place of transit become evident as the story unfolds.

With quickened pulse Coronado and his men moved to the
north bank of the River of Quivira. They crossed at the ford
previously used by buffaloes and Indians from time immemorial,
and in after years by travelers, pack train traders, and mule-
team freighters on the renowned Santa Fe Trail from Missouri
to Colorado, New Mexico, Chihuahua, Sonora, and California.
First among Europeans to tread the sands of this noble stream
were Coronado and his Chosen Thirty.

At the bend the general swung northeast and followed the
river downstream along its northern bank, which at that season
presented a charming scene of rolling prairies and extravagant
verdure. Here as elsewhere for the last three or four hundred
miles, buffaloes were doubtless seen on every hill. Incidentally,
along this stretch Coronado was for some distance on the route
of the Santa Fe Railway, built nearly three and a half centuries
later, and of present day Highway No. 45. He was now marching from twelve to fifteen miles a day, his pace quickened perhaps by his approach to the Promised Land—promised by that
son of Ananias called the Turk.

Another exciting moment! Three days beyond the ford—

this would be on July 2—they came upon Quivira Indians out
hunting buffalo meat to take to their village, "which was three
or four days farther downstream." These Quivirans were evidently met between the sites of Kinsley and Larned. Some of
the hunters "even had their women with them," to skin the
slaughtered animals, no doubt, and to carry home the products
of the chase, privileges rarely claimed by their lords.

The natives were taken quite by surprise, as one can readily
understand, for Europeans and horses had never visited their
country before, although it is possible, and even probable, that
rumors had reached them of the spectacular doings of the
Spaniards in Pueblo Land. News traveled far among Indians.
Seeing the strange apparition—centaurs with helmets, swords,
and firearms—the Indians began to shout and run away. But
their terror was short-lived, for when Sopete gave chase and
harangued them in his native tongue they understood him, and
thereupon approached the visitors without further signs of fear.
Coronado made camp near by and engaged the Quivirans in
friendly conversation, by signs and through Sopete as interpreter.

"When both Spaniards and Indians had come to a halt, the
general exhibited the Turk," says Jaramillo. Possibly this was
to see if the Quivirans would recognize their fellow-tribesman,
but more likely it was to present him as an example of what
happened to anyone who offended representatives of his Majesty
the King of Spain. Quite in contrast with that of the manacled
Turk, Sopete's home-coming was a personal triumph. "Seeing
the good appearance of the land, and indeed it was charming—
not only this among the cattle but also that farther back and
from here forward, Isopete felt no little satisfaction." And well
he might! His story was being verified, his credit was rising, his
worst enemy was publicly humiliated, Sopete himself was nearing his native land, and he was proudly guiding a distinguished
visitor from a distant country—reasons enough for elation. The
general's hopes were likewise stimulated. Quivira was at hand!

According to the story as it was retold in Spain, Coronado
now sat down beside the trail and solemnly wrote a letter to the

"governor of Harahey and Quivira," evidently regarding him as ruler of both regions and "believing that he was a Christian from the wrecked fleets of Florida." Perhaps some of Narváez's men, unknown to Vaca, had escaped from the Texas hurricane, conquered the interior tribes, and set up a court! "The form of government and society which El Indio had described led us to entertain this opinion," says reliable Jaramillo. That is to say, the Wichita Indians met here might now be subjects of Spaniards! Herrera tells us that in his letter Coronado informed the supposed Europeans of the journey he was making and of the place he had reached; requested "advice and report" of their doings; summoned to him "those Christians if perchance such they were," or that they should tell him what help they needed "to escape from their captivity." Here might be a knightly deed for Coronado to perform. Herrera adds that the letter was sent to the Great Chief by Sopete, "the faithful one of the two Indians." Just where he rejoined the general does not appear, but he was soon again in the picture. Coronado did not know that at this very time, July 2, De Soto was at Pacaha, west of the Mississippi River, where he remained in camp a month, till July 28, but his presence there may have been the basis of the rumor.

The next stage of Coronado's expectant march took him past Pawnee Rock, that imposing landmark which at a later date was notable in the annals of the Santa Fe Trail, past the Great Bend of Arkansas River, and, a short distance farther downstream, to the first of the Quivira villages. The general had abandoned hope of finding great cities—for this he had been prepared by the confession of the Turk and by the testimony of Sopete and Xabe—but there still might be gold or other precious metals. Therefore, says Jaramillo, "the Indians having left for their homes, which were at the distance mentioned"— three or four days' travel from the place where Coronado was now camped (or thirty leagues from the crossing of the Arkansas) —"we proceeded by our regular marches until we reached the settlements. We found them along streams which, although they did not carry much water, were good, had fine banks, and flowed into the larger one I have mentioned," that is to say, into the River of Quivira, now called the Arkansas.

In terms of the modern map, this march of three or four days from the hunters' camp to the settlements was northeastward to Great Bend, then eastward across several tributaries of the Arkansas Rivers, on which the first Quivira villages were situated, in the vicinity of Lyons, Kansas. These small streams are easy to identify. Just west of here are found Cow Creek, Little Cow Creek, and their affluents, all of which flow into the Arkansas. East of Lyons are Long Branch and Jarvis Creek, and a few miles still farther east and north is Little Arkansas River, all likewise tributaries of the Arkansas. Jaramillo's location of the first Quivira villages on these unmistakable streams is borne out by significant archaeological remains in the area, made known by the research of Udden, Jones, Hodge, and Wedel. The general reached these first settlements about July 6, that is, three or four days after leaving the hunters' camp, thirty-five days after starting north from Palo Duro Canyon, and seventy-seven days after setting forth from Tiguex. Of the hubbub which was no doubt caused by the arrival of the strangers the records make no mention, but we may be sure that while mongrel dogs barked, naked children scurried to cover, and from safe retreats inquisitive women peered at the armored Spaniards and their strange mounts, a delegation of headmen in ceremonial array welcomed the visitors with the matchless dignity characteristic of the native American.

What Coronado saw here did not tally with the picture which the Turk while in Tiguex had painted in such glowing terms. The country in its summer verdure was beautiful beyond description, but there were no substantial houses, no signs of wealth of the kind he sought, no crowned ruler waiting to bid him welcome. Instead the general beheld a settlement of scattered round lodges, thatched with grass and emitting smoke from holes in the roofs. From these primitive dwellings there emerged to greet him dark-skinned, tattooed, and nearly naked Wichita Indians, little different in general appearance from the

wandering Querechos and Teyas he had met in the Texas plains
—fine specimens of physical manhood and womanhood, yes, but
of a primitive culture. Sopete's truthfulness now stood out
in bold contrast with the Turk's mendacity.

In this first group of Quivira villages, according to Jaramillo,
there were six or seven settlements some distance apart, and
situated on and between Cow Creek and Little River. The
general wrote to the Emperor that "in this province, of which
my guides are natives, I was peacefully received." The Quivirans
"gave allegiance to your Majesty and placed themselves under
your royal authority." Presumably this was done with the
formality prescribed for such occasions, just as had been the
case in Cíbola and Tiguex. Another "kingdom" was thus
added to the Spanish Empire. Perhaps there were better things
farther on. There were other Quivira settlements to see, and
Coronado had asked for a conference with Tatarrax, whom
the Turk had pictured as a great ruler with a sumptuous Court.
Besides, he must pursue the rumors of Christians in the interior.
So he went forward. Having traveled five or six days and twenty-
five leagues among the villages, he came to another stream
"carrying more water and having a larger population than the
others" just passed. During the twenty-five days spent in Quivira
Coronado saw or heard of twenty-five towns. He had swung
northeastward across Little River, struck the waters of Smoky
Hill River, and reached the vicinity of Lindsborg.

This interpretation of the route through Quivira, on the
basis of documentary evidence, is sustained and clarified by
archaeological testimony, as is admirably set forth by Wedel
of the National Museum, and Jones of Lyons, Kansas. They
describe results of the excavation of Wichita sites along this
route, four miles west of Lyons, northward of there on Little
River, and on Paint Creek, a small stream flowing north into
Smoky Hill River. It is significant that in all these sites fragments of sixteenth-century pottery from the Pueblo region of
New Mexico have been found, showing communication between
these two areas. Moreover, several of the sites have yielded bits
of late fifteenth or early sixteenth century chain mail armor—a

very significant fact. The first of these fragments was unearthed by archaeologist Udden prior to 1890 in a refuse heap on Paint Creek four miles southwest of Lindsborg. Other fragments were found in 1940 by Wedel in Rice County in a cache pit and a nearby refuse heap at the Tobias site on Little Arkansas River, about twenty-five miles west of Paint Creek. Udden's specimen was lost—accidentally thrown away by a house-maid at Lindsborg, it is said, but from a surviving photograph and description it is seen to have been like the relics found in Rice County. The metal rings of the armor in each case averaged about an inch in diameter. Two other early Spanish expeditions are known to have visited Quivira, one in 1593 and another in 1601, but they reached the Arkansas River much farther southeast, in the vicinity of the city of Wichita. The chain mail armor found in the sites between Lyons and Lindsborg, antiquated in Coronado's day, would have been still more outmoded at these later dates. The strong probability is that it was left there by Coronado's men, and Wedel's findings are more significant than his modesty has permitted him to claim.

Here at the terminus of this march, writes Jaramillo, "we came to the end of what they said was the remotest region of Quivira, to which they had taken us, saying it was of much importance," and expressing it by the word *teucárea.* Scholars have long believed that the Quivirans were Wichitas, and now we can be more emphatic in this view. I have recently acquired the significant eyewitness testimony that the last settlement reached by Coronado was called *Tabás,* which is but another spelling of Towásh, or Taováyas, the well-known name of a Wichita group at a later date. Moreover, one suspects that the word which some copyist wrote as *teucárea* (without an accent), is a mistranscription of *taováias*—that is, Taováias, or Towásh. Anyone who will mouth these words with a heavy accent on the main syllable will see that they all are equivalents. A scientist can identify a human being by a drop of his blood. A linguist can do analogous things by phonetics.

In due time arrived the Indian whom Gómara calls Tatarrax,

the well-known title for a Wichita chief. He, too, was disappointing, for he bore little resemblance to the grandiose potentate of whom the Turk had told such impressive tales. "A man already aged," he wore an ornament of copper at his neck, "this being his only wealth." But even so, he was a personality—"a huge Indian with a large body and limbs in proportion." With him came two hundred warriors, armed with bows and arrows. Jaramillo, who was present, says "they wore I do not know what over their heads," in addition to very slender breechclouts round their middles. Another witness tells us this headdress which was beyond Jaramillo's vocabulary was made of feathers. A modern commentator has suggested that the reference may be to the Pawnee custom of roaching the hair, and to that tribe this Indian has been thought to have belonged. But *tatarrax* was a Wichita word for head man, and Tatarrax was doubtless a Quivira chief. On inquiry about copper, such as that hanging from the neck of the giant, Coronado was informed that this metal existed farther on. "Near the pueblo of Arae [Harahey], according to what El Indio [the Turk] told us, there was more of it, judging by the good signs that he made." But as to copper, the Spaniards "found no more signs nor news of it."

Tatarrax was not the only giant seen by the Spaniards in Quivira. Coronado wrote: "The people are large. I had some Indians measured and found they were ten spans tall. The women are comely, with faces more like Moorish than Indian women." Some of their descendants now are handsome and wealthy oil queens in Oklahoma. Ten spans would be six feet and eight inches for the height of the men the general measured! Perhaps to some of the smallest of the Spaniards they looked even taller. At Salina, Kansas, a few miles beyond Lindsborg, there is a museum exhibit consisting of skeletons *in situ* in an ancient burying ground. Some of them are giantesque, but anthropologists have concluded that they are of another culture than that of the Wichitas, which Quivira represented.

The guides told Coronado the plains beyond Tabás soon

came to an end, and it is true that north and east of Lindsborg there is some relatively rough country. They said also that beyond Quivira there was nothing but Arahey (Harahey), which had "the same settlements and size" as Quivira, "except that some of the houses of Arahey were of straw and hides." So the Turk's Harahey, like his Quivira, was very much deflated, and the general decided, for the present at least, not to go to see it. By some scholars Harahey is thought to have been a settlement of Pawnees in Nebraska. The Quivirans informed Coronado of other tribes nearby. They said that "down the river" there were people who did not plant crops but lived by hunting. And they told of Taraque, "whose people had straw houses." Hodge concludes that these Taraques, like the Quivirans, were probably Wichitas, they being the only tribes in that general region who customarily lived in grass lodges. But one inevitably wonders if Taraque is not just another form of the name Harahey.

Now some of my readers will be shocked. The traditional statement that Coronado sent explorers beyond the Quivira settlements is not justified by the fuller records of the expedition which we now possess, hence all conjectures about long marches east or north of Tabás fall to the ground. One author, discussing Coronado's visit to Quivira, writes that after exploring Quivira for twenty-five leagues, he "*sent out captains in many directions*, but they failed to find that of which they went in search." He adds: "There is no reason to suppose that Coronado's party went beyond the limits of the present state of Kansas." As a matter of fact, there is no reason for thinking that any explorers were despatched from Quivira, or that Coronado or his men got beyond Lindsborg. We now know that the phrase italicized above refers to the exploring parties, including those of Tovar, Cárdenas, Alvarado, and others sent out in the Pueblo region before the march to the Texas Panhandle and Quivira.

Light is shed on this subject by unpublished records of an inquiry made in 1544 in the investigation of the management of Coronado's expedition. The questions asked witnesses were obviously modeled on the phrase in Coronado's letter regarding the sending of "captains and men to explore," and they were framed by Coronado's attorney in conference with Don Francisco.

The witnesses were asked whether they knew that Coronado, having reached Cíbola, and finding there no place in which to increase the royal patrimony of his Majesty, sent "captains and men in various directions to seek lands where settlements might be made . . . and these lands having been seen and traversed, and no place suitable for settlement having been found, the governor went five hundred leagues beyond Cíbola to Quivira." In reply to this question the witnesses told of exploring excursions made by Tovar, Cárdenas, Alvarado, Ovando and Mondragón. We know that all of these except Mondragón were sent out to explore in Pueblo Land before Coronado started from Tiguex for Quivira, and by implication that was true also in his case.

The men who testified were Hernando del Valle, Juan Bermejo, Melchior Pérez, Pedro de Ledesma, Pedro de Castro, Juan Ruíz, Juan Galeas, Juan Pastor, Froilán Vermúdez, Gaspár Saldaña, and García Rodríguez. It is noteworthy that of these eleven witnesses all but two (Hernando del Valle and Pedro de Castro) are known to have been among the Chosen Thirty who went with Coronado to Quivira. They told about the expeditions of Tovar, Cárdenas, Alvarado, Ovando, and Mondragón in the Pueblo Region. But not a word was said about explorations beyond Tabás, where the Turk was executed. Their silence is significant. The Quivira excursion being the supreme exploring effort of the whole Coronado expedition, and especially of the Chosen Thirty, it is inconceivable that they should have overlooked what would have been the best evidence of their own bravery and patriotism, their ultimate effort. Moreover, it is explicitly stated in the testimony of the witnesses named, that all the excursions listed were made *before starting for Quivira,* whither Coronado went because "the explorers sent out" had found no suitable place for settlement. So we must conclude that in Quivira no exploring parties were detached from the main body of the Chosen Thirty, because, as they testified, they "had not dared" to go any farther inland.

It must be remembered in this connection that in Quivira Coronado had only thirty-odd men, and that he knew the Turk was urging his people to destroy the Spaniards. It is doubtful whether the general could have spared any of his force for excursions, and whether small bands of explorers would have been safe under the circumstances. Indeed, Castañeda specifically tells us that Coronado "had not dared" to go farther inland, "because it was densely populated and he did not feel strong enough."

Although the Spaniards did not find in Quivira the things of which the Turk had boasted, and were sorely disappointed in consequence, they recognized the fertility and beauty of the country, and revealed their nostalgia by pointing out its resemblances, real or imagined, to beloved Old Spain. Next to the Turk, who as salesman has seldom been outclassed, Jaramillo deserves to be regarded as the original "booster" of Kansas, for he among these first Europeans was loudest in its praise. A yearly Jaramillo Festival in the Sunflower State would be highly appropriate, but to insure its correct pronunciation perhaps his name should be spelled with an initial *H*. "This country has a fine appearance," he writes, "the like of which I have never seen anywhere in our Spain, in Italy, or in any part of France where I have traveled in the service of his Majesty." Our chronicler was a cosmopolite, and wrote from wide experience. "It is not a hilly country, but has table-lands, plains, and charming rivers with fine waters. It greatly pleased me, and I am of the belief that it will be very productive of all sorts of commodities." His prediction was entirely sound, though its verification was long delayed. "As for the cattle"—which by now were commonplace to Coronado's men, who of all Europeans in the world had ever seen these immense herds of the American bison—"we have proof that vast numbers exist there, as many as anyone could imagine."

And there were other assets. "We found plums, of a variety

not exactly red, but shading off from reddish to green. **The** tree and its fruit are surely Castilian, the plums being of excellent flavor. In the cattle country we found a sort of flax growing wild in small clusters some distance apart. Since the cattle do not eat it, there it remains, with little heads of blue flowers. Although small, it is excellent. . . . Along some of the creeks there are grapes of fairly good flavor, considering the fact that they are not cultivated. The houses of the Indians are of grass, differing in size and shape. Most of them are round, the grass hanging to the ground like a wall. Annexed on the outside they had a sort of chapel or sentry-box, with a doorway where the Indians were seen either seated or lying down." Castañeda said these arbors resembled "barbacoas, under the roofs of which the inhabitants sleep and keep their belongings." The Wichitas continued to live in the same sort of grass lodges down to modern times.

Another member of Coronado's party was less eulogistic. "At Quivira there is a bestial people without any order in their dwellings or anything else. The houses are of straw like Tarascan huts, in some towns there being as many as two hundred clustered together. The natives have maize, beans, and calabashes, but they do not have cotton or turkeys, nor do they bake bread on griddles, but under ashes." But with all its drawbacks, —even its lack of griddles—the same witness put the country ahead of the Pueblo country. "Quivira is a better land, with more savannas and not so cold, although it is farther north." But he had never wintered in Kansas, or swallowed one of its blizzards.

Coronado had been in Quivira nearly a month, and it was time to think of returning to Tiguex. Nothing he had heard about Harahey or any other region justified going farther at this time, or with so small a force. The three divisions of his expedition were hundreds of miles apart, in Sonora, Tiguex, and Quivira, and all were many other hundreds of miles from their base in central Mexico. For thirty men, poorly provisioned, to remain alone in a land of giants would be hazardous and foolhardy. And these men from the semi-tropical South imagined that winter in the latitude of Quivira would be early and Arctic. Moreover, the Quivirans had manifested a growing hostility.

So Don Francisco held a council of war to consider the situation. It was convened at his northernmost camp on the border of the province, at the village of Tabás, near Lindsborg on Smoky Hill River. The decision was reached in the usual democratic way. "Taking note of the opinions of various persons," says Jaramillo, "the general asked them what we ought to do, remembering that we had left the army behind and we were here." The answer was unanimous and wholly sound. "It seemed to everybody that, since it was almost the beginning of winter, for if I remember correctly it was past the middle of August [it was in fact early in August]; and since there were so few of us to establish winter quarters there; and because of the scantiness of our provisions . . . and in order that winter might not obstruct the roads with snow and make the rivers impassable; moreover, not knowing the circumstances of the people left behind"—that is to say, the army sent from the Barrancas back to Tiguex under Arellano—"we unanimously decided that his Lordship ought to turn back in search of them . . . learn of their situation, spend the winter there, and at the beginning of summer return to that land to explore and cultivate it." Castañeda adds that Coronado would have gone farther inland to explore, but "had not dared. . . ." So "he turned back, with the intention of leading his men there after the rainy season."

Coronado still had the Turk to deal with. In Quivira this rascal had found himself in a most unpleasant predicament. His plans had not worked out according to program, and he had a grievance that burned deep down in his soul. The general, when he marched northeast along the Arkansas River, had prepared for a ceremonious meeting with King Tatarrax—another Montezuma perhaps. The wealth of Quivira might yet materialize, in which case the Turk would be restored to favor as a true prophet. But El Turco knew better. He knew that the real wealth of Quivira—endless green pastures and countless buffaloes, which made the Kansas prairies indeed an Indian paradise—was not what the Spaniards were looking for; and he knew that his lies would soon overtake him. So he turned for rescue to his own people and plotted to induce them to drive the Spaniards from the land or even to exterminate them. He would incite the Quivirans to starve out the strangers, or to slaughter their horses, which would be just as effective, for thirty men on foot would be easy marks for myriad Quivira arrows and war clubs.

The Turk was kept in chains and as much as possible out of sight. Alvarado, his original captor, was still his custodian, and at night he kept the prisoner at his own tent. Meanwhile Sopete remained a partisan of the Spaniards and did all he could to humiliate the Turk, whom he hated. So, handicapped though he was, El Turco had no sooner reached the Quivira settlements than he began to carry out his plan. One day when the Spaniards were at the very first village near Cow Creek, the Turk, pointing to Alvarado's big horse, said to some of the natives, *"Tit-ley*—Kill him." This was a gesture of ominous import.

As Coronado proceeded northeast across Quivira, new rumors of the Turk's machinations reached the ears of the Spaniards, chiefly through Sopete. In proportion as prospects for the promised gold declined, Spanish ill feeling against El Turco increased, and tales of his intrigues multiplied. Diego López, his tentmate Juan de Zaldívar, and Gómez Suárez, several times urged Coronado to execute the tricky Quiviran. But Coronado demurred. "What honor would be gained by killing the Indian?" he asked. For the general was far from bloodthirsty or vengeful—really a gentleman conqueror if there was one—and he still nursed a stubborn hope that El Turco might possess valuable information, which he could not impart if he were dead.

Such tenderness for the Turk, after all his guile, caused impatience among the soldiers. Gaspár de Saldaña declared that "what most irritated all the Spaniards was the great partiality shown by the general for El Turco; indeed, if it had not been for this the comrades would have killed the Indian long before this, for there was a refrain among the Christians"—perhaps in unprintable rhyme—"which said that the general was sustaining the Turk." Sopete, chief tale-bearer, kept the Spaniards informed of El Turco's intrigues, reporting them to Troyano and certain others, "who knew how to speak some in the Turk's language and he in Mexican." We know that in the course of the expedition Troyano had acquired an Indian consort; and though it is not known just where Don Juan found this American belle, it is possible that she helped out as an interpreter in Quivira.

Things came to a head at Tabás, the last Quivira village visited in the north. Here the shortage of maize was serious. When Coronado inquired why the natives did not supply him as they previously had done, he was told that the Turk had urged the Quivirans not to give him any more, saying that without it the horses would soon die, leaving the Spaniards helpless; for, since the strangers were so few, once the mounts were dead the massacre of their riders would be easy. He urged them especially to keep an eye on certain of the best horses, such as Alvarado's powerful mount, and kill them first.

Coronado at last yielded and ordered López to investigate the new charges against the Turk. If they should be verified he was to execute the prisoner, first explaining to him the reason why. López made the inquiry and the Turk confessed, at the same time implicating the pueblo of Pecos in the plot. The secret now came out! They asked him why he had lied to them and misguided them so perversely. He replied that when Coronado was on his way to Quivira the people of Cicúique, or Pecos, who also had a deep-seated grievance, urged him to take the Spaniards out on the plains and lead them astray. Then, through lack of provisions, their horses would die and the Spaniards would become so weak that on their return the Pecos pueblo could easily dispose of them, and so obtain revenge for what the Spaniards had done to them. This, said the Turk, was the reason why he had misled them, "believing they would not

know how to hunt nor be able to survive without maize."
Bigotes, war chief of Pecos, had not forgotten his handcuffs, his
long imprisonment at Alcanfor, or the wounds inflicted upon
his body and his spirit by the dogs of the Spaniards, a base return for all he had done for them! Here was Bigotes' chance to
get even!

The confession of the Turk was promptly followed by his
execution, regarding which we now have intimate details formerly lacking. We know who did it and how it was done. One
afternoon at Tabás the prisoner was removed from the tent of
Alvarado and taken to the one shared by López and Zaldívar.
That night Coronado called his head groom from his customary
place at the door of the general's tent. When Contreras responded, rubbing his eyes, Coronado told him to go and tell
López and Zaldívar that if they thought it was a propitious hour
to execute the Turk they should proceed with the unpleasant
business; but it must be done with great secrecy, so there would
be no outcry, and that it would not be known in the camp. Contreras carried the message, and he tells us what he saw. "And so
this witness went to the tent of the persons named and reported
what Coronado had ordered him to tell them. And he saw that
they took the Indian called El Turco from the place where he
was imprisoned, and told him that since he had lied to them
and led them astray," his doom was sealed; "and they asked
him the whereabouts of the gold and the wealth of which he
had told them in Tiguex."

The Turk grasped at this last straw. He might save his
neck after all. With his usual ingenuity he replied "that the
town having gold and other riches was farther on, and that he
had led the Spaniards by way of Quivira merely to get his wife,
who was there, in order to take her along." *Mas allá!* This explanation might once have worked, but no longer. López had
heard enough lies from the Turk, and "without waiting for
any more talk" he proceeded with the execution. "A soldier
named Pérez," none other than Don Melchior Pérez, the governor's son, who had been with Alvarado on **his boisterous excur-**

sion to the Buffalo Plains, "by order of Diego López and Juan de Zaldívar, from behind put a rope around the Turk's neck, twisted it with a garrote, and choked him to death." Several witnesses at a later time declared that the garrote was turned by Francisco Martín, the butcher from Mexico City. Perhaps the honors were divided, Pérez adjusting the rope around the Turk's swarthy neck and Martín twisting the stick. Contreras added that they buried El Turco near the tent of López and Zaldívar, "and when this witness departed," after delivering Coronado's message, "the sepulchre was already dug." So far as we know, the Turk bore no mark that might be recognizable by some future archaeologist—but *quién sabe?* Archaeologists perform remarkable feats. The Turk might have had some telltale pocket-piece.

Coronado was much grieved by the execution of the Turk, for he had repeatedly opposed those who said he ought to be killed. Sopete, on the other hand, was gleeful, "because the Turk had always said that he was a scoundrel who didn't know what he was talking about." The junior guide by his talebearing had more than evened up scores. But we must not forget the Turk's side of the story. He had experienced rough sledding.

The drama of the approach of two rival conquerors toward each other from opposite directions is now evident. Just fifteen days after Coronado left Tiguex on April 23, 1541, bound for Quivira, De Soto reached the Mississippi River, as we have seen. While Coronado was marching down Canadian River to the Texas Panhandle, De Soto was building his fleet of barges and in them crossing the Mississippi River into Arkansas. As Don Francisco moved north from the Barranca Grande with the Chosen Thirty, Don Hernando traveled upstream, and reached Pacaha in northeastern Arkansas on June 29, the very day when Coronado arrived at the Ford of the Arkansas River. A few days later, when Coronado despatched a letter northeastward to whomsoever it might concern—the Spaniards of whom he had heard rumors—De Soto's men from the Pacaha base were seeking Coluça in northern Arkansas. The two expeditions were nearest together when Coronado was at Tabás and De Soto at Coluça. They were then less than three hundred miles apart air line; thereafter the distance between them increased. De Soto now traveled south to the mouth of Arkansas River, ascended that stream to the vicinity of Little Rock, thence went west to Tula, near Caddo Gap, and then to winter quarters on the Ouachita River in southern Arkansas. There is no evidence that either Coronado or De Soto had specific knowledge of the movements of the other.

Chapter XXVI

REUNION IN PUEBLO LAND

Having summarily disposed of the Turk, with what degree of justice or injustice will always be a matter of varied opinion, Coronado hastened from the land he had found so disappointing. He feared revenge for the execution of the luckless Indian, which could not long be kept a secret; and with only thirty men he could not afford to risk an attack by the huge Quivirans. Moreover, from the Turk's confession he had learned of the plot of Pecos to destroy the Spaniards in Pueblo Land, and this might already have happened to the army led by Arellano!

So the Chosen Thirty by common consent turned their faces toward Tiguex, leaving behind them their dispelled delusions, their deflated hopes and an undying tradition in Kansas. "In view of the agreement we had reached," says Jaramillo, "we marched back—I do not know whether it was two days or three, to a place where we obtained a supply of . . . green and dried maize for our return." Here a cross was erected, "at the foot of which some letters were cut with a chisel saying that Francisco Vázquez de Coronado, general of the army, had reached this place." Fray Juan Padilla was with Coronado, and we may assume that he blessed the standard. Presumably it was made of wood, and was displayed in some conspicuous place along the trail. Since the carving was done with a chisel, and was at the foot of the cross, one infers that it was cut in rock on which the Christian symbol stood, although this is not certain. Presumably, also, the village where the monument was erected had a considerable population, since it was here that Coronado obtained his supply of maize for the homeward march. This being the case, the site of the settlement should be well marked by archaeological remains. In all likelihood Coronado was travel-

ing pretty fast these days and was near the southwestern Quivira villages when he stopped to get provisions. From all the
known data it seems probable that the historic cross was erected
at the village on Cow Creek near Lyons, Kansas, where Coronado had been welcomed by the Wichitas before he turned
north from Arkansas River on his way to Tabás. The "Quivira
Stone," reported a few years ago and thought by some persons
to be the one carved at the foot of the cross, looks like a clumsy
fraud. Moreover, it is said to have been found in northeastern
Kansas, perhaps a hundred miles or more beyond any point
reached by Coronado. Of course, it might have been carried
there from its original site, but we have no reason to assume
that such was the case.

At the place where the cross was raised, Sopete, "the faithful guide," requested that he be permitted to remain, as had
been promised him. This may have been his native village.
Coronado kept his word, and because it was Sopete who had
disclosed the Turk's plot, he was rewarded by a good present,
with which he was greatly pleased. Here again imagination
roams. "And he offered to serve on other occasions whenever it
might be asked of him," especially when Coronado should return the next summer—if he came.

Now, with six Quivira Indians "to guide him to the flat-
roofed houses" of Pecos, the general said a final good-bye and
went on his way. Gómara remarks, "the fraud of these riches
thus exposed to the Spaniards, they returned to Tiguex without
seeing any cross or trace of Christianity." In other words, they
saw nothing of the shipwrecked Christians of whom they had
heard on the way northeast.

It was about the middle of August, 1541, when Coronado
and the Chosen Thirty, guided by the young Quivirans, set out
from the site of the cross to rejoin the army. "Thus," says Jaramillo, "they took us back over the same route by which we had
come as far as . . . the river of San Pedro y San Pablo," on the
march to Quivira—that is, to the crossing at the bend of the Arkansas near the present town of Ford, Kansas. It is this point
from which writers have drawn a line two degrees east of south

by which to locate the Barrancas, on the basis of a wrong guess as to the declination of the compass needle, by which Coronado had traveled from Palo Duro Canyon to the historic ford.

On the next stretch of the return march Coronado broke a new trail for which he will long be remembered. "Here," continues Jaramillo, "they abandoned our previous route"—the northward march on the way to Quivira—"and, taking off to the right, they led us by watering places, among the cattle, and over good road," through the Oklahoma and Texas Panhandles, "although there is no good road anywhere unless it be the paths of the cattle. *Finally we arrived at and recognized the place where, as I said at the beginning, we found the ranchería where the Turk led us away from the route we ought to have followed.*"

The words of Jaramillo italicized above are priceless. They are the key not only to the problem of Coronado's return route from the crossing of Arkansas River, but likewise to that of his march from Tiguex to the plains and to the Barrancas. The ranchería mentioned was the second Querecho village seen by Coronado on his journey to Quivira, and was situated on the Canadian River near the Texas-New Mexico boundary. Modern map names are here used for purposes of identification. This ranchería was the place where the Turk had urged Alvarado to turn northeast to Quivira, at the time when he told Don Hernando about the golden bracelet. It was the place where, next year, puzzled Coronado on his eastward march was led by the Turk away from the direct route to Quivira and became lost on the plains. And it was the place where Coronado now arrived at the Canadian River on his return from Quivira. It was a pivotal point in all three of the journeys east of Pecos River. We have therefore established the two ends of Coronado's return route from the Arkansas River to the Canadian River, one at the bend of the Arkansas River near Ford, and the other on the Canadian River just west of the Texas-New Mexico line. The trail is approximated now by the Chicago, Rock Island, and El Paso Railway, for whose survey Coronado's heirs might claim payment—a suggestion which might here be omitted for a suitable consideration.

On this return march Coronado raised the curtain of history for a score or more present day towns and cities. Leaving the Arkansas River at Ford, in Kansas he passed through or near the sites of Bloom, Minneola, Fowler, Plains, Kismet and Liberal; in the Oklahoma Panhandle, Tyrone, Hooker, Optima, Guymon and Goodwell can claim him as their discoverer; in the Texas Panhandle he passed the sites of Texhoma, Stratford, Conlen, Dalhart, Middlewater and Romero. Crossing the line, in New Mexico he brought into history the sites of Nara-Visa, Obar, and Logan, on the north bank of Canadian River, opposite the place where the Turk first led him astray on his march to Quivira. For some distance after leaving the Arkansas River Coronado's return route was not far west of his northward line of march to the same stream.

"Thus," says Jaramillo, "omitting further details, we arrived at Tiguex." The presumption is that from the Querecho village Coronado traveled by his former road, in reverse, to the bridge at Pecos River and thence upstream to Pecos village. As he neared Bigotes' home town he was, of course, on the *qui vive*, for the Turk in his confession at Tabás had told him of the hostility of that pueblo, of its connivance with the Turk to lead the Spaniards astray on the Llano Estacado, and of Pecos to slaughter them if they should return.

It has been customary for writers to say that from the ford of the Arkansas River Coronado returned to Tiguex by what in later years became known as the Cimarron Trail to Santa Fe, which cut across a corner of Colorado, but this is manifestly incorrect. The Cimarron Trail of bullwhacking days was altogether distinct from and well north of Coronado's return route as described above. It left the Arkansas at the famous crossing near Ford, or sometimes near the site of Dodge City a little farther west, ran west-southwest across a corner of Colorado to Upper Cimarron Spring, near the northwestern corner of the Oklahoma Panhandle, and did not enter the Texas Panhandle, through which Coronado traveled fully half the length

of his cut-off. In fact, Coronado's route after leaving the ford of
Arkansas River did not touch the Cimarron Trail until he
reached the site of later-founded San Miguel, a few miles down
Pecos River below the town of Pecos. Thus, the two routes,
starting from the Arkansas River near the same point, constantly diverged, until, at the western edge of the Oklahoma and
Texas Panhandles, they were not less than a hundred miles
apart. In other words they were entirely separate for more
than three hundred miles. A corollary to this conclusion is
that Coronado did not touch the soil of Colorado. For upsetting
a fondly nursed tradition in that beautiful State one can only
say "I'm sorry!"

The *Relación del Suceso* gives an interesting estimate of the
saving of distance by this Querecho cut-off on the way back
from Quivira. "We returned by a more direct route, for on the
way out we traveled three hundred and thirty leagues," or some
eight hundred and fifty miles, "whereas on the way back we
covered not more than two hundred leagues," or some five hundred and twenty miles. The difference of one hundred and
thirty leagues, or about three hundred and forty miles of hard
travel, is what the Turk's lies had cost Coronado and his men
when they went to Quivira. El Indio's unpopularity when his
deceit was discovered is not difficult to understand, for the
travelers measured this extra distance in terms of aching muscles, hunger, blistered feet, and saddle galls. But, if he had not
played the trick we should lack the drama of the Llano Estacado,
the Barrancas, the march north by the needle, and the return
of the army by way of the chain of marvelous salt lakes. With
out the villain, the play would lack much of its flavor.

While Coronado and the Chosen Thirty were experiencing
new adventures and meeting disappointment in Quivira, Arellano, having reached Tiguex before the middle of July, made
preparations to care for the army during the coming winter. He
set about gathering supplies, for it was now the harvest season.
To this end he sent Captain Velasco de Barrionuevo, who had
served as his maestre de campo on the journey from Compostela,

on a tour among the northern pueblos. Don Velasco was "a caballero from Granada," and was one of those who went on the expedition under the banner of the general, "as befitted distinguished persons." He seems to have been a competent man, and he left his mark on the history of the pueblo region.

Barrionuevo visited the province of Xémez, in the valley of that name, then consisting of seven pueblos. The inhabitants, in keeping with their previous relations with the Spaniards, came out peacefully and furnished provisions. Presumably at this time they returned the cannons left by Coronado in their custody. From Xémez Don Velasco ascended the Rio Grande to Yuque-Yunque. While the soldiers were establishing camp the natives fled, abandoning two beautiful pueblos on opposite sides of the river, and took refuge in the sierra, where they had four strong towns that could not be reached by the horses because of the rough terrain. In them the Spaniards, going on foot, found abundant provisions and glazed pottery "of many decorations and shapes." The soldiers found also *ollas* or jars filled with a shiny metal used by the Indians in glazing their pottery. This, says Castañeda, "was an indication that silver mines would be found in that region if they were sought." Half a century later Yuque-Yunque was a Tewa pueblo on the site of present Chamita, where the Chama River joins the Rio Grande, and perhaps was in the same place when visited by Barrionuevo. Apparently Castañeda's prediction about silver deposits there has never been verified on any grand scale.

Twenty leagues farther upstream Barrionuevo visited the large pueblo of Brava which Alvarado had discovered, and of which we get an interesting account by Castañeda, who perhaps was in Barrionuevo's party, since he did not go to Quivira. The Spaniards now dubbed the place Valladolid, in honor of the famous city in Spain. A small stream flowed through the middle of the town and was spanned by wooden bridges made of square pine timbers. Braba, the famous pueblo now called Taos, still consists of two towns close together, on opposite sides of the creek. Alvarado, it will be remembered, described only one of them. Taos today—now a mecca for tourists and artists—does not occupy exactly the same site as in Barrionuevo's time, but conditions are similar, since the pueblos are still separated by the stream. The ruins of the two house groups of Coronado's day lie a few hundred yards west of the present North and South towns. It has been suggested that the name Braba came from the Spanish word *brava*, meaning brave or fearless; or possibly from "the pueblo's abrupt scenic background." A simpler and perhaps equally accurate if less romantic explanation would be that Braba in the mouth of an Indian was what the name Taos sounded like to Spanish ears. From here Barrionuevo returned downstream to Alcanfor, "leaving all those provinces at peace," and glad to see his back!

Another captain, whose name does not appear, but who may have been Mondragón, for he is known to have made an expedition among pueblos not otherwise accounted for, was sent by Arellano down the Rio Grande in search of settlements which the people of Tutahaco said were a few days' journey from there. Passing pueblos on the way, he reached a place where the river disappeared under ground, "like the Guadiana in Extremadura," making him homesick. This phenomenon of nature was on the later celebrated Jornado del Muerto, now covered by the waters imprisoned by Elephant Butte Dam in the vicinity of Hot Springs, New Mexico. He did not continue to where the Indians said it reappeared as a large stream, because his commission was limited to eighty leagues. Thus Barrionuevo and this "other captain," perhaps Mondragón, while awaiting Coronado, had visited most of the pueblos on the Rio Grande between Taos and El Paso—no small feat of exploration!

When Arellano thought it was nearly time for Coronado to arrive from Quivira, he left Barrionuevo in command at Tiguex and accompanied by forty men went east to meet the general. With him went Xabe, the young Quivira guide who had returned from the Barrancas with the army. When Don Tristán reached Cicúique the inhabitants sallied forth to fight, in keeping with the plot of Bigotes and the Turk when Coronado started for Quivira. The captain accepted the challenge, and in the skirmish that followed two prominent Indians were killed.

The natives now withdrew and refused to come out in the open, so Arellano fired a few shots into the pueblo, killing some more of the Indians. In this way four days were spent. We are not told whether Bigotes and Cacique were among the slain, but presumably they were not, for the death of men so prominent as they would almost certainly have been mentioned, an inference from which we may obtain satisfaction, for these men were real heroes. They deserve a memorial in the land they so patriotically served.

In the meantime news came that Coronado was approaching, so, to prevent an attack on the general's small company of some forty men, Arellano waited for him at Cicúique. Coronado soon arrived and was welcomed with great rejoicing by the Spaniards and even more by young Xabe. When he heard that Don Francisco was approaching he exclaimed: "Now that the general is returning you will see that there *is* gold and silver in Quivira, although not as much as the Turk pretended." When Coronado arrived and Xabe learned that nothing of value had been found, he was sad and dejected, but he still maintained there was gold and silver in the land of the Turk. Castañeda adds that, since Coronado had not gone beyond Quivira, Xabe made many persons believe that if he had gone a little farther he would have found gold—as El Turco in his last moments had declared. Perhaps like the Turk, Xabe wanted to escape from his enslavement and go home. After a brief stop at Cicúique Coronado went on his way, "leaving the pueblo much more calm, for now the people came out readily to talk with the general in a friendly way." The Turk's plan for the massacre of the Spaniards on their return had failed.

Arriving at Tiguex near the middle of September, Coronado set about establishing quarters for another cold and uncomfortable winter there. Like Xabe, when they heard the news, the men of the army "were not satisfied to think there was no gold" in Quivira. "On the contrary, they were of the belief that it was to be found farther inland, because the people had a name for it, calling it *acochis*." Assuming an air of optimism as a means of sustaining the morale of his men during the long winter they now faced, Coronado said he had reports of large settlements and mighty rivers beyond Quivira, and promised to return thither in the spring with his whole army, by the short route he had discovered, of course. The men needed some ray of hope after more than a year and a half of hardship and disappointment. But surely Don Francisco had seen and heard in Quivira nothing to justify any expectation of a harvest of ready-to-hand wealth either there or beyond.

Coronado was in fact disillusioned and disheartened. He had gambled and lost. For the Cíbola enterprise others than himself had been chiefly responsible. The Seven Cities had proved to be anything but golden, but for this Coronado could not be blamed. He had been sent by the viceroy to conquer them, and they were what nature and the natives had made them. The Tiguex War had been distressing to the general, but it was not of his seeking. The destruction of Arenal was tragic, but it was an incident in rebellion and war, and such matters cannot always be controlled. Battles are seldom fought by Marquis of Queensberry rules.

The Quivira expedition was a different matter. The final responsibility for making the hard march to that far-distant land was Coronado's own, although it was in keeping with the spirit of his instructions and the wishes of the men in his army. In the adventure he had been misled—duped if one wishes so to call it. He had listened to the Turk, whose mendacity has made him remembered through four centuries. By this unsurpassed liar Coronado had been induced to travel nearly two thousand painful miles from Cíbola, only to learn that the gold of Quivira was a pure fabrication, and from the standpoint of its immediate objectives the expedition was a wild goose chase. On the other hand, if, after hearing all the Turk's seductive tales Coronado had declined to go to Quivira, his men would have made a resounding protest, perhaps even to the point of mutiny, and he would scarcely have dared to show his face again in Mexico. This was a day of El Dorados, and it was a part of Coronado's business to seek the new one so glowingly advertised by the Turk.

Now it was the general's unpleasant duty to report the Quivira expedition to his superiors, so he sat down and reviewed the whole story in a letter to Charles V and in another to Viceroy Mendoza. The despatch to the Emperor was penned at Alcanfor on October 20, 1541, a month or more after Coronado's return to Tiguex. Written modestly and simply, it gives us insight into the qualities of the man who wrote it. Not confining himself to the Quivira venture, he summarized in general the results of his whole enterprise to date. He recalled the stories told by the Turk which had caused him to go to Quivira, recounted his march to the plains, told of the vast buffalo herds, the Querechos, their dog trains, his wandering astray misled by the Turk, the march of the Chosen Thirty to Quivira, what he saw and did there, the Turk's confession, and the return to Tiguex by a shorter route.

The new El Dorado was not what the Turk had represented it to be. Coronado wrote: "After traveling seventy-seven days over these barren lands, our Lord willed that I should arrive in the province called Quivira, to which the guides were taking me. They had pictured it as having stone houses many storeys high; not only are there none of stone, but, on the contrary, they are of grass, and the people are savage like all I have seen and passed up to that place. They have no woven fabrics, nor cotton with which to make them. All they have is the tanned skins of the cattle they kill, for the herds are near the place where they live, at a fair-sized river. They eat raw meat like the Querechos and Teyas. They are enemies of one another, but all are of the same type, except that the people of Quivira are superior to these others in their houses and in the growing of maize. In that province, of which my guides are natives, I was peacefully received.

"Although when I set out" for Quivira "I was told I could not see it all in two months, in it there are not more than twenty-five towns, with grass houses, nor any others in all the rest of the country I have seen and learned about." Apparently he now took no stock in the Turk's tales of Harahey. "They gave allegiance to your Majesty and placed themselves under your authority. . . . The natives gave me a piece of copper which an Indian chief wore suspended from his neck"—this of course was Tatarrax. "I am sending it to the viceroy of New Spain, for I have not seen any other metal . . . except this and some copper bells which I am forwarding to him. I am sending also a small amount of metal which resembles gold, but I could not find out where it was obtained, although I believe the Indians who gave it to me got it from the servants who accompanied me, for I cannot otherwise account for its presence or its origin." In other words, it had been brought with the expedition from Mexico.

"Withal, after visiting the land of Quivira, and obtaining the informaton regarding the region farther on, [Harahey] mentioned above, I returned to this province to look after the people I had sent back here, and to give your Majesty a report of the nature of the land, as I informed you I would do as soon as I had seen it. I have done everything within my power to serve you, as your faithful servant and vassal, and to discover some country where God our Lord might be served by extending your royal patrimony."

Before closing, Coronado reviewed the Cíbola expedition as a whole to date, his efforts, difficulties, and the general results. He emphasized especially the exploring parties which he had sent out at various times, before going to Quivira, in an effort to follow up every clue and discover a region of wealth. "As I have been obliged to send captains and men to many places in this country"—the whole of Pueblo Land—"to find out whether there was anything by which your Majesty might be served, the diversity of languages spoken in this region and the lack of people who understand them has been a great handicap to me, since the natives in each pueblo speak their own. And although we have searched with all diligence we have not found nor heard of any pueblos except those in these provinces," of Cíbola and Tiguex, "which do not amount to very much."

"From the moment I arrived in the province of Cíbola, where the viceroy of New Spain had sent me in the name of your Majesty, I began to explore this region for two hundred leagues and more around and beyond Cíbola, since nothing of what Fray Marcos had reported was found there. The best country I have discovered is this Tiguex River and the settlements where I am now camping. But they are not suitable for colonizing, for, besides being four hundred leagues from the North Sea and more than two hundred from the South Sea, thus prohibiting all intercourse, the land is so cold, as I have informed your Majesty, that it seems impossible for anyone to spend the winter here, since there is no firewood, nor any clothing with which the men may keep themselves warm, except the skins which the natives wear, and some cotton mantas, few in number." Where he was writing the elevation is more than five thousand feet.

"I am sending to the viceroy of New Spain a report of everything I have seen in the lands I have traversed. And, since, Don García López de Cárdenas, after working diligently and serving your Majesty well in this expedition, is leaving to kiss your hands, he will inform you of everything here, as a man who has seen it, and I leave the matter in his hands." That is, Cárdenas was planning to see Charles V in person.

"May our Lord protect the sacred Cæsarean Catholic person of your Majesty, increasing your kingdoms and dominions, as we, your faithful servants and vassals, desire. From this province of Tiguex, October 20, 1541.

"Your Majesty's humble servant and vassal, who kisses your royal feet and hands.

FRANCISCO VÁZQUEZ DE CORONADO
Sacred Cæsarean Catholic Majesty."

Coronado's report was modest, accurate, and straightforward, and his discouragement is not difficult to understand. Moreover, neither Cortés nor Pizarro could have done more than he had accomplished.

Chapter XXVII

REBELLION IN SONORA

Soon after Coronado reached Tiguex on his return from Quivira in the fall of 1541, Captain Pedro Tovar arrived there from Sonora, whither he had been sent to quiet disturbances at San Gerónimo, bring back part of the soldiers stationed there, and with them follow the general to Quivira. In April and May, while Coronado and the army had moved out upon the Buffalo Plains, Tovar had retraced the already familiar trail through Ácoma, Cíbola, the Great Forest, Chichilticale, up Rio San Pedro, thence to San Gerónimo II, in Sonora Valley. Here he found affairs in a sad state, for Alcaráz once more had proved himself unfit to rule. The alienated natives of the province killed a soldier with a poisoned arrow. When Alcaráz sent a squad of men to look into the matter they were resisted by the Indians. Thereupon Tovar sent Alcaráz with a small force to apprehend the leading men of a rebellious town at Valle de los Vellacos—Valley of the Rogues. He arrested the chief men of the place, and then released them on condition that they should furnish clothing and other things needed by the garrison. This was a fatal mistake, for as soon as the chiefs were liberated they renewed hostilities with increased vigor. Alcaráz attacked the Indians, but as they were fortified and used poisoned arrows they put the Spaniards to rout and killed a number of them as they were fleeing for safety. If the soldiers had not been aided by Indian allies they would have fared still worse. When they reached the protection of the stockade at San Gerónimo they had left behind seventeen men, dead from the poisoned arrows of the Sonorans. From very small wounds they died in terrible agony, their flesh rotting with a foul stench.

Realizing that the garrison would no longer be safe in

Sonora Valley, especially since some of the men were to be taken to reinforce Coronado, Tovar moved the post northward and upstream forty leagues—perhaps a hundred miles—to Valle de Suya. This new settlement, for convenience, Sauer has called San Gerónimo III. The site apparently was about at present-day Bacuachi.

Taking half of the soldiers from San Gerónimo, Tovar now set out for Tiguex to follow Coronado to Quivira, whither he would be guided, as he supposed, by the crosses the general had promised to erect as roadsigns on the way. We are told that "because he needed good men with whom to follow the general to the land of the Indian called the Turk, he did not take the rebellious or troublesome ones, but chose the most trustworthy men he could find." This was not the highest praise, for Arellano on his way to Cíbola already had sifted the human grain at San Gerónimo, and now Tovar repeated the process, still further lowering the level of the soldiery left behind in that ill-fated garrison. The Sonora Valley base for the support of Coronado was henceforth on the defensive and far from secure.

But Tovar and his men were now bound for Quivira to join Coronado, with their backs to rebellious Sonora and its poisonous plant. As they traveled north and east those autumn days, they probably sat erect in their saddles and urged their mounts forward, talking of the bags of gold they would have when they reached Quivira, and telling how they would spend it in Mexico or old Spain. What a dash they would cut! As Castañeda put it, they went "with their noses in the air, thinking they would find the general in the rich country of the Turk." Learning when they arrived at Tiguex that Coronado had already returned with unfavorable reports of Quivira their disappointment knew no bounds. But when the general told them he had plans for going again in the spring to the Land of El Turco, they "consoled themselves with the hope of the journey they were to make, and lived . . . in anticipation . . . that the departure of the army for Quivira would be soon"— such optimists are gold-seekers of every variety in every land and every clime. They get their pay in advance, which, after all, is not bad business.

Tovar carried to Tiguex important despatches from Mexico City, which some unnamed courier had brought to Sonora Valley over the long, difficult, and now very dangerous trail. Some of the communications were from Viceroy Mendoza, and others from private individuals. We may assume that there were letters for Coronado from Doña Beatríz, and for many of the soldiers from wives, friends, or sweethearts. By one of the letters Captain Cárdenas was notified of the death of his oldest brother and was called to Spain to take possession of a large inheritance there. With the summons came the viceroy's permission to respond to the call. Since Cárdenas was badly crippled by his broken arm, and thus incapacitated for military service, he decided to go to the old homeland, and with that intent he set out at once for Mexico, taking with him ten or twelve others who were returning for various reasons. From a military standpoint their depatrure was no loss, "there being not one among them who was able to fight." On the other hand, their withdrawal would be a relief for the commissary department. Many more would have been glad to go, but very humanly they refrained from doing so "in order not to appear weak-kneed." In the disillusioned band, now led by Cárdenas over the back track, were Alonso Sánchez, his *soldadera* wife Francisca de Hozes, and their children, of whom there were now two, one having been born in Tiguex or somewhere on the trail.

But Cárdenas did not get far on his way to Mexico, for when he reached San Gerónimo he found the Sonora country up in arms, the settlement destroyed and deserted, Alcaráz and other Spaniards killed by Indians, and the rebels in control of the mountain passes, making it impossible for Don Lope to continue his journey. Most of the Spanish survivors had fled toward Culiacán; others were met by Cárdenas as they escaped north toward Tiguex. In short, the Ópatas of the Sonora Valley had arisen in a general rebellion and driven the Spaniards out, and Cárdenas and his companions, now in grave danger, hurried back to Pueblo Land. Don Lope's fortune in Spain would have to wait.

This uprising of the Ópatas was the result of the continued ineptness of Alcaráz, the reduction of manpower in the valley by Tovar when he took part of the company to Tiguex, and the inferior quality of the garrison, of which only the dregs of the original detachment were now left. The Indians at San Gerónimo complained of the exaction of heavy tribute by way of supplies and personal services, including the seizure of provisions without consent or remuneration. Most galling of all was the conduct of the soldiers toward the native women, whom they impressed as servants and as tent mates. On this last score Alcaráz was said to be a chief offender.

Not all the blame should be charged to the commander for, as Castañeda tells, us, after the two winnowings of the garrison, only "the worthless, turbulent and seditious people" remained; and "although some honorable men were left in the administrative posts . . . scoundrels got the upper hand." These malcontents held assemblages and formed plots, saying they had been sold out, and that if they stayed there they would not be profitably employed, since the north country was now being entered through another part of New Spain, "better situated than this one." They referred to the opening of mines in the Central Plateau of Mexico on the way toward Pueblo Land. But Castañeda, a West Coast patriot, declared that this was not true, since Sonora was "on an almost direct route" to El Dorado. His geography was a little defective.

In the course of these disturbances, restive soldiers chose Pedro de Ávila as their leader and fled to Culiacán, leaving Alcaráz at San Gerónimo with a handful of invalids, and "no able-bodied men to pursue them or beg them to return." On the way south some of the fugitives were killed by Indians. The retreat of the deserters was like jumping from the frying pan into the fire, for when they reached Culiacán they were arrested by the alcalde mayor, who was expecting Juan Gallego to arrive from the capital with a force of men who, the alcalde hoped, would take the deserters back to their Sonora post. Fearing such an event, some of the fugitives fled in the night toward Compostela. Juan Gallego, it will be remembered, had journeyed south from Tiguex with Díaz and Fray Marcos just about a year earlier. He had continued on his way to Mexico City to get supplies for Coronado's army, and his return through Culiacán was now anticipated.

Besides the actual happenings at San Gerónimo, the difficulty there may be considered as a part of the mutinous conduct of the Indians in all the western area, as epitomized in the uprising known as the Mixton War. This, says one writer, "was the most formidable and widespread struggle for liberty ever made by the native races in any part of Mexico. The Jalisco tribes killed their encomenderos, abandoned their towns, and took refuge in the fortified peñoles, or cliffs, believed to be impregnable. At the end of 1540 Guadalajara . . . was the only place north of the [Santiago] river and east of the sierra still held by the Spaniards. Strong forces of soldiers under different leaders were repeatedly repulsed by native warriors. [Pedro de] Alvarado marched rashly inland only to be defeated and killed. Mendoza was alarmed for the safety not only of New Galicia but of all New Spain"; and even now, while Alcaráz was experiencing such tribulations at San Gerónimo III, the viceroy had found it necessary to take to the field in person at the head of a considerable army of Spaniards and native allies in an effort to quell the uprising.

Meanwhile Alcaráz, now ill, was unable to maintain himself at Suya even if he had wished to do so, because the Indians of the vicinity were attacking the Spaniards with arrows dipped in the deadly poison of the *yerba pestífera*, which had given Sonora such unflattering fame. The natives, knowing the weakness of the soldiery, no longer obeyed them. Coming at this time, the uprising was doubly unfortunate. Veins of gold had been discovered in the neighborhood of San Gerónimo, but because of Indian hostility they were not worked, for the handful of Spaniards had all they could do to save their own skins. Otherwise Sonora might have become the scene of a profitable gold rush and a permanent Spanish settlement from that time forward.

At Suya, Alcaráz had been warned of an impending attack, "but, being dull, and obstinate in his blindness," he failed to take the necessary measures for defense. The contemporary historian Obregón attributed this "to the fact that God our Lord willed it, in order to punish the loose conduct and the iniquitous example they were setting the people whom they had appointed to discipline them and attract them to our Holy Catholic Faith." It seems rather unfair to lay the blame on God for the deviltry of such a scoundrel as the commander.

To manifest their hatred for the Spaniards and their contempt for Alcaraz, the natives at San Gerónimo now fashioned an insulting effigy of him, set it up in a conspicuous place, and shot it full of arrows, meanwhile shouting, "Capitán! Capitán!" and emitting volleys of native ribaldry. Then dragging the crude statue to a safe place, they indulged in an orgy made boisterous by draughts of liquor brewed from the tunas which were abundant in the vicinity.

When the war spirit had been fanned to a white heat, the final blow at the Spaniards was struck. One night the defenders of Suya were surprised by seeing some inexplicable fires in the nearby hills. The watches were now redoubled, but nothing happened, and toward morning the sentries relaxed their vigilance. Thereupon hostile Indians slipped into town unobserved and began to plunder and murder. Some of the Spaniards managed to flee toward the plain, among them Alcaráz, who was mortally wounded in his effort to escape. According to a story current in later tradition, when the attack occurred Alcaráz was in bed with two native women. Hearing the alarm they hustled the captain into his *lesquipil*, a form of native cotton armor, then made themselves heroines among the Ópatas by firing poisoned arrows between the seams of the armor of Alcaráz and thus causing his death. So ended an inglorious career. Many of his contemporaries would say that Alcaráz got what he deserved, for he had been a sinister influence ever since the days when he mistreated Cabeza de Vaca.

Some of the Spaniards rallied on horseback, turned on the rebels and rescued a few persons, but "the enemy departed with the booty and without suffering any harm, having killed three Spaniards, numerous servants, and more than twenty horses."

The surviving Spaniards now fled on foot, some toward the north where they met Cárdenas on his way to Mexico, and others toward the south in the wake of Ávila and his deserters. This latter group found it necessary to avoid the roads and to go without food until they reached Corazones. Here the natives, like the faithful friends they had always been, furnished them provisions. After untold hardships the refugees succeeded in reaching Culiacán, where the alcalde mayor welcomed them and lodged them to the best of his ability. He now had on his hands two sets of fugitives from Suya, deserters and patriots.

Trapped north of San Gerónimo, but "escaping from the Indians through good fortune and diligence," Cárdenas hurried back to Tiguex to report the situation to Coronado. Señora Sánchez, who was one of the refugees, sheds a little light on the retreat. She says the rebels would have killed Cárdenas and all those with him if they had not turned back, and if they had not been succored by another captain who was coming near by." The identity of this other captain is not disclosed, but apparently he too was fleeing with some of the Sonora colonists from the wrath of the rebels. Just when they reached Tiguex in their retreat does not appear in the records. Cárdenas's fortune in Spain still had to wait.

Apropos of the Sonora rebellion, Obregón moralizes on the evils common to the dealings of the early conquistadores with the natives of America. Of course, we must remember that when he wrote, forty years after the disaster, he was applying for the job of conquistador himself, as Coronado's successor in Pueblo Land. One of the chief points emphasized by him was the relation of Spaniards with the native women of regions explored and conquered in the New World.

Juan Gallego now caused a sensation. Late in 1541 he

reached Culiacán on his way to Tiguex with a supply train, half a dozen Spaniards, and a few Indian allies. Of his march north to relieve Coronado's army, Castañeda wrote: ". . . there are events which have happened recently in these parts to our Spaniards, in conquests and clashes with the natives, that surpass, as deeds of amazement, not only . . . books of chivalry, but even those written about the Twelve Peers of France. One might well complain that in the preceding chapter I have passed over in silence the exploits of Captain Juan Gallego and the twenty companions who went with him. We shall tell of them here in order that those who in the future may read and talk about them may have a reliable author on whom to depend, an author who does not write fables, like some we nowadays read in books of chivalry."

When Gallego arrived at Culiacán, some of the refugees from Suya were still there, and from them he learned that the Indians on the road north were in revolt. He therefore needed more men, and, under guarantee of pardon for rebellion or desertion, he enlisted enough of the fugitives to make a total of twenty-two in his force, not counting a contingent of Indian allies and servants. By no means formidable in numbers, this little band made themselves remembered on the West Coast to this day, four centuries later.

Hastening north, Gallego traveled through country now violently hostile toward the Spaniards, having almost daily clashes with the natives encountered on the way. Indeed, it was only the boldness of Gallego and his handful of men that enabled them to win safely through with supplies for Coronado and the army. Castañeda gives a graphic account of the lightning blows struck by Gallego on his way up the coast and of the terror he spread there. The natives might well have thought Guzmán had broken jail and returned from Spain to his former empire. Gallego's method of travel was to leave the baggage behind with two-thirds of his men, "while he . . . led the advance guard with six or seven Spaniards and without any of the allies." His technique was to secure safety through terror, which is sometimes the only means of keeping one's head on one's shoulders. These commandos forced their way into the hostile Indian towns, killing, destroying, applying the torch, and falling upon the enemy so suddenly that they had no time to assemble. By these tactics Gallego and his men "became so greatly feared that not a pueblo dared to oppose them. On the contrary, the natives fled from them as from a powerful army. Thus, Gallego traveled for ten days entirely through inhabited country, without an hour of rest, and all this was accomplished with only seven companions. When the men followed with the baggage they found nothing to do but plunder, since the advance guard had already killed or apprehended all the people they had been able to lay hands on; the rest had fled." Gallego and his demoniacal seven halted nowhere, so that even when towns were forewarned they had no chance to organize for resistance. In the region of Suya he executed a large number of Indians as a punishment for rebellion. In all this raid Gallego did not lose a single man, and only one was wounded. This one, "while despoiling a dying Indian was hit by him on the eyelid and the skin was broken. Since the weapon was poisoned, he would have died had he not been given some quince juice. As it was, he lost his eye."

Writing a quarter of a century later, Castañeda remarked: "These deeds were such that those people will remember them as long as they live. This will be particularly true of four or five friendly Indians who left Corazones with them. They were so amazed they thought the Spaniards more divine than human."

Chapter XXVIII

A SADDLE GIRTH BREAKS

When Coronado returned from Quivira to Pueblo Land he again made his headquarters at Alcanfor, where they had been first established by Cárdenas and reoccupied by Arellano after his heroic march from the Barrancas. Living accommodations were hardly ideal from the standpoint of the sons of noblemen in the army, but there was nothing better available. The soldiers were presumably domiciled in the upper storeys of the pueblo, since the ground level apartments were built for storage only, although in a pinch they might serve as barracks. One can imagine Coronado, geared with helmet and coat of mail, climbing up a wooden ladder to his humble quarters and stooping over when inside to adjust his stature to the low ceilings. It was a far cry from here to his aristocratic home in Mother Spain or to the *casa* of Doña Beatríz in Mexico.

The second winter spent by the Spaniards at Tiguex was a severe strain on human endurance. It was a long period of hardship, discouragement, and what was worse, of idleness and ennui. Existence lacked the flavor given it the previous winter by the Tiguex War. Life now was chiefly a matter of waiting in the continued misery of hunger and cold. Before spring came, the army was ragged and on the brink of starvation. They had the jerked buffalo meat Arellano had gathered in the great hunt near the Barrancas the previous June, and the provisions Barrionuevo had assembled from the remote pueblos up and down the Rio Grande, but these stores did not last indefinitely. There are indications of a winter buffalo hunt on the eastern Plains, and of new foraging expeditions among distant pueblos which had not been abandoned by the natives. But no supplies had come from Mexico since the adventurers first reached

Cíbola a year and a half before, and such as had not been consumed were now stale or even rotten. The arrival of Juan Gallego with his pack train was anxiously awaited, but Indian hostilities on the route to Mexico caused great uncertainty. The return of crippled Cárdenas with his fugitives from Sonora added to the general's cares. Not the least of these was due to the sharp tongue of Doña Francisca de Hozes, who assumed the rôle of critic and trouble maker, and whom he, as a gentleman, could not discipline.

In his need of supplies Coronado invited the conquered Tiguex Indians to make peace with the Spaniards, hoping they might aid him, but they were distrustful and sullen. Their pueblos had been destroyed, their people alienated, and their fields laid waste, so they now had neither the disposition nor the ability to relieve the hunger of the intruders. Coronado tried to pacify certain unnamed pueblos which were "restless," but without avail. He made efforts with some success to obtain from other pueblos clothing for the soldiers who were shivering with cold and plagued with lice. "As necessity knows no law," says Castañeda, who was one of the sufferers, soldiers were sent to gather the needed garments from the unwilling natives. Just where these supplies were procured we are not informed, but apparently the Xémez towns and some of those farther up the Rio Grande were still friendly, or at least not openly hostile. This may have been true also of some of those downstream. But the chief reliance for food and clothing was the dwindling herd of cattle and the flock of sheep brought from Mexico with the army and not yet exhausted, having been materially replenished by one or two new crops of calves and lambs in the course of some three thousand miles of wayfaring. And we wonder if among them there were any of the cross-breed stock which Goodnight long afterward called *cattalo*. Fresh beef, veal, and mutton might become monotonous, but, even if tough, they contained essential vitamins, and apparently there was little sickness in camp. Clothing made of hide and hair was not always artistic, but it gave welcome protection against the biting cold of a Tiguex winter.

Discomfort and idleness had a serious effect upon morale and discipline in the camp, much as was the case more than two centuries later in that terrible winter spent by Washington and his tatterdemalion army at Valley Forge—a gap in space and time which helps to give us historical perspective. Here, as there, tempers became short, and small matters led to irritation, bickering, and intrigue, as all soldiers who have been long idle in camp will readily understand. Under these circumstances the general lost some of his former popularity with his men. Castañeda, who was present that winter as a common soldier, though an uncommon man, tells us that hitherto "Coronado had been among his captains and soldiers the most beloved leader who had ever ventured forth in the Indies," and there is good ground for thinking this was true. But now, troubles great and small led to abuses for which Don Francisco, justly or unjustly, was held responsible. The outcome was a rift between officers and men. It was charged that the captains who were sent among the natives to gather clothing distributed it unfairly, taking the best for themselves, their friends, or their own servants, leaving the "discards" for the others. "Ill feeling and harsh words soon developed," says Castañeda. Soldiers complained that men of social standing were exempted from menial tasks and sentry duty, and fared better than others as to food and clothing— complaints which have been heard in all armies ever since recorded history began. For this Coronado was likewise blamed. At the bottom of it all were tedium and loss of incentive. Everybody, officers and men alike, had enlisted under Coronado's banner as seekers of treasure in the fabulous land advertised by Fray Marcos, visualizing at the end of the rainbow a pot of gold. But there had been a succession of disappointments. Cíbola—no gold! Tusayán—no gold! Tiguex—no gold! And now Quivira—no gold! A later version of the oft-told story was "Pike's Peak or bust—Busted, by God!" Thus does history repeat itself.

Coronado had declared his intention to return in the spring to Quivira with a view to going farther inland, and he still talked of doing so. But he was half-hearted in the matter, and so were most of his men. What he had seen in Kansas left the general pessimistic regarding prospects farther on—a feeling that was shared by the majority of the men who were shivering and scratching in Tiguex. Now, being idle, disillusioned, and hungry, most of them were homesick and ready to give up the quest. A few, perhaps among them recent arrivals from Sonora, and some others not included in the saddle-galled Chosen Thirty on the jaunt to Kansas, wanted their fling at further adventure and a chance to prospect for themselves. These had their own special grievance and favored a new expedition to Quivira. Buffer of all brands of malcontents was the formerly much-loved general. Don Francisco was paying a high price for transitory glory.

With a lurking hope but slender confidence in the outcome, Coronado went forward with plans for a return to the prairies of the northeast. Just what he expected to find there it is difficult to say. Judging from what he had seen and heard it promised little, but it was his duty to follow every clue. To him Mendoza had committed the task of uncovering the secrets of this Tierra Nueva, and he must prove himself worthy of the great viceroy's confidence. And there was Doña Beatríz, whose admiration must be retained and her fortune restored. More immediately to the point, any change from idleness to activity would improve the morale of his camp-weary men, a consideration which has accounted for many a thousand miles of otherwise pointless marching by armies. "Keep 'em moving!" So Coronado proposed to spend the winter preparing to set forth to learn what was beyond the disappointing lands he had already seen in Kansas. Clothing had to be mended, armor refurbished, and scouting parties sent out anew to gather supplies for the return to Quivira. While all this was going on, the western horizon was anxiously scanned for a sight of long-overdue Juan Gallego with his pack train of supplies and news from Mexico.

But, as Castañeda understood it, a higher authority now intervened. "Since nothing in this world depends upon the plans of men, but upon the will of Almighty God, it was His design that our desires should not be fulfilled." Castañeda, it will be remembered, had not been to Quivira, and by his reference to "our desires" we infer that he was one of the few remaining optimists regarding what was *mas allá*. Or perhaps the fact that he had not been in at the capture of Cíbola, nor at the battle of Arenal, nor included among the Chosen Thirty, may have colored his comments on some of these matters. Be that as it may, Fate now took a hand in events.

"It happened that on a holiday"—St. John's day, December 27, says one chronicler—"the general rode out on horseback as he often did, to find recreation. Mounted on a spirited horse" —a sorrel steed—"he raced by the side of Don Rodrigo Maldonado," the gallant discoverer of the Barranca in the Llano Estacado where the hailstorm had occurred. Coronado's servants "had put in a new saddle girth, which, because of having been in stock so long, must have become rotten. During the race it broke, and the general," being ahead of his competitor, it may be noted, "fell on the side where Don Rodrigo rode, and when passing over him the horse struck him on the head with a hoof. As a result Francisco Vázquez was on the point of death, and his recovery was slow and uncertain." Thus, twice at least in the course of his great adventure Coronado had faced Eternity, once in the battle of Cíbola, and now at Tiguex near the Rio Grande. Another version of the same episode is that it occurred when Coronado was racing his horse in the presence of his men, "giving lessons . . . and animating them in order that they might be ready for whatever was important in matters of war." Be this as it may, the result was the same.

This accident marks a decisive turning point in Coronado's career. He was never again quite himself, and most of the misfortunes which thereafter attended his steps can be traced to the fatal moment when he fell under the hoof of Maldonado's steed. This is the opinion of Castañeda, one of the general's critics, and of several other witnesses. Coronado now became gloomy and uncertain, he was ill many days, and his mind never recovered its buoyancy and vigor. For the present the accident left López, the maestre de campo, in actual command of the expedition.

It was while Coronado was confined to his comfortless bed in the loft of the pueblo that Cárdenas, who had set out for Mexico and Spain, returned fleeing in double-quick time from Sonora, where he had found the natives in revolt, Alcaráz killed, and San Gerónimo deserted by the Spaniards. When the officers at Tiguex learned the distressing news they kept it from Coronado, dreading the consequence of reporting it to him. Their fears proved to be well founded. When the general had somewhat recovered and was able to leave his bed, he was told about affairs in Sonora. Thereupon he became violent, and swore he would hang anybody who might abuse Indians as Alcaráz was said to have done. Indeed, the news "affected him so deeply that he had a relapse, which may have induced him to make the decision he did, as was later believed." The decision referred to was not to return to Quivira, but instead to pull up stakes and lead his army back to Mexico.

What followed should be no cause for surprise to anybody who knows human nature. Unscrupulous persons now took advantage of the sick man's weakness; and crippled Cárdenas, his ablest lieutenant, was no longer in a position of authority where he might sustain the general in his hour of need.

The real Coronado was no more, and henceforth we are telling the story of another man. From this point forward, judgment of his acts must be on a new plane. He now became homesick, longed to return to Doña Beatríz, and brooded upon his past, finding mystery and significance in trifling and even long-forgotten incidents. One such example is recited by Castañeda: "It happened that when he found himself in this situation he remembered that at Salamanca a mathematical friend had told him that he would find himself in strange lands, that he would become great and powerful, and that he was to suffer a fall from which he would never recover." The prophecy seemed to have come true. "The thought of death now made him wish to return to die near his wife and children"—this from a man who hitherto had proved himself to be as hardy as any good soldier.

The secret now came out—if it was a secret. Not Coronado alone, but most of his followers, especially the rank and file, also wanted to go home, and they took advantage of the general's condition to bring it about. In his weakness, when out of his head, he talked too much about his troubles, and his ravings were capitalized by other homesick men. His garrulous doctor was the go-between. Not important enough to be remembered by name—perhaps he was Dr. Ramos, who already has entered our story—the *médico* is preserved for history by his wagging tongue. "As the physician and surgeon who attended him was a gossip," says Castañeda, the general learned from him about the grumbling among the soldiers, "and then he connived secretly . . . with some of the caballeros of his own way of thinking to bring about a return to New Spain. . . . This led to holding conferences, and to presenting the general . . . petitions signed by all the soldiers. Since they had discussed the whole matter in detail, it was not necessary to waste much time, for many were already inclined to return." To them the wealth of Quivira was a mirage now dispelled, and home was next door to heaven!

Castañeda, looking back after two decades, portrayed Coronado's further part in the procedure as duplicity. Perhaps it was, but his acts were all directed toward doing what he well knew was desired by a large majority of the men, who took advantage of his illness to achieve their own ends. The show was over and they wanted to go home. When they presented a petition to this effect, Coronado declared he would not consent to it "unless it was approved by all the caballeros and captains in a signed statement"—a very correct procedure it would seem. "As some were in on the secret, they readily consented, and even induced the others to do likewise. They expressed their opinion that they ought to return to New Spain, since they had not found any wealth or any settled area where repartimientos"— Indians to exploit—"could be provided for the whole army. As soon as the general had the signatures, the return to New

Spain was announced." The decision was made by a majority vote of officers, caballeros, and common soldiers, in an orderly manner.

Under some impulse, part of the soldiers afterwards changed their minds, tried to back out of their bargain, and sought by various means to recover their signatures from Coronado. The episode would have been ludicrous had it not been pathetic from the point of view of the sick general whom his men were using for their own purposes. But Coronado "guarded the signatures so closely that he never left his chamber, pretending that his ailment was much more serious" than actually was the case, "placing guards about himself and his room, and at night about the upper storey where he slept. In spite of all this they stole his strong box from him, but it was said they failed to find any signatures in it because he kept them hidden in his mattress." This was perhaps just camp gossip. Incidentally, it may be remarked that it is easy for anyone to say but difficult to prove that a person is not as sick as he pretends.

A handful of the dissenters now made a compromise proposal. They told the general that if he would give them sixty chosen men they would remain in Tiguex and hold the country until the viceroy should send them reinforcements or recall them. Another suggestion was that Coronado should take sixty men to escort him to Mexico, leaving the rest of the army in Tiguex, a plan to which only a very small minority of the men would have subscribed. These overtures were made chiefly by officers, whether through patriotism or personal ambition it is not clear. "But the soldiers would not remain there under any circumstances," says Castañeda. In other words, Coronado had the rank and file on his side. "In the first place, they had already set their prow toward New Spain, and in the second place, they clearly saw that discord would arise over the question as to who should command. So the caballeros—we do not know whether it was because they had sworn loyalty to Coronado, or because they thought the soldiers would not support them— although they felt aggrieved, were forced to submit and abide by the decision." Castañeda adds: "Thenceforth, however, they did not obey the general as they formerly had done, and he was now disliked by them. He catered to the soldiers and flattered them, thus achieving the result he sought, namely, the return of the entire army." So we may say that, crazy or not, Coronado had prevailed against his opponents, and that he had the majority of the army on his side. They had hoped to find ready-to-hand wealth and were disillusioned. The Cíbola bubble had burst, and Quivira had proved to be even more disappointing. They now wanted to go home! Having won out in the contest, Coronado ordered everybody to be ready to begin the return march to Mexico early in April, 1542. This was a little more than two years after they had started north from Compostela.

In viewing this episode it must be remembered that the Coronado Expedition, though military in form, was not primarily such in its purposes. Its members were colonists, some of them with their families, and accompanied by native families from Mexico who had been recruited under promise that they might return home whenever they wished. Under the circumstances, Coronado made the only justifiable decision.

Chapter XXIX

FRIARS REMAIN IN THE NEW LAND

When Coronado announced his intention to lead his followers back to Mexico, Fray Juan de Padilla informed him that some of the friars had decided to stay in the country to work among the natives. This bold declaration should not surprise us. The Coronado expedition was intended in no small part as a missionary venture, for Mendoza was deeply interested in the conversion of the Indians. It was mainly because of his wish, supported by the zeal of Bishop Zumárraga, that several friars were sent with Coronado under the leadership of Marcos de Niza. And he, as Franciscan provincial, before departing from Cíbola for Mexico had authorized the missionaries to go among the Indians to convert them. Indeed, it was for this they had enlisted in the venturesome expedition.

Padilla hoped some of the soldiers might remain in Tierra Nueva with him and his companions, but when such a plan was suggested it was overruled by Coronado. Francisca de Hozes at a later time declared that the general mistreated and put in shackles many Spaniards who wished to stay with Fray Juan, "and that of these there must have been about sixty, among them being this witness and her husband, whom he threatened to hang if they remained or even said any more about it." The story of the shackles lacks confirmation. Perhaps Señora Sánchez talked too much and got on Coronado's nerves. Certainly she had exercised woman's prerogative of changing her mind, for it will be remembered that she and her spouse were among those who some time previously had set out for Mexico with Cárdenas and were driven back to Tiguex by the Sonora uprising. The number sixty here mentioned suggests that this scene was a part of the dispute over remaining in the New Land which Castañeda described.

Although the petition of the sixty soldiers was vetoed by the general, Padilla went ahead with his plans. To stay alone in that distant land without military protection was a brave thing to do, and called for downright nerve; but fearlessness was characteristic of the missionaries. By some of the soldiers these friars who now declared their intention to devote their lives to work among the Indians were doubtless called foolhardy or crazy; by most of them they were applauded as saintly men courting martyrdom for the Faith.

Three friars, according to later Franciscan chroniclers, were left among the Indians when the army withdrew. They were Fray Juan de Padilla, superior, Fray Luís de Escalona (also called Ubeda), and Fray Juan de la Cruz. Padilla, the fighting friar, was an ordained priest, with all the authority of that high office. The others were lay brothers. They could not say Mass, but could expound the Christian doctrine, baptize dying natives, and teach the rudiments of European civilization, which was an important part of their duty among the heathen.

A few other members of the expedition, persons of humble rank, obtained Coronado's permission to remain with the missionaries. Most of these, in fact, had come to Tierra Nueva as assistants to the friars, and now continued in the same capacity. Among them were two Indian *donados* (lay brothers wearing the habit of friars) named Lucas and Sebastián. They were from the monastery at Zapotlán, where they had been trained in their boyhood by Father Padilla, and were now his personal aids. Two or more Negroes also figured in the missionary story, among them being one named Cristóbal belonging to Jaramillo, and another named Sebastián who was a slave of Melchior Pérez, the governor's son. Sebastián had with him a wife and children. Most notable among the laymen who remained to assist the missionaries was Andrés do Campo, a Portuguese soldier, gardener by occupation, who was listed at Compostela as possessing three horses, native weapons, and a buckskin coat.

Having approved the plan of the friars to cast their lot with the Indians of the New Land, Coronado generously assisted them with an outfit and with escorts to their respective provinces. Jaramillo, the chronicler, was a warm friend of Fray Luís and personally helped to equip him for his exile among the natives. He also devoted to the cause his young slave Cristóbal, whom the friar especially wished to have with him. In fact, Fray Luís "desired no other companion for his comfort . . . saying that Cristóbal would soon learn the language of the vicinity if the natives would assist him." The friar knew that learning to speak a new tongue is child's play, whereas it is the despair of an adult. Fray Luís was so eager to obtain Cristóbal, says Jaramillo, "that I could not refuse him."

Available evidence regarding the deeds of these brave friars who remained in the New Land to work among the Indians is scanty and not altogether clear. It is found chiefly in later Franciscan chronicles and may be regarded as partly based on documentary sources, and partly on tradition as it grew and was recorded in the sixteenth, seventeenth, and eighteenth centuries. Whatever may be the shortcoming of these chronicles, it is mainly from them we must write this chapter of our story.

Fray Luís de Escalona told Coronado he desired to work at the terraced houses, that is, in the Pueblo country, "saying that with the chisel and an adze which he still possessed he would erect crosses in those towns, and would baptize the children whom he might find on the verge of death, thus sending them to Heaven." This did not imply an expectation of great success among adult natives, which the friar well knew was a more difficult matter. He pinned his hopes on the young, as do all discerning teachers. For his headquarters Fray Luís chose Cicúique, the famous settlement on Pecos River, home of Bigotes and Cacique, where so many things had happened during the stay of the Spaniards in Pueblo Land. He said those Indians, in spite of the distressing occurrences there, seemed to have some leaning toward Christianity, "and since he was old he would employ the short time that might still remain to him in saving the souls of those people." This does not imply that he was what we would now call aged. He may have been fifty.

Escalona was escorted to Pecos by soldiers furnished him by Coronado, and by them he was left alone with Cristóbal. What little we know about his stay there can be quickly told. Before the army left Tiguex for Mexico, when a party of men took Fray Luís a little flock of sheep, they met him accompanied by people of Pecos on his way to visit pueblos fifteen or twenty leagues from his mission. If the men with the sheep met Escalona on their way eastward, the friar manifestly was going westward, perhaps to Galisteo Valley, or possibly northwestward, to settlements up the Rio Grande. "This gave rise to no little hope that he was in the good graces of the pueblo and that his teaching would be fruitful." Nevertheless, Fray Luís complained that the old men were already deserting him "and he believed they would end by killing him," a prospect which he seems to have cheerfully faced.

Mota Padilla, writing long afterward, says that Escalona lived at Pecos in "a hut . . . or cave, where the Indians ministered to him his meager sustenance, consisting of tortillas, beans, and a little atole. His death has not been reported, but everybody who knew him remembered his perfect life." Castañeda, who knew Fray Luís as a fellow traveler, wrote: "as for myself, I believe that since he was a man of good and saintly life, Our Lord would protect him and grant him grace to convert some of the people, and upon his demise he would leave someone to maintain them in the Faith. And there is no reason to believe otherwise, since the natives in the vicinity are merciful and in no way cruel. On the contrary, they are faithful . . . and opposed to cruelty. They keep their word and are loyal to their friends." What really happened to Fray Luís at his lonely outpost must be left to the imagination, for we have no further knowledge except that he never returned to civilization.

The sojourn of Fray Juan de la Cruz in the Pueblo country is even more shadowy than that of Fray Luís. In fact, it is not certain that he was with the Coronado expedition at all, and we can only repeat here what we are told by the later chroniclers. Mendieta, the Franciscan historian, writes that "of the servant of God Fray Juan . . . nothing more is known than that he remained alone in that pueblo of Tiguex . . . to instruct the Indians in matters of our Faith and of Christian life, at which they were greatly pleased; and as a sign of rejoicing they embraced him and gave other demonstrations of satisfaction. It is to be understood that he died a martyr. He was a religious of devout and approved life, and therefore very much respected by everybody; so much indeed that Captain Francisco Vázquez Coronado had ordered his soldiers to bare their heads whenever they might hear the name of Fray Juan de la Cruz—certain evidence of his great merit." The last rumor of Fray Juan was that he died pierced by Indian arrows, "for not all of them had embraced his teachings and the counsels by which he urged them to detest their barbarous customs, although in general he was greatly esteemed by the chiefs and the rest of the natives, who had witnessed the veneration with which the general, captains, and soldiers treated him." Such is the legendary story of Fray Juan de la Cruz.

The hero in this chapter of missionary history was red-blooded Father Padilla, who has already figured so prominently in the Coronado story. Fray Juan chose Quivira as his field of endeavor, from which we infer that while in that distant region with Coronado he had formed a good opinion of the tall Wichitas, or was deeply impressed by their special need of his ministrations, for either of these considerations would be to him a challenge. He took as companions the Portuguese Andrés do Campo and the two Indian lay brothers, Lucas and Sebastián, whom he had personally brought from Zapotlán. Besides these went a mestizo, a free Negro interpreter, and a few other servants—just who or how many is not known. In his outfit, furnished by Coronado, Padilla took pack mules, a horse, a flock of sheep, church ornaments, and other equipment. Some of these sheep perhaps had walked all the way from Mexico to the Rio Grande, across the Buffalo Plains to the Barrancas and back to Tiguex, and now started on another journey of six or seven hundred miles to Quivira. If so, we wonder what was the condition of their hoofs. Others perhaps were young animals born in Pueblo Land or along the trail, woolly wayfarers in the vineyard of the Lord. Padilla requested of Coronado and was given as guides the six young Wichita braves who had conducted the general and his Chosen Thirty on the return from Quivira to Pueblo Land by the cut-off between the Arkansas River and the Canadian. Presumably they now led Padilla back over the same trail. In fact, we are told that they went "by the shorter route." The journey was made in the spring of 1542. It must have lasted a month or more, for the sheep would probably not average more than twelve or fifteen miles a day.

Arriving at Quivira, Fray Juan was well received by the natives, and he established himself at the village where Coronado had erected a cross on the return trip. It was two or three days' travel southward from Tabás, the last settlement reached by the Chosen Thirty, where the Turk had been executed that gruesome midnight in the previous August. That is to say, the village was probably on Cow Creek in the vicinity of Lyons, Kansas. We are unable to say whether or not Father Padilla was welcomed there by Sopete.

After working successfully here for a short time, restless Fray Juan decided to visit people farther on, toward the east, and thought to have been the Gaus, the tribe later known as the Kaws or Kansas. In the face of protest by the natives at the mission, Padilla set forth accompanied by Do Campo, Lucas, Sebastián, and some servants, "to see with his own eyes" the country about which he had been told. It was an exploring trip. But he had traveled only a short distance—a day or a few days —when he was set upon by Indians he met on the trail. What tribe they belonged to is not known. Says Mendieta, "They must have been enemies of the others," the Quiviras, "who had peacefully welcomed the servants of God, and accepted them as spiritual fathers and teachers of the Faith."

When Padilla saw these Indians coming toward him in war-like array he realized his fate. Not wishing his companions to risk their lives in an effort to save him, he begged Do Campo, who had a horse—the only one—to flee, together with Lucas and

Sebastián. Then "the servant of God fell on his knees, and, beginning to pray, he awaited the fury of the barbarians who were coming near, commending his soul to that Lord for whose love and faith he offered it. The cruel butchers in a twinkling filled him with arrows, and thus the unfortunate man died." Lucas and Sebastián went back and with the consent of the murderers buried Fray Juan, it is said, and then fled to overtake Do Campo. The date of the martyrdom is given by Mota Padilla as 1542, the same year in which Fray Juan returned to the Quivira country. A monument to Father Padilla has been erected at Herington in eastern Kansas. Though the exact spot where the friar was slain is not known, the site chosen for the memorial to the illustrious pioneer is in the general vicinity where he met his fate. Of Do Campo and the lay brothers we shall have an exciting tale to tell later on.

The memory of Padilla lived on among the Indians of Pueblo Land and among the Spaniards who returned in after years to colonize the country that Coronado had discovered and explored. Fact and fiction gradually became fused into a legend which is still recounted. Jones, a few years ago, gave one version of the story which will serve as an illustration. While Kansans assume that the friar's bones lie buried in the vicinity of Herington, "the town of Isleta, New Mexico, is just as certain those bones are contained in a rude coffin, constructed from the trunk of a cottonwood tree, and buried in the dirt floor of an old Spanish mission there. In Isleta they say that a party of Franciscans went to Kansas not many years after the massacre, located the grave and brought the remains of the friar to their town for interment.

"And that isn't all they say. They are willing to affirm on oath that every 20 years the cottonwood coffin works to the surface of the dirt floor and has to be reburied by the padre in charge of the chapel. Five times in the past 100 years the miracle has been observed. The padre of the old mission will take you into the chapel and point out to you, at one side of the altar, the spot under which the bones of Father Padilla now rest. He will not swear that they move upward with the passing of the years, but he was told that on one occasion the archbishop, with some thirty priests and a physician from Albuquerque, opened the grave and found the coffin very close to the surface. There was a hole in the cottonwood sarcophagus and one foot was gone from the partially mummified body. A scrap of the departed father's robe was taken and placed in a reliquary. He does not know where the reliquary is now but he can give you the address of a photographer in Albuquerque who took a picture of the coffin with the body exposed. The last time the enthralled spirit of the courageous Franciscan made an attempt to break its bounds and return to Kansas was in 1914."

Annoyed by these folk-tales, the authorities of the Catholic Church in New Mexico have recently made a careful study of the matter, and have officially published the conclusion that the Father Padilla who entered into the Isleta story was a later priest of the same name, and that the facts in the case were of a nature wholly foreign to the story of Juan Padilla, protomartyr of Kansas. But we may safely predict that the legend will persist indefinitely, for such is the way with folk-tales.

CHAPTER XXX

BACK TRACK TO MEXICO

Soon after Padilla left Tiguex for Quivira, General Coronado prepared to set forth on his return march to Mexico City. There was one last matter to attend to. In the course of nearly two years' residence among the pueblos some of the Spaniards had acquired native servants who had been captured in the Tiguex War. What had been the basis of their distribution does not appear. They had accompanied the expedition to the Texas Plains and trudged back with Arellano from the Barrancas to Tiguex. Before leaving Cíbola for the return to Mexico, Coronado ordered all these Indians released. Probably, in view of Mendoza's instructions regarding treatment of the natives, he feared unpleasant consequences if they should be taken to the capital. "In my opinion," says Castañeda, ever a loyal son of the Church, "in this they erred, for it would have been better if they had been taught among Christians." Some of the servants were women living with the soldiers, notwithstanding the scandal raised by Villegas, which had been an alleged cause of the Tiguex War. In spite of Coronado's order to release the Indians, Juan de Troyano, the red-blooded comrade of Alvarado in the discovery of the Buffalo Plains, who had acquired a companion somewhere in Tierra Nueva, now took her with him to Mexico, and years later he boasted that he was the only member of the Coronado expedition who thus clung to his Indian consort at the time of the departure from Tiguex. When he wrote, they were still happy partners in matrimony and living in Mexico City. The inference is that Troyano was not the only soldier whose loneliness had been relieved by some native beauty, all of Mendoza's solicitude to the contrary notwithstanding.

The day appointed for the departure from Pueblo Land arrived. It was early in April, 1542, a little more than two years since the expedition had left Compostela bound for the Seven Cities. Everybody being equipped for the trail as well as circumstances would permit, the caravan set forth westward over the road to Cíbola, driving in its train the dwindling remainer of the herd of stock, for food on the long march through hostile country. Spirits were a mixture of disappointment at failure to have realized the dreams of wealth in Tierra Nueva, and pleasant anticipation of again seeing friends and home in sunny Mexico. The travelers passed and once more marveled at Ácoma the Sky City, threaded their way through the *malpais*, skirted Corn Mountain (Tówayálane), and descended Zuñi Valley to Háwikuh, scene of their first battle in Tierra Nueva, where some of the now veteran soldiers had been decorated with badges worn forever after in the form of battle scars.

On this leg of the journey a new misfortune occurred. "It was that although the horses had started out well broken to toil, fat and beautiful, in the course of the ten days it took them to reach Cíbola more than thirty of them died, for there was not a day when two, three, or even more did not succumb. Later, until they reached Culiacán, a large number of them perished, something which had not happened before in the course of the whole expedition." To these lovers of horses the loss was only less deeply felt than their unlucky gamble with Fortune. Of the nature of the epidemic no hint is given, but it might be a subject of real interest to veterinary science. It has been suggested that the malady was due to the well-known loco weed, which is common in the region through which they were passing, But this is only a guess, and guesses make bad history, however interesting they may be.

Coronado found Cíbola "pacified and calm." Some of the Indian allies from Mexico in his following remained here, and were absorbed into the Zuñi tribe which still occupies the same little valley where it then lived. Before leaving Háwikuh, forces were reorganized for the back track through the uninhabited area between there and Chichilticale. Says Castañeda: "Leaving now astern, as we may say, the first settlements that had been discovered in the Tierra Nueva, namely, . . . the seven towns of Cíbola, the first to be seen and the last to be left behind, the army set forth through the Despoblado." For two or three days the Cíbolans "never ceased to follow the rear guard of the army to pick up stray baggage or Indian servants, for although they remained peaceful and had been good and faithful friends, yet, when they saw we were abandoning the country they rejoiced at keeping some of our people"—Indians or mixed bloods of course. "However, it is believed that it was not to harm them, as was learned from some who refused to remain behind, although they had been invited and importuned by them" to do so. Castañeda adds, writing in Mexico with a practical retrospect, "As a result there must be fine interpreters there now." And there were, as was subsequently learned.

Without noteworthy incident the return march was continued over the now well-known trail, each familiar scene recalling some episode in the journey to Cíbola and bringing forth a laugh, a sigh—or a well-rounded oath—through the "Bad Pass," site of the midnight attack on Cárdenas and his advance guard, where the nervous greenhorns had put their saddles on hind side before; down Zuñi River, across the Little Colorado, where Coronado had been met by the soft-voiced Zuñi spies; past the gruesome Camp of Death where Espinosa had been buried beside the trail and later exhumed by coyotes; through the Great Forest, where the hungry Indian allies had roasted the live horse suspended between trees; by the detour around La Barranca, which left a sharp crook in the trail down White River to the day of modern bridges; across the deep-canyoned branches of Gila River; then over the main stream and through the mountain pass to Chichilticale. Here, doubtless, Zaldívar had vivid memories of his frigid winter camp there with stalwart Melchior Díaz some three years before, and Castañeda of his vain effort to capture mountain sheep. Of all the returning company Zaldívar was the veteran on this stretch of the trail, for Díaz now lay buried far to the west beside the

Camino del Diablo, a forbidding route whose fame increased in after years with the heroic exploits of Kino, Garcés, and Anza.

Two days beyond Chichilticale, near San Pedro River, Coronado met Juan Gallego and his dare-devil band returning from Mexico. Hats and loud cheers went up in Coronado's caravan. Gallego, on the other hand, was both surprised and disappointed to see the retreating adventurers, for he had assumed that Coronado by this time was in Quivira reaping a harvest of gold, and hoped to join him there. Castañeda remarks: "If our army had not met Gallego as it did, he and his men would have gone clear to the land of the Turk, for which they were bound. And they would have reached it without great risk, such was Gallego's discipline and leadership, and so well were his men trained and experienced in war." They would have followed him through hell and high water! Incidentally, Coronado now got Gallego's pack train load of supplies, which he had long and anxiously awaited, and on which his followers feasted as they had not done for many a lean month in their long peregrination.

The meeting with Gallego reopened the question of remaining in Tierra Nueva. The captain and his men had visualized their arrival in Quivira where they would help Coronado scoop up the gold reported by the Turk, but now they saw their chance to get rich going a'glimmering. On the other hand, the arrival of the pack train with supplies gave the malcontent caballeros with Coronado an excuse for again proposing to stay in the country. When Gallego saw the army was returning to Mexico, says Castañeda, "the first word he uttered was not, 'I am glad you are coming back,' nor did he express any regret." But when, after having spoken to the general, he mingled with the soldiers, "there was not lacking some restlessness among the men on account of that aid." In other words, with new supplies, the argument over retreating to Mexico broke forth again among the captains, causing the general renewed worries, and apparently Gallego encouraged the discontent. The dissenting sixty now saw another chance to realize their desire to remain in Tierra Nueva—or at least to be noticed, which so often is the real aim of objectors. "There were debates, and proposals to establish a settlement somewhere in that vicinity, sending a report to the viceroy to inform him what was taking place" and awaiting his decision. But the homesick rank and file of the army were as determined as before, and "would not agree to anything except to return to New Spain." They had seen enough of hardship and too little of gold. So "nothing came of the plans advanced in these discussions, and although there were some disturbances, in the end the men calmed down." Coronado without bluster again had won and he breathed more easily.

With Gallego came the fugitives from Suya whom he had enlisted at Culiacán and who may have had some misgivings with regard to the reception they might meet. But, Castañeda writes, "they were protected and guaranteed by Gallego's word, and even if the general had wished to impose some punishment upon them, his authority was slight, for he was now disobeyed and little respected. He again began to be afraid, and, pretending that he was ill, he surrounded himself with guards." Indeed, much of the way to Mexico Coronado was actually too infirm to ride a horse and was carried in a cowhide litter swung between mules driven tandem. Castañeda spoke with too much assurance on a subject which Don Francisco knew better than he.

Accompanied now by Gallego and his fighting devils, Coronado resumed his march southward over the Cananea divide and down the old trail through Sonora. The Indians were still hostile, for they had not forgotten Alcaráz, nor had they been completely intimidated by Gallego. They made a number of attacks on the retreating Spaniards, killing several horses and wounding others. In one of these encounters Arellano was personally involved. Two Indians killed his horse with poisoned arrows, and would have slain the captain himself if he had not been rescued by his men. Punishment was swift and terrible. One of the two Sonorans having been captured, Don Tristán ordered his nose and hands cut off and sent him thus maimed to his companions in rebellion, to frighten them, "because they were still following and shooting at the army with arrows poisoned with the *yerba braba y pestifera,*" whose effects were so awful that "of all those wounded with it nobody escaped, for within twelve hours they died swollen and raving."

The terrors of the *yerba pestifera* were reduced somewhat by the discovery in the course of this retreat of what was considered an antidote for the pest, a contribution to *materia medica.* Coronado's men found that quince juice, which they carried among their provisions, was a good remedy for the poison. For at a narrow pass the hostile Indians shot a Spaniard named Mesa, "and although it was a deadly wound infected with fresh venom, and it was more than two hours before he was attended to, he did not die," thanks to the quince juice, it was believed. Nevertheless, the part infected by the poison rotted away and the flesh dropped off, leaving bones and tendons bare, with a terrible stench. The wound was on Mesa's wrist; but before he recovered, the infection had reached his shoulder.

Swinging eastward now to avoid the fearsome gorge of Senoquipe and the Ópata settlements farther down Sonora Valley, Coronado reached Batuco, whither the natives of Corazones—the beloved of Cabeza de Vaca—went a long distance overland to see the homeward-bound Spaniards. "They came to meet the general like the friends they had always been. For thus they had treated all the Spaniards who had passed through their land, furnishing them with needed supplies and even with men when necessary. So they had always been well treated and rewarded by our men on this expedition." Such is Castañeda's tribute to the loyal hosts of Cabeza de Vaca who lived in the Town of Hearts at the end of the river gorge, where Ures now stands.

From Batuco the army traveled at a rapid pace and without stopping to rest, for the Indians in this region also were in revolt. Coronado rejoined his northbound trail at Soyopa and retraced it southward, crossed Mayo River, passed the rock of the vigilant Frailes near the site of Alamos, later famed for its silver mines, forded Rio Fuerte, and arrived at Petatlán on Rio Sinaloa, where the Indians were peaceful. At this place he rested a few days and obtained new provisions, then continued to Culiacán.

The major hardships of the long journey here came to an end, partly because the travelers had reached settled country, with some of the conveniences and amenities of civilized life, and partly because, being now within the jurisdiction of Nueva Galicia, Coronado as governor was able to use his authority in that capacity to aid his way-worn men. Culiacán was pleasantly remembered by the returning gold-seekers for the sham battle with which they had been welcomed on their way north, and for the generous hospitality accorded them by the citizens at that time. And no doubt there were sly remarks about Trujillo's vision of Doña Beatríz, through which the trickster had been discharged by Coronado and thereby escaped several thousand miles of weary travel.

Here at Culiacán the army was formally disbanded, as we are explictly told by Cárdenas, and the men were free to fall out of the ranks. From this we conclude that Castañeda, when he wrote years later, overdrew the impression that the army fell apart because of Coronado's lack of authority. In other words, the expedition as a military enterprise was over. "Each one now conducted his own affairs in his own way, so that when the general went to a pueblo ten leagues distant"—perhaps to get supplies—"many persons, or most of them, remained in the valley to rest." A number of Coronado's soldiers were residents of Culiacán, and they now rejoined their families. Others, having no ties in the capital, where they had been floaters, here started life anew. An official inquiry made later in Mexico City regarding the whereabouts of Diego López and Francisco Martín, who were wanted as witnesses, brought forth the rumor that they were among those who had remained at Culiacán.

From now on the soldiers gradually readjusted themselves to civilian life, dropping out of the ranks at one frontier outpost after another and settling down in good pioneer style. It was like the return of adventurers from any gold rush in other parts of the Western Hemisphere in other days. In this way disappeared some of the problems which had worried Viceroy Mendoza when the expedition was organized, and the capital was relieved of many restless men whose departure with Coronado had been regarded as "good riddance." Castañeda tells us that some of Coronado's men, while here in Culiacán, very humanly "began to square accounts for the arrogance that had been shown them by some of the captains"—evidently not all of the officers were angels—"and even some of the captains under the command of the general did likewise." This has happened in other times and places. Ask the G. I. Joes.

Such was the attraction of life at Culiacán that, although it solved one problem, it raised another. Coronado feared he would have no following to Compostela and the capital, a situation which would be humiliating. Therefore, according to Castañeda, he resorted to a ruse. "He pretended to be ill and remained in bed in order that persons who wished to conduct business with him might speak to him and he to them more freely and without hindrance or observation. He did not neglect to send for some citizen friends, urging them to speak to the soldiers and persuade them . . . to accompany him on his way to New Spain, and to tell them he would commend them to the viceroy, Don Antonio de Mendoza, and that he, himself, would favor those who might settle there." Castañeda, who was repeating the accumulated gossip of twenty years, perhaps overplayed this theme. Indeed, he was one of those who left the army and became a resident here, and it was here that he wrote his famous narrative of the Coronado expedition.

The general's known love of a fine horse was again reflected in his sojourn at Culiacán. While there he was visited by a priest named Jiménez, who offered to present the governor with a handsome young chestnut. He said he had raised it as a colt with the intention of sending it to the general in Tierra Nueva. Now that Coronado was returning, Jiménez begged Coronado to accept the animal. Don Francisco decently protested, but as Jiménez was insistent he finally yielded, giving the padre a note for forty pesos in gold bullion—*oro de minas*—to be paid whenever Jiménez might pass through Compostela, the governor's capital. Otherwise, Coronado would return the horse. It might be surmised that Jiménez was a good businessman, or that Coronado lacked sales resistance. A still different explanation was given at a later time, as will appear.

His business at Culiacán being finished, Coronado, carried in a litter, set out for Compostela with the dwindling remains of his army. He started on the Feast of San Juan, June 24, 1542, at the beginning of the rainy season. The numerous rivers he had to cross on the way were now dangerously in flood, besides being infested with fierce alligators. While in camp at one of these streams, apparently the mighty Santiago, a soldier who tried to ford it was carried away by one of these monsters within sight of everybody, and the onlookers were unable to rescue him. In the same or another stream the chestnut horse obtained at Culiacán from Father Jiménez, while being led by one of the general's servants, was drowned in the turbulent flood, much to the owner's sorrow. Somewhere on the way from Cíbola, the horse given to Coronado by Oñate also died. In each case Don Francisco felt the loss as of a comrade. When the general arrived at Compostela, still too weak to ride a horse, he was welcomed by numerous friends. Francisco de Godoy, provincial treasurer and therefore one of the official family, was especially touched by his superior's sufferings, and did all he could to assist and care for him.

Having rested sufficiently to be able to continue his travels, even though he must still be carried, Coronado resumed his way to Mexico City. When he was about to set out from Compostela, Godoy, realizing the governor's infirmity, offered him for the journey a gentle horse with an easy gait—*paseaba llano*—saying that on the way he might sometimes wish to leave the litter and ride for a change. Coronado thanked his friend and accepted the animal as a loan, to be returned when he should come back to Compostela to resume his work as governor of Nueva Galicia. And so he added one more to the list of his numerous equine loves. The fact that, famous horseman though he was, he welcomed a gentle mount for the journey to the capital, reveals the degree of his infirmity.

Castañeda says that Coronado "arrived in Mexico with less than a hundred men, to report to the viceroy, Don Antonio de Mendoza, by whom he was not very cordially welcomed," for he brought no gold with which to repay the viceroy's investment in the expedition. In the same vein, Gómara wrote that Don Antonio was much grieved that Coronado had returned to Mexico, abandoning the Tierra Nueva, "because he had spent more than sixty thousand gold pesos on the enterprise, much of which he still owed, and they did not bring . . . a sign of gold or any other wealth."

But Coronado was by no means so completely out of favor as Castañeda implied. It is true that Mendoza was sadly disappointed over the outcome of the expedition and that he momentarily displayed his discomfiture, but this was not so much censure of the general's performance as chagrin at his own bad gamble in the supposed wealth of Cíbola. Mendoza well knew that if he had led the expedition himself he would have found in Cíbola, Tusayán, Tiguex, the Llano Estacado, the Great Barrancas, and Quivira just what Coronado found there, and if he had gone beyond Quivira, which Don Francisco refrained from doing, he too would have discovered no gold. Doña Beatríz was perhaps as much disappointed as Mendoza, for Don Francisco had invested a goodly slice of her fortune in Tierra Nueva and lost it. We do not know how many tears she shed, nor how much she may have scolded her spouse behind the curtain. But in public she stood by him as faithfully as Jessie Benton, the "Immortal Wife," three centuries later championed her John C. Frémont.

That Coronado was not long if at all in personal disfavor with the viceroy, and that he still had entrée into Mendoza's home, is shown by the fact that soon after he arrived at Mexico City he attended, at the viceroy's palace, the wedding of Mendoza's sister, Doña María. The viceroy sustained Coronado in the investigations which followed the Cíbola expedition, and on the other hand, Don Francisco was a star witness for Mendoza in his own residencia which soon was held. His support in that episode was much appreciated by the viceroy, and his testimony carried great weight with the judge who conducted the inquiry. Clearly, Castañeda overstated Mendoza's anger at Coronado for the outcome of the expedition to Tierra Nueva.

In the returning army were the Indian allies who had gone with Coronado from Mexico, still almost in full quota, for only one small contingent had withdrawn from the New Land ahead of Coronado, leaving with permission and escorted by a soldier guard, as they had been promised. Perhaps this had occurred just before the army set out from Tiguex for Quivira. On this count Don Francisco had made a remarkable record. When he reached Mexico he was able to say that he had scrupulously complied with Mendoza's orders regarding the good treatment of the natives he had led to Cíbola. He had taken "special care to look after them, to provide for the sick, and to keep a list of the dead," and "according to the reckoning . . . not thirty Indians had died in the expedition, including the stops on the way and journey there and back." This was indeed a record.

As has been the case after most wars, many of Coronado's soldiers spent the rest of their lives begging the government for pensions or other rewards for their services. One such disappointed soul was Francisco de Santillana, who went to Cíbola with Coronado as blacksmith and veterinary surgeon. To equip himself with servants, arms, and horses had cost him a considerable sum, and for his work as blacksmith and horse doctor—"one of the best in New Spain"—he received no compensation. At Tiguex he was wounded so badly by an arrow that he was never again able to use his right arm. After his return to Mexico the King appointed him doorkeeper of the Royal Audiencia for life with a yearly salary of five hundred dollars in gold, but since Mendoza had already given the post to someone else, the order never took effect. Twenty-six years after Santillana arrived home from Tierra Nueva, his son was trying to collect the reward of which his father had been defrauded. This case was typical of many of Coronado's followers to Cíbola. Some of Coronado's men remained on the western frontier, some went to Spain, and others went to Peru to take part in the wars and the gold rush there.

CHAPTER XXXI

LATER NEWS FROM THE NORTH

Nearly a year behind Coronado and his men, the survivors of De Soto's adventure straggled into Mexico. Hitherto rivals in conquest, they now were companions in disappointment and need. Don Hernando had spent the winter of 1541–1542 on Ouachita River in Arkansas, while Coronado and his followers were shivering at Tiguex after their return from Quivira. Spring came; and in March De Soto continued downstream. Of the six hundred who had come with him from Spain he now had left not over three hundred efficient men nor more than forty horses. So he resolved to go to the Gulf coast, which he thought was near by. On its shore he would build two ships, one to be sent to Mexico for aid and the other to Cuba, there to refit and return to explore farther westward, with a view to reaching the Pacific Ocean. It was now three years since De Soto had been heard of by his wife, Doña Isabel, so he did not know how she fared in Cuba. Shortly after Coronado abandoned Tiguex and started for Mexico, De Soto reached Guachoya, near the mouth of Red River in Louisiana. But he went no farther, for his hour had struck. On May 21, 1542, he died and was buried in a hollowed-out log in the Mississippi River, the incomparable stream he had discovered. Before passing away he named as his successor Luís de Moscoso. A few years ago a journalist-turned-historian wrote of finding De Soto's coffin, now of copper, at the bottom of Mississippi River, near the shore of Illinois, but he did not explain how the historic sarcophagus had floated several hundred miles upstream nor how the log had been transformed into copper. Historians still await confirmation of the story.

The travels of De Soto's followers were by no means over.

Moscoso decided to try to lead them to Mexico by land, and on June 5, 1542, he moved westward, headed for Pánuco, about the time when Coronado was in the vicinity of Culiacán on his way back to the capital. Moscoso and his men crossed northern Louisiana and arrived again at Red River near the site of Shreveport. They now swung southward, traveled among the Caddo (Tejas) villages of eastern Texas, veered southwest again, and reached a large river, probably the Trinity. Here as in Arkansas they heard of the Buffalo Plains beyond, but did not reach them. Here, too, they got news of Coronado in an interesting manner. It will be remembered that after Don Francisco and his Chosen Thirty started north for Quivira from the Barrancas in the Texas Panhandle, a captive Indian girl belonging to Juan de Zaldívar, having been left behind by him, hid in the canyons and escaped. This is not reported here to suggest a broken romance. Castañeda, who heard the story after he reached Mexico, tells us that Zaldívar's woman, having fled eastward from the Barrancas, came into the possession of the Moscoso party in eastern Texas. She "told them she had fled from other Spaniards nine days distant and she named the captains." The chronology indicated has raised some questions, but the main facts in the case are clear. Zaldívar's girl, by her flight across Texas, was a personal link between the explorations of Coronado and the men of De Soto. The two expeditions had spanned the Continent.

In October, 1542, Moscoso turned back to the Mississippi River, reaching it near the place where Don Hernando had died. Here he built a fleet of seven brigantines. Timber was felled, a forge set up, and iron chains converted into spikes. A Portuguese carpenter who had some saws cut planks with the aid of helpers. A Genoese sailor served as shipwright. Another Genoese and a Sardinian calked the seams with "oakum got from a plant like hemp, called enequén"; a sick cooper made for each of the seven ships two half-hogsheads to hold fresh water. Sails were fashioned from woven hemp and skins, and anchors from stirrups. In June, 1543, the ships were launched, and twenty-two horses taken on board; the rest, being worn out and unfit for service, were killed and used for food.

Thus, early in July, 322 Spaniards and one hundred Indian slaves set sail on the Mississippi River, the rest of the captives having been released. Natives along their course several times beset the vessels and ten Spaniards were killed. Seventeen (or nineteen) days after leaving Aminoya the refugees reached the Gulf of Mexico. At first they sailed westward, skirting the shore-line, then steered for the open, but turned again to the coast. They experienced hunger and thirst, doubts and fears, and storms at sea. Fierce head winds forced them to spend two weeks in a shelter inlet on the Texas coast [where they discovered petroleum], and when the wind changed in their favor they "very devoutly formed a procession for the return of thanks," not for the petroleum but for their survival we assume.

More than two months after launching their ships on the Mississippi River (on September 10, 1543, to be exact), Moscoso and his men entered Pánuco River, which flows into the Gulf north of Veracruz. It waters the Tampico region, today made golden by its harvest of petroleum. But for oil Moscoso did not care. He had reached civilization! Indians "in the apparel of Spain" told the refugees in the Spanish language there was a Christian settlement fifteen leagues inland. "They felt as though life had been newly given them; many, leaping on shore, kissed the ground; and all, on bended knees, with hands raised above their heads and their eyes to heaven, were untiring in giving thanks to God." Weatherbeaten and toil-worn, they entered Pánuco, each man clad in deerskins, "tanned and dyed black," and carrying his pack on his shoulders. Three hundred and twelve men were warmly welcomed by their countrymen and given the best the place afforded. The event deserves commemoration by a monument and an annual celebration in the historic old town.

Leaving Pánuco, the refugees crossed the plain westward, climbed the Sierra Madre Oriental, perhaps by the route of the present automobile highway, turned south down the plateau and arrived at Mexico City, where they were shown the warmest hospitality. A wealthy caballero named Xaramillo took eighteen men to his house, dressed them with cloth of Segovia, and gave each one a bed with mattress, sheets, blankets, and pillows, with comb, brush, and everything else necessary for a soldier, "for all the city was much grieved to see them attired in deerskins and cowhides; and they showed them this honor and charity because of the great hardships they had suffered in La Florida. On the other hand," says one of the refugees, believing tales current in Mexico, "they refused to show any favor to those who had gone with ... Coronado ... to discover the Seven Cities, and who had come out a little before our people, because without any necessity they had returned to Mexico, not wishing to settle." Thus De Soto's men, who had left Spain as rivals of those sent out by Mendoza, ended their journey as welcome refugees in the viceroy's realm.

There were still other stragglers from the northern interior. A few years after Moscoso's men reached Pánuco, Do Campo, the Portuguese who had remained in the New Land with Fray Juan Padilla, also found his way to that port on the Gulf. Most of the friar's companions were never heard of again, but Do Campo and the Indian *donados,* Lucas and Sebastián, fled from the scene of Fray Juan's martyrdom in Kansas, and, after heroic experiences, all three reached central Mexico in safety. In fact, it was their hair-raising tales, recounted to wide-eyed listeners, that gave the first news in Mexico of the fate of the martyred friar.

Gómara, a contemporary who wrote in Spain from official sources, tells in brief the story of Do Campo's remarkable peregrination. "The Portuguese, although he escaped death at the time, did not escape captivity, for they seized him at once; but ten months later, during which period he was a slave, he fled with two dogs. On the way he blessed people with a cross, to which they made generous offerings, and wherever he went they gave him alms, shelter, and food. He arrived at the land of the Chichimecas"—the wild tribes north of the sedentary Aztecs— "finally made port at Pánuco," and from there went to the capital. "When he reached Mexico his hair was very long and his beard hung in braids. And he reported the strange things of the lands, rivers, and mountains."

Lummis and others write of Do Campo's "nine years" of wandering between Quivira and Pánuco, this being an unwarranted inference from the fact that Gómara told the story in the first edition of his *Historia*, which covered events to 1551. We now know that this is an error by at least four years, for on March 1, 1547, Jerónimo López, a high royal official, wrote from Mexico telling the story of Do Campo's adventure, and of his presence at that time in the capital. How long the fugitive had been there is not stated, but since the event was reported as "news," it may be concluded that his return to civilization was recent. His odyssey therefore ended not nine but less than five years after the death of Padilla, during nearly one year of which he had been in captivity. The story caused a sensation in Mexico and renewed interest in Quivira. López writes: "Very great are the things told of by a Portuguese who escaped from a province where the Indians killed a friar, and who, not knowing where he was going, by the will of God was brought to this city, with such great news of the land and its people that everybody marvels. . . . This Portuguese says that if the Indians killed the friar it was due to their arrogance and because they despised the people of that country"—that is, they were enemies of the Wichitas. Do Campo evidently had spoken well of Kansas in spite of his harrowing sojourn there.

The donados, Lucas and Sebastián, also reached Mexico after experiences strikingly similar to those of Do Campo, as the story is told. Indeed, at least one account states that Do Campo and the donados escaped together to Pánuco; in the narratives of both adventures a cross, miracles, and dogs play analogous parts. In each instance the main features of the story appear to be well founded on fact. According to Mendieta, a later Franciscan chronicler, when Do Campo was captured by the Indians, Lucas and Sebastián were left to shift for themselves, which they did with great competence. "Seeing they were without the help of their good father and master," they fled toward their native land and miraculously succeeded in reaching it. Since they were without guide other than the sun, they made a wooden cross and carried it on their backs, "trusting that with such company they could not become lost." And, says the chronicler, "the cross served and guided them so well that"—many months later—"when they least expected it they found themselves in . . . the land of Christians." As they traveled they were aided in getting food by a faithful dog, "for he hunted hares and rabbits on which they lived during all that time." Returning to their monastery in the west, these two lay brothers acquired great fame. Sebastián soon died, noted and long remembered for his adventures, his piety, and his Christian character. Lucas for many years continued his work as a lay brother, "much loved by everybody, by Spaniards, both secular and religious, as well as by Indians. He made journeys inland, won many souls among the heathen people," and finally died of old age. With his customary brilliance and hyperbole, Lummis compares the wanderings of Do Campo with those of Cabeza de Vaca. "The walk of Alvar Núñez Cabeza de Vaca, the first American traveler, was surpassed by the achievement of the poor and forgotten soldier Andrés Docampo. Cabeza de Vaca tramped much more than ten thousand miles, but Docampo much over *twenty* thousand."

Castañeda, writing with a knowledge of the explorations of both Coronado and De Soto, gives us an unmistakable clue to Do Campo's route. He says the Portuguese "traveled over the plains until he crossed the cordillera of the North Sea, keeping always to his left the land discovered by Don Hernando de Soto. This man never saw the Espíritu Santo River"—that is, the Mississippi. "After crossing the cordillera of the North Sea [the Gulf of Mexico] he came upon Pánuco. If he had not gone in search of the North Sea he would have come to the borders of the land of Zacatecas." Putting Do Campo's remarkable hike in terms of the modern map, he turned south from Quivira, left Kansas, crossed Oklahoma and Texas, passed the Rio Grande, perhaps at Eagle Pass, crossed Coahuila and Nuevo León, near the site of Monterrey cut through the Sierra Madre

Oriental into Tamaulipas, reached Pánuco, turned westward, ascended the Sierra Madre Oriental, perhaps by the route of the modern automobile highway, then traveled south across the states of Hidalgo and Mexico to Mexico City.

Meanwhile another great expedition, auxiliary to that of Coronado, had been made up the Pacific Coast and returned. In the autumn of 1540, about the time when Alarcón got back from his voyage to Colorado River, Pedro de Alvarado arrived from Guatemala with a large fleet to take part in northern exploration. Stopping at Navidad, he went inland and had a conference with Mendoza. Formerly rivals, they now made a "fifty-fifty" agreement, by which they joined forces, each to receive half the profits of the other. This arranged, Alvarado, who was always spoiling for a fight, took part in the Mixton War then raging. In the episode he lost his life, thus leaving his fleet in possession of Mendoza.

With some of the ships Villalobos crossed the Pacific and reached the Philippine Islands. The *San Salvador* and the *Victoria* were assigned to Cabrillo, a skilled mariner who had been in the service of Alvarado in Central America, with orders to explore the northern coasts and to seek news of Coronado. As chief pilot went Bartolomé Ferrelo. On June 27, 1542, about when Coronado was at Culiacán on his way back to Mexico, Cabrillo sailed from Navidad. Soon thereafter they passed each other on the way, one going north filled with hope, the other headed south, weighed down by illness and discouragement.

Reaching the southern point of the Peninsula of California, Cabrillo continued up the outer shore. At San Quentín the Indians made signs understood to mean they had seen or heard of Spaniards before—men with beards, dogs, and Spanish weapons, and that they were five days inland. They must be some of Coronado's party, it was thought. To communicate with these men, Cabrillo left a letter to be delivered by the natives. Perhaps the rumor was genuine, and referred to Díaz' men, who some months previously had crossed the Colorado River into Lower California.

Continuing up the coast, Cabrillo discovered San Diego Bay, and here again natives told him of Spaniards in the interior, imitating horsemen by prancing around. Farther north the mariner discovered the Channel Islands off the coast of Upper California, and took formal possession of the mainland for Spain. On San Miguel Island he suffered a broken arm, but ascended to Cabo de Pinos near Fort Ross. Turning south, exploring as they went, the party wintered at San Miguel Island, where Cabrillo died on January 3, 1543. Ferrelo now took command and sailed north to the vicinity of Rogue River, Oregon. Between them, Cabrillo and Ferrelo had discovered most of the capes and harbors of Lower and Upper California above the point reached by Ulloa—explorations which were corollary to the Coronado expedition. On April 2, 1543, about six months before Moscoso's men landed at Pánuco, both of Cabrillo's vessels reached Navidad, on the coast of Mexico, whence they had set out in the previous June. Thus was completed one of the great series of discoveries in that era of Splendid Wayfaring in North America, at the center of which was the Coronado Expedition.

CHAPTER XXXII

GOSSIPS AND LAWYERS

After a few months' rest in Mexico City, Coronado returned to Nueva Galicia as governor in the fall of 1542, taking with him his wife, their two daughters, and a retinue of servants. Though reared in luxury, Doña Beatríz was not afraid to brave the hardships of frontier life. As a horsewoman, Queen Isabella had set her a shining example, attested by the number of her saddles still on display in the museums of Spain. Incidentally, it may be remarked that Coronado took with him the steed with the easy gait which he had borrowed from Godoy and promised to return. He now established his residence at Guadalajara, which had outgrown Compostela and was nearer to Mexico City, the capital of the viceroyalty.

The governor was met a day's journey outside the town by a delegation of citizens who went to do him honor and escort him to his new home. Among them was Juan de Villareal. Having kissed the governor's hand, Don Juan took from his chest a golden chain with a jewel attached and, with courtly bow, hung it round the neck of Doña Isabel, Coronado's daughter, a child of four or five, who was standing nearby. Don Francisco thanked Villareal, but said that since he was governor he must not accept presents, and that Don Juan must take the necklace back. Villareal replied that it was not for Coronado but for Doña Isabel. The governor subsided, the young lady kept the jewelry, and Coronado settled the account by sending to the wife of Villareal "a piece of silver which weighed about three marks, as payment for the little chain." Such were some of the amenities in what was then the Wild West of North America.

For two more years, in spite of ill health, Coronado contin-

ued to exercise his office as governor, being occupied in the
details of administration, making tours of inspection, coping
with Indian uprisings, promoting public works, and playing
cards with his friends. There is ample material for a significant
volume on the Nueva Galicia frontier in this period of Coronado's career, but space is available here for only a few illustra-
tions.

During Coronado's absence in Tierra Nueva major Indian
insurrections had been pretty thoroughly stamped out through
hard fighting by Mendoza, Oñate, and Pedro de Alvarado in the
Mixton War. But there were still occasional disturbances. One
such occurred near Purificación in the summer of 1543, and it
is mentioned here as an example of Coronado's activities. When
news of the trouble reached the governor he was in Compostela. On short notice in frontier style he assembled a squad
of citizen-soldiers and hurried south to the scene, making Purificación his headquarters for some forty days.

In all that time Coronado and his following—soldiers, Negro
and Indian servants, horses and mules—lived off the country,
chiefly as guests of the settlers of Purificación, where Juan
Hernández de Ijar was alcalde mayor and big shot of the
district. Coronado and his men occupied the home of Melchior
Vázquez, which must have been spacious if not *de luxe*. Meanwhile the citizens of the town supplied the governor and his
company with all the food they needed, "each one furnishing
whatever he had, whether wine, fowls, sheep, calves, bread,
maize or other things necessary, giving it *gratis*, without asking
or accepting any pay."

The donors' list would have looked well in the society
column, for it included the names of Melchior Vázquez, Juan
de Almesto, Iñigo de Zúñiga, Fernán Ruíz de la Peña, Martín
de Rifarache, and of course Juan Hernández de Ijar, a member
of whose family three centuries later contributed a chapter to
the history of Alta California. Almesto supplied Coronado with
two young bulls and forty sheep, sixteen of which were consumed by the visitors, the rest being returned. The bulls were
worth three *pesos* each, and the sheep, two *tomines*. Melchior

Vázquez came forth with maize, fowls, oysters, and fish as a gift, and sent Coronado half an *arroba* of wine as a loan, to be paid back in kind. Others furnished bread and a variety of other edibles. Almesto estimated that the daily supplies afforded Coronado, one day with another, were worth at least a *peso de oro común*, which in the present day looks like a small sum. But it must be remembered that a peso then—like the U.S. dollar in the good old days—had high purchasing value. Provisions were not cheap, but money was dear. As to the wine, Almesto did not know how much was furnished nor how much it would be worth, "for everybody who had any supplied Coronado with it." The wine and meat left over at the end of the forty days the governor took with him for use on his return journey to Guadalajara. The settlers were generous hosts but they afterward sent in the bill, from which we learn the details of the story.

Like all administrators, Coronado had his troubles and his critics—more especially since Nueva Galicia was a roaring frontier democracy. When he tried to compose personal quarrels the governor sometimes won the enmity of all parties and the thanks of none. One illustration will suffice. Attorney Sánchez, in the name of Andrés de Villanueva, complained before Coronado in the city of Compostela. The written charge declared that Diego de Colio, alcalde of Guadalajara, had imprisoned Villanueva and put him in manacles. Colio then assaulted Villanueva, thus manacled, dealing to him poniard stabs and fisticuffs. It was complained that Coronado not only dissimulated the offense, but failed to punish the offender. As a result the governor was accused of partiality. Coronado explained that when the charge was made he asked Sánchez for information regarding the matter, but none was given, and only conflicting gossip came to his ears, so he did not proceed against any of the persons implicated. In consequence he was criticized by partisans on both sides of the quarrel.

It was the governor's duty to see that the Indians of his province were properly instructed in the Christian Faith, and encouraged in the ways of civilized life. Therefore "knowing it was very saintly to assemble the Indians from their crags and breaks," Coronado brought more friars to the province and urged them to gather the Indians into villages. With the same end in view, and as the King desired, he ordered all Spaniards having natives in service to build churches in the Indian pueblos, and charged them to take great pains to teach the natives in matters of the Faith.

In the interest of material improvement Coronado proclaimed a royal order requiring every holder of repartimientos of Indians to build a substantial home in a Spanish city or town within the district of his grant, the house to be of stone or adobe wherever possible. Highways and roads were a matter of Coronado's care. The difficulty of fording the rivers, especially Rio de Santiago, was a serious obstacle to travel and communication. Moreover, the river crossings were dangerous to human life. For lack of bridges and ferries, each year many natives and some Spaniards and their horses had been drowned and eaten by alligators, as Coronado had experienced on his return from Pueblo Land.

So important was this matter of the rivers that the King provided funds for building a bridge across Rio Santiago near Guadalajara. Coronado went in person to inspect the site and learned that recently another person had been drowned there. Thereupon he assigned to nearby towns the task of constructing the bridge, distributing the royal appropriation among them. He also recommended a salary for a keeper of the river-crossing at Centispac, where floods and alligators had made him so much trouble in his expedition to and from Cíbola. These were just a few of the multitudinous activities of Coronado in the rough and tumble province in the two years after his return from Tierra Nueva. During all this time the governor still clearly showed the ill effects of the fall from his horse in Tiguex, suffering many bad days.

Don Francisco was loyal to his followers to Pueblo Land, and frequently helped them out in their needs, which were often grave. It was declared by one of these veterans that Coronado "clothed many caballeros and hidalgos who had returned broke, restored them to health, and lodged them in his house, dressing them according to the rank of their persons, and giving them horses, Negroes, and money."

Meanwhile a storm was gathering round the young governor's aching head. His return to Mexico had been followed by complaints regarding the Cíbola expedition. His men had expected to get rich from the much-heralded gold, silver, and precious stones of that new El Dorado, but none had been found. This was through no fault on the part of Coronado, but by critics he was held responsible, nevertheless. He ought to have returned from Tiguex to Quivira, some persons said, and from there continued to Harahey. There was the gold! Why, of course! It was also charged that there had been abuses in the management of the expedition. Let Coronado take the blame! Just at this time the Spanish Court was resounding with the discourses of Las Casas which brought about the promulgation of the celebrated New Laws for the protection of the Indians—a movement toward which Fray Marcos had contributed his bit, and of which Don Francisco was one of the first victims in Mexico. These complaints and the new attitude in Spain toward Indians resulted in an official inquiry into Coronado's leadership of the expedition to Tierra Nueva, and also into his administration as governor of Nueva Galicia. Incidentally the inquiry did much to bring Coronado forth as a human being in other capacities than as commander of a great exploring expedition.

To conduct the investigation the Emperor appointed Lorenzo de Tejada, a judge of the Royal Audiencia of Mexico, the august body which exercised authority only less than that wielded by Mendoza and of which Mendoza himself was president. Tejada's commission was signed at Valladolid, Spain, on September 7, 1543, about a year after Coronado had returned from Tierra Nueva to Mexico City, and a few months after he went back to his governorship of Nueva Galicia. The document said it had been reported "that in the expedition which

Francisco Vázquez de Coronado made to the province of Cíbola he and the Spaniards who went with him committed, both going and returning, great cruelties upon the natives of the land through which they passed," hence the investigation was demanded.

By the royal order, Tejada was instructed to investigate the management of the Cíbola expedition, making inquiry in Mexico City, Nueva Galicia, or any other place where he might think best, in order to learn "what cruelties and robberies" were committed by Coronado and his followers, and at whose orders they were perpetrated. If he should discover any culpable persons he must arrest them bodily, hear their defense, and send it to the Audiencia of Mexico, together with any report he might wish to make. By the same royal order, Tejada was appointed judge of the residencia or formal review of Coronado's administration as governor of Nueva Galicia. The residencia was a customary procedure, and did not necessarily imply that any charges had been made against the official concerned.

So Coronado was in for a scrutiny of his record both as governor of Nueva Galicia and as captain-general of the Cíbola expedition. It was now open season for enemies and gossips, and tongues began to wag, as tongues so happily do. It is significant that Tejada's commission arrived from Spain in the same ship that brought Tello de Sandoval, visitor general, who came to hold the residencia of Mendoza and other high officials, and to enforce the New Laws regarding Indian labor and tributes. Coronado was not the only target of the lawyers. He had plenty of good company, for Spain had embarked on a general campaign of reform in her Indian policy in the Americas, and before the crusade ended many a worthy administrator was ruined in pocket and in reputation.

Coronado's residencia and the investigation of the Cíbola expedition proceeded simultaneously, and they required the presence of Tejada in Mexico City and Guadalajara, for essential witnesses were to be found in both places. The judge was ordered to go to Nueva Galicia as soon as possible, suspend

Coronado and other officials for the time being, take the rods of authority into his own hands and for forty days hold an investigation of the conduct of the governor and other officials of the province, listening to anyone who might have complaints to register against them.

After making preliminary inquiries in Mexico the judge set out for Nueva Galicia on July 19, 1544, to continue his investigations there. By August 8 he had reached Guadalajara and taken up lodgings in a hostelry facing the plaza. Apparently he had arrived some little time previously, for on that day a group of officials and other citizens gathered at his quarters to hear what he had to say. The assemblage included some of the chief characters in the serio-comic drama which was enacted in that historic place during the next forty days, a number of them having been summoned from long distances for the occasion. For, indeed, an occasion it was.

Tejada now made his official bow. We may be sure he was decked out with appropriate wig, robe, and other insignia of his great office. With due formality, in the presence of the assemblage, he delivered his commission to Pedro de Requena, royal notary, who had accompanied him from Mexico City. Requena broke the seal and read the long screed to the patient listeners "who said they would obey it and did obey it," with appropriate gestures of obeisance. They probably kissed the document, placed it above their heads, and repeated a prescribed formula. Thereupon Tejada with all solemnity took to himself the rods of justice from Plasencia, Zaldívar, and the other alcaldes. With all those canes he must have felt impressive.

This ceremony over, the judge ordered everybody to go to the plaza, where he would publish to the general populace the forthcoming inquiry, together with other royal dispatches which he had brought with him. The expectant group having reassembled, Tejada "by the voice of Hernando, a Negro, in loud and clear tones proclaimed his commission." Such was the morning paper in Guadalajara at that date. In the same way Tejada published the New Laws, just then the sensation in all

Spanish America; and another solemn royal edict "to the effect that blasphemers should be punished according to law." For the time being men kept their profanity *sotto voce*, and their language was fit for ladies and children to hear. Having thus announced the residencia to the citizens *en bloc*, the judge made known his errand individually to Coronado and the other officials whose record in office was about to be investigated. They declared they would obey the royal order, "and they did obey it with due reverence," placing the document above their heads and repeating the required formula.

The show had begun. For the next forty days it was open season for anybody who had a grudge against Coronado and other officials now being investigated. The event, of course, made a stir in the frontier town. A man of note had honored the place by his presence. More to the point, what scandal would the judge uncover? That was the question in everybody's mind if not on his lips. We can readily imagine the state of nerves in Guadalajara during the next six weeks when tale-bearing was at a premium, and we may safely guess there was more than one log-rolling session outside of court while the ordeal lasted. "You shield me and I'll shield you!" But who could be trusted when the investigation was being made behind closed doors?

Tejada had his case well formulated on the basis of the general objects of his inquiry and of the investigations he had made in Mexico before starting west. It is also evident that gossips in Guadalajara worked pretty fast, for by August 10 the judge had prepared an *interrogatorio*, or questionnaire, by which witnesses were quizzed, and a number of the questions had a distinctly local odor, manifestly having been suggested by someone after the judge's arrival. Tale-bearing was the evil genius of the secret residencia. Coronado testified in his own defense before Tejada on September 1. He was defended by attorney Pero Ruíz de Haro, who was given only a week to prepare his case. Ruíz asked for more time, because some of the needed witnesses were in Mexico City and others elsewhere, but Tejada denied the request, saying he was in a hurry. So on September 8 Ruíz presented an *interrogatorio* containing eighteen points by which he questioned eighteen witnesses, some of whom testified also for the prosecution.

The document prepared by Tejada contained twenty-five questions touching upon such matters as graft, bribery, public and private morals, administration of justice, treatment of the natives, their instruction in the Faith, freedom of elections, and care for public highways. Some of the testimony given was trivial, but it sheds interesting light on life and society on that new frontier. This, indeed, is more important to the historian than any question of Coronado's innocence or guilt. Official shortcomings and legal technicalities are no new things.

The examination of Tejada's witnesses began on August 11. Twenty-eight persons were questioned regarding some or all the points listed, several of them being recalled for cross-examination. Each witness was sworn to tell the truth before God, Holy Mary, and the sign of the Cross, touching this sacred symbol with his right hand, according to law. No women were formally quizzed, but this does not mean they could not have contributed interesting information, which, indeed, they probably did in unofficial sessions, for some of the charges have a peculiarly feminine flavor.

Of the twenty-eight citizens who testified for the prosecution, nine gave their address as Guadalajara, seven as Compostela, in the west, and seven as Purificación, in the south. Several of the witnesses were old-timers in the province, having been there fourteen or fifteen years, participating in the conquest in the days of Cortés and Guzmán, and more recently in the Mixton War, regarding which the death of gallant, red-headed, Pedro de Alvarado was a vivid and sorrowful memory. Some of the witnesses were well acquainted with Coronado, knowing him *"por vista, habla, trata y conversación."* Seven had known him before he became governor of Nueva Galicia, or ever since his arrival in Mexico in 1535; but most of them, having preceded him to the west, first met him after he took charge of the province three years later.

If we may judge from their testimony, one concludes that these twenty-eight witnesses were as good a pioneer group as one would find on any American frontier. Sun-browned, hardy, and battle-scarred, they were direct in their words, and by reading their depositions we come to feel on speaking terms with the founders of the vigorous society which grew up in Nueva Galicia and gave the region a stamp which has persisted to the present. It is interesting to note that of all the twenty-eight, only one was unable to write—*"no sabía escribir."* He was Pedro Sánchez, a blacksmith of Guadalajara. It is doubtful if many comparable Anglo-American outposts could excel this record for literacy.

The proceedings followed legal models. Tejada framed leading questions, generally indicating the answers he desired—a lawyer's trick—and some of the witnesses said little more than "yes" to statements which Tejada had formulated for them. Other witnesses, flouting the august judge, took off their coats and told in forthright manner what they knew or thought, sometimes for and sometimes against the governor. Most of the charges made against him in the residencia were for things done after his return from Pueblo Land, when, because of the fall from his horse in Tiguex, he was not altogether in his right mind. They did not apply to the real Coronado—a fact which Judge Tejada recognized and generously stated in writing.

There was a very special factor in the case which cannot be overlooked. When Coronado became governor of Nueva Galicia and was made head of the spectacular Cíbola expedition he was a rising star. He was popular in both official and unofficial circles. Numerous persons gave him presents, and showed him other favors, in some cases just out of friendly admiration and respect, and in other cases, no doubt, in the hope of ascending with Fortune's child, a human motive as old as the Garden of Eden. But Coronado's expedition to Tierra Nueva, although a truly great feat of exploration, was a financial flop, involving all the disillusioned participants. Coronado was no longer able to bestow important favors, and the good-will investments in Don Francisco's enterprise in his golden days had now turned sour. Moreover, since his fall from his horse, Coronado was a greatly changed man, with traits he never before had manifested. So laudation and flattery gave way to complaints and gossip, poured into the ears of Judge Tejada in the secret sessions of the residencia. But this does not mean that Coronado did not still have many and loyal supporters.

Much of the testimony given by witnesses was based on hearsay. "Somebody told me thus and so. And somebody else told Fulano de Tal." It was like what goes on around us every day, by intent perhaps just as innocent and in effect just as vicious. There are indications that personal grudges and dislikes sometimes colored the testimony. This, too, is human. Most of us would have felt at home in that sixteenth-century atmosphere.

In the inquiry Coronado was his own worst witness. At the time when he testified he was ill and his mind was under a cloud. His memory was bad and he failed to take advantage of evidence that would have strengthened his case. Frequently he denied things, or said he did not know, when the facts would have counted in his favor.

The matter of Coronado's salary as governor of Nueva Galicia *in absentia* was a sore spot with Oñate and his friends. Coronado had held that office four or five years. Of the period he had been nearly two and a half years in Tierra Nueva, and besides he had spent several months in going to Mexico City after his return, to give his report to Mendoza and take his family back to Guadalajara. During all this time Oñate as lieutenant-governor had held the fort in Nueva Galicia. But Coronado had collected his full salary as governor ever since his first appointment, at the rate of one thousand ducats a year during eight months and at fifteen hundred ducats from the time of his "second appointment," when he became head of the Cíbola expedition.

In the residencia several old-timers rather testily declared it was "public and notorious" that Coronado's salary had been collected by him in full, "whether present or absent," whereas Oñate, pinch-hitter for more than two years, had been paid nothing more than his former salary. Dignified Oñate merely testified that Coronado had been governor four or five years and had received the salary all that time, "present or absent." Clearly, there had been neighborhood gossip about the matter. The fault was not Coronado's. Leading the Cíbola expedition was his main duty as governor of Nueva Galicia in the period of his absence, and for the expedition he received no extra pay. The trouble was that the government had made no provision for adequately remunerating Oñate as acting governor. Tejada evidently took this view of the case, for after hearing testimony on the subject he made no charges against Don Francisco.

Coronado's friends had given him so many presents that suspicion of bribery had been whispered. So Tejada asked the witnesses whether Coronado while governor had accepted gifts from litigants or other persons in the province for himself, wife, children, or dependents. To be explicit, had Coronado obtained as bribes for expected favors the horses he acquired from Samaniego, Ijar, Oñate, and Jiménez—four mounts which had figured prominently and almost personally in the Cíbola expedition? Don Francisco's horses, dead or alive, were now brought forth on judicial display. Different witnesses told variant stories. After hearing the testimony Tejada charged Coronado with accepting Jiménez's colt valued at a hundred pesos in gold bullion, on condition that Coronado should not remove the priest from his post at Culiacán; with obtaining *gratis* from Cristóbal de Oñate the black horse valued at a hundred pesos in gold bullion; with receiving from Juan Hernández de Ijar the chestnut-colored horse, worth thirty pesos in gold bullion; and with accepting from Francisco de Godoy the dappled horse with a smooth gait, using it on his journey to Mexico City, keeping it for nearly two years, and not returning it until he heard his residencia was to be held. Coronado plausibly answered the charges, but Tejada was only partly convinced. In his decison he absolved the governor on the first count, with regard to the colt obtained from Jiménez, which had been drowned, and on the fourth, involving the horse borrowed from Godoy. But on the others he was not satisfied, and he fined Coronado 150 pesos for the transaction regarding Oñate's black horse, and sixty pesos for that regarding Ijar's fast-travel-ing chestnut. Villareal's locket was put in the same category with the horses, and for it Coronado was fined another sixty pesos. Considering the then high value of the peso it must have been a handsome jewel.

Coronado's manners and morals came under inquiry. He could get angry under provocation. He was once heard to say: "Shut up, Plasencia! I know all about you! Shut up!" Sánchez, the blacksmith, intimated there was a matter of Coro-nado's relations with a married woman which "ought to be complained of in the residencia." Tejada let the subject pass, and the two persons most competent to testify were not ques-tioned. Here the judge showed plain common sense.

Diego Vázquez declared the governor had not punished gamblers as he ought. Horrors! In fact, Coronado himself shuffled the pasteboards! "Many times he had seen him gamble in his own house! And he has heard it said that he played for as much as a hundred or two hundred gold pesos. . . . And those who gambled with the governor were Juan Ruíz de Ijar, Juan de Villa Real, Juan de Hojeda, and Francisco de Godoy!" But it was much ado about nothing. Witnesses for the defense testi-fied that although Coronado sometimes played *primera* and *triunfo*, it was always for small stakes, a few dollars in cash or an arroba or two of wine; he never played *dados* (dice), *dob-ladilla*, *parar* (lansquenet), or other prohibited games. Moreover, they declared, the charge that Coronado's gambling interfered with the duties of his office was untrue, for if a citizen with business to transact happened to find the governor at cards, he always dropped the game and attended to the client. Coronado himself admitted that he played for small stakes in his own house but never in public, and never at prohibited games. Still more convincing, Diego Vázquez said the governor always lost, "whether the stakes were high or low." Evidently Coronado was a bad player but a good loser, and on that score was pop-ular.

Several of the charges made against Coronado related to the administration of the New Laws regulating the exploitation of

Indian labor by miners and hacienda owners. Resistance to the new code was widespread all over Spanish America at the time, and in some instances it went to the extremes of rebellion. Coronado, as governor of Nueva Galicia, was inevitably involved in the matter, and was caught between the reform movement and the settlers, whose vested interests were disturbed by the New Laws. In this respect he shared the fate of many contemporary officials.

The result of the residencia was that on twelve of the thirty-four charges made against Coronado, Tejada absolved him. On thirteen counts the governor was fined a total of 650 pesos. Seven charges, because they contained dynamite, or difficult points of law, were referred for decision to the Council of the Indies. Let the officials in Spain take the responsibility. As much on account of his broken health as because of his record, Coronado was removed from his governorship and ordered to go to Mexico to live. He was stripped of all the encomiendas he claimed. But at once he appealed his case to the King and the request was granted, subject to a deposit of the amount of the fines imposed.

Meanwhile an investigation of the management of the Cíbola expedition was going forward. Before starting for Guadalajara, Tejada had begun taking testimony regarding the matter "in the great city of Temistitán, Mexico." On May 27 he swore in as witnesses Francisca de Hozes and her husband, Alonso Sánchez, whom she always held on leash. Others called to testify in the capital between that date and June 25 were Juan de Paradinas, Juan de Contreras, Rodrigo Simón, Cristóbal de Escobar, Juan de Troyano, and Rodrigo de Frías. At Guadalajara, in August, Melchior Pérez, Juan de Zaldívar, Pedro de Ledesma, and Coronado himself testified. All these witnesses had been members of the Cíbola expedition, and some of them had played conspicuous parts in the drama. Whether or not they were chosen for their known opinions does not appear. But the indications are that this was not the case, for there were differences of view among them on various points, and individual deponents gave testimony which counted sometimes for and sometimes against Don Francisco. Apparently Tejada took his witnesses wherever he could find them.

The inquiry was designed to ascertain the extent of Coronado's responsibility for any abuses that occurred during the great reconnoissance, and for his failure to discover the riches of which Fray Marcos had told. This last was no minor consideration. Indeed, if he had hit such good fortune as fell to Cortés or Pizarro, the trial might never have been held. Much of the information elicited in the legal process has been utilized in the foregoing pages, and it has added immensely to the data hitherto available regarding nearly every major episode of the Coronado expedition. It is a priceless source of knowledge for many subjects formerly shadowy in the extreme or completely in the dark. At numerous points it gives us a close-up view of events and of personalities, and is a good illustration of what every historian knows, namely, that when people begin to dispute we learn something about what they have been doing. The questions asked the witnesses centered around the episodes of the expedition in which there was friction between Spaniards and natives, with the purpose of learning just what happened and who was to blame for anything that was blameworthy. It is interesting to note that the first witness called was dauntless Señora Sánchez, who had ridden *á caballo* all the way from Mexico City to the Barrancas in the Texas Panhandle and back —a good seven thousand miles! Although she had entered Cíbola with the rear guard, when it came to talking, she was right up in front. True to form, her colorless husband followed her to the witness stand and echoed her opinions.

The impression conveyed by most of those who gave testimony is that the Cíbola expedition was admirably conducted in the main, and that, with the exception of the skirmish at Chiametla, where Samaniego was killed, it proceeded without serious mishaps until Háwikuh was reached. There the natives resisted. It was the consensus of opinion, with minor differences, that the battle of Háwikuh was brought on by the natives themselves, in spite of all Coronado's efforts to avoid trouble. Of course this was the white man's point of view but it seems to have been well founded in fact. The Indians not only refused peacefully to accept Spanish rule, which it was Coronado's duty to impose, but they twice attacked the Spaniards, who had been altogether conciliatory. The general then ordered the assault on the pueblo which, after a brief fight, was abandoned by the natives. But they soon returned, and thereafter relations of Cíbola with the invaders were peaceful. Coronado's bravery in the battle was lauded by most of the witnesses, and all testified to the seriousness of the wounds he received.

It was in the course of this inquiry that Juan de Troyano and Melchior Pérez gave their hitherto unknown accounts of Alvarado's dashing expedition to Tiguex, Taos, Pecos, and the Buffalo Plains, and of the sensational episode of the golden bracelet. The pivotal question at this point was who set the dogs on Bigotes and Cacique and by whose order? The general opinion was that Alvarado actually unleashed the dogs, which belong to Tovar, but that it must have been with Coronado's knowledge, for the incident occurred right in front of his lodgings, and he was so strict that without his approval nobody else would have dared to do such a thing. This view of Coronado as a disciplinarian is manifest throughout the inquiry.

The testimony of witnesses illuminates the origin and the main episodes of the Tiguex War. Cárdenas found the natives outwardly friendly, to the extent of vacating a pueblo for the use of the Spaniards. The affair of Villegas and the Indian woman, and the harsh levy of supplies took place before Coronado's arrival, and Melchior Pérez and others in their depositions absolved Coronado on both counts. When asked if these acts were approved by Coronado after he arrived, Pérez replied emphatically in the negative. "On the contrary, he had heard it said that the captains and men tried to prevent the general from learning about the rape and the robbery, because they feared he would hang Villegas and punish the others who were implicated."

The high point of the investigation of the Tiguex War was the burning of the Indians at Arenal, and the outcome casts doubt upon Castañeda's later story regarding the part played in the episode by Cárdenas. The general tenor of the evidence was to the effect that Coronado, who was busy at another pueblo, did not know about the burning of the Indians until it was reported to him by a messenger. As to who executed the Turk and why, the testimony clearly shows that Coronado was reluctant to put him to death, but yielded when urged by his captains; and that Alvarado, Diego López, and Zaldívar carried out the order. Señora Sánchez and her spouse were the only witnesses who told about the sixty men who wished to remain in Tierra Nueva with Father Padilla, an incident which they dramatized.

The governor himself was interrogated by Tejada regarding the Cíbola expedition at Guadalajara on September 3, 1544. Many of the questions implied much more than was warranted by the facts. In his answers Coronado was restrained, and at several points his memory, as in the residencia, was obviously bad, the result, it was admitted even by the prosecution, of his accident in Tiguex.

Having completed the examination in Guadalajara, Tejada ordered Coronado to appear in Mexico within the next fifty days. In compliance Don Francisco rode once more to the capital, accompanied by Doña Beatríz, the rest of his large household, and, apparently, by Tejada. We hear no more of borrowed or gift horses now. On February 26, 1545, the judge ordered Coronado, under penalty of twenty thousand pesos, to "remain in his home in the city of Mexico as if in jail," a nominal rather than a real imprisonment. At the same time Tejada summoned Hernando de Alvarado to appear before the Royal Audiencia within thirty days, and decreed that the fiscal of his Majesty should make charges against both him and Coronado. But so far as is known, Alvarado was never held for trial.

Tejada realized that Coronado was a broken man, and he put this view on paper. When on March 11, 1545, he made a report to his Majesty, he wrote: "Francisco Vázquez came to his home, and he is more fit to be governed in it than to govern outside of it. He is lacking in many of his former fine qualities,

and he is not the same man he was when your Majesty appointed him to that governorship. They say this change was
caused by the fall from a horse which he suffered in the exploration and pacification of Tierra Nueva." This judgment
is amply sustained by other evidence. Coronado had paid a
high price for his great adventure in the service of the King.

On the basis of the inquiries thus far completed, Cristóbal
de Benavente, royal fiscal or prosecuting attorney, appeared before Tejada on March 21, 1545, and made formal charges
against Coronado for mismanagement of the Cíbola expedition. He was declared culpable for (1) hanging the Indians at
Chiametla; (2) failure to put a suitable person in command at
San Gerónimo instead of incompetent Alcaráz; (3) waging war
on Háwikuh; (4) setting dogs on Bigotes and other Indians at
Tiguex and thus causing the rebellion; (5) the execution of the
Turk, especially because it was done in secret; (6) failure to
colonize Quivira or to permit to settle there some Spaniards
who wished to do so; and (7) abandoning the lands he had discovered, after having used up all his supplies, and thus causing
great loss to the royal treasury. As to the appointment of Alcaráz as alcalde of San Gerónimo, it should be noted that this
was done by Díaz, while Arellano was there and after Coronado had gone forward to Cíbola. Díaz had already paid his debt
in full, and was sleeping in an unknown grave on the Camino
del Diablo.

Benavente recommended proceedings against Coronado,
who appeared before Tejada and answered the charges, chiefly
repeating his previous testimony. The matter was next referred
to the Royal Audiencia of Mexico, of which Mendoza was president. That august body made short work of Benavente's recommendation. After reviewing the case, the judges on February
19, 1546, in the following terms completely absolved Coronado on all the charges:

"In view of the proceedings and the merits in the case, we
find that . . . the fiscal did not prove the accusations and charges
he made against the said Francisco Vázquez de Coronado with
respect to the offenses the fiscal says he committed in Tierra

Nueva; we find them not proved; and that the said Francisco Vázquez de Coronado proved his exceptions and rejoinders; and we find and pronounce them well proved. Therefore we must and do absolve the said Francisco Vázquez of all he has been . . . charged with in this case by the said fiscal, whom we enjoin to perpetual silence, so that neither now nor at any time in the future may he accuse or bring charges against him for anything contained . . . in this our sentence. Thus we pronounce and order.—*Don Antonio de Mendoza, Licentiate Tello de Sandoval, Licentiate Ceynos, Licentiate Tejada, Licentiate Santillan.*"

Coronado's triumph was complete. It will be noted that Tejada was one of the judges who signed this report. So it may be inferred either that he had not taken too seriously his own statement of the case, or that the decision of the Audiencia must have greatly deflated his ego.

Chapter XXXIII

CÁRDENAS TAKES THE COUNT

Coronado had been exonerated. But Tejada was not satisfied that justice had been served. Somebody ought to be held responsible; and it would help Tejada's record as a lawyer. The testimony given in the course of the previous investigation, he said, established the guilt of García López de Cárdenas, but since Don García was now in Spain he was not available "to be punished as justice demands."

It will be remembered that while in Tiguex. after he had suffered a broken arm in the Buffalo Plains, Cárdenas got news of the death of his brother in Spain and of his inheritance of the family fortune—the worst luck that ever fell to him. His first attempt to answer the summons was frustrated by the Sonora uprising, which had forced him to hurry back to Tiguex with hostile Indians at his heels. But he returned to Mexico with Coronado in the summer of 1542, and from there sailed for Spain, where he was known as García Ramírez de Cárdenas. So Tejada prepared a copy of the entire bale of documents pertaining to the Coronado investigation and sent it to the Council of the Indies in Madrid, in order that its learned judges might do whatever to them seemed proper with regard to Don García.

Ships and the wheels of government moved slowly, and almost a year had passed before the next major step was taken—a delay which was symbolic of the fate of Cárdenas. Then, on January 7, 1546, nearly four years after Don García had finally departed from Pueblo Land, Villalobos, fiscal or prosecuting attorney of the Council of the Indies, presented to that august body a long list of charges against Cárdenas, based upon the documents forwarded from Mexico by Tejada, supplemented by a lively imagination and gross inaccuracy on the part of the fiscal. Cárdenas was wealthy, and a good prospect for increasing the royal revenue.

"To the best of my ability, and as it is my duty," Villalobos piously wrote, "I bring criminal charges against Don García López, resident of this city of Madrid." He now accused Cárdenas of nearly everything of which Coronado had been exonerated, adding a lot of absurdities which would have been laughable if they had not proved so harmful to Cárdenas. Specifically Villalobos charged that in the Cíbola expedition, both going and returning, Cárdenas being maestre de campo, he and his men committed "robberies, burnings, cruelties and many other offenses against the natives of the lands through which they passed, killing many of them, taking their women by force and against their will and that of their husbands and parents, and lying with them carnally." Whatever the facts may have been, it should be said in passing that with the exception of the Villegas case no such charge as the last had been made against anybody in the Coronado trial, nor was any evidence adduced to sustain the accusation. Moreover, said Villalobos, they set dogs on the Indians, confiscated their food and clothing, drove them from their homes, burned twelve or thirteen pueblos, and forced them into rebellion. Thereupon Cárdenas attacked the Indians with fire and sword. In the course of the battle of Arenal more than eighty Indians surrendered to him under promise of amnesty, a pledge which was sealed with the sign of the Cross. Then Cárdenas broke his promise, took to his tent the Indians who had surrendered, tied more than thirty of them to stakes, burned them alive, and killed those remaining in the tent with lance and sword thrusts.

All this was done, said Villalobos, as a result of Don García's greed for gold and silver, because he had heard that Bigotes wore a gold bracelet and other ornaments. "And because two other friendly Indian chieftains, one named the Turk and the other Ysopete, did not give him gold or silver, nor take him to the place where these metals could be found, he killed them all." Still worse, said Villalobos, as a result of the Indian rebellion Tierra Nueva was not colonized, the spread of the Faith was hindered, and "the royal patrimony lost an opportunity to obtain more than 500,000 ducats in gold and other things." He concluded by saying that Cárdenas ought to be subjected to the heaviest penalties, executed upon his person and his property, both as a punishment for himself and as a warning to others. Specifically he recommended that Cárdenas be sentenced to pay into the royal treasury "up to the sum of 500,000 ducats . . . the amount at which I appraise and reckon the damages and costs." One would be interested to know just how Villalobos arrived at the particular figure which he gave for his Majesty's financial losses in Tierra Nueva. One suspects that it corresponded with his estimate of the value of Don García's fortune. Cárdenas was now promptly jailed in the nearby fortress of Pinto, there to await trial. He had a long sojourn in prison and plenty of time to ponder the vicissitudes of mundane existence.

These charges of Villalobos invite a few comments. It is clear that he or his clerks very carelessly if at all read the documents sent him by Tejada, otherwise he could not have been so misinformed on a number of points. Most of his accusations fall by the evidence already set forth. He implied that Cárdenas was responsible for abuses of the Indians on the return journey from Tiguex to Mexico. But, in the first place, there is little indication that any serious irregularities occurred at that time. In the second place, Cárdenas was not in charge of the army during this period, nor had he been in command since the day when he broke his arm on Canadian River. Diego López, and not Cárdenas, was then maestre de campo. Moreover, the burning of the pueblos was not a cause, but a result of the Tiguex revolt, as everybody knew.

There were other absurdities and falsifications. Villalobos said that Bigotes had provided the Spaniards "with very good lodgings" at Tiguex. But, except for the friendliness he had shown, Bigotes had nothing whatever to do with providing the army with winter quarters, for at the time when Cárdenas established camp at Alcanfor, Bigotes was at his home on Pecos River. Most stupid of all, the fiscal said that because the Turk and Sopete did not give Cárdenas gold and silver or take him where these metals could be found, he put them all to death, by implication including Bigotes among the slain. What a lawyer! Bigotes was not executed, nor had anybody asserted or even suggested that this was the case. It was commonplace knowledge of everybody in the expedition, and was clearly stated in the records sent by Tejada to Spain, that Sopete was not killed by the Spaniards but, instead, was rewarded by them; and that when the Turk was garrotted in Quivira, Cárdenas was in Tiguex, some five hundred miles away. In fact, Cárdenas never went to Quivira, having turned back from the Barrancas to Tiguex with Arellano, because of the injury to his arm. Such disregard of the evidence right before him raises a well founded suspicion of insincerity on the part of Villalobos. If it was not insincerity it was monumental incompetence.

The steps in the trial that followed may be briefly summarized. Villalobos directed the prosecution of Cárdenas; and Benavente, who had lost his case against Coronado, represented the Council in Mexico. To act for him in America, Cárdenas appointed Luís del Castillo and Coronado, one of numerous indications that the general and Don García stood by each other through thick and thin. In Spain the prosecution and the defense each drew up an *interrogatorio* by which their respective witnesses were to be quizzed. Coronado's men were now scattered, and witnesses had to be hunted up, which was time-consuming. Most of the veterans were still in Mexico City, but some were in Spain and others had gone off to the wars in Peru. Still others were in Nueva Galicia, where they had remained on the way back from Quivira. Some of them could not be found. The investigation shows how Coronado's men had scattered after the expedition.

Time passed. On February 20, 1546, Cárdenas made his deposition in his prison cell in the fortress of Pinto. Juan de Vitoria, being at court, was questioned by the prosecution in Madrid on May 15. Francisco Gorbalán, García del Castillo, and Pedro de Navarro were found at Guadalajara, Spain, where they testified on June 16. Pablos de Melgosa, of Grand Canyon fame, who had been in Flanders for a time, told his story at Burgos on October 5. Their testimony was sent to Mexico, where the examination of witnesses for the prosecution was continued on January 21, 1547. Between that date and March 26, twelve more of Coronado's men testified, namely Hernando de Orduña, Cristóbal de Escobar, Hernando de Alvarado, Rodrigo Maldonado, Alonso de Valderrey, Hernando de la Cadena, Juan de Jaramillo, Rodrigo Simón, Gaspár de Saldaña, Domingo Martín, Pedro de Ledesma, and Rodrigo de Frías. On April 26, Benavente reported that he could find no more witnesses, "some of them having gone to Peru and some to other places." In Mexico on December 9 of the same year Sebastian Vázquez, acting for Cárdenas, began examining witnesses for the defense. By January 24, 1548, eleven veterans had testified: Hernando de Alvarado, Pedro de Ledesma, Juan de Beteta, Juan Galeras, Juan de Fíoz, Rodrigo de Frías, Domingo Martín, Hernán Paez, Luís de Vargas, Gaspár de Saldaña, and Gerónimo Mercado de Sotomayor. This last-named adventurer, it will be remembered, had been appointed official historian of the Coronado expedition, and was one of the discoverers of Grand Canyon. On January 26 Sebastian Vázquez stated that for the time being he did not wish to present any more witnesses, and no more were examined thereafter. It will be noted that five men, Alvarado, Saldaña, Martín, Ledesma, and Frías, were questioned by both the prosecution and the defense.

Cárdenas in his deposition at Pinto reviewed his early career in the Indies, his appointment as maestre de campo by Coronado, the march of the advance guard, the capture of Cíbola, his discovery of Grand Canyon (modestly told in ten lines), the uprising of the Indians at Tiguex, his efforts to induce them to submit peacefully, their refusal, and the battle of Arenal, in which he had played a major part. The crux of the inquiry at this point was the burning of thirty or more Indians in that fierce combat, and whether this was done, as charged by Villalobos, after Cárdenas had promised them amnesty if they would surrender, the pledge being sealed by the sign of the Cross, according to a story told by Contreras, Pérez and Troyano in the

Coronado trial. Cárdenas declared that before the battle he exhorted the Indians to submit peacefully, but they refused;
thereafter he did not exhort them again, nor did the Indians
sue for peace during the combat. Whoever told this story of
the cross was spreading a malicious untruth! To drive the Indians out of the pueblo it was set on fire and some Indians were
burned by the soldiers. He did not punish his men for this
deed because it was done in the heat of battle, a circumstance
which all soldiers would understand. Being asked "whether it
was true that Melchior Pérez told him that if he did not intend
to keep his pledge to the Indians he should not make promises
to them by the sign of the Cross, and he replied that he was not
making the crosses in good faith," Cárdenas declared that he
never told Pérez any such thing. Here was a flat denial on a
question of fact. The testimony of Pérez, Contreras, and Troyano carries less weight when we learn that all three were
known to be bitter enemies of Cárdenas because he had punished them for misdemeanors, the nature of which is not disclosed. It is still further weakened by conflicting statements. For
example, Castañeda said in his narrative that it was Pablos
de Melgosa and Diego López, and not Cárdenas, who had
promised the Indians amnesty. So there was uncertainty, to
say the least.

The questions which were asked the witnesses for the prosecution both in Spain and Mexico closely paralleled the charges
made against Cárdenas by Villalobos. Some of them, like the accusations, were based upon assumptions contrary to well-known
facts. They implied that the burning of the pueblos was a cause
instead of a result of the uprising; that Cárdenas killed Bigotes,
the Turk and Sopete, which everybody knew was false; that the
rebellion entailed "a loss to the royal patrimony of half a million ducats in gold, silver, and other things." Witnesses were
asked to estimate what the crown might have obtained if the
colonization of Tierra Nueva had not been prevented by the
deeds of Cárdenas.

Here Villalobos could have found little comfort in the testimony even of his own witnesses, for most of it flatly contradicted

the charges he had made against Cárdenas. In other words, it backfired. In general the witnesses for both the prosecution and the defense took the position that the Indians of Tiguex had rebelled against the authority of his Majesty and that Cárdenas had punished them, as by his orders he was required to do. With few exceptions they stood consistently by Cárdenas, declaring that he led the army well and always treated the Indians kindly. What he did at Arenal was justified by the rules of war.

As to the King's losses, the witnesses made the charges of Villalobos look ridiculous. He had declared the Tiguex rebellion prevented the settlement of Tierra Nueva and the spread of the Faith, whereby the "royal patrimony missed the opportunity to obtain more than 500,000 ducats in gold, silver, and other things." When the witnesses were quizzed on this point they must have laughed—unless perhaps they swore vigorous oaths. At any rate their replies were emphatic. "Let the witnesses say and declare what they think his Majesty and the royal patrimony lost, and what they might have obtained if the country had been explored and pacified, and had not been disturbed by the war and the mistreatment inflicted upon the Indians. Let them tell what they know." They told! And how!

Alvarado said that "after the service of God and his Majesty, what many of the hidalgos and caballeros who went in the army desired was to make a living and improve their status; and if in that country there had been what is declared in the question, they would not have . . . abandoned it." Juan de Jaramillo said he did not know what was charged because it was not true. "Instead, he knows just the opposite . . . and is certain that in abandoning that country a service was rendered to both God our Lord and his Majesty, because the land is so poor and sterile, and . . . so far from the sea and from any place whence they might have obtained succor." Villalobos must be dreaming! Hernando de Orduña "believed that if they had remained in that country, in a short time everybody would have died because of the extreme cold and sterility of the land." Talk about royal profits from such a region was absurd! He added: "This was the opinion held by all the army, judging from what he had many times heard them say in conversation." Hernando de la Cadena looked at the ledger and saw the balance in deep red. If Coronado had remained in Tierra Nueva, "his Majesty would have had to support that country, and in peopling it . . . would have spent more than the half million ducats . . . and from it would never have had any profit or anything else." In short, "Coronado ought to be regarded as having rendered his Majesty a great service by not having colonized the country, because it is sterile and worthless." New Mexicans today may not like Cadena for this opinion of their beautiful country.

Pedro de Ledesma said he never saw any gold or silver in all the distance he had covered, nor any metal "except a piece of copper"—the ornament worn by Tatarrax—and that if the Spaniards had remained there it would have cost the King a pretty penny just to keep them alive, "for his Majesty is most Christian and he would not have permitted them to die of hunger." García del Castillo said he never saw gold, silver, nor pearls. In fact, he did not bring back as much as the value of a copper cent—"no trujo blanca." Juan de Fíoz declared he never saw "a speck of gold nor any precious stones." On the contrary, the natives had "huge grinding stones . . . with which they . . . broke the heads, arms and legs of the soldiers."

During the many months required to find witnesses, take depositions in both Spain and Mexico, and assemble all the evidence in Madrid, Cárdenas was either in prison or out on bail. When first incarcerated in the fortress at Pinto, a suburb of Madrid, he was ill, and the alcaide, or warden, did not wish to be responsible for him; moreover, he had not been told what manner of confinement he was expected to impose upon the distinguished prisoner. On the other hand, Cárdenas complained of excessive living costs at the fortress. So he begged the Council of the Indies to order him imprisoned in his own home in Madrid, under any guaranty that might be required, "for he was a man of honor and would not break jail." In case this request were not granted, he asked permission to go freely about the fortress without manacles or guard. The Council ruled (February 26, 1546) that if Don García would furnish bail for twenty thousand ducats as guaranty that he would not leave prison "on his own feet or the feet of anybody else," and would seal the promise by swearing homage, the petition would be granted. Bondsmen with imposing titles of nobility were found, and Cárdenas pledged homage in the hands of Pero Zapata Osorio, "once, twice, thrice; once, trice, thrice; once, twice, thrice," whereupon his petition was approved. He could now move freely about and calm his fretful spirit.

But the troubles of Cárdenas were not over, and for nearly two and one-half years, while his case was being considered, he spent a goodly portion of his time asking for new leaves of absence or removal from one to another place of incarceration. Some of these petitions were granted and some denied. A few examples are illustrative. Two weeks after he had been given freedom to move about the fortress—that is to say, on March 14, 1546—Cárdenas asked permission to leave Pinto for ten or twelve days to visit his prospective father-in-law, the noble Conde de Coruña, who was gravely ill in Guadalajara, making it necessary to arrange before it was too late the dowry which Cárdenas would receive with Doña Ana. With his petition he offered the same bail as before and ample evidence of the gravity of the Conde's condition. But the Council was unmoved and coldly ruled: *No ha lugar!* Petition denied!

Next time Cárdenas had better luck. A few days after meeting this blunt rebuff he made a new appeal to the Council. Rodríguez, his attorney, reported to that body that his client was suffering from "a broken arm and other infirmities which befall those who are in the Indies." Moreover, his right leg was so swollen and painful that he could not stand on it. The trouble was attributed to the dampness of the fortress, which in good medieval style was surrounded by a water-filled moat. So, offering the same bail as before, he again begged permission to be imprisoned at his home in Madrid, where he could have proper treatment for his infirmities. In proof of his illness, numerous witnesses made sworn statements. Luís de Oviedo, his servant, declared that Cárdenas's right leg was badly swollen, and so sore that he could not put his foot to the ground. Oviedo had cared for him in the night, applying hot cloths and other remedies. Dr. Pedro Torres testified that his patient's left arm was "very much withered, and drier than the other." Torres had prescribed for him a poultice, and many powders and herbs. He had treated him for a fever which was due to a fall, and had frequently bled him, but had never dared to bleed the withered arm. Dr. Alonso Díaz, bolder than Torres, had recommended bleeding that member "because by drawing out the blood the limb would become warm and therefore stronger." Díaz added that if Cárdenas were not removed from the damp fortress he was in danger of being a cripple for life—as indeed was the case.

Yielding to all this testimony, the Council ruled that if Cárdenas would renew his bail and pledge of homage, promising to regard his house as a prison, and not to leave it without special permission, the request would be granted—"but he must arrive in Madrid at night and without torches"—so that nobody would know how soft the officials were becoming. The pledge of homage had already been attended to, and on April 5, at Pinto, "the very magnificent Señor don García Ramírez" obligated himself to remain in his house, giving his oath by "the Scriptures and the sign of the Cross, on which he put his hand," and at the same time he did homage "once, twice, thrice; once, twice, thrice; once, twice, thrice, in the hand of Juan de Cárdenas, *hijo dalgo*."

Now followed several leaves of absence from jail, alternating with flat refusals. Meanwhile Cárdenas had the satisfaction of keeping the royal officials busy. After a new appeal he was released for twelve days to go to Guadalajara to visit the Conde de Coruña, but he must start before daybreak and return at night. Later he was given leave for sixty days to visit Guadalajara to look after a mill he owned there, and another of four months to attend to his interests in Andalucía and Granada. On the occasion of his marriage, permission to move freely about Madrid for six months was granted. On December 5, 1548, he was given leave for three months to journey to Valladolid with the Duque de Maqueda; and on July 4, 1549, he was permitted to go again to that city to await the decision of his case.

The wheels of justice turned thus slowly. Cárdenas had made his deposition regarding his part in the Cíbola expedition at Pinto on February 20, 1546. Rodríguez, after having presented several vigorous statements in defense of Don García, wrote to the Council on July 15, that his client, who was "without guilt," had long been imprisoned, greatly to his injury. On August 15 and again on October 2 of the same year he urged that the charges against Cárdenas be withdrawn, "he having given . . . better and truer evidence than that which your fiscal gave . . . for arresting and holding him in prison for so long a time."

Tardily the depositions made in Mexico by the witnesses of Cárdenas arrived in Spain; and on September 19, 1548, Rodríguez presented them to the Council, "signed and sealed." Another new year was ushered in. On January 24, 1549, Rodríguez declared that by the evidence Cárdenas was absolved, and demanded that his client be acquitted, but Villalobos refused to yield. Finally, on December 20, 1549, after six years of uncertainty and delay, a decision was announced by the Council. It was hard-boiled. Cárdenas was declared guilty on all the charges, and sentenced to serve his Majesty for thirty-three months at Orán, in Africa, with his person, arms, and horse, and at his own expense. He was sentenced also to pay eight hundred gold ducats—not the half-million of which Villalobos had dreamed—one half of the amount to be used to pay the passage of friars to the Indies and the other half to be spent in charitable work in New Spain. In this way his crime would serve a pious cause.

Cárdenas appealed the decision, urging that the place of service be changed to Navarre. The hearts of the Council mellowed somewhat, and on July 17, 1551, they ordered an amended sentence, "not in justice," Cárdenas was reminded, but in mercy. The thirty months' service in Orán was changed to one year on the frontiers of Navarre, and the fine of eight hundred ducats was reduced to two hundred. At the same time Cárdenas was banned from the New World for a period of ten years, an unnecessary precaution, we may assume. Cárdenas protested that the climate of Navarre was bad for his health, so he was sent instead to Vélez Málaga, a little town on the north shore of the blue Mediterranean some twenty miles east of Málaga, and there he served his term. Thus, counting the time spent in jail or out under bond, he had been a prisoner for some seven years. He had paid a high price for his treasure hunt in Tierra Nueva. But he had a tale of adventure to tell, and we hope that from it he found some satisfaction to offset the heavy price he had paid.

The basis for the decision in the trial of Cárdenas is not clear, for little attention was paid to the evidence presented. This is particularly true of the charges made against the defendant by Villalobos, the prosecuting attorney. It would seem, moreover, that either the Council of the Indies did not credit the witnesses for defense, or that it had decided, regardless of the evidence, to make Cárdenas an example for future conquistadores. In the main the Coronado expedition had been quite exemplary—mild and gentle as compared with acts committed by Cortés, Pedrarias, Guzmán, De Soto, or the Pizarros. But the burning of the Indians at Arenal was a distressing event, even though it was an accident of war.

There were other factors in the case. Although Coronado was commander-in-chief of the expedition, and was close at hand when the holocaust occurred at Arenal, he was completely exonerated. But Coronado was tried in Mexico and Cárdenas in Spain. In America, Indians were realities and not exactly what Las Casas had painted them at the Court of Charles V in Europe. Moreover, the chief justice of the court which exonerated Coronado was Mendoza, his patron. Furthermore, Mendoza himself at the very same time was under investigation, and Coronado was one of his star witnesses. Cárdenas, on the other hand, was tried in Spain, where Las Casas had preached with such vigor that he brought about the enactment of the famous New Laws designed to remedy the many abuses to which the natives of America had been subjected.

The sentence of Cárdenas may be regarded as an incident in the putting of teeth into the New Laws. Let Don García be made an example! Let it be known that the swashbuckling days were over!

Chapter XXXIV

IN PERSPECTIVE

Because Coronado found no precious metals in the regions he explored it has been the fashion to regard his expedition as a pointless jaunt. Nothing could be farther from the truth. Exploration was a necessary antecedent to the colonization, exploitation, and social development of any part of the New World. Before the Wright brothers invented an airplane that would work, more than one Darius Green made a flying machine that failed to function. Before Cortés and Alvarado entered the interior of Mexico and Central America, numerous apparently profitless voyages had been made around the shores of the Gulf and the Caribbean. Before the English pioneers crossed the mountains and established homes in the Ohio Valley, it was visited by a whole galaxy of Daniel Boones and by them made known to the people on the eastern seaboard as a Promised Land. In the long perspective of history no exploring expedition was entirely profitless, even if it netted no contemporary a dollar. Negatively or positively, each reconnoissance of any region helped to prepare the way for the next step in the historical process by which the New World became what it is today.

Coronado made one of the significant expeditions of that remarkable era of the opening of the Western Hemisphere by Europeans. He performed in North America a service analogous to what was done in South America by Pizarro, Almagro, Belalcázar, or Quesada; or in Middle America by Balboa, Alvarado, or Cortés. He converted the old trail up the West Coast Corridor into a well-known road that is still in use, and in its time and place just as significant as the Wilderness Road over the mountains to Kentucky. To the map of the interior of North

America he added Cíbola, Tusayán, Tiguex, the Llanos del Cíbola, and Quivira, regions which were later combined by Anglo-Americans under the name of the Southwest, or the Spanish Borderlands. Historical tradition in this vast area, all the way from California to Nebraska, runs back to the reconnoissance made by the gallant conquistador.

A notable contribution of Coronado to the larger features of North American geography was the discovery of the Continental Divide—the watershed between the Pacific and the Atlantic Oceans from which two river systems run in opposite directions. Jaramillo observed and correctly stated that in the latitude where they crossed it the Divide was just east of Zuñi. He says that "all the springs, rivers, and arroyos we have found as far as Cíbola, and perhaps also those one or two days beyond, flow to the South Sea, and those farther on to the North Sea." As a matter of general interest it would be appropriate to erect a marker of the Continental Divide on the road leading east from Zuñi where Jaramillo noted the watershed, and on it record his important discovery.

It was Coronado who first acquired a relatively accurate knowledge of the width of the continent in the latitude of his travels. Contemporary maps made in Europe showed North America as very narrow in this area. Cabeza de Vaca's long journey westward from Florida to Arizona had not dispelled the notion that north of Mexico the oceans were close together. Then a new idea dawned. Coronado while he was still at Cíbola was visited by native ambassadors from the Pecos River some two hundred miles farther east, who told of the great Buffalo Plains still beyond. Don Francisco now formed a generally sound opinion regarding Cíbola's relation to both oceans. He wrote from there: "I have gained no information about the North Sea [Atlantic Ocean] nor about the one in the west, nor am I able to tell your Lordship which one we are nearest, but I should judge we are closer to the Western Sea. It appears to me that it cannot be less than 150 leagues from here to there, and that the North Sea must be much farther away." This is a definitely more accurate estimate than the one revealed by Mendoza's instructions to Fray Marcos. The man who furnished the initial data for this important geographical news was no other than our young friend Bigotes, chief of Pecos. He deserves a place in the history of cartography alongside of Jaramillo.

After going east to far-distant Quivira, Coronado concluded that the Tiguex pueblos were "four hundred leagues from the North Sea, and more than two hundred from the South Sea, thus prohibiting all intercourse." This would put Tiguex, on the upper Rio Grande, about one-third of the distance from the Pacific to the Atlantic, which is fairly accurate, and his estimate of six hundred leagues for the total width of the continent, though still too small, was a vast improvement over some of the contemporary maps. Nor was Coronado's opinion a guess; it was based on his long journey from Arizona to Kansas, during which he and his horses had measured every mile of the way in terms of sweat, sore muscles, and bodily fatigue. If by the North Sea Coronado meant the Gulf of Mexico, as apparently is the case, his calculation of distance was not far from correct.

This idea of the immense span of the continent acquired by Coronado on the basis of his own travels was substantiated and made more exact by the contemporary expedition of De Soto from the eastern seaboard to and across the Mississippi into the regions now called Arkansas, Louisiana, and eastern Texas. Thus the approximate width of the continent was now established on the basis of actual exploration by the two armies which almost met. To the same result Zaldívar's Indian woman contributed her bit. Having fled from the Barrancas of the Panhandle, later on she reached Moscoso's men in eastern Texas, as was learned by Coronado's men after they returned to Mexico. "Thus," Castañeda remarks, "we are led to believe that we were not far from the region they discovered. . . . So it is estimated that the land in that latitude must be more than six hundred leagues wide from sea to sea"—a very fair estimate of the distance from the Gulf of California to the Gulf of Mexico. In the short space of three years these two rival explorers had made known to the world in broad outline nearly a third of the area now contained in the United States, and in several important respects had changed current ideas regarding the entire land mass of North America and its geographical relation to the rest of the globe.

By a strange misunderstanding, recorded by Ramusio and adopted by Gómara, European map makers absurdly reversed the direction of Coronado's long eastward march from Cíbola and the order of the pueblos seen by him, transformed the River of Quivira into a lake, and then shifted the province of Quivira to the shores of the Pacific Ocean, where for several decades it roamed up and down the map. As a corollary to this blunder, Coronado's River of La Señora [the Rio Grande] was shown as flowing west into the Pacific Ocean in northern California—categorical statements by Coronado, Jaramillo, and Castañeda to the contrary notwithstanding. It is safe to say that Coronado never told Mendoza what Ramusio attributed to him. Both Ramusio and Gómara deserve a prominent place in a Southwestern joke book.

Relatively unimportant though these curious mistakes of the map makers may have been, they make it clear that Coronado and his contemporaries had contributed more to North American geography than Europeans could quickly digest. The government of Spain was partly at fault by reason of its secretive policy with respect to the work of its explorers, for after Gómara's history, little was published regarding the Coronado expedition for several decades. French, Portuguese, English, and Russian explorers in America also suffered from the ignorance of their officials in Europe.

It must not be concluded from the strange errors made by map makers that the explorers themselves did not know where they had been, or that they did not understand the relative position of their discoveries with respect to Mexico and adjacent areas. On the contrary, the chroniclers of the Coronado expedition, contemporary Mexican officials, and contemporary frontier promoters had a generally clear idea of what both Coronado and his *vis à vis,* De Soto, had done; and they made use of the new information in the discussion of problems which immediately arose. More important than the difficulty of educating Europeans was the widening of the horizon of the colonists in New Spain, who made practical use of the new data acquired.

Coronado on his march from the Barranca Grande to the Arkansas River made an interesting contribution to knowledge of the declination of the compass needle in that region and at that date. Writers hitherto have generally approached the problem of the identity of the Barranca Grande backward. Not knowing the topography of the region, in order to locate the great canyon, and noting that Coronado said he traveled by the needle, they consulted scientists regarding the declination of the compass needle in 1541. On confessedly inadequate data the scientists conjectured that the declination along Coronado's route from the Barranca Grande was some two degrees west of true north. In accordance with that guess historians placed the Barranca Grande far east and south of its true location. But the Barranca Grande was unmistakably Palo Duro Canyon. From here Coronado traveled on the high plain, near the escarpment of the Llano Estacado, which runs about eleven degrees east of true north. This happens to be about the average declination of the needle along Coronado's route for the last century, for which we have accurate data based on astronomical observations. The obvious conclusion is that it was about the same in Coronado's day. Hence his record has enabled us to answer a question for which scientists have had no reliable data.

There is a widespread impression, often expressed in print, that the horses in use by the Plains Indians in the seventeenth and eighteenth centuries were descended from the animals left behind when the Coronado expedition withdrew to Mexico. But this opinion, as Aiton states, does not appear to be well founded. In the first place, as has already been noted, among the horses taken to New Mexico by Coronado and his men there were very few mares. In the muster roll of the army drawn up at Compostela when the expedition started north, out of some five hundred mounts listed, only two mares were mentioned. There probably were others but the number apparently was small. Since mounts were at a premium they no doubt were carefully guarded in the course of the long march and at the winter camps in Pueblo Land. In the available records of the expedition there is mention of the disappearance of two or three horses besides those killed by the Pueblo Indians in the Tiguex War. Had there been others, it is reasonable to suppose they also would have been noted. Moreover, in the accounts of the Spanish expeditions to the Southwest and Kansas in the later sixteenth and early seventeenth centuries no mention is made of horses or mounted Indians, which, if encountered, would have been sure to attract attention. It would seem, therefore, that the horses ridden by the Plains Indians in the eighteenth century as far north as the prairies of Canada were descended from stock which strayed or was obtained from the Spanish settlements after the permanent colonization of New Mexico and Texas in the seventeenth century.

The notion of vast wealth in Tierra Nueva would not down. In spite of Coronado's reports, and of the emphatic testimony of his followers as to the lack of ready-to-hand riches—namely, gold, silver, and precious stones—Don Francisco was criticized for withdrawing to Mexico, and within five years of his return there was official talk of sending a new expedition to colonize Quivira. Contributory motives were the desire to relieve Mexico City of idle adventurers, including some of Coronado's own men, and fear of another intrusion from the east such as that of De Soto. The route to Quivira now proposed was the direct one by which Do Campo had fled to Pánuco and which was paralleled by Moscoso. "Of all this wealth they give great news," wrote a high official of Mexico in 1547, "and it is very proper that your Majesty should order all that country peopled. . . . Now the route is certain and the land so healthful and fertile and abounding . . . with so many provisions and so many millions of cattle which God has scattered there that it appears to me . . . another Promised Land." Do Campo's trail from Quivira to Mexico City was not more than half as long as the one followed by Coronado, hence the route proposed for a return to Kansas.

But the defense of Florida at the moment was more urgent,

and to this task attention was now given. Mendoza requested Moscoso's men to return thither overland, "offering them whatever was necessary to establish themselves in that distant land," but many of them went instead to Peru. A colony for Florida was raised in Mexico in 1559, and the man chosen to lead the adventurers was no other than Don Tristàn de Luna y Arellano, who had made a good record with Coronado and had high family connections. Six of his captains had been with De Soto, acquired Alabama wives, and with them now accompanied Arellano. Thus Don Tristán was a personal link between Coronado and Florida. The Do Campo-De Soto route was at first contemplated, but the expedition was finally sent by water, which under existing circumstances was more practicable. The wide gap overland was not bridged till long afterward, but the idea persisted and it was initially based on the exploits of Do Campo, De Soto, and Moscoso.

If Coronado may appear less efficient than some of his contemporary conquistadores, it is partly due to his finer sense of the rights and dignity of human beings. He was not a swashbuckler. Don Francisco had many unquestionable qualifications for leadership. When he set forth on his great expedition he was only thirty years old. With five years of American experience behind him, he was still in the bloom of early manhood, and had those precious attributes that make youth so competent, so engaging, and so enviable. He was attractive, optimistic, and unsoured by the hard knocks and disappointments that come with sordid worldly contacts. There is abundant evidence that Coronado organized his army well, and led it in an orderly manner all the way to Cíbola, Tiguex, the Buffalo Plains, and Quivira. His treatment of the Indian allies whom he took in his train was notably more humane than that practiced by some of the conquerors of the period. Mendoza's orders regarding this matter were strict, and Coronado was zealous in carrying them out. He was so successful in this particular that on the long march of more than four thousand miles, from Mexico City to eastern Kansas and back, and embracing a period of more than two years, including two cold and hungry winters in Tiguex, few Spaniards were lost and not more than thirty Indian allies were sacrificed. No other contemporary record could match this one.

Coronado was reputed by his followers to be a strict disciplinarian, even something of a martinet, and it is well known that he sometimes punished his soldiers for misconduct, especially for offenses against the Indians. But on only one occasion, so far as the available record goes, was he charged with being harsh and arbitrary with his men. This was when some of the soldiers opposed his decision to abandon conquest and return with the whole army to Mexico. When, as we have seen, some sixty men on that occasion proposed to remain in Tiguex, or to return to Quivira with Father Padilla, Coronado threatened to punish—even to hang—anyone who remained or so much as talked about remaining. He had decided to return to Mexico for what he regarded as good reasons, and now it was his duty to enforce his orders.

If Don Francisco had been an incompetent leader some of his followers might well have clamored to turn back after the shocking disappointment experienced at Cíbola, when they saw the much advertised city was nothing but a "huddle of mud huts"; and they might have done the same after new disappointments at Tiguex, or after the hardships of the first winter there. But not many faltered, and apparently nobody deserted except some of the men left with brutal Alcaráz in Sonora Valley. Without a commander who inspired confidence and enthusiasm for the gamble this could not have been true.

There is no doubt of Coronado's dash and nerve, qualities which endeared him to his soldiers, and made them willing to follow him through thick and thin. At Cíbola he led his men into battle, receiving blows and wounds which caused his comrades to despair of his life, and to admire him all the more in consequence. His conduct in the Tiguex War was brave and soldierly. It took real stamina to march with only thirty men through unknown country from the Barrancas of the Texas Panhandle five or six hundred miles to Quivira, whose ruler had been represented as a powerful monarch who commanded an army of giants and inflicted awful punishment upon anyone who opposed his will.

The testimony of Coronado's comrades was put in phrases that leave no doubt of the loyalty and admiration of his followers. Hernando del Valle declared that the general, in the course of the expedition, "suffered great hardships from hunger, cold, heat, and loss of blood from many wounds which the natives of those lands gave him and from which he was at the point of death; and many times his life was put in great peril and danger in the service of his Majesty." Juan Bermejo, royal notary of the expedition, at Cíbola saw Coronado "at the point of death, and beyond the hope of all who went with him on the expedition, because the Indians of that valley wounded him with arrows in many places." Melchior Pérez "saw that the natives of the principal pueblo of Cíbola wounded the governor . . . when he went to enter it, because he was in the vanguard. And such were the wounds and blows they gave him on his head and his body that he lost much blood; and they carried him on their shoulders as dead to the Spanish camp." Pedro de Castro testified that at Cíbola when Coronado was leading the van and encouraging his men, the natives gave him so many wounds that they thought him dead. "They carried him out in their arms and he became very ill from his wounds." Juan Pastor declared that "in all the encounters . . . Coronado, like a good captain, was always in the vanguard, and that . . . he many times came out wounded, and was at the point of death, as is notorious among the men who went in that army." All these and many more testimonials to Coronado's qualities and deeds were given in a secret and not wholly sympathetic inquiry, conducted with a view to obtaining frank expression of opinions.

It is not without human interest to learn how the chief participants in this truly great exploring expedition passed their last days, and what was their reward. Coronado spent the few remaining years of his short life in Mexico City, nursing his broken health and taking part in the government of the capital. He resumed his duties as a member of the council and was elected by that body to serve as procurator mayor for two different years, 1545 and 1551. Don Francisco seems to have made his second term of office noteworthy chiefly by the erection of a pillory in the plaza of the city. A stir was created in the council by the former governor when, in the spring of 1545, he was notified he must carry the city banner in a procession on the feast of San Hipólito. Coronado objected that inasmuch as he had been absent in Jalisco on the King's business when his turn had come up, he was not liable for such service until the duty had made its full rounds. He apparently was not flattered by the honor. The argument continued for more than two months, but at last, on July 3, Don Francisco agreed to function as standard-bearer.

Coronado retained the friendship of Viceroy Mendoza, and in 1547 he was one of the most important witnesses for the defense in the great official's residencia. Two years later, on February 14 and again July 5, presumably because of this friendship, Coronado was designated by the council to visit Mendoza, who was ill at Guastepec, and consult with him on certain matters of city business. In the same year, 1549, in spite of Tejada's condemnation, Coronado received a royal grant of Indians in encomienda "for meritorious services in discovery and conquest." He regarded this as only a partial vindication, and in 1551 he was still pressing his suit to regain the estates of which he had been deprived by Tejada. His health continued to decline, and on June 5, 1553, he obtained permission to leave Mexico City in an effort to improve his condition, for he had never fully recovered from the effects of his accident in Tiguex. By August 1, however, weary though he was, he had again taken up his duties in the cabildo. The records of the council show that Don Francisco was absent for some time during the early months of 1554, and on June 21 the sick man petitioned the King to appoint as regidor in his place Bernaldino de Bocanegra, who was betrothed to Coronado's daughter Doña Isabel, of chain and locket fame. Don Francisco gave ill health as the reason for his resignation but promised to continue to serve the King to the best of his ability until formal appointment of a successor should be made. This was not to be for very long, for although, in accordance with his pledge, he appeared in council meetings on July 3, 6, and 9, "Francisco Vázquez de Coronado died and passed from this present life on the night of a Saturday which was accounted the 22nd day of September of this year of 1554."

The remains of Don Francisco, his celebrated wife, Doña Beatríz, and other members of the explorer's family lie buried in Mexico City in the famous church of Santo Domingo, three blocks north of the Cathedral and across the street from the old Inquisition building. Paul A. Jones and Joaquín Meade y Sáinz Trapaga recently identified the Coronado shrine. With justifiable gratification, Jones writes: "When a Kansas country editor and a Mexico City building contractor had satisfied themselves from the only available records that they knew the spot where all that is mortal of Francisco Vázquez de Coronado now reposes, they went to Santo Domingo church and stood at the gospel or left side of the main altar, confident and proud that they were the first two living persons, representing the two most interested nations, to make the pilgrimage and pay such homage to a brave man across a span of nearly four hundred years. The editor, visibly affected, felt that years of travel and research had been rewarded."

With the death of Francisco Vázquez de Coronado, the central figure of one great episode in the pageant of the New World passed from the scene. Many another actor in that vast drama, who had played a part either large or small in the Coronado sequence, already had made his final exit or was soon to spin out his rôle. After his release from the prison into which Pérez de la Torre had ordered him thrown, Nuño de Guzmán, founder of Coronado's province of Nueva Galicia, returned to Spain at the King's command, and spent his remaining years in an attempt to vindicate himself and urge his rights to a share in the northern conquests. There in poverty he died in 1544.

Cortés, the ablest of the conquerors, Guzmán's bitterest enemy, and Coronado's rival in the race for the Seven Cities, likewise passed his last years in Spain, pressing the recognition of his claims in the New World. He left Mexico in 1540 never to return, although just before his final illness he was making plans to set sail for the land he had won for his king. The Marquis of the Valley died, an old man at sixty-two, on December 2, 1547, in the village of Castillejo de la Cuesta, near Seville.

Just a few months later, on June 3, 1548, after twenty illustrious years in Mexico in the service of the Church, the venerable Bishop Zumárraga expired. It was he who had sponsored Fray Marcos and urged Mendoza to put the Coronado expedition into effect. The weight of the Bishop's opinion had been an important factor in the genesis of the great adventure. Highest honors had come to the prelate—but too late. Only nine days before his death, documents arrived naming him first archbishop of Mexico, but he was so feeble that he could not accept the imposing office.

In 1551 Coronado said a last farewell to his good friend, Antonio de Mendoza, with whom he had so carefully and so hopefully planned the expedition north to see the wonders reported by Cabeza de Vaca and Fray Marcos. The parting was far different from that which took place at Tepic in 1540 when the viceroy, having seen Coronado and the army well on their way to the Seven Cities, had turned back to his capital and his official duties. For several years Mendoza had petitioned the King for release from those duties and permission to return to Spain. At last another viceroy was appointed for Mexico, but only death could free Don Antonio from service to his King, for he was now requested to go to Lima to become the viceroy of Peru. Ill and longing for his homeland, the loyal servant of His Majesty set sail from one of the ports on the Pacific Coast of Mexico and arrived at his new capital on September 12, 1551. Less than a year later he died there, on July 21, 1552, and was laid to his final rest in the cathedral beside Pizarro, the conquistador who had found gold at the end of his rainbow.

Soon after Coronado's death—probably in 1556, according to his biographer, Morris Bishop—Cabeza de Vaca ceased his earthly wanderings. He had returned to Spain to get permission to conquer Florida, only to learn that Hernando de Soto, over whom the waters of the mighty Mississippi were soon to roll forever, had already won the post. One would assume that Vaca had seen enough of that land of his misfortune. As an alternative to Florida, he was appointed governor and captain-general to rule at Asunción in Paraguay, South America. His luck there was no better, and after a free-for-all fight with his enemies he returned to Spain defeated and a prisoner. On January 20, 1546, not quite three weeks after he had brought charges against Cárdenas in connection with the Coronado expedition, Villalobos, the King's fiscal and enemy of conquerors, filed suit against Cabeza de Vaca before the Council of the Indies. The case dragged on, and it was not until 1551 that Vaca was finally released from prison, to spend his last years in penniless obscurity.

Meanwhile, in Mexico, Fray Marcos, who with Vaca's black companion, Stephen, had gone to verify the wonders of which the Narváez castaways had told, was nearing the end of a trail which had led him across the wide Atlantic Ocean, west to Guatemala, south to Peru, and north to Cíbola. After his return from the Pueblo country Fray Marcos became crippled, with paralysis, it is said, and repaired to Jalapa to profit by its warm climate. Later he went to live in a monastery at Xochimilco, the suburb of Mexico City, famous for its so-called floating gardens. In 1546, in response to a plea from the friar telling of his illness, Bishop Zumárraga promised to furnish him an arroba of wine each month as long as he, the bishop, should live. Two years later Zumárraga died. Who concerned himself about Marcos's ills during the last decade of the friar's life we do not know. The date of his death is reported by Vetancurt as March 25, 1558.

Cristóbal de Oñate, over whose failure to receive a salary for his services as lieutenant-governor for Coronado in Nueva Galicia there was so much talk during the governor's *residencia*, with the discovery in 1546 of rich mines at Zacatecas, became one of the wealthiest persons in America—perhaps a millionaire. Ironically, it was the man who had stayed behind when the treasure-seekers trailed north searching for cities of gold, on whom Fate bestowed her munificence. Just how long a time was allotted Don Cristóbal to enjoy his wealth we do not know, having evidence only that he was still living in 1550.

At Culiacán, that outpost so important in Coronado tradition, Don Pedro de Tovar, who had been chief ensign of the expedition and discoverer of the Hopi pueblos, lived for many years. As alcalde mayor, the old post of Melchior Díaz, his former companion in arms who had long lain buried far in the north beside the Camino del Diablo, Tovar won distinction. Described as "the most virtuous and accomplished gentleman in that kingdom," he married Doña Francisca de Guzmán, daughter of a former governor of Cuba and, says one chronicler, "a lady of much Christian fervor, courage, discretion, and beauty, so perfect in every respect that I doubt if there was any one in those regions who could equal her in virtue or quality." When Tovar died is not known, but Tello informs us that the event occurred in Culiacán and that Don Pedro was buried there, as was so fitting.

Like Coronado and Cárdenas, ill and travel-weary, Tristán de Arellano, who had been in command of the main army for many miles in the Cíbola enterprise, made his way back to Mexico City. After recuperating at the home of a friend, Luís de Castilla, Don Tristán went to Oaxaca, where, in 1545, he married a wealthy widow, Doña Isabel de Rojas. Three years later, while Coronado was attending town council meetings in Mexico and Cárdenas was alternately in and out of jail in Spain, Arellano put down a serious Indian uprising in Oaxaca. Ten years later, as we have seen, he was commissioned governor and captain-general of Florida by Viceroy Luís de Velasco, with instructions to lead an expedition to that region and establish a bulwark against foreign intrusions into territory claimed by Spain. As the fortune of Doña Beatríz had been poured into the Cíbola venture, that of Doña Isabel now dissolved in the Florida gamble. The expedition having failed, Don Tristán went to Madrid in 1561 to regain favor, but without success. Poverty-stricken, he returned to Mexico about 1567, and, until his death on September 16, 1573, was again given a home and cared for by his old friend, Luís de Castilla. Arellano's will made provision for the repayment of this debt, but so depleted was the estate of the man who had been cast in leading rôles in two great expeditions in the New World that even his funeral expenses had to be met by his benefactor. Not republics alone are ungrateful to their servants.

Chapter XXXV

RETURN TO PUEBLO LAND

The permanent occupation of Pueblo Land by Spain came about through the northward advance of settlement up the Central Plateau of Mexico, an historical epic analogous to our Anglo-American Westward Movement two centuries later. With the opening of mines and stock-raising in Durango and Chihuahua the outposts of settlement by 1580 reached north-flowing Conchos River, which gave a new approach to El Dorado, more direct than Coronado's roundabout trek up the Pacific Coast. Missionaries, miners, and traders from Chihuahua ascended Rio Grande, finding Tiguex rebuilt and called Puaray. These adventurers revisited most of the pueblos seen by Coronado, traded with the natives, reexplored the buffalo plains, and revisited Quivira.

Meanwhile Don Juan de Oñate, son of Coronado's mainstay in Compostela, became a man of great wealth, perhaps a millionaire, in the mines of Zacatecas, and married an heiress of Montezuma. Then, in 1595, he was appointed by the King of Spain to colonize Pueblo Land. With a caravan of some four hundred persons, eighty-three wagons, and seven thousand head of stock, he led the historic trek.

At El Paso, the crossing of Rio Grande, in the name of ascetic Philip II, Oñate took formal possession "of all the kingdoms and provinces of New Mexico." There was a sermon, a religious celebration, and much rejoicing; a comedy written on the spot by Captain Farfán was enacted, and the royal standard was blessed. Farfán's pageant has been called the beginning of drama in the United States, a statement which will bear scrutiny by some scholar on the Atlantic Coast.

From El Paso Oñate went ahead with sixty men, and at the

Pueblo of Caypa, rechristened San Juan, he established his capital. On August 18, the main body of the colony arrived, and on September 9, a general assembly of chiefs from all the country round was held. Rods of office were given to the chiefs, and Franciscan missionaries were assigned to the various districts. Pueblo Land had become a Spanish province. Oñate revisited most of the pueblos, the Llano Estacado, Quivira, and the Colorado River of the West.

Fiction is always more intriguing than fact. Father Escobar, who was with Oñate on his expedition to Colorado River, recorded faithfully what he saw, but when he narrated what a native chief named Otata said about the people living on the stream he let his imagination soar. According to the friar, Otata told him of a tribe using bowls made of silver, a lake where the natives wore golden bracelets, a tribe whose ears dragged on the ground, another with only one foot, another who lived on smells, another who slept under water, another who roosted in trees, and still another who slept standing up bearing burdens on their heads. The ruler of the nearby Island of California, which Cortés had sought, was a giantess named Ciñaca Cohota who had enormous feet. The men there were bald, "and with them the monstrosities ended." One suspects that Father Escobar was drawing on Pliny. On his way back from Colorado River Oñate exquisitely carved his name and the date high up on Inscription Rock where the record is still conspicuous, and is annually admired by hundreds of sight seers. Don Juan revisited the Llano Estacado and Quivira, finding there only what Coronado had reported.

Oñate's first capital was at San Juan, on upper Rio Grande, but in 1610, three years after the founding of Jamestown, it was moved south to Santa Fe, where it still is today. For two and one half centuries Spaniards and Pueblo Indians lived side by side in the picturesque region. Then, a century ago the Gringos came and contributed their blood and their institutions to a unique society in the Pueblo Land first made known to the world by Coronado.

APPENDIX

PUEBLO SOCIETY

The Pueblo tribes of historic times, beginning with Coronado, lived in the area extending from northwestern Arizona to Pecos River in New Mexico, and intrusively into western Kansas, and from Taos, New Mexico, on Rio Grande, to and below El Paso. In Utah and Colorado there are remains of prehistoric cliff dwellings once occupied by ancestors of the Pueblo folk visited by Coronado and of their present day descendants. Pueblos (towns or villages) are so-called because of the formal settlements of these people, as distinguished from temporary camps or scattered villages of less substantial dwellings common to most of the Indian tribes north of Mexico. The term *pueblo,* which in Spain and Spanish-America means *town,* was applied by the Spaniards and later adopted by English-speaking people to designate the Indians who now are living or once lived in permanent stone or adobe houses forming compact villages in New Mexico, Arizona, and adjacent Mexican territory. The historic pueblos of the area described comprise the Tanoan, Keresan (Queres), and Zuñian linguistic families of New Mexico, and the Hopis of Shoshonean affinity in northeastern Arizona.

The dwellings of the Pueblos varied according to available building materials and topography. In the Northern area the houses were generally built of sandstone quarried nearby. In the south, especially along the Gila and Salt rivers, adobe was the material most commonly used. Pueblo dwellings were generally compact structures of several storeys, with many small rooms or compartments because of the scarcity of timber and means of transporting it, for before the coming of the Spaniards to the Southwest the natives had no beasts of burden except the dog. Pueblos were primitive apartment houses, generally built in terraces, pyramidal in shape, each tier of houses being narrower than the one below it. The ground floor was used for storage and for defensive purposes, and was without doors. Entrance to this storey was by ladders from the ground to the flat roof, then through a hatchway and down a ladder to the ground floor inside. The upper storeys were reached by moveable ladders or by masonry steps built against the outer walls and resting on the roofs of the houses next below. In the more ancient pueblos fireplaces were usually in the form of a shallow box or pit in the middle of the floor, the smoke escaping through the hatchway, which is still the case in some of the kivas, as the ceremonial chambers are called. Corner fireplaces were also used, but chimneys, out-door ovens, and paneled doors and shutters were derived from the Spaniards after Coronado's day. Floors were paved with flat stones or plastered smooth with adobe mortar, like the walls of the terraces. The houses were built and owned by the women, the men assisting in the heavy work, such as quarrying stone, and hauling and placing the beams. Each pueblo had at least one kiva, and it is believed by some scholars that the kivas formed the nuclei of the ancient pueblos.

The Pueblo folk were well advanced in many elements of civilization. They made good basketry, but not equal to that of some of the tribes of northern California. Some of the Hopis made basket plaques in two styles of weaving, artistically ornamented in colors derived from native substances, now mainly replaced by commercial dyes. As potters and weavers the Pueblos have not been excelled by any Indians north of Mexico. Their earthen vessels, ancient and modern, exemplify practically every form known to the aborigines, from large, rough, cooking and storage vessels to delicately modeled and elaborately painted jars, bowls, platters, bottles, ladles, and box-shaped utensils.

Many of the ancient Pueblos, especially those of the northern area, were horticulturists rather than agriculturists, so intensive was their cultivation. Small fields were irrigated from living streams or from storage reservoirs, the chief crop being maize,

Cotton was also raised, the fibre being woven into everyday clothing, ceremonial cloaks, kilts, and leggings, which were extensively traded to other tribes. The Hopis were and still are the chief cotton weavers of all the Pueblos, but the native cotton formerly used has given place almost entirely to modern trade stuff. It is believed that weaving was introduced among the Navajos by Pueblo women adopted into that tribe. Today many so-called "Navajo blankets" are really produced on Hopi and Zuñi looms operated by both men and women.

In the southern Pueblo area, agriculture was conducted on a large scale, with elaborate and extensive systems of irrigation. Such works, utilized by an entire community, were constructed under a communal system, still largely followed by all the Pueblos. Besides fields of maize, wheat, pumpkins, melons, etc., garden patches of onions, beans, chile, etc., are cultivated near the houses, water being daily carried to them in jars by the women. to whom the gardens as well as the houses belong.

To supplement the products of their agriculture, the Pueblos hunted wild game, the deer, antelope, bear, and mountain lion being among the larger animals sought. The eastern Pueblos hunted also the buffalo in the eastern plains, as the men with Coronado tell us so graphically. Cottontails and jack rabbits abounded everywhere in the Pueblo country and were hunted by individuals as well as by large groups of men and boys, who surrounded a wide area, gradually drew together, cornered the rabbits and killed them with sticks shaped like boomerangs. The "rabbit stick" is even now a well known weapon. Traps were also used, especially for catching small mammals and birds, including eagles, prized for their feathers for ceremonial purposes. Fish and other products of the water were never eaten, and certain animals were tabooed as food by some clans. Turkeys were domesticated, large flocks being "herded." These birds, as well as eagles were and still are kept in captivity for their feathers. The only other domestic animal was the dog, but there is no evidence that the Pueblos used the dog as a beast of burden, as was customary among the tribes of the Plains. Horses, burros, cattle, sheep, and goats, like wheat, peaches and apples, now commonly raised, were not known to the Pueblo Indians before the coming of the Spaniards in the sixteenth century.

The ancient clothing of Pueblo men consisted of a short tunic of deerskin, trousers of the same material reaching to the knees, leggings of skin or cotton, fastened at the knees with woven garters, and deerskin moccasins with rawhide soles, neatly sewn with sinews. Fur moccasins, hairy side in, were worn in snowy weather. All the men and boys wore breech cloths. Warriors sported close-fitting skin caps, ventilated with holes and gaily decorated with feathers. Garments of skilfully woven yucca fibre were also used in ancient times.

The hair of the Pueblo men was then, as now, banged above the eyes, cut horizontally at the neckline, the back hair being tied with a woven band into a knot behind. A headband is always worn by men and boys in the western pueblos, whereas those of the Rio Grande Valley wore their hair in plaits without a headband. Robes of twisted strands of rabbit or wild cat skin were donned in cold weather and used also for bedding. The men loved finery, and wore ornaments of shell and turquoise beads; the turquoise came especially from mines at Los Cerrillos, New Mexico, the Queres tribe being the chief turquoise traders. The men wore also ear and neck pendants of the same materials, and beautiful mosaic, shell, turquoise and other colored stones. Metal work processes were later derived from the Spaniards.

The women now wear a woolen dress of native weave, knee length, in the form of a blanket, the two ends sewn together, worn over the right shoulder and under the left, belted at the waist with a long woven sash, fringed at the end and tucked in; a cotton shirt extending to the knees, deerskin leggings wrapped round and round, from knee to ankle, and forming part of the moccasin of the same material. The leggings of the women, unlike the men's, are not dyed. The women wear also a light cotton mantle. Among some of the Pueblos, the hair of married women is banged in front and wrapped in coils behind the ears. Marriageable girls wore their hair in two large whorls, one at each side. Among the Hopis these are called squash blossoms, symbols of fertility. Other Pueblo women do not bang their hair, but part it in the middle and braid it at the sides. Necklaces, pendants, bracelets, and earrings were worn by the women.

Every pueblo was and is composed of a number of clans based on descent in the female or male line, respectively, the number of clans varying in different pueblos. In Zía, for example, there are sixteen clans still existing. Most of the clans are named from natural objects or elements, especially plants and animals. The Zuñis have many organizations pertaining to war, healing, hunting, agriculture, magic, religion, and other matters. In their ceremonials the cardinal points play a prominent part. Each society has its own rites and ceremonies, some performed in secret, some in public.

All the Pueblos are monogamists, and the status of women among them is much higher than in most native American tribes. Among the Pueblo tribes in which descent is reckoned through the mother, the home belongs to the woman, and her sons-in-law make it their home. Marriage is contracted with little ceremony, divorce is lightly regarded, and the wife can dismiss her spouse on slight pretext, whether sentimental or practical. Labor is divided as equitably as circumstances permit. Like the houses, the gardens belong to the woman in case of divorce. Originally, Pueblo government was controlled by the priesthood, but this was changed somewhat with the coming of the Spaniards. Since statistics were first recorded in the early eighteenth century, Pueblo population has not changed greatly, the available figures ranging between about 12,000 in the year 1749, and 9,000 in 1887.

Each pueblo has one or more secret chambers called *kivas,* whose location is generally indicated by two ladder poles of unequal length projecting above the roof. These kivas are temples for holding sacred ceremonies, and lounging places or club rooms for men and boys. Coronado and his successors called them *estufas* or hot rooms, evidently regarding them as sweat houses. Castañeda, who was with Coronado, described one at Taos as containing "twelve pillars, four of which, in the center, were as large as two men could reach around." He added that some of the kivas were "large enough for a game of ball." The Spaniards said the young men lived in the *estufas,* and if a man repudiated his wife, he went to the *estufa* to live. Women were not permitted to enter the kivas for any other purpose than to take food to their husbands or sons. This is still true, except that in a few cases women use the kivas for religious rites or enter them to witness certain ceremonies performed by the men.

The oldest kivas were circular, as is still the case with some of them in the Rio Grande pueblos. At Zuñi and the Hopi towns, on the other hand, they are rectangular. The Hopi kivas are partly or wholly underground, and usually are isolated from the center of the pueblos. Originally, those of the Zuñi tribe were in the plazas or courtyards of the towns, but now they are hidden among the dwellings of the one pueblo where the descendants of all the Zuñi tribe are congregated. The number of kivas in a pueblo varied with the size and number of religious organizations using them. The Hopi kivas, of which in 1907 there were thirty-three, are usually built on a north and south line and are subterranean or nearly so. Oraibe then had thirteen kivas, but some of the smaller towns have only one. Kivas are entered by an outside ladder to the roof and another through a hatchway, with a ladder reaching to the ground below. The roof is supported by beams covered with osiers or with boards and adobe mortar, the floors being of smooth sandstone slabs. The walls are sometimes decorated with paintings of symbolic meaning. All or part way round the room runs a stone-capped adobe bench, and a shallow fire pit occupies the center of the floor, the smoke escaping through the hatchway. At the end of some of the kivas, facing the ladder, there is a round hole in a stone or cottonwood slab, called the *sipapú* symbolizing the place of origin and final departure of the Pueblo peoples, and the means of communicating with the underworld. Behind this orifice there is usually an altar, and sometimes, in front of it a dry painting, and other symbolic apparatus.

It was once assumed that until the coming of the Spanish

missionaries, irrigation was not practiced by the natives of the arid Southwest, except to a very limited extent. But recent archaeological research has made it plain that agriculture was practiced there in prehistoric times with the aid of extensive canals, reservoirs, and dams. The most notable of these irrigation works were in the valleys of Gila River and its tributaries in southern Arizona, where many miles of canals are still traceable, and sometimes extending more than ten miles from the mother stream. It has been estimated that in the Salt River valley alone, 200,000 acres were thus cultivated before the coming of Europeans. Some of the ancient canals were seven feet deep and four feet wide at the bottom. The sides of the canals sloped gradually, rising in steps or terraces, giving the ditch a width of thirty feet at the top. The sides and bottom of the canals were plastered with clay to prevent waste through seepage. Remains of what are thought to have been wooden headgates have been discovered by excavation. Several of these ancient canals have been used for modern irrigation. For example, at Maricopa, Arizona, $20,000 or more was saved by using an ancient irrigation canal that cut through a volcanic knoll for three miles, and at one point for several hundred feet cut a channel twenty-five feet deep through solid rock. Similar ancient irrigation works were constructed in the valleys of Rio Verde and Hassayampa River near Phoenix. Water was carried to pueblos several miles by means of canals, each village along the way having a reservoir, some of them being a mile long and half a mile wide.

In the valleys of the Rio Grande and its tributaries in New Mexico, small reservoirs were the chief means of supplying water to the ancient Pueblos. At Peñasco Blanco, an ancient ruin in northwestern New Mexico, the early inhabitants diverted water from the Chaco River by a ditch that supplied a reservoir built in sand, and prevented seepage by lining its bed with slabs of stone and clay. There, five pueblos were artificially provided with water for irrigation. At one of these towns water was diverted from the sandy wash to a natural depression, and thence to fields two miles away by a ditch dug around a mesa or plateau. The ditch was chiefly earthenwork, but in some places it was reinforced by stone walls. Kinyaah, in the same valley, was supplied with two large reservoirs and a canal twenty-five or thirty feet wide.

Hand irrigation was and still is practiced by the Pueblo Indians. Zuñi women, to raise their crops of onions, chile, etc., carry water long distances in earthen jars on their heads and pour it on the plants with gourd ladles. At the middle mesa villages of the Hopis, garden patches are watered in much the same way, except that here the gardens are near springs, and are irrigated by the women by means of a gourd vessel fastened to the end of a long pole.

Throughout the Southwest where pueblos occupied the summits of mesas or elevated plateaus, the inhabitants constructed reservoirs, and according to tradition some of them were ingeniously filled in winter by rolling into them numerous huge snowballs which melted with the coming of spring. For hundreds of years, Ácoma, "the sky city," has derived its entire water supply from a natural depression in the rock which receives the rain-fall from the mesa summit.

Some of the ancestors of the Pueblo people of historic times were Cliff Dwellers. The plateau country of Arizona, New Mexico, Colorado, and Utah abounds in natural recesses and shallow caverns weathered in the faces of high cliffs. Primitive tribes, on taking possession of the area, in many cases occupied these ready-made shelters for residence, storage, and burial, and for hiding and defense in times of danger. This occupancy led in time to the building of marginal walls for protection and houses for dwelling, to the enlargement of rooms and later to the excavation of commodious dwellings, such as now are found deserted in many places in the arid region of the Southwest, both within and outside of the area occupied by the Pueblo people now and in Coronado's day.

Archaeologists distinguish between a cliff-house and cavate dwellings excavated in cliffs. It is believed that agricultural tribes of pre-Spanish times, who had built large towns and developed an irrigation system, went to the cliffs not from choice but because of the encroachment of warlike tribes, who probably were non-agricultural people without a permanent abode. On the other hand, many of the cliff sites were near streams and fields, were natural dwelling places, and were occupied for the shelter and protection they afforded. Some of the cliff-houses thus utilized were storage places for maize and other property, while others were look-outs from which the fields below could be watched, and the approach of enemies observed.

In some regions there is evidence of post-occupancy of these sites—walls of houses built on deposits accumulated since sheep were introduced, and adobe bricks, which were not used in prehistoric times. A well authenticated tradition exists among the Hopis that in the eighteenth century the Asa clans of that tribe, because of an epidemic, moved to Canyon de Chelly, where they occupied a cliff shelter for a time and intermarried with the Navajos.

The area in which the cliff-dwellings occur is practically co-extensive with that in which now are found traces of town building, and relics attributable to the Pueblo tribes. Noteworthy among these groups of built dwellings are those found in the canyons of Mesa Verde in Colorado, in Hovenweep, Mc-Elmo, and Montezuma canyons in Colorado and Utah, in Canyon de Chelly and its branches in northeastern Arizona, and, of the cavate variety, in the cliffs of Jémez plateau facing the Rio Grande in New Mexico, and in the Verde Valley of Arizona. In these cliff-dwellings there are local differences in style of building, construction, plan, and finish, but the main characteristics are the same everywhere. Corresponding differences with general likeness are observed in implements, utensils, and ornaments found in the ruins.

Owing to differences in the rocky strata, the cliff-dwellings varied greatly in character. Many were mere horizontal crevices or isolated niches, large enough only for men to crawl into and build small stone lodges. There are extensive chambers with level floors, "and with roofs opening out in great sweeps of solid rock surface, more imposing than any structure built by human hands," and accommodating "not merely single households, but communities of considerable size. The niches occur at all levels in the cliffs, rising to nearly a thousand feet, and are approached with great difficulty from below, or, in rare cases from above. When the way was very steep, niche stairways were cut in the rock face—and ladders of notched logs were also used." Some of the rooms served as kivas. The masonry is excellent, gathered sometimes from distant sites. The walls were sometimes plastered inside and out, and finished with clay paint. Windows or outlook apertures were numerous and generally small.

Notable among cliff-dwellings are Cliff Palace in Walnut Canyon, Spruce Tree House in Navajo Canyon, Casa Blanca in Canyon de Chelly, and Montezuma Castle in Beaver Creek, Arizona. Near most of these cliff-dwellings there are ruins of pueblos identical with those seen by Coronado in the open country.

Cavate cliff-houses were not built, but dug in the cliffs. Natural openings were enlarged or excavated in places where there were no natural openings. Large natural openings in the cliffs were walled up and supplied with doors and windows. The typical cavate dwelling is entered through a small hewn doorway. The floor is often below the level of the threshold, and both floor and walls are sometimes plastered. Sometimes, too, there are crude fireplaces. These cavate dwellings are most numerous on the east side of Jémez plateau, facing the Rio Grande. They are numerous also along Rio San Juan and its tributaries in New Mexico and Colorado, and in the valley of Rio Verde in Arizona. Others are found near Flagstaff, Arizona. Coronado did not get far into the cliff-dwelling area.

ACKNOWLEDGMENTS

No historian ever writes a book without becoming indebted to others, and I am no exception. When I began my work on Coronado, intending to write only a brief sketch as a contribution to the Coronado Cuarto Centennial Celebration, no comprehensive synthesis of the subject had appeared. Winship had laid the foundations for a study of the expedition to Cíbola and Quivira when in 1896 he published his monumental source book containing most of the essential documents at that time known. In 1907 and 1933, the greater part of these were published in translation by Hodge, with editorial notes and interpretations based on his wide knowledge of archaeology and ethnology.

In more recent times, incidental to his work on Viceroy Mendoza and other subjects, Aiton has discovered and published vital and previously unknown documents in the archives of Spain, notable among them being the Muster Roll of Coronado's army at Compostela before starting for Cíbola in 1540. Sauer in 1932 published his *Road to Cíbola,* which laid down securely at most points Coronado's route from Compostela to the Gila River, and in subsequent articles he has made studies of the journey of Fray Marcos to the Arizona region which have not been set aside by writers who have dissented from his conclusions. Jones wrote an excellent account of Coronado's doings in Kansas, and of his final resting place in Mexico City; Wedel has made important contributions regarding archaeological evidences in the Kansas area. France V. Scholes, Lansing Bloom, and other scholars have written valuable articles on special phases of the subject.

A new era began in 1940, when Hammond and Rey published in translation a comprehensive volume of Coronado materials including, besides the major items previously known, extensive selections from the formerly little used records of the residencia of Coronado's administration as governor of Nueva Galicia and of the criminal trials of both Coronado and Cárdenas on charges emanating from the expedition to Cíbola and Quivira. A large body of these documents which Hammond and Rey acquired but did not publish they generously turned over to me, and they have been used for the first time in the writing of this book. The difficult paleographic work of transcribing them from the original sixteenth-century manuscripts has been done by expert Professor Agapito Rey, of the University of Indiana.

After I had begun this work, Day brought out his admirable *Coronado's Quest,* of whose forthcoming I had not had the least intimation, believe it or not, although it was published on my own campus. In order to be independent in my findings, I refrained from reading Day's book until this one was well along. Excellent though I found his narrative to be, it did not greatly modify my conclusions, some of which, because of my more complete sources and more extensive field work, are at variance with his and with those of all my predecessors. Hitherto, students of Coronado's career, other than the early chroniclers of Nueva Galicia, have paid slight attention to him except as leader of the great expedition to Cíbola and Quivira, whereas he was also a prominent figure in Mexico. Before the appearance of the documents published by Hammond and Rey, little was known about the legal investigations after Coronado's return from Tierra Nueva, to which two chapters are devoted in this volume.

The greater part of the terrain covered by Coronado in his truly prodigious expedition has long been familiar ground to me, as is evidenced by several publications based on field work and archival research on the historical geography of the Pacific Slope and the Spanish Southwest. Nevertheless, in the preparation of this book I have re-examined almost the entire area with special reference to Coronado. In this pastime I have had assistance from numerous persons and organizations mentioned elsewhere. The University of California has been liberal in providing me with funds. The National Park Service has encouraged my work, and, jointly with the officials of the New Mexico Coronado Cuarto Centennial, it has aided me in a new reconnaissance of most of Coronado's route all the way from Compostela to central Kansas and return. Generous coöperation was given me by the Honorable Clinton P. Anderson, then Managing Director of the United States Coronado Exposition Commission, and now Senator from New Mexico; and by Mrs. Marguerite Rockwell and other members of the Arizona Coronado Commission. I am indebted to Mr. J. Evetts Haley for valuable data regarding travel routes and water supply in Oklahoma and the Texas Panhandle. Helen Harding Bretnor has generously read part of the manuscript with reference to the unification of spelling and other matters.

My deepest gratitude for assistance and forbearance in the long task of preparing this book is due to Maxine Chappell Bethel, my secretary, who herself is a competent scholar and an accomplished writer. She has not only borne the drudgery of typing—yea, and much retyping—but has participated vitally in the research at every turn, and in giving the manuscript its final form. For reading proof and other important help I am deeply indebted to Miss Virginia E. Thickens and Miss Margaret Mollins.

From the American Philosophical Society I have received a generous grant for research in the history of the West Coast Corridor, of which this book is the first major episode, and is to be followed by others in the same sequence.

HERBERT E. BOLTON

RETRACING THE TRAIL

In January and February, 1940, with Dr. George P. Hammond, then Dean of the Graduate School of the University of New Mexico, Dr. Russell C. Ewing, of the University of Arizona, Dr. Aubrey Neasham, and W. Ward Yeager of the National Park Service, and Harold Walter of the United States Coronado Commission, I retraced most of the Coronado trail from Compostela to the United States border. This being a very wet season we appreciated some of the difficulties encountered by the general and his caravan on their return from Cíbola in 1542. Drs. Emil Haury and Harold Spicer of the University of Arizona aided me on the trail through southern Arizona. With Drs. Hammond and Neasham, later in 1940, in several trips which need not be recounted here in detail with all their diverting incidents, I followed the entire trail from the Mexican border to central Kansas: To Chichilticale, Gila River, Ash Creek, Fort Apache, Little Colorado River, Háwikuh, and the Hopi Mesas; from Háwikuh to Acoma, Bernalillo, and Taos; from Bernalillo to Pecos, Antón Chico, to the Texas line, along Canadian basin, up the mesa to Vega, across the Llano Estacado to the First Barranca (Tule Canyon) to the Second Barranca (Palo Duro Canyon), up the Texas Panhandle, across Oklahoma and Kansas to the Arkansas River at Ford, down the Arkansas to Lyons, northward across Little River to Smoky Hill River at Lindsborg, and to Salina; back to Ford, thence by Coronado's cut-off to Canadian River. With Dr. William R. Hogan, now of Tulane University, I examined the route from Clifton to St. John, concluding that this was no part of Coronado's trail.

In another trip with Dr. Hammond, I went to Lubbock, and with the help of Professor W. C. Holden we made a reconnoissance of the terrain in that vicinity and in and eastward of there in Brazos and Blanco canyons, concluding that Coronado did not reach those regions. Going back to Castro County we retraced the route of Coronado's army past the salt lakes on its return from Tule Canyon to Pecos River.

After all this work on the trail, in April, 1944, I made a further examination of the region of the Barrancas, a key area in the whole problem of Coronado's route. The keen interest which the subject by this time had aroused is indicated by the number and prominence of the men who joined me in the enterprise. There were Hillory A. Tolson, M. R. Tillotson, and Herbert E. Kahler, of the National Park Service; President J. A. Hill, Professor L. F. Sheffy, and Boone McClure, of the West Texas State College; Frank B. Quinn, Secretary of the Texas State Parks Board; Frank Miller and Fred Emory, of the Palo Duro State Park; Byrle Elliston, formerly of the staff of the Palo Duro State Park; Bishop L. J. FitzSimon, George Autry, John Boyce, Joe Jenkins, Guy Carlander, and Floyd V. Studer, of Amarillo; and E. D. Posey, of Hereford. With the help of these men I reëxplored Tule Canyon, Palo Duro Canyon, and the terrain between them. Then, with Messrs. Tolson, Tillotson, Quinn, and Kahler, I again went over the terrain between Canyon and Lubbock, and the escarpment southeastward of there.

As to the route of Alarcón on the Colorado River and Díaz' journey from Sonora Valley to find him, I may remark that in my researches on Kino, Anza, and Garcés, I have followed the banks of the Colorado River all the way from the mouth to Needles and explored in great detail the Camino del Diablo and adjacent areas.

REFERENCES

CHAPTER I

PUBLISHED DOCUMENTS: Carranza, "Relación sobre la jornada que hizo Nuño de Guzmán"; Castañeda, in Winship, 416-417—English translation, Hammond and Rey, 195-196; Cortés, *Escritos sueltos,* 127-165; [Flores], "Cuarta relación anónima de la jornada que hizo Nuño de Guzmán"; Diego de Guzmán, "Relación"; Nuño de Guzmán, "Carta al emperador [Chiametla, January 16, 1531]"—"Provanza ad perpetuam, sobre lo de la villa de la Purificacion"; G. Lopez, "Relación del descubrimiento y conquista que se hizo por . . . Nuño de Guzmán"; "Proceso del Marqués del Valle. . . ."

OTHER REFERENCES: Anghiera, *De Orbe Novo, the Eight Decades of Peter Martyr;* Arciniegas, *The Knight of El Dorado;* "Autos del Marqués del Valle, Pánfilo de Narváez"; Bancroft, *Mexico,* I, II, 43-64, 254-272, 341-374, 410-427—*North Mexican States,* I, 1-59; A. F. Bandelier, *The Gilded Man,* 1-124; Beaumont, *Crónica,* II, libro I, caps. XXI-XXII, XXIV; Gómara, *Historia general,* caps. XIII-CLXXXVII, CCXII; Herrera, *Historia general;* Kelly, *Pedro de Alvarado;* Las Casas, *Historia de las Indias;* López-Portillo y Weber, *La conquista de la Nueva Galicia;* Mendieta, *Historia eclesiástica indiana;* Mota Padilla, *Historia,* 23-106; Oviedo y Valdés, *Historia general,* libro XXXIV; Pilar, "Relación de la entrada de Nuño de Guzmán"; Prescott, *Mexico—Peru;* Tello, *Libro segundo,* 65-184, 188-265; Wagner, *Cartography of the Northwest Coast,* I, 13-16—*Spanish Voyages,* 1-8, 289-292.

CHAPTER II

PUBLISHED DOCUMENTS: Cabeza de Vaca, *Relación;* Cabeza de Vaca, Maldonado, Dorantes de Carrança, "Joint report."

OTHER REFERENCES: Bancroft, *North Mexican States,* I, 60-70; A. F. Bandelier, "Alvar Núñez Cabeza de Vaca"—*Contributions,* 24-67—*The Gilded Man,* 125-136; F. Bandelier, *The Journey of . . . Cabeza de Vaca;* Barcía, *Ensayo cronológico,* Dec. III, años XXXII-XXXVII; Baskett, "A study of the route of Cabeza de Vaca"; Beaumont, *Crónica,* libro II, cap. II; Bishop, *Odyssey of Cabeza de Vaca;* Bolton, *Spanish Borderlands,* 19-45; Coopwood, "The route of Cabeza de Vaca"; Davenport, "The expedition of Pánfilo de Narváez"; Davenport and Wells, "The first Europeans in Texas"; Hallenbeck, *Alvar Núñez Cabeza de Vaca;* Herrera, *Historia general,* Dec. IV, libro IV, caps. IV-VII, libro V, cap. V, Dec. V, libro I, caps. VII-VIII, libro VII, caps. III-IV, Dec. VI, libro I, caps. III-VII, IX;

Hodge and Lewis, *Spanish Explorers*, 3-123; Lowery, *Spanish Settlements*, 172-212; Oviedo y Valdés, *Historia general*, libro XXXV; Ponton and McFarland, "Alvar Núñez Cabeza de Vaca"; Sauer, "Discovery of New Mexico reconsidered," 271-277—*Road to Cíbola*, 1-21; Tello, *Libro segundo*, 185-187; Twitchell, *Leading Facts of New Mexican History*, I, 53-134; Winship, 345-348.

CHAPTER III

PUBLISHED DOCUMENTS: *Actas de cabildo*, libro IV, 130-148; Aiton and Rey, "Coronado's testimony," 288-290; Bloom, "The Coronado-Bocanegra family alliance," 401-405; Castañeda, in Winship, 417-418—English translation, Hammond and Rey, 196-197; Ciudad Rodrigo, "Certification of Fray Marcos' 'Relation'"; Coronado, "Appointment . . . as alderman of Mexico City"; Hodge and Lewis, *Spanish Explorers*, 3-126; "Información de los méritos . . . de los capitanes Andrés Dorantes y Don Sancho Dorantes de Carranza"; Mendoza, "Carta á la emperatriz [Mexico, February 11, 1537]"—"Carta al emperador [Mexico, December 10, 1537]"—"Lettere scritte . . . alla maesta dell' Imperadore [1539]"; "Proceso del Marqués del Valle . . ."; Zumárraga, "Carta á un eclesiástico desconocido [Mexico, April 4, 1537]."

OTHER REFERENCES: Aiton, *Antonio de Mendoza*, 3-42, 116-119; Avalos Guzmán, *Don Antonio de Mendoza*; Bancroft, *Mexico*, II, 375-385, 457-467—*North Mexican States*, I, 69-70; A. F. Bandelier, *The Gilded Man*, 136-138; Bishop, *The Odyssey of Cabeza de Vaca*; Day, *Coronado's Quest*, 21-32; Hammond and Rey, 1-3; P. A. Jones, *Coronado and Quivira*, 166-173; Mota Padilla, *Historia*, 103-110; Pérez Bustamante, Pereyra, Blanco Rivero, *Antonio de Mendoza*; Tello, *Libro segundo*, 298-304; 310-314; Wagner, "Fr. Marcos de Niza," 184-201; Winship, 348-351, 379-381.

CHAPTER IV

MANUSCRIPTS: A. G. I. Justicia, legajo 336, *Proceso de pleito . . . por parte de . . . Coronado:* Royal cédula, no date. A. G. I. Justicia, legajo 339, pieza 1, *Residencia tomada á . . . Coronado:* Section 1, Tejada's *Interrogatorio*—Testimony of Melchior Pérez; Section 2, Coronado's testimony—*Interrogatorio* in the matter of Coronado's *descargos*—Testimonies of Pedro Cuadrado, Hernando de Valle, Toribio de Bolaños, Salvador de Estrada, Alonso de Toro, Bartolomé García, Pedro de Ledesma, Juan de Alaejos, Cristóbal Romero, Francisco Cornejo, Alonso Lorenzo, Juan de Subía, Cristóbal de Valle, Alonso de Plasencia, Francisco Olivares, Diego Hurtado—Ruíz de Haro's *Interrogatorio*—Testimonies of Fray Onorato, Juan de Villareal, Cristóbal Romero, Alonso de Torio, Pedro de Ledesma, Juan de Zaldívar, Pedro Cuadrado, Francisco Cornejo. A. G. I. Justicia, legajo 1021, pieza 4, *Información contra . . . Coronado:* Testimony of Juan Troyano.

PUBLISHED DOCUMENTS: Aiton, "Coronado's first report"; Castañeda, in Winship, 418-419—English translation, Hammond and Rey, 197-199;

Coronado, "Appointment as governor"—"Copia delle lettere . . . al Signor Antonio de Mendozza [San Miguel, March 8, 1539]"—"Letter to the emperor, December 15, 1538"—"Letter to the emperor, July 15, 1539"—"Residencia," 375-376, 378; Marcos de Niza, "Relación"; Mendoza, "Instruccion (al Fray Marcos de Niza)"—"Lettere scritte . . . alla maesta dell' Imperadore [1539]."

OTHER REFERENCES: Arteaga y S., "Fray Marcos de Niza"; Baldwin, "Fray Marcos de Niza"; Bancroft, Arizona and New Mexico, 27-33; A. F. Bandelier, Contributions, 106-178—"The discovery of New Mexico by Fray Marcos de Nizza"—The Gilded Man, 136-162—"An outline of the documentary history of the Zuñi tribe," 2-20; Bartlett and Colton, "A note on the Marcos de Niza inscription"; Bloom, "Was Fray Marcos a liar?"; Day, Coronado's Quest, 32-61—"Gómara," 349; Gómara, Historia general, cap. CCXIII; Herrera, Historia general, Dec. VI, libro VII, caps. VII-VIII; Hodge, "The first discovered city of Cibola"—History of Háwikuh, 6-29—in Winship, Journey of Coronado, xiv-xvii; Lowery, Spanish Settlements, 253-282, 464-468; Sauer, "The credibility of the Fray Marcos account"—"Discovery of New Mexico reconsidered," 277-287—Road to Cíbola, 21-32; Twitchell, Leading Facts of New Mexican History, I, 139-160; Vetancurt, Teatro mexicano, IV, 117-118; Wagner, Cartography of the Northwest Coast, 16-18—"Fr. Marcos de Niza," 201-217—"A 'Fray Marcos de Niza' note"; Winship, 353-362, 381.

CHAPTER V

PUBLISHED DOCUMENTS: Aiton and Rey, "Coronado's testimony," 310-311, 322; Alarcón, "Relación del armada . . ."; "Autos del Marqués del Valle . . . Año de 1526"; De Soto, "Asiento y capitulación"; Gentleman of Elvas, in Smith, Career of . . . de Soto (Bourne ed.), 3-22, and Hodge and Lewis, Spanish Explorers, 135-146; Preciado, "Relatione"; "Proceso del Marqués del Valle . . ."; "Royal cédula—Barcelona, April 17, 1535"; Ulloa, "Record and narrative"; Wagner, Spanish Voyages, 11-14, 51-56.

OTHER REFERENCES: Bancroft, Central America, II, 203—North Mexican States, I, 77-82; Day, Coronado's Quest, 65-69; De Soto, Final Report of the . . . Commission, 65-92, 97-102, 304; Garcilaso de la Vega, La Florida del Ynca, libro I; Herrera, Historia general, Dec. VI, libro VII, cap. IX, libro IX, caps. VIII-X; Lowery, Spanish Settlements, 213-219; Maynard, De Soto, 14-139; Mota Padilla, Historia, 119; Swanton, Indians of the Southeastern United States, 39-40; Tello, Libro segundo, 349-353; Twitchell, Leading Facts of New Mexican History, I, 163-169; Wagner, "California Voyages," in California Historical Society Quarterly, III, 307-314—Cartography of the Northwest Coast, I, 20-24; Winship, 352, 362-373.

CHAPTER VI

MANUSCRIPTS: A. G. I. Justicia, legajo 336, Proceso de pleito . . . por parte de . . . Coronado: Coronado's reply to Benavente's charges—Mendoza's commission to Coronado, Mechuacán, January 6, 1540—Royal provision, Vallid, September 29, 1550—Testimonies of Hernando del Valle, Juan Bermejo, Melchior Pérez, Pedro de Ledesma, Pedro de Castro, Juan Ruíz, Juan Galeas, Juan Pastór, Juan Fernández Verdejo, Jorge Ceron Carabajal, Salvador de Estrada, Froilán Vermúdez. A. G. I. Justicia, legajo 339, pieza 1, *Residencia tomada á* . . . *Coronado:* Section 1, Tejada's *Interrogatorio*—Testimonies of Cristóbal de Oñate, Juan Hernández de Ijar, Juan de Samaniego, Juan Gallego; Section 2, Coronado's testimony— *Interrogatorio* in the matter of Coronado's *descargos*—Testimonies of Hernando de Valle, Juan Bermejo, Alonso Palomeque, Toribio de Bolaños, Hernando Martel, Rodrigo de Tamara, Salvado de Estrada, Cristóbal Pérez, Alvaro de Bracamonte, Juan Gallegos, Martín Cano, Alonso de Toro, Pedro de Ledesma, Cristóbal Romero, Francisco Cornejo, Cristóbal de Valle, Pedro de Cuadrado, Francisco Olivares—Ruíz de Haro's *Interrogatorio*—Testimonies of Juan de Villareal, Alonso de Toro, Pedro de-Ledesma, Juan de Zaldívar, Cristóbal de Oñate. A. G. I. Justicia, legajo 1021, pieza 1, *Acusación contra* . . . *Cárdenas:* Coronado's appointment by the king. A. G. I. Justicia, legajo 1021, pieza 2 (b), *Relación sacada de la probanza presentada por parte de* . . . *Coronado:* Testimony of Rodrigo Maldonado. A. G. I. Justicia, legajo 1021, pieza 4, *Información contra* . . . *Coronado:* Testimony of Francisca de Hozes. A. G. I. Justicia, legajo 1021, pieza 5, *Probanza hecha en Méjico a pedimento de* . . . *Cárdenas:* Testimonies of Hernando de Alvarado, Pedro de Ledesma, Juan de Beteta, Juan Gallego [this should be Galeras or Gálves], Juan de Fioz, Rodrigo de Frias, Domingo Martín, Diego de Madrid, Hernando de Paez, Luís de Vargas, Gaspár de Saldaña, Gerónimo Mercado de Sotomayor, Juan de Vitoria, Francisco Gorbalán, García del Castillo, Pedro Navarro, Pablo de Melgosa. A. G. I. Justicia, legajo 1021, pieza 6, *Probanza del Fiscal contra* . . . *Cárdenas:* Benavente's *Interrogatorio*—Testimonies of García Rodríguez, Gaspar de Saldaña, Rodrigo Maldonado—Villalobos's *Interrogatorio*—Testimonies of Hernando de Alvarado, Juan de Jaramillo, Hernando de Orduña, Alonso de Valderrey, Cristóbal de Mayorga, Cristóbal de Escobar, Rodrigo Ximón, Gaspár de Saldaña, Domingo Martín, Pedro de Ledesma, Juan de Fioz, Juan de Paradiñas, Hernando de la Cadena, García Rodríguez, Rodrigo de Frias, Rodrigo Maldonado.

PUBLISHED DOCUMENTS: *Actas de cabildo,* libro IV, 172-182; Aiton and Rey, "Coronado's testimony," 314-317; A. F. and F. Bandelier, *Historical Documents,* I, 45-47; Castañeda, in Winship, 419-420, 422—English translation, Hammond and Rey, 199-200, 204; Coronado, "Appointment . . . as commander of the expedition"—"Residencia," 370-371; Mendoza, "Carta al emperador [Jacona, April 17, 1540]"—"Residencia," 118-120; "Proceso del Marqués del Valle . . ."; Suárez de Peralta, *Tratado del descubrimiento de las Yndias,* 144, 148-149; Ximénez de San Esteban, "Carta á Santo Tomás de Villanueva"; Zumárraga, "Tres cartas familiares [letter of August 23, 1539]."

OTHER REFERENCES: Bancroft, *Central America,* II, 202-203—*North Mexican States,* I, 82-83; A. F. Bandelier, "An outline of the documentary history of the Zuñi tribe," 21-27; Benitez, "Conquistadores de Nueva Galicia," 322; Day, *Coronado's Quest,* 63-65, 69-73—"Mota Padilla," 91;

Hammond and Rey, 7-8, 12; Icaza, *Diccionario*, II, nos. 987, 1302; P. A. Jones, *Coronado and Quivira*, 19-22; Lowery, *Spanish Settlements*, 285-287; Mota Padilla, *Historia*, 111; Tello, *Libro segundo*, 325-326; Twitchell, *Leading Facts of New Mexican History*, I, 169-173; Winship, 363-367, 373-377.

CHAPTER VII

MANUSCRIPTS: A. G. I. Justicia, legajo 339, pieza 1, *Residencia tomada á . . . Coronado:* Section 1, Tejada's *Interrogatorio*—Testimony of Juan de Samaniego; Section 2, *Interrogatorio* in the matter of Coronado's *descargos*—Testimonies of Pedro Cuadrado, Hernando de Valle, Hernando Martel, Rodrigo de Tamara, Cristóbal Pérez, Alvaro de Bracamonte, Alonso de Toro, Bartolomé García, Antonio de Aguiar, Pedro de Ledesma, Juan de Alaejos, Cristóbal Romero, Francisco Cornejo, Alonzo Lorenzo, Juan de Subía, Cristóbal de Valle, Alonso de Plasencia, Francisco Olivares, Diego Hurtado. A. G. I. Justicia, legajo 339, pieza 3 (a), *Una información sobre ciertos pueblos que pertenecieron a Cristóbal de Oñate:* Tejada's *Interrogatorio*—Testimonies of Diego Hurtado, Tomás Grióz, Melchior Pérez, Francisco Vázquez de Coronado, Fernando de Palencia, Francisco de Godoy, Francisco Cornejo. A. G. I. Justicia, legajo 339, pieza 3 (b), *Una información sobre ciertos pueblos que . . . Coronado y . . . Bracamonte tuvieron en compañia:* Bracamonte's *Interrogatorio*—Testimonies of Cristóbal de Oñate, Francisco de Godoy, Alonso Valiente, Alonso Rodríguez, Pedro de Ledesma, Alonso de Toro, Juan Durán. A. G. I. Justicia, legajo 1021, pieza 3, *Relación sacada de la probanza hecha por parte de . . . Cárdenas:* Testimonies of Juan Gálves, Juan de Fioz, Rodrigo de Frias, Domingo Martín. A. G. I. Justicia, legajo 1021, pieza 5, *Probanza hecha en Méjico a pedimento de . . . Cárdenas:* Testimonies of Juan Galego [Gálves or Galeras], Juan de Fioz, Domingo Martín, Diego de Madrid, Hernando de Paez, Luís de Vargas, Gerónimo Mercado de Sotomayor, Francisco Gorbalán, García del Castillo, Pedro Navarro, Pablo de Melgosa. A. G. I. Justicia, legajo 1021, pieza 6, *Probanza del Fiscal contra . . . Cárdenas:* Benavente's *Interrogatorio*—Testimony of Rodrigo Maldonado.

PUBLISHED DOCUMENTS: *Actas de cabildo*, libro IV, 181-182; Aiton, "Coronado's commission as captain general"—"Coronado's muster roll"; Aiton and Rey, "Coronado's testimony," 311-312; Castañeda, in Winship, 420-422—English translation, Hammond and Rey, 201-204; Coronado, "Appointment . . . as commander of the expedition"—"Coronado's testimony," 319-320; Cuebas, *Muster Roll;* "Información del virrey de Nueva España"; Jaramillo, "Relación," in Pacheco y Cárdenas, XIV, 304—English translation, Hammond and Rey, 295; Mendoza, "Carta al emperador [Jacona, April 17, 1540]"—"Residencia," 102.

OTHER REFERENCES: A. F. Bandelier, *The Gilded Man*, 164-165; Conway, "A Scotsman in America"; F. S. Curtis, Jr., "Spanish arms and armor," 107-111; Day, *Coronado's Quest*—"Mota Padilla," 91-92; Hammond and Rey, 6-14; Herrera, *Historia general*, Dec. VI, libro IX, cap. XL; P. A. Jones, *Coronado and Quivira*, 23-29; Mendieta, *Historia eclesiás-*

tica indiana, 742-743; Mota Padilla, *Historia,* 110, 112; Obregón, *Historia,* 17-19—English translation, Hammond and Rey, *Obregón's History,* 13-14; Tello, *Libro segundo,* 67-68, 78, 88, 100, 137, 201, 326-327, 484; Twitchell, *Leading Facts of New Mexican History,* I, 173-176.

CHAPTER VIII

MANUSCRIPTS: A. G. I. Justicia, legajo 336, *Proceso de pleito . . . por parte de . . . Coronado:* Coronado's reply to Benavente's charges; Testimony of Juan Pastor. A. G. I. Justicia, legajo 1021, pieza 1, *Acusación contra* . . . *Cárdenas:* Confession of Cárdenas. A. G. I. Justicia, legajo 1021, pieza 3, *Relación sacada de la probanza hecha por parte de . . . Cárdenas:* Testimonies of Hernando de Alvarado, Pedro de Ledesma, Juan Beteta, Juan Gálves, Juan de Fioz, Rodrigo de Frias. A. G. I. Justicia, legajo 1021, pieza 4, *Información contra* . . . *Coronado:* Testimony of Juan de Zaldívar, A. G. I. Justicia, legajo 1021, pieza 5, *Probanza hecha en Méjico a pedimento de* . . . *Cárdenas:* Testimonies of Hernando de Alvarado, Pedro de Ledesma, Juan Beteta, Juan Gallego [Gálves or Galeras], Juan de Fioz, Rodrigo de Frias, Domingo Martín, Diego de Madrid, Hernando de Paez, Luís de Vargas, Gaspar de Saldaña, Francisco Gorbalán, García del Castillo, Pedro Navarro, A. G. I. Justicia, legajo 1021, pieza 6, *Probanza del Fiscal contra* . . . *Cárdenas:* Benavente's *Interrogatorio*—Testimony of Rodrigo Maldonado—Villalobos's *Interrogatorio*—Testimony of Hernando de la Cadena.

PUBLISHED DOCUMENTS: Cárdenas, "Testimony," 341-343; Castañeda, in Winship, 422-424—English translation, Hammond and Rey, 204-207; Coronado, "Charges against Coronado," 394—"Coronado's testimony concerning the expedition," 320; Jaramillo, "Relación," in Pacheco y Cárdenas, XIV, 304—English translation, Hammond and Rey, 295; Mendoza, "Carta al emperador [Jacona, April 17, 1540].

OTHER REFERENCES: Day, *Coronado's Quest,* 84-95—"Mota Padilla," 92; Hammond and Rey, 340-341; P. A. Jones, *Coronado and Quivira,* 29-30, 39; Lowery, *Spanish Settlements,* 296-298; Mota Padilla, *Historia,* 112; Sauer, *Road to Cíbola,* 32-33; Tello, *Libro segundo,* 327-329; Twitchell, *Leading Facts of New Mexican History,* I, 176-178.

CHAPTER IX

MANUSCRIPTS: A. G. I. Justicia, legajo 336, *Proceso de pleito . . . por parte de* . . . *Coronado:* Testimonies of Hernando del Valle, Juan Bermejo, Melchior Pérez, Pedro de Ledesma, Pedro de Castro, Juan Ruíz, Juan Galeas, Froilán Vermúdez. A. G. I. Justicia, legajo 1021, pieza 2 (a), *Relación sacade de la probanza . . . que trata con . . . Cárdenas:* Testimonies of Hernando de Alvarado, Juan de Jaramillo, Hernando de Orduña, Hernando de la Cadena. A. G. I. Justicia, legajo 1021, pieza 2 (b), *Relación sacada de la probanza presentada por parte de . . . Coronado:* Testimonies of Gaspar de Saldaña, García Rodríguez, Rodrigo Maldonado. A. G. I. Justicia, legajo 1021, pieza 3, *Relación sacada de la probanza hecha por parte de* . . . *Cárdenas:* Testimony of Diego de Madrid. A. G. I. Justicia, legajo 1021, pieza 4, *Información contra* . . . *Coronado:* Testimonies of Domingo Martín, Juan de Contreras, Rodrigo Ximón, Cristóbal de Escobar, Juan Troyano, Rodrigo de Frias, Melchior Pérez, Pedro de Ledesma, Juan de Zaldívar, Alonso Alvarez.

PUBLISHED DOCUMENTS: Cárdenas, "Testimony," 343; Castañeda, in Winship, 424, 448-450—English translation, Hammond and Rey, 207-208, 249-252; Coronado, "Coronado's testimony concerning the expedition," 321-322—"Relatione . . . quel che successe nel viaggio [August 3, 1540]," in Ramusio, III, 359-360—English translation, Hammond and Rey, 162-167; Jaramillo, "Relación," in Pacheco y Cárdenas, XIV, 304-307—English translation, Hammond and Rey, 295-298; "Relación del suceso," in Pacheco y Cárdenas, XIV, 318-320—English translation, Hammond and Rey, 284-286; "Relación postrera," in Winship, 566—English translation, Hammond and Rey, 308; "Traslado de las nuevas," in Pacheco y Cárdenas, XIX, 529-530—English translation, Hammond and Rey, 179-180.

OTHER REFERENCES: Bancroft, *Arizona and New Mexico*, 37-42; A. F. Bandelier, *The Gilded Man*, 166-185—"An outline of the documentary history of the Zuñi tribe," 29-30; Day, *Coronado's Quest*, 97-111—"Mota Padilla," 90-91; Dellenbaugh, "True route of Coronado's march," 406-412; Hammond and Rey, 15-17; Herrera, *Historia general*, Dec. VI, libro IX, cap. XL; Hodge, "Coronado's march to Quivira"—*History of Hawikuh*, 30-33—in Winship, *Journey of Coronado*, xx-xxi; P. A. Jones, *Coronado and Quivira*, 31-32; Lowery, *Spanish Settlements*, 298-300, 455-456, 470-472; Mota Padilla, *Historia*, 112-113; Sauer, *Road to Cíbola*, 33-37; Tello, *Libro segundo*, 329-335; Twitchell, *Leading Facts of New Mexican History*, I, 184-186; Winship, 386-388.

CHAPTER X

MANUSCRIPTS: A. G. I. Justicia, legajo 336, *Proceso de pleito* . . . *por parte de* . . . *Coronado:* Coronado's reply to Benavente's charges. A. G. I. Justicia, legajo 1021, pieza 4, *Información contra* . . . *Coronado:* Testimonies of Domingo Martín, Juan Troyano, Pedro de Ledesma.

PUBLISHED DOCUMENTS: Cárdenas, "Testimony," 343-344; Castañeda, in Winship, 424—English translation, Hammond and Rey, 208; Coronado, "Coronado's testimony concerning the expedition," 322—"Relatione . . . quel che successe nel viaggio [August 3, 1540]," in Ramusio, III, 360—English translation, Hammond and Rey, 167.

OTHER REFERENCES: A. F. Bandelier, "An outline of the documentary history of the Zuñi tribe," 30; Day, *Coronado's Quest*, 111-112; Hodge, History of Hawikuh, 32-33—in Winship, *Journey of Coronado*, xxi; Lowery, *Spanish Settlements*, 300; Twitchell, *Leading Facts of New Mexican History*, I, 186-187.

CHAPTER XI

MANUSCRIPTS: A. G. I. Justicia, legajo 336, *Proceso de pleito* . . . *por* monies of Melchior Pérez, Pedro de Castro, Juan Ruíz. A. G. I. Justicia, *parte de* . . . *Coronado:* Coronado's reply to Benavente's charges—Testi-

legajo 1021, pieza 2 (b), *Relación sacada de la probanza presentada por parte de . . . Coronado:* Testimony of Gaspar de Saldaña. A. G. I. Justicia, legajo 1021, pieza 4, *Información contra . . . Coronado:* Testimonies of Francisca de Hozes, Domingo Martín, Juan de Contreras, Rodrigo Ximón, Cristóbal de Escobar, Juan Troyano, Rodrigo de Frias, Melchior Pérez, Pedro de Ledesma, Juan de Zaldívar, Alonso Alvarez.

PUBLISHED DOCUMENTS: Cárdenas, "Testimony," 344-346; Castañeda, in Winship, 424-425, 450-451—English translation, Hammond and Rey, 208-209, 252-253; Coronado, "Coronado's testimony concerning the expedition," 322-324—"Relatione . . . quel che successe nel viaggio [August 3, 1540]," in Ramusio, III, 360-362—English translation, Hammond and Rey, 167-175; Jaramillo, "Relación," in Pacheco y Cárdenas, XIV, 307-309—English translation, Hammond and Rey, 298-299; "Relación del suceso," in Pacheco y Cárdenas, XIV, 319-320—English translation, Hammond and Rey, 285-286; "Relación postrera," in Winship, 566—English translation, Hammond and Rey, 308-309; "Traslado de las nuevas," in Pacheco y Cárdenas, XIX, 530-532—English translation, Hammond and Rey, 180-181.

OTHER REFERENCES: Bancroft, *Arizona and New Mexico,* 42-45; A. F. Bandelier, *The Gilded Man,* 185-186—"An outline of the documentary history of the Zuñi tribe," 30-39, 41-56; Day, *Coronado's Quest,* 113-130—"Gomara," 350—"Mota Padilla," 93-94; Gómara, *Historia general,* cap. CCXIII; Herrera, *Historia general,* Dec. VI, libro IX, cap. XL; Hodge, *History of Hawikuh,* 33-58—"The six cities of Cíbola," in Winship, *Journey of Coronado,* xxi-xxv; Lowery, *Spanish Settlements,* 300-303; Mota Padilla, *Historia,* 113; Tello, *Libro segundo,* 335-336; Twitchell, *Leading Facts of New Mexican History,* I, 187-191; Winship, 388-390.

CHAPTER XII

MANUSCRIPTS: A. G. I. Justicia, legajo 336, *Proceso de pleito . . . por parte de . . . Coronado:* Testimony of Melchior Pérez. A. G. I. Justicia, legajo 1021, pieza 2 (b), *Relación sacada de la probanza presentada por parte de . . . Coronado:* Testimony of Gaspar de Saldaña.

PUBLISHED DOCUMENTS: Cárdenas, "Testimony," 346-347; Castañeda, in Winship, 428-430, 451—English translation, Hammond and Rey, 213-217, 253; Coronado, "Relatione . . . quel che successe nel viaggio [August 3, 1540]," in Ramusio, III, 362—English translation, Hammond and Rey, 175-176; Jaramillo, "Relación," in Pacheco y Cárdenas, XIV, 308—English translation, Hammond and Rey, 299; "Relación del suceso," in Pacheco y Cárdenas, XIV, 320-322—English translation, Hammond and Rey, 286-288.

OTHER REFERENCES: Bancroft, *Arizona and New Mexico,* 46-48; A. F. Bandelier, "Final report," II, 367-369, 376-377—*The Gilded Man,* 197-199; Bartlett, "How Don Pedro de Tovar discovered the Hopi"; Day, *Coronado's Quest,* 135-346; Dellenbaugh, *Romance of the Colorado River,* 32-35; Hammond and Rey, 18-19; Hargrave, "The Jeddito valley"; Obregón, *Historia,* 24—English translation, Hammond and Rey, *Obregón's History,* 22-23; Simpson, "Cornado's march," 316-317; Tello, *Libro segundo,* 407-408; Twitchell, *Leading Facts of New Mexican History,* I, 192-194, 197-198; Winship, 390.

CHAPTER XIII

Manuscripts: A. G. I. Justicia, legajo 336, *Proceso de pleito . . . por parte de . . . Coronado:* Coronado's reply to Benavente's charges—Testimony of Pedro de Castro. A. G. I. Justicia, legajo 1021, pieza 4, *Información contra . . . Coronado:* Testimonies of Juan Troyano, Juan de Zaldívar, Juan de Paradinas, Domingo Martín, Juan Contreras. A. G. I. Justicia, legajo 1021, pieza 6, *Probanza del Fiscal contra . . . Cárdenas:* Benavente's *Interrogatorio*—Testimony of Rodrigo Maldonado.

Published Documents: Castañeda, in Winship, 418-419, 425-426—English translation, Hammond and Rey, 198-199, 209-210; Coronado, "Coronado's testimony concerning the expedition," 320—"Relatione . . . quel che successe nel viaggio [August 3, 1540]," in Ramusio, III, 362-363—English translation, Hammond and Rey, 176-178; Jaramillo, "Relación," in Pacheco y Cárdenas, XIV, 307-308—English translation, Hammond and Rey, 297-298; "Relación del suceso," in Pacheco y Cárdenas, XIV, 321—English translation, Hammond and Rey, 286.

Other References: Bancroft, *North Mexican States,* I, 87-88; A. F. Bandelier, "Fray Juan Padilla," 551—*The Gilded Man,* 188-189; Day, *Coronado's Quest,* 131-135—"Mota Padilla," 94; Hammond and Rey, 20; Mota Padilla, *Historia,* 114; Obregón, *Historia,* 147, 155-156—English translation, Hammond and Rey, *Obregón's History,* 162, 171-173; Tello, *Libro segundo,* 408; Twitchell, *Leading Facts of New History,* I, 194; Vetancurt, *Teatro mexicano,* IV, 119; Winship, 391-392.

CHAPTER XIV

Published Documents: Alarcón, "De lo que hizo por la mar Hernando de Alarcón"—"Relación del armada del Marqués del Valle"—"Relatione della navigatione & scoperta"; Castañeda, in Winship, 421—English translation, Hammond and Rey, 202-203; Mendoza, "Instrucción que debia observar el capitan Hernando Alarcón."

Other References: Bancroft, *North Mexican States,* I, 90-95; A. F. Bandelier, *Final Report,* I, 107-109—*The Gilded Man,* 173-174; Day, *Coronado's Quest,* 167-187; Dellenbaugh, *Romance of the Colorado River,* 11-27; Freeman, "The conquistadores," 6-17; Herrera, *Historia general,* Dec. VI, libro IX, caps. XIII-XV; Leigh, *Forgotten Waters,* 17-18; Lowery, *Spanish Settlements,* 289-296; Simpson, "Coronado's march," 315-316; Sykes, *The Colorado Delta,* 8-9; Twitchell, *Leading Facts of New Mexican History,* I, 179-184; Wagner, *Cartography of the Northwest Coast,* I, 30-32 —"Voyage of Hernando de Alarcón"; Waters, *The Colorado,* 143-145; Winship, 385-386, 403-406.

CHAPTER XV

Manuscripts: A. G. I. Justicia, legajo 336, *Proceso de pleito . . . por parte de . . . Coronado:* Testimony of Pedro de Castro. A. G. I. Justicia, legajo 1021, pieza 2 (a), *Relación sacada de la probanza . . . que trata con*

Cárdenas: Testimony of Hernando de Orduña. A. G. I. Justicia, legajo 1021, pieza 4, *Información contra . . . Coronado:* Testimony of Domingo Martín. A. G. I. Justicia, legajo 1021, pieza 6, *Probanza del Fiscal contra . . . Cárdenas:* Villalobos's *Interrogatorio*—Testimony of Hernando de Orduña.

PUBLISHED DOCUMENTS: Castañeda, in Winship, 426-427, 438—English translation, Hammond and Rey, 210-212, 231-232; "Relación del suceso," in Pacheco y Cárdenas, XIV, 321—English translation, Hammond and Rey, 287.

OTHER REFERENCES: Bancroft, *North Mexican States*, I, 88-89; A. F. Bandelier, *The Gilded Man*, 189-190; Day, *Coronado's Quest*, 159-165— "Mota Padilla," 94-96; Dellenbaugh, *Romance of the Colorado River*, 28-32; Freeman, "The conquistadores," 18-21; R. L. Ives, "Melchior Díaz"; Lowery, *Spanish Settlements*, 305-307; Mota Padilla, *Historia*, 158-159; Sauer, "Communication"; Simpson, "Coronado's march," 314-315; Sykes, *The Colorado Delta*, 9; Tello, *Libro segundo*, 408-411; Twitchell, *Leading Facts of New Mexican History*, I, 194-197; Winship, 406-408.

CHAPTER XVI

MANUSCRIPTS: A. G. I. Justicia, legajo 336, *Proceso de pleito . . . por parte de . . . Coronado:* Testimony of Melchior Pérez. A. G. I. Justicia, legajo 1021, pieza 2 (b), *Relación sacada de la probanza presentada por de . . . Coronado:* Testimony of Gaspár de Saldaña. A. G. I. Justicia, legajo 1021, pieza 4, *Información contra . . . Coronado:* Testimonies of Francisca de Hozes, Alonso Sánchez, Juan de Paradinas, Domingo Martín, Juan de Contreras, Rodrigo Ximón, Cristóbal de Escobar, Juan de Troyano, Rodrigo de Frias, Melchior Pérez, Pedro de Ledesma, Juan de Zaldívar, Alonso Alvarez.

PUBLISHED DOCUMENTS: Hernando de Alvarado, "Relación de lo que Hernando de Alvarado y Fray Joan de Padilla descubrieron"; Cárdenas, "Testimony," 349-350; Castañeda, in Winship, 430-431—English translation, Hammond and Rey, 217-220; Coronado, "Coronado's testimony concerning the expedition," 324-329; "Relación del suceso," in Pacheca y Cárdenas, XIV, 322-324—English translation, Hammond and Rey, 288-289.

OTHER REFERENCES: Bancroft, *Arizona and New Mexico*, 49-51; A. F. Bandelier, *Documentary History, New Mexico Historical Review*, IV, 305-323—see also, Bandelier and Hewett, *Indians of the Rio Grande Valley*, 143-155—*The Gilded Man*, 201-208—*Historical Introduction to Studies among the Sedentary Indians of New Mexico;* Day, *Coronado's Quest*, 147-159—"Mota Padilla," 99; Hammond and Rey, 19-20; Lowery, *Spanish Settlements*, 312-316; Mota Padilla, *Historia*, 160-161; Sedgwick, *Acoma, the Sky City*, 58-60; Simpson, "Coronado's march," 318-319; Tello, *Libro segundo*, 416-417; Twitchell, *Leading Facts of New Mexican History*, I, 198-204; Winship, 390-391.

CHAPTER XVII

MANUSCRIPTS: A. G. I. Justicia, legajo 1021, pieza 2 (a), *Relación sacada de la probanza . . . que trata con Cárdenas:* Testimonies of Hernando Alvarado, Alonso de Valderreina. A. G. I. Justicia, legajo 1021, pieza 2 (b), *Relación sacada de la probanza presentada por parte de . . . Coronado:* Testimony of Gaspar de Saldaña. A. G. I. Justicia, legajo 1021, pieza 3, *Relación sacada de la probanza hecha por parte de . . . Cárdenas:* Testimonies of Francisco Gorbalán, Juan Beteta. A. G. I. Justicia, legajo 1021, pieza 4, *Información contra . . . Coronado:* Testimony of Francisca de Hozes, Alonso Sánchez, Juan de Paradinas, Domingo Martín, Juan de Contreras, Rodrigo Ximón, Cristóbal de Escobar, Juan Troyano, Rodrigo de Frias, Melchior Pérez, Pedro de Ledesma, Juan de Zaldívar, Alonso Alvarez. A. G. I. Justicia, legajo 1021, pieza 5, *Probanza hecha en Méjico a pedimento de . . . Cárdenas:* Testimonies of Juan Beteta, Francisco Gorbalán. A. G. I. Justicia, legajo 1021, pieza 6, *Probanza del Fiscal contra . . . Cárdenas:* Benavente's *Interrogatorio*—Testimony of Gaspar de Saldaña.

PUBLISHED DOCUMENTS: Cárdenas, "Testimony," 347, 349-352; Castañeda, in Winship, 427-428, 432—English translation, Hammond and Rey, 212-213, 220-221; Coronado, "Coronado's testimony," 325-329; Jaramillo, "Relación," in Pacheco y Cárdenas, XIV, 308-309—English translation, Hammond and Rey, 299; "Relación del suceso," in Pacheco y Cárdenas, XIV, 324—English translation, Hammond and Rey, 289-290.

OTHER REFERENCES: Bancroft, *Arizona and New Mexico,* 54-56; A. F. Bandelier, *Documentary History, New Mexico Historical Review,* IV, 323-329—see also, Bandelier and Hewett, *Indians of the Rio Grande Valley,* 155-158—*The Gilded Man,* 208-212—*Historical Introduction to Studies among the Sedentary Indians of New Mexico,* 21-22; Day, *Coronado's Quest,* 189-194; Hammond and Rey, 21-23; Hodge, *History of Hawikuh,* 42—in Winship, *Journey of Coronado,* 26, n. 1; Lowery, *Spanish Settlements,* 316-318; Sedgwick, *Acoma, the Sky City,* 60-61; Simpson, "Coronado's march," 319-320; Tello, "Libro segundo," 417; Twitchell, *Leading Facts of New Mexican History,* I, 204-208.

CHAPTER XVIII

MANUSCRIPTS: A. G. I. Justicia, legajo 336, *Proceso de pleito . . . por parte de . . . Coronado:* Coronado's reply to Benavente's charges. A. G. I. Justicia, legajo 1021, pieza 1, *Acusación contra . . . Cárdenas:* Rodríguez's appeal of Cardenas's sentence (Vallid, January 7, 1550). A. G. I. Justicia, legajo 1021, pieza 2 (a), *Relación sacada de la probanza . . . que trata con . . . Cárdenas:* Testimonies of Alonso de Valderreina, Hernando Alvarado, Juan de Jaramillo, Hernando de la Cadena, Hernando de Orduña, Cristóbal de Mayorga. A. G. I. Justicia, legajo 1021, pieza 2 (b), *Relación sacada de la probanza presentada por parte de . . . Coronado:* Testimonies of García Rodríguez, Gaspar de Saldaña. A. G. I. Justicia, legajo 1021, pieza 3, *Relación sacada de la probanza hecha por parte de . . . Cárdenas:* Testimonies of Francisco Gorbalán, Hernando de Alvarado, Pedro de

Ledesma, Juan Beteta, Juan Gálves, Juan de Fioz, Rodrigo de Frias, Diego de Madrid, Hernan Paez, Luis de Vargas, Gaspar de Saldaña, Gerónimo de Sotomayor, García del Castillo, Pedro Navarro, Juan de Vitoria. A. G. I. Justicia, legajo 1021, pieza 4, *Información contra* . . . *Coronado:* Testimonies of Francisca de Hozes, Alonso Sánchez, Juan de Paradinas, Domjngo Martín, Juan de Contreras, Rodrigo Ximón, Cristóbal de Escobar, Juan Troyano, Rodrigo de Frias, Melchior Pérez, Pedro de Lgdesma, Juan de Zaldívar, Alonso Alvarez. A. G. I. Justicia, legajo 1021, pieza 5, *Probanza hecha en Méjico a pedimento de* . . . *Cárdenas:* Testimonies of Hernando de Alvarado, Pedro de Ledesma, Juan Beteta, Juan Gallego [Gálves or Galeras], Juan de Fioz, Rodrigo de Frias, Diego de Madrid, Hernando de Paez, Luís de Vargas, Gaspar de Saldaña, Gerónimo Mercado de Soto-mayor, Juan de Vitoria, Francisco Gorbalán, Garcia del Castillo, Pedro Navarro, Pablos de Melgosa. A. G. I. Justicia, legajo 1021, pieza 6, *Probanza del Fiscal contra* . . . *Cárdenas:* Benavente's *Interrogatorio*—Testimonies of Gaspar de Saldaña, Rodrigo Maldonado—Villalobos's *Interrogatorio*—Testimonies of Hernando de Alvarado, Juan de Jaramillo, Hernando de Orduña, Alonso de Valderrey, Cristobal de Mayorga, Hernando de la Cadena.

PUBLISHED DOCUMENTS: Cárdenas, "Testimony," 347-349, 351-358; Castañeda, in Winship, 432-435—English translation, Hammond and Rey, 222-227; Coronado, "Coronado's testimony," 329-335; "Relación del suceso," in Pacheco y Cárdenas, XIV, 324-325—English translation, Hammond and Rey, 290.

OTHER REFERENCES: Bancroft, *Arizona and New Mexico,* 56-57; A. F. Bandelier, *Documentary History, New Mexico Historical Review,* IV, 329-334, V, 38-40, 47—see also, Bandelier and Hewett, *Indians of the Rio Grande Valley,* 158-163, 168—*The Gilded Man,* 213-214; Day, *Coronado's Quest,* 194-202—"Mota Padilla," 100—Hammond and Rey, 23-25; Hodge, in Winship, *Journey of Coronado,* 28, n. 2; Mota Padilla, *Historia,* 161; Simpson, "Coronado's march," 320; Tello, *Libro segundo,* 418-419; Twitchell, *Leading Facts of New Mexican History,* I, 208-212.

CHAPTER XIX

MANUSCRIPTS: A. G. I. Justicia, legajo 336, *Proceso de pleito* . . . *por parte de* . . . *Coronado:* Coronado's reply to Benavente's charges. A. G. I. Justicia, legajo 1021, pieza 2 (a) *Relación sacada de la probanza* . . . *que trata con* . . . *Cárdenas:* Testimonies of Hernando de Orduña, Cristóbal de Mayorga. A. G. I. Justicia, legajo 1021, pieza 2 (b), *Relación sacada de la probanza presentado por parte de* . . . *Coronado:* Testimonies of Gaspar de Saldaña, García Rodríguez. A. G. I. Justicia, legajo 1021, pieza 3, *Relación sacada de la probanza hecha por parte de* . . . *Cárdenas:* Testimonies of Hernando de Alvarado, Pedro de Ledesma, Juan Beteta, Juan de Fioz, Rodrigo de Frias, Domingo Martín, Diego de Madrid, Hernan Paez, Luís de Vargas, Gaspar de Saldaña, Gerónimo de Sotomayor, Francisco Gorbalán, García del Castillo, Pedro Navarro. A. G. I. Justicia, legajo 1021, pieza 4, *Información contra* . . . *Coronado:* Testimonies of Alonso

Sánchez, Domingo Martín, Juan de Contreras, Rodrigo Ximón, Cristóbal de Escobar, Juan Troyano, Rodrigo de Frias, Melchior Pérez, Pedro de Ledesma, Juan de Zaldívar, Alonso Alvarez. A. G. I. Justicia, legajo 1021, pieza 5, *Probanza hecha en Méjico a pedimento de . . . Cárdenas:* Testimonies of Hernando de Alvarado, Juan Beteta, Juan de Fioz, Diego de Madrid, Luís de Vargas, Gaspar de Saldaña, Juan de Vitoria. Francisco Gorbalán, García del Castillo, Pedro Navarro, Pablos de Melgosa. A. G. I. Justicia, legajo 1021, pieza 6, *Probanza del Fiscal contra . . . Cárdenas:* Villalobos's *Interrogatorio*—Testimony of Cristóbal de Mayorga.

PUBLISHED DOCUMENTS: Cárdenas, "Testimony," 358-361; Castañeda, in Winship, 435-437, 452—English translation, Hammond and Rey, 227-231, 256; Coronado, "Coronado's testimony," 332-334; "Relación del suceso," in Pacheco y Cárdenas, XIV, 325—English translation, Hammond and Rey, 290.

OTHER REFERENCES: Bancroft, *Arizona and New Mexico,* 57-58; A. F. Bandelier, *Documentary History, New Mexico Historical Review,* V, 40-50 —see also, Bandelier and Hewett, *Indians of the Rio Grande Valley,* 163-169—*The Gilded Man,* 215-217; Day, *Coronado's Quest,* 202-210, 218— "Gomara," 351-352—"Mota Padilla," 100-102; Gómara, *Historia general,* cap. CCXIIII; Lowery, *Spanish Settlements,* 320-322; Mota Padilla, *Historia,* 161-162; Tello, *Libro segundo,* 419-427; Twitchell, *Leading Facts of New Mexican History,* I, 212-218; Winship, 393.

CHAPTER XX

MANUSCRIPTS: A. G. I. Justicia, legajo 1021, pieza 2 (a), *Relación sacada de la probanza . . . que trata con . . . Cárdenas:* Testimony of Hernando de Orduña. A. G. I. Justicia, legajo 1021, pieza 6, *Probanza del Fiscal contra . . . Cárdenas:* Testimony of Hernando de Orduña.

PUBLISHED DOCUMENTS: Castañeda, in Winship, 438-440—English translation, Hammond and Rey, 232-234; Coronado, "Carta . . . al emperador [October 20, 1541]," in Pacheco y Cárdenas, III, 363—English translation, Hammond and Rey, 185—"Coronado's testimony," 328, 331; Jaramillo, "Relación," in Pacheco y Cárdenas, XIV, 312—English translation, Hammond and Rey, 302; Peramíldez, "Carta al secretario Juan de Sámano"; "Relación del suceso," in Pacheco y Cárdenas, XIV, 325—English translation, Hammond and Rey, 290-291.

OTHER REFERENCES: Bancroft, *North Mexican States,* I, 89; A. F. Bandelier, *The Gilded Man,* 217, 219-220; Day, *Coronado's Quest,* 217, 220-223—"Gomara," 351—"Mota Padilla," 99, 102; Gómara, *Historia general,* cap. CCXIIII; Mota Padilla, *Historia,* 160-161, 163; Tello, *Libro segundo,* 417-418, 427; Twitchell, *Leading Facts of New Mexican History,* I, 218-219; Winship, 394-395.

CHAPTER XXI

MANUSCRIPTS: A. G. I. Justicia, legajo 1021, pieza 4, *Información contra . . . Coronado:* Testimony of Juan de Zaldívar.

PUBLISHED DOCUMENTS: Castañeda, in Winship, 429-440, 452-454, 456—English translation, Hammond and Rey, 234-236, 256-258, 261-262; Coronado, "Carta . . . al emperador [October 20, 1541]," in Pacheco y Cárdenas, III, 363-364—English translation, Hammond and Rey, 186; Jaramillo, "Relación," in Pacheco y Cárdenas, XIV, 309-310—English translation, Hammond and Rey, 300-301; "Relación del suceso," in Pacheco y Cárdenas, XIV, 327-328—English translation, Hammond and Rey, 310-311.

OTHER REFERENCES: Bancroft, *Arizona and New Mexico*, 59-60; A. F. Bandelier, *The Gilded Man*, 220-226; A. F. Bandelier and Hewett, *Indians of the Rio Grande Valley*, 182-183; Baskett, "A study of the route of Coronado," 225, 227, 235-240; Day, *Coronado's Quest*, 225-237—"Gomara," 352, 354-355—"Mota Padilla," 102-104; Gómara, *Historia general*, caps. CCXIIII-CCXV; Herrera, *Historia general*, Dec. VI, libro IX, cap. XI; P. A. Jones, *Coronado and Quivira*, 45-60; Lowery, *Spanish Settlements*, 323-326; Mota Padilla, *Historia*, 164-165; Scisco, "Coronado's march," 237-240; Tello, *Libro segundo*, 427-433; Twitchell, *Leading Facts of New Mexican History*, I, 219-220; Winship, 395.

CHAPTER XXII

MANUSCRIPTS: A. G. I. Justicia, legajo 1021, pieza 2 (b), *Relación sacada de la probanza presentada por parte de . . . Coronado:* Testimony of García Rodríguez. A. G. I. Justicia, legajo 1021, pieza 3, *Relación sacada de la probanza hecha por parte de . . . Cárdenas:* Testimony of Juan de Fioz. A. G. I. Justicia, legajo 1021, pieza 6, *Probanza del Fiscal contra . . . Cárdenas:* Benavente's *Interrogatorio*—Testimonies of García Rodríguez, Gaspár de Saldaña.

PUBLISHED DOCUMENTS: Cabeza de Vaca, Relación, in Ramusio, III, 324—English translation, F. Bandelier, *Journey of . . . Cabeza de Vaca*, 128-130, 132-133; Cárdenas, "Testimony," 362; Castañeda, in Winship, 440-442, 456, 466-467—English translation, Hammond and Rey, 236-238, 262, 278-279; Coronado, "Carta . . . al emperador [October 20, 1541]," in Pacheco y Cárdenas, III, 364—English translation, Hammond and Rey, 186; Jaramillo, "Relación," in Pacheco y Cárdenas, XIV, 310-311—English translation, Hammond and Rey, 301-302; "Relación del suceso," in Pacheco y Cárdenas, XIV, 326—English translation, Hammond and Rey, 291; "Relación postrera," in Winship, 568—English translation, Hammond and Rey, 311.

OTHER REFERENCES: Baker, *Geology . . . of the Northern Llano Estacado;* A. F. Bandelier, *The Gilded Man*, 226-227; Baskett, "A Study of the route of Coronado," 223, 225-226, 228, 237-240, 249-250; Bryan, "The Llano Estacado"; Day, *Coronado's Quest*, 237-242—"Gomara," 352—"Mota Padilla," 104-105; Donoghue, "Route of the Coronado expedition," *New Mexico Historical Review*, IV, 77-89; Gómara, *Historia general*, cap. CCXIIII; Gould, *Geology . . . of the Eastern Portion of the Panhandle of Texas—Geology . . . of the Western Portion of the Panhandle of Texas;* Hallenbeck, *Journey . . . of Cabeza de Vaca*, 169-177; Herrera, *Historia general*, Dec. VI, libro IX, cap. XI; W. D. Johnson, "The high plains";

P. A. Jones, *Coronado and Quivira*, 61, 66, 69; Lowery, *Spanish Settlements*, 326-327; Mota Padilla, *Historia*, 165; Scisco, "Coronado's march across the high plains," 240-241; Tello, *Libro segundo*, 434-435; Twitchell, *Leading Facts of New Mexican History*, I, 220-221.

CHAPTER XXIII

PUBLISHED DOCUMENTS: Castañeda, in Winship, 442-443—English translation, Hammond and Rey, 238-240; Coronado, "Carta . . . al emperador [October 20, 1541]," in Pacheco y Cárdenas, III, 365—English translation, Hammond and Rey, 186-187; Jaramillo, "Relación," in Pacheco y Cárdenas, XIV, 310-311—English translation, Hammond and Rey, 301-302; "Relación del suceso," in Pacheco y Cárdenas, XIV, 326—English translation, Hammond and Rey, 291.

OTHER REFERENCES: A. F. Bandelier, *The Gilded Man*, 228; Day, *Coronado's Quest*, 240-246—"Mota Padilla," 104-105; Herrera, *Historia general*, Dec. VI, libro IX, cap. XI; P. A. Jones, *Coronado and Quivira*, 60-62, 69; Mota Padilla, *Historia*, 165; Tello, *Libro segundo*, 434-436; Winship, 395-396.

CHAPTER XXIV

PUBLISHED DOCUMENTS: Cárdenas, "Testimony," 362; Castañeda, in Winship, 443-445, 466—English translation, Hammond and Rey, 240-243, 279; "Gentleman of Elvas," in Smith, *Career of . . . de Soto* (Bourne ed.), 22-145—also, Hodge and Lewis, *Spanish Explorers*, 146-223; "Relación del suceso," in Pacheco y Cárdenas, XIV, 326—English translation, Hammond and Rey, 291.

OTHER REFERENCES: A. F. Bandelier, *The Gilded Man*, 229-231; Day, *Coronado's Quest*, 246-247, 255-259—"Mota Padilla," 105; De Soto, *Final Report of the . . . Commission*, 139-257; Donoghue, "Route of the Coronado expedition," *New Mexico Historical Review*, IV, 89-90; Garcilaso de la Vega, *La Florida del Ynca*, libros II-IV; Herrera, *Historia general*, Dec. VI, libro VII, caps. X-XII, Dec. VII, libro I, caps. X-XV, libro II, caps. I-IV, libro VII, cap. I; P. A. Jones, *Coronado and Quivira*, 63-64; Lowery, Spanish Settlements, 331-332; Maynard, *De Soto*, 140-250; Mota Padilla, *Historia*, 165; Swanton, *Indians of the Southeastern United States*, 40-55; Tello, *Libro segundo*, 436; Twitchell, *Leading Facts of New Mexican History*, I, 228-229.

CHAPTER XXV

MANUSCRIPTS: A. G. I. Justicia, legajo 336, *Proceso de pleito . . . por parte de . . . Coronado:* Coronado's reply to Benavente's charges—Testimonies of Hernando del Valle, Juan Bermejo, Pedro de Ledesma, Juan Ruíz, Juan Galeas, Froilán Vermúdez. A. G. I. Justicia, legajo 1021, pieza 2 (a), *Relación sacada de la probanza . . . que trata con . . . Cárdenas:* Testimony of Alonso de Valderreina. A. G. I. Justicia, legajo 1021, pieza 2 (b), *Relación sacada de la probanza presentada por parte de ... Coronado:* Testimonies of Gaspár de Saldaña, García Rodríguez. A. G. I. Justicia, legajo 1021, pieza 3, *Relación sacada de la probanza hecha por parte de ... Cárdenas:* Testimonies of Juan Gálves, Luís de Vargas, Gaspár de Saldaña, Francisco Gorbalán, Pedro Navarro. A. G. I. Justicia, legajo 1021, pieza 4, *Información contra ... Coronado:* Testimonies of Francisca de Hozes, Alonso Sánchez, Juan de Paradinas, Domingo Martín, Juan de Contreras, Rodrigo Ximón, Cristóbal de Escobar, Juan Troyano, Rodrigo de Frias, Melchior Pérez, Pedro de Ledesma, Juan de Zaldívar. A. G. I. Justicia, legajo 1021, pieza 5, *Probanza hecha en Méjico a pedimento de ... Cárdenas:* Testimonies of Juan Gallego [Galeas or Galeras], Diego de Madrid, Luís de Vargas, Francisco Gorbalán. A. G. I. Justicia, legajo 1021, pieza 6, *Probanza del Fiscal contra ... Cárdenas: Benavente's Interrogatorio*—Testimony of García Rodríguez, Gaspár de Saldaña—Villalobos' *Interrogatorio*—Testimony of Alonso de Valderrey.

PUBLISHED DOCUMENTS: Cárdenas, "Testimony," 362-363; Castañeda, in Winship, 443-444, 446, 456-457—English translation, Hammond and Rey, 241-242, 245, 262-263; Coronado, "Carta . . . al emperador [October 20, 1541]," in Pacheco y Cárdenas, III, 365-368—English translation, Hammond and Rey, 187-189; Jaramillo, "Relación," in Pacheco y Cárdenas, XIV, 312-315—English translation, Hammond and Rey, 302-305; "Relación del suceso," in Pacheco y Cárdenas, XIV, 326-327—English translation, Hammond and Rey, 291-292.

OTHER REFERENCES: A. F. Bandelier, *The Gilded Man*, 235-237; Baskett, "A study of the route of Coronado"; Brower, *Harahey—Quivira;* Day, *Coronado's Quest*, 247-255—"Gomara," 352—"Mota Padilla," 105; Donoghue, "Coronado, Oñate, and Quivira"—"The location of Quivira"; Gómara, *Historia general,* cap. CCXIIII; Herrera, *Historia general,* Dec. VI, libro IX, caps. XI-XII; Hodge, "Coronado's march to Quivira"; Hodge and Lewis, *Spanish Explorers,* 337-338; H. Jones, "Quivira"; P. A. Jones, *Coronado and Quivira*, 71-124; Lowery, *Spanish Settlements*, 328-330, 468-470; Mooney, "Quivira and the Wichitas"; Mota Padilla, *Historia,* 165-166; E. C. Ross, "The Quivira village"; Schott, "Letter on question of magnetic declination"; Tello, *Libro segundo,* 436-437; Twitchell, *Leading Facts of New Mexican History,* I, 226-228; Wedel, *Archaeological Remains in Central Kansas*—"In search of Coronado's province."

CHAPTER XXVI

PUBLISHED DOCUMENTS: Castañeda, in Winship, 445-446—English translation, Hammond and Rey, 244-246; Coronado, "Carta . . . al emperador [October 20, 1541]," in Pacheco y Cárdenas, III, 363-369—English translation, Hammond and Rey, 185-190; Jaramillo, "Relación," in Pacheco y Cárdenas, XIV, 315-316—English translation, Hammond and Rey, 305-306; "Relación del suceso," in Pacheco y Cárdenas, XIV, 327—English translation, Hammond and Rey, 292.

OTHER REFERENCES: Bancroft, *Arizona and New Mexico,* 62-65; A. F. Bandelier, *The Gilded Man,* 231-234, 237; Day, *Coronado's Quest,* 255,

260-267—"Gómara," 352: Gómara, *Historia general,* cap. CCXIII; Herrera, *Historia general,* Dec. VI, libro IX, cap. XII; P. A. Jones, *Coronado and Quivira,* 124-129; Lowery, *Spanish Settlements,* 330-333; Simpson, *Coronado's March,* 322-323; Twitchell, *Leading Facts of New Mexican History,* I, 228-234.

CHAPTER XXVII

MANUSCRIPTS: A. G. I. Justicia, legajo 1021, pieza 4, *Información contra . . . Coronado:* Testimonies of Francisca de Hozes, Alonso Sánchez, Juan de Paradinas, Domingo Martín, Juan de Contreras, Rodrigo Ximón, Cristóbal de Escobar, Juan Troyano, Rodrigo de Frias, Melchior Pérez, Pedro de Ledesma, Juan de Zaldívar.

PUBLISHED DOCUMENTS: Cárdenas, "Testimony," 363-364; Castañeda, in Winship, 458-461, 464-466—English translation, Hammond and Rey, 264-270, 276-278; "Relación del suceso," Pacheco y Cárdenas, XIV, 328— English translation, Hammond and Rey, 293.

OTHER REFERENCES: A. F. Bandelier, *The Gilded Man,* 239-242; Day, *Coronado's Quest,* 267-269, 273, 287-291—"Mota Padilla," 106; Mota Padilla, *Historia,* 166; Obregón, *Historia,* 147-148, 152-153—English translation, Hammond and Rey, *Obregón's History,* 162-163, 168-169; Tello, *Libro segundo,* 437-439; Twitchell, *Leading Facts of New Mexican History,* I, 237-238; Winship, 399.

CHAPTER XXVIII

MANUSCRIPTS: A. G. I. Justicia, legajo 336, *Proceso de pleito . . . por parte de . . . Coronado:* Coronado's reply to Benavente's charges—Testimonies of Hernando del Valle, Juan Bermejo, Melchior Pérez, Pedro de Ledesma, Pedro de Castro, Juan Ruíz, Juan Galeas, Juan Pastor, Froilán Vermúdez. A. G. I. Justicia, legajo 1021, pieza 4, *Información contra . . . Coronado:* Testimonies of Francisca de Hozes, Alonso Sánchez.

PUBLISHED DOCUMENTS: Castañeda, in Winship, 458-460—English translation, Hammond and Rey, 264-268; Jaramillo, "Relación," in Pacheco y Cárdenas, XIV, 316—English translation, Hammond and Rey, 306—"Relación del suceso," in Pacheco y Cárdenas, XIV, 328—English translation, Hammond and Rey, 293.

OTHER REFERENCES: Bancroft, *Arizona and New Mexico,* 65-66; A. F. Bandelier, *The Gilded Man,* 239-243; Day, *Coronado's Quest,* 270-277—"Mota Padilla," 106-107; P. A. Jones, *Coronado and Quivira,* 127-129; Lowery, *Spanish Settlements,* 333-335; Mota Padilla, *Historia,* 166; Tello, *Libro segundo,* 439-441; Twitchell, *Leading Facts of New Mexican History,* I, 234-237; Winship, 400.

CHAPTER XXIX

MANUSCRIPTS: A. G. I. Justicia, legajo 1021, pieza 4. *Información contra . . . Coronado:* Testimonies of Francisca de Hozes, Alonso Sánchez.

PUBLISHED DOCUMENTS: Castañeda, in Winship, 461-466—English translation, Hammond and Rey, 270-271; Jaramillo, "Relación," in Pacheco y Cárdenas, XIV, 316-317—English translation, Hammond and Rey, 306-307; "Relación del suceso," Pacheco y Cárdenas, XIV, 329—English translation, Hammond and Rey, 294; Troyano, "Carta al rey," Paso y Troncoso, X, 277.

OTHER REFERENCES: Bancroft, *Arizona and New Mexico*, 66-67; A. F. Bandelier, *Documentary History, New Mexico Historical Review*, V, 174-185—see also, Bandelier and Hewett, *Indians of the Rio Grande Valley*, 193-200—"Fray Juan de Padilla"—*The Gilded Man*, 243-245; Day, *Coronado's Quest*, 278-283—"Gomara," 353—"Mota Padilla," 107-109; Foik, "Fray Juan Padilla; proto-martyr"; Gómara, *Historia general*, cap. CCXIIII; Herrera, *Historia general*, Dec. VI, libro IX, cap. XII; P. A. Jones, *Coronado and Quivira*, 141-146; Lowery, *Spanish Settlements*, 401-408; Lummis, *Spanish Pioneers* (ed. 1914), 118-123; Mendieta, *Historia eclesiástica*, 743-745; Mota Padilla, *Historia*, 167-168; Tello, *Libro segundo*, 484-492; Twitchell, *Leading Facts of New Mexican History*, I, 238-245; Vetancurt, *Teatro mexicano*, IV, 386-387; Winship, 400-401; Zarate Salmeron, "Relaciones," XI, 9.

CHAPTER XXX

MANUSCRIPTS: A. G. I. Justicia, legajo 339, pieza 1, *Residencia tomada á . . . Coronado:* Section 1, Tejada's *Interrogatorio*—Testimonies of Juan de Hojeda, Melchior Pérez, Hernando de Palencia, Cristóbal de Oñate, Pedro de Ledesma, Francisco Cornejo, Francisco de Godoy, Rodrigo Alvarez, Alvaro de Bracamonte, Pedro de Plasencia, Juan Hernández de Ijar, Diego Vázquez; Section 2, Coronado's petition, September 6, 1544—Coronado's testimony—*Interrogatorio* in the matter of Coronado's *descargos*—Testimonies of Hernando de Valle, Francisco Italiano, Juan Bermejo, Luís de Montesinos, Alonso de Palomeque, Toribio de Bolaños, Martín Paez, Hernando Martel, Rodrigo de Tamara, Salvado de Estrada, Cristóbal Pérez, Francisco Mejía, Alvaro de Bracamonte, Alonso de Toro, Juan de Cantoral, Bartolomé García, Antonio de Aguiar, Pedro de Ledesma, Juan de Alaejos, Cristóbal Romero, Francisco Cornejo, Alonso Lorenzo, Juan de Subía, Cristóbal de Valle, Alonso de Plasencia, Francisco Olivares, Diego Hurtado—Ruíz de Haro's *Interrogatorio*—Testimonies of Francisco de Godoy, Alonso de Torio, Pedro de Ledesma, Alvaro de Bracamonte. A. G. I. Justicia, legajo 1021, pieza 4, *Información contra . . . Coronado:* Testimonies of Juan de Paradinas, Juan de Contreras, Alonso Sánchez.

PUBLISHED DOCUMENTS: Aiton and Rey, "Coronado's testimony," 297-298, 316; Castañeda, in Winship, 462-464—English translation, Hammond and Rey, 271-276; Coronado, "Residencia," 369-372; "Relación del suceso," in Pacheco y Cárdenas, XIV, 328-329—English translation, Hammond and Rey, 293-294; Suárez de Peralta, *Tratado del descubrimiento de las Yndias*, 156.

OTHER REFERENCES: Bancroft, *Arizona and New Mexico*, 68; A. F.

Bandelier, *The Gilded Man,* 246-251; Day, *Coronado's Quest,* 285-287, 293-298—"Gómara," 353-354—"Mota Padilla," 110; Gómara, *Historia general, cap.* CCXIIII; Herrera, *Historia general,* Dec. VI, libro, IX, cap. XII; Hodge, in Winship, *Journey of Coronado,* 70, note 1; P. A. Jones, *Coronado and Quivira,* 130-135; Lowery, *Spanish Settlements,* 335-336; Mota Padilla, *Historia,* 169; Tello, *Libro segundo,* 484-499; Twitchell, *Leading Facts of New Mexican History,* I, 238-239; 245-247; Winship, 401-402, 409-412.

CHAPTER XXXI

PUBLISHED DOCUMENTS: P. Alvarado, "Asiento y capitulaciones"; Cabrillo, "Relación . . . de la navegación"; Castañeda, in Winship, 468— English translation, Hammond and Rey, 281; Gentleman of Elvas, in Smith, *Career of . . . de Soto* (Bourne ed.), 141-219, and Hodge and Lewis, *Spanish Explorers,* 221-270; Jaramillo, "Relación," in Pacheco y Cárdenas, XIV, 317—English translation, Hammond and Rey, 306-307; J. López, "Carta al rey [Mexico, March 1, 1547]," Paso y Troncoso, V, 11-12; Paez, "Relación . . . de la navegación que hizo . . . Cabrillo."

OTHER REFERENCES: Bancroft, *Mexico,* II, 494-502; A. F. Bandelier, *The Gilded Man,* 245-246; Bolton, *Spanish Borderlands,* 69-78; Day, *Coronado's Quest,* 283-284—"Gómara," 353—"Mota Padilla," 109; De Soto, *Final Report,* 258-280; Garcilaso de la Vega, *La Florida del Ynca,* libro IV, cap. XVI, libro VI, cap. XIX; Gómara, *Historia general,* cap. CCXIIII; Herrera, *Historia general,* Dec. VI, libro IX, cap. XII, Dec. VII, libro V, caps. III-IV, Lowery, *Spanish Settlements,* 409-410; Lummis, *Spanish Pioneers* (ed. 1914), 123-124; Maynard, *De Soto,* 251-278; Mendieta, *Historia eclesiástica,* 744-745; Mota Padilla, *Historia,* 168; Swanton, *Indians of the Southeastern United States,* 55-59; Tello, *Libro segundo,* 367-373, 490; Vetancurt, *Teatro mexicano,* IV, 387; Wagner, *Cartography of the Northwest Coast,* I, 41-42.

CHAPTER XXXII

MANUSCRIPTS: A. G. I. Justicia, legajo 336, *Proceso de pleito . . . por parte de . . . Coronado:* Benavente's charges—Coronado's reply and absolution. A. G. I. Justicia, legajo 339, pieza 1, *Residencia tomada á . . . Coronado.* A. G. I. Justicia, legajo 1021, pieza 1, *Acusación contra . . . Cárdenas:* Judgment freeing Coronado, A. G. I. Justicia, legajo 1021, pieza 2 (b), *Relación sacada de la probanza presentada por parte de . . . Coronado.* A. G. I. Justicia, legajo 1021, pieza 4, *Información contra . . . Coronado.*

PUBLISHED DOCUMENTS: Coronado, "Absolutory sentence"—"Charges . . . resulting from the investigation into the management of the expedition"—"Coronado's testimony concerning the expedition"—"Residencia . . . Charges brought against . . . Coronado"—"Sentence of . . . Coronado on residencia charges"; Tejada, "Appointment . . . as judge of residencia" —"Carta al principe [Mexico, August 31, 1545]"—"Carta al principe . . .

avisando haber recibido los despachos de la comisión [Mexico, May 24, 1544]"—"Carta al rey . . . haciendo relación de todo lo que había proveído en la visita hecha á la Nueva Galicia [Mexico, March 11, 1545]"—"Tejada's commission."

OTHER REFERENCES: Aiton, "The later career of Coronado," 299-302— "Report on the residencia of the Coronado government in New Galicia"; Day, *Coronado's Quest*, 303-307; Hammond and Rey, 28-30.

CHAPTER XXXIII

MANUSCRIPTS: A. G. I. Justicia, legajo 1021, pieza 1, *Acusación contra . . . Cárdenas*. A. G. I. Justicia, legajo 1021, pieza 2 (a), *Relación sacada de la probanza . . . que trata con . . . Cárdenas*. A. G. I. Justicia, legajo 1021, pieza 3, *Relación sacada de la probanza hecha por parte de . . . Cárdenas*. A. G. I. Justicia, legajo 1021, pieza 5, *Probanza hecha en Méjico a pedimento de . . . Cárdenas*. A. G. I. Justicia, legajo 1021, pieza 6, *Probanza del Fiscal contra . . . Cárdenas*.

PUBLISHED DOCUMENTS: Cárdenas, "Amended sentence"—"Sentence . . . in the lawsuit between Licentiate Villalobos . . . and . . . Cárdenas"— "Testimony . . . concerning charges brought against him." The transcript of these documents comprises several hundred pages.

CHAPTER XXXIV

MANUSCRIPTS: A. G. I. Justicia, legajo 336, *Proceso de pleito . . . por parte de . . . Coronado:* Testimonies of Hernando del Valle, Juan Bermejo, Melchior Pérez, Pedro de Ledesma, Pedro de Castro, Juan Ruíz, Juan Pastor, Froilán Vermúdez. A. G. I. Justicia, legajo 339, pieza 1, *Residencia tomada á . . . Coronado:* Section 2, *Interrogatorio* in the matter of *Coronado's descargos*—Testimonies of Pedro Cuadrado, Juan Bermejo, Rodrigo de Tamara.

PUBLISHED DOCUMENTS: *Actas de cabildo,* libro V, 71-313, Libro VI, 3-152; Castañeda, in Winship, 444-445, 457—English translation, Hammond and Rey, 243, 263; Coronado, "Carta . . . al emperador [October 20, 1541]," in Pacheco y Cárdenas, III, 368—English translation, Hammond and Rey, 190—"Relatione . . . quel che successe nel viaggio [August 3, 1540]," in Ramusio, III, 361—English translation, Hammond and Rey, 172; Garcia Icazbalceta, *Nueva colección*, II, 292-293; Jaramillo, "Relación," in Pacheco y Cárdenas, XIV, 308-310—English translation, Hammond and Rey, 299-300; J. López, "Carta al rey [March 1, 1547]," in Paso y Troncoso, V, 11-12 —"Carta al rey [November 15, 1547]," *Ibid.*, 45-46; Mendoza, "Instruccion (al Fray Marcos de Niza)," in Pacheco y Cárdenas, III, 326-327—English translation, Hammond and Rey, 60; Priestley, *The Luna Papers;* Ruíz, "Testimony," in Sauer, *Road to Cíbola*, 55.

OTHER REFERENCES: Aiton, *Antonio de Mendoza*, 188-192—"The later career of Coronado"; Bancroft, *Mexico*, II, 458-461, 476-479, 556; Barcia, *Ensayo cronologico*, Año M.D. XLIII; Bishop, *The Odyssey of Cabeza de Vaca*, 276-291; Bloom, "The Coronado-Bocanegra family alliance," 406-

408; Day, *Coronado's Quest,* 368-369, 382-383—"Gomara," 353; Gómara, *Historia general,* CCXIIII; P. A. Jones, *Coronado and Quivira,* 183-187, 201-207; Lowery, *Spanish Settlements,* 351-377; Mecham, *Francisco de Ibarra,* 47-48; Obregón, *Historia,* 93-95—English translation, Hammond and Rey, *Obregón's History,* 105-107; Priestley, *Tristan de Luna,* Ramusio, *Navigationi et viaggi,* I (ed. 1554), 414; Vetancurt, *Teatro mexicano,* IV, 119; Winship, 403—also, the following maps: Plate XLIII, between 160-161, Plate XLI, between 368-369, Plate XLV, between 372-373, Plate XLVI, between 376-377, Plate L, between 392-393.

CHAPTER XXXV

PUBLISHED DOCUMENTS: A. F. and F. Bandelier, *Historical Documents,* I, 193-483; Bolton, "Father Escobar's relation of the Oñate expedition"; Castaño de Sosa, "Memoria"; Espejo, "Relación del viage"; Mecham, "Supplementary documents"; Pérez de Luxán, *Expedition into New Mexico;* Sotelo de Betanzos, "Carta al rey [Mexico, June 5, 1566]"—"Carta al rey [Temazcaltepeque, December 9, 1567]"—"Relación [Temazcaltepeque, December 9, 1567]"; "Testimonio dado en Méjico sobre el descubrimiento de doscientas leguas adelante, de las minas de Santa Bárbola"; Villagrá, *Historia de la Nueva Mexico.*

OTHER REFERENCES: Bancroft, *Arizona and New Mexico,* 72-157—*North Mexican States,* I, 99-112; A. F. Bandelier, *Documentary History, New Mexico Historical Review,* V, 240-262, 333-385; see also, Bandelier and Hewett, *Indians of the Rio Grande Valley,* 200-241; Bartlett, "Notes upon the routes of Espejo and Farfán"—"Oñate's route across west central Arizona"; Bolton, *Spanish Borderlands,* 165-181—*Spanish Exploration,* 137-280; Hammond, *Don Juan de Oñate;* Hull, "Castano de Sosa's expedition"; Lummis, *Spanish Pioneers* (ed. 1914), 125-148; Mecham, "Antonio de Espejo"—*Francisco de Ibarra*—"The second Spanish expedition to New Mexico"; Mota Padilla, *Historia,* 193-210; Obregón, *Historia;* Sedgwick, *Acoma,* 62-87; Twitchell, *Leading Facts of New Mexican History,* I, 252-332; Zarate Salmeron, "Relaciones," 9-11, 21-38.

BIBLIOGRAPHY

MANUSCRIPT MATERIALS [1]

A. G. I. Justicia, legajo 336, *Proceso de pleito que se trató en la real audiencia del nuevo reino de Galicia por parte de Francisco Vázquez de Coronado, gobernador que fué de la dicha Nueva Galicia, contra el fiscal sobre los pueblos de Aguacatlán, Xala y Suchepil y los demas en su demanda contenidos; que va para ante su magestad, ó para ante los señores de su alto Consejo de Indias.*

———, legajo 339, pieza 1, *Residencia tomada á Francisco Vázquez de Coronado del tiempo que fue gobernador del Reyno de la Nueva Galicia.*

———, legajo 339, pieza 3, (a) *Una información sobre ciertos pueblos que pertenecieron á Cristóbal de Oñate.* (b) *Una información sobre ciertos pueblos que Francisco Vázquez de Coronado y Alvaro de Braçamonte tuvieron en compañia.*

———, legajo 339, pieza 4, *Nombramiento del licenciado Tejada como juéz de residencia de Nueva Galicia.*

———, legajo 1021, pieza 1, *Acusación contra don García López de Cárdenas por ciertas crueldades que cometió en la jornada de Cíbola.*

———, legajo 1021, pieza 2, (a) *Relación sacada de la probanza hecha por parte del Licenciado Villalobos, fiscal de su magestad en el real consejo de las Indias, en el pleito que trata con don García Ramírez de Cárdenas, maeso de campo, que fué en el descubrimiento de Cíbola.* (b) *Relación sacada de la probanza presentada por parte de Francisco Vázquez de Coronado, en la cual estan ratificados tres testigos de el fiscal, que son Gaspár de Saldaña, y García Rodríguez y don Rodrigo Maldonado.* [See, A. G. I. Justicia, legajo 1021, pieza 6.]

———, legajo 1021, pieza 3, *Relación sacada de la probanza hecha por parte de don García Ramírez de Cárdenas en el pleito que contra el trata el Licenciado Villalobos, fiscal de su magestad en el Consejo real de Indias, sobre las causas y razones en el proceso del dicho pleito contenidas.*

———, legajo 1021, pieza 4, *Información contra Francisco Vázquez de Coronado.*

———, legajo 1021, pieza 5, *Probanza hecha en Méjico a pedimento de*

[1] The abbreviation A. G. I. used in identifying the location of these source materials refers to the Archivo General de Indias, Seville, Spain. These manuscript documents when transcribed filled several hundred typed pages.

don García Ramírez (López) de Cárdenas para rebatir los cargos que le hizo el fiscal Villalobos.
[The *Interrogatorio* and testimony in this pieza are essentially the same as those in legajo 1021, pieza 3. However, because in copying more detail was given sometimes in one and sometimes in the other pieza, both are cited.]
——, legajo 1021, pieza 6, *Probanza del Fiscal contra don García Ramírez (López) de Cárdenas.*
[The *Interrogatorios* and testimony in this pieza are essentially the same as those in legajo 1021, pieza 2. However, because in copying more detail was given sometimes in one and sometimes in the other pieza, both are cited.]

PRINTED MATERIALS

Abert, James William, "Report of Lieut. J. W. Abert, of his examination of New Mexico in the years 1846–'47," Emory.

Actas de cabildo del ayuntamiento de México, 1538–1554. Mexico, 1884–1905.

Aguila, Vicente del, "Relación breve de la misión de Cinaloa, Archivo General de México, Historia vol. 308," Sauer, *Road to Cíbola.*

Aiton, Arthur S., *Antonio de Mendoza, First Viceroy of New Spain.* Durham, N. C., 1927.

—— "Coronado's commission as captain-general," *Hispanic American Historical Review,* vol. xx, February, 1940.

—— "Coronado's first report on the government of New Galicia," *ibid.,* vol. xix, August, 1939.

—— "Coronado's muster roll," *ibid.,* vol. xliv, April, 1939. *See also,* Juan de Cuebas.

—— "The later career of Coronado," *ibid.,* vol. xxx, January, 1925. Reprinted without notes under title "The last days of Coronado," in Paul A. Jones.

—— "Ordenanzas hechas por el Sr. Visorrey don Antonio de Mendoza sobre las minas de la Nueva España, 1540," *Revista de Historia de America,* no. 14, June, 1942.

—— "Report on the Residencia of the Coronado government in New Galicia," *Panhandle Plains Historical Review,* vol. XIII, 1940.

—— "The secret visita against Viceroy Mendoza," *New Spain and the Anglo-American West,* vol. I, Los Angeles, 1932.

—— and Agapito Rey, "Coronado's testimony in the Viceroy Mendoza residencia," *New Mexico Historical Review,* vol. XII, July, 1937.

Alarcón, Hernando, "De lo que hizo por la mar Hernando de Alarcón, que con dos nauios andaua por la costa por orden del visorrey don Antonio de Mendoça," Herrera, Dec. VI, lib. IX, cap. XIII.

—— Instrucción [May 31, 1541]." *See,* Mendoza.

—— "Relación del armada del Marqués del Valle, capitaneada de Francisco de Ulloa . . . y de la que el virey de Nueva España envió con un Alarcón," *Collección de España,* vol. IV.

——— "Relatione della navigatione & scoperta che fece il capitano Fernando Alarcone per ordine della illustrissimo signor Don Antonio di Mendozza vice re della Nuoua Spagna," Ramusio, III, (ed. 1556). French translation, Ternaux, IX. English translations, Hakluyt, III (ed. 1600); IX, (ed. 1914); Hammond and Rey. See also, Herrera, Dec. VI, lib. IX, caps. XIII-XV (ed. 1730).

Alegre, Francisco Javier. *Historia de la Compañía de Jesús en Nueva España,* 3 vols. Mexico, 1841.

——— *Memorias para la historia de la provincia que tuvo la Compañía de Jesús en Nueva España,* 2 vols. Mexico, 1940–41. Published for the first time from a manuscript in the library of Federico González Suárez.

Alvarado, Hernando de. "Relación de lo que Hernando de Alvarado y Fray Joan de Padilla descubrieron en demanda de la Mar del Sur, agosto de 1540," Pacheco y Cárdenas, vol. III; Smith, *Colección.* English translations, Hammond and Rey; Winship (reprinted in *Journey of Coronado* and *Journey of Francisco Vázquez de Coronado, 1540–1542*). Translation by Winship appears also in *Boston Transcript,* October 14, 1893.

Alvarado, Pedro de, "Asiento y capitualaciones, entre el virey de Nueva España, D. Antonio de Mendoza, y el adelantado, D. Pedro de Alvarado, para la prosecución del descubrimiento de tierra nueva, hecho por Fr. Marcos de Niza, Pueblo de Tiripitío de la Nueva España, 29 noviembre, 1540," pacheco y Cárdenas, vols. III, XVI.

Anghiera, Pietro Martire d', *De Orbe Novo, the Eight Decades of Peter Martyr d'Anghiera;* translated from the Latin with notes and introduction, by Francis Augustus MacNutt. New York and London, 1912.

Arciniegas, Germán, *The Knight of El Dorado: The Tale of Don Gonzalo Jiménez de Quesada;* translated by Mildred Adams. New York, 1942.

Ardoino, Antonio. *Examen apologético de la historica narración de los naufragios, peregrinaciones, i milagros de Alvar Nuñez Cabeza de Baca, en las tierras de la Florida, i del Nuevo México.* Madrid, 1736.

Arteaga y S., Armando, "Fray Marcos de Niza y el descubrimiento de Nuevo Mexico," *Hispanic American Historical Review,* vol. XII, November, 1932.

Audiencia de México, "Carta al rey, del presidente y oidores de la Audiencia de México, consultando ciertas dudas sobre el castigo de los indios, libertad de los esclavos, exención del pago de la sisa que pretendían algunos hijosdalgo y sucesión en las encomiendas: dan su parecer sobre los servicios de Francisco Vázquez de Coronado y Alonso del Castillo [Mexico, February 20, 1548]," Paso y Troncoso, vol. V.

"Autos del Marqués del Valle, Pánfilo de Narvaez . . . Año de 1526," Pacheco y Cárdenas, vol. XVI.

Avalos Guzmán, Gustavo, *Don Antonio de Mendoza . . . Primer Virrey de la Nueva España. Morelia,* Mexico, 1941.

Baker, Charles Laurence, *Geology and Underground Waters of the North ern Llano Estacado,* Bulletin of the University of Texas, No. 57 Austin, 1915.

Baldwin, Percy M., "Fray Marcos de Niza and his discovery of the seven cities of Cibola," *New Mexico Historical Review,* vol. I, April, 1926.

Bancroft, Hubert Howe, *Arizona and New Mexico, 1530–1888.* San Francisco, 1888.

—— *History of Central America,* 3 vols. San Francisco, 1882–87.

—— *History of Mexico,* 6 vols. San Francisco, 1883–87.

—— *History of the North Mexican States and Texas,* 2 vols. San Francisco, 1884–89.

Bandelier, Adolph F., "Alvar Nuñez Cabeza de Vaca, the first overland traveler of European descent, and his journey from Florida to the Pacific Coast, 1528–1536," *Magazine of Western History,* vol. IV, July, 1886.

—— *Contributions to the History of the Southwestern Portion of the United States,* Papers of the Archaeological Institute of America, American Series, vol. V. Cambridge, Mass., 1890.

—— "The discovery of New Mexico by Fray Marcos of Nizza," *Magazine of Western History,* vol. IV, September, 1886; reprinted in the *New Mexico Historical Review,* vol. IV, January, 1929.

—— *Documentary History of the Rio Grande Pueblos,* "Bibliographic Introduction" issued separately as No. 13 of the Papers of the School of American Archaeology, 1910; published without the "Bibliographic Introduction" in *New Mexico Historical Review,* vol. IV, October, 1929; vol. V, January, April, July, October; reprinted with "Introduction" and without author's footnotes, but annotated by L. B. Bloom, in Bandelier and Hewitt.

—— *Final Report of Investigations among the Indians of the Southwestern United States,* 2 vols, Papers of the Archaeological Institute of America, American Series, vols. III-IV. Cambridge, Mass., 1890–92.

Bandelier, Adolph F., "Fray Juan de Padilla, the first Catholic missionary and martyr in eastern Kansas," *American Catholic Quarterly Review,* vol. XV, July, 1890.

—— *The Gilded Man,* New York, 1893.

—— *Historical Introduction to Studies among the Sedentary Indians of New Mexico,* Papers of the Archaeological Institute of America, American Series, vol. I. Boston, 1881.

—— "An outline of the documentary history of the Zuñi tribe," in J. Walter Fewkes, *A Journal of American Ethnology and Archaeology,* vol. III. Boston and New York, 1892.

—— "Quivira," *Nation,* vol. XLIX, October 31 and November 7, 1889.

—— *Report on the Ruins of the Pueblo of Pecos,* Papers of the Archaeological Institute of America, American Series, vol. I. Boston, 1881.

Bandelier, Adolph F., and Fanny Bandelier. *Historical Documents Relating to New Mexico,* edited by Charles D. Hackett, I. Carnegie Institution, Publication No. 330. Washington, D. C., 1923.

Bandelier, Adolph F., and Edgar L. Hewett, *Indians of the Rio Grande Valley,* Handbook of Archaeological History, No. 3. Albuquerque, 1937.

Bandelier, Fanny (translator), *The Journey of Alvar Nuñez Cabeza de*

Vaca and His Companions from Florida to the Pacific, 1528–1536. New York, 1905. Translated from 1542 imprint.

Barcia, Andrés Gonzalez, *Ensayo cronologico para la historia general de la Florida.* Madrid, 1723.

Barra, Luís L. de la, "The Coronado genealogy," Paul A. Jones.

Bartlett, Katharine, "How Don Pedro de Tovar discovered the Hopi and Don García López de Cárdenas saw the Grand Canyon, with notes upon their probable route," *Plateau,* vol. XII, January, 1940.

—— "Notes upon the routes of Espejo and Farfán to the mines in the sixteenth century," *New Mexico Historical Review,* vol. XVII, January, 1942.

—— "Oñate's route across west central Arizona," *Plateau,* vol. XV, January, 1943.

—— and Harold S. Colton. "A note on the Marcos de Niza inscription near Phoenix, Arizona," *ibid.,* vol. XII, April, 1940.

Baskett, James Newton, "A study of the route of Cabeza de Vaca," *Texas Historical Association Quarterly,* vol. X, January, April, 1907.

—— "A study of the route of Coronado between the Rio Grande and Missouri Rivers," *Collections of the Kansas State Historical Society,* vol. XII, 1912.

Beaumont, Pablo de la Purísima Concepción, *Cronica de la provincia de los santos apostoles S. Pedro y S. Pablo de Michoacan,* 5 vols. Mexico, 1873–74.

Benitez, Jose R. "Conquistadores de Nueva Galicia y fundadores de Guadalajara," *Boletin de la Junta Auxiliar Jalisciense de la Sociedad Mexicana de Geografia y Estadistica,* vol. VII, 1941–1942.

Betanzos. *See,* Sotelo de Betanzos.

Biedma, Luys Hernando de, "Relación del suceso de la jornada que hizo Hernando de Soto, y de la calidad de la tierra por donde anduvo," Smith, *Colección.*

Bishop, Morris. *The Odyssey of Cabeza de Vaca.* New York, 1933.

Bloom, Lansing B., "Was Fray Marcos a liar?" *New Mexico Historical Review, vol.* XVI, April, 1941.

—— "The Coronado-Bocanegra family alliance," *ibid.,* vol. XVI, October, 1941.

—— "Who discovered New Mexico?" *ibid.,* vol. XV, April, 1940.

Bolton, Herbert E., "Father Escobar's relation of the Oñate expedition to California," *Catholic Historical Review,* vol. V, April, 1919.

—— *The Spanish Borderlands,* Chronicles of America, vol. XXIII. New Haven, Conn., 1921.

—— *Spanish Exploration in the Southwest 1542–1706,* Original Narratives of Early American History. New York, 1916.

Brackenridge, H. M., *Early Discoveries by Spaniards in New Mexico Containing an Account of the Castles of Cibola.* Pittsburgh, 1857.

Branch, E. Douglas, The Hunting of the Buffalo, New York, 1929.

Brower, J. V., *Harahey,* Memoirs of Explorations in the Basin of the Mississippi, vol. II. St. Paul, Minn., 1899.

—— Kansas. *Monumental Perpetuation of Its Earliest History, 1541–1896, ibid.,* vol. VII. St. Paul, Minn., 1903.

—— *Quivira, ibid.,* vol. St. Paul, Minn. 1898.

Bryan, Frank, "The Llano Estacado: The geographical background of the Coronado expedition," *Panhandle Plains Historical Review,* vol. XIII, 1940.

Cabeza de Vaca, Alvar Núñez, *La relación que dió Aluar Núñez Cabeça de Vaca de lo acaescido en las Indias en la armada donde yua por gouernador Pamphilo de Narvaez.* Zamora, 1542; reprinted Valladolid, 1555; various other editions. Italian translation, Ramusio, III. French translation, Ternaux, vol. VII. Paraphrased from Ramusio into English by Purchas, Part IV, Book VIII, chapter I; also paraphrased into English in Hallenbeck, *Álvar Núñez Cabeza de Vaca.* English translations, *see,* Smith, *Relation,* and F. Bandelier, *Journey.*

—— Alonzo del Castillo Maldonado, Andres Dorantes de Carrança. "Joint report," Oviedo y Valdés, III, lib. XXXV. A summary of a report now missing.

Cabrillo, Juan Rodríguez, "Relación ó diario, de la navegación que hizo Juan Rodríguez Cabrillo con dos navíos al descubrimiento del paso del Mar del Sur al norte . . . ," Smith, *Colección;* also Pacheco y Cárdenas, vol. XIV. English translations, Bolton, *Spanish Exploration; U. S. Geological Survey West of the One Hundredth Meridian* (translated by R. S. Evans and edited by H. W. Henshaw), VIII; Wagner, *Spanish Voyages. See also,* Herrera.

Cárdenas, López de, "Amended sentence of Cárdenas in the lawsuit between Doctor Berastegui, his majesty's fiscal, on the one side, and Don García Ramírez de Cárdenas, resident of Madrid, and Sebastián Rodríguez, his attorney, on the other," Hammond and Rey.

—— "Sentence of López de Cárdenas in the lawsuit between Licentiate Villalobos, his majesty's fiscal, on the one side, and Don García Ramírez de Cárdenas, resident of the city of Madrid, and Sebastián Rodríguez, his attorney, on the other," *ibid.*

—— "Testimony of López de Cárdenas . . . concerning charges brought against him for the excesses he committed while he was maestre de campo of the expedition to Cíbola . . . ," *ibid.*

Carranza, Pedro de, "Relación sobre la jornada que hizo Nuño de Guzmán, de la entrada y sucesos en la Nueva Galicia [1531]," Pacheco y Cárdenas, vol. XIV.

Carreño, Alberto Maria, *Don Fray Juan de Zumárraga primer obispo y arzobispo de Mexico.* Mexico, 1941.

—— "Nuevos documentos inéditos de don Fray Juan de Zumárraga y cédulas y cartas reales en relación con su gobierno," *Divulgacion Historica,* vol. III, December, 1941.

Castañeda, Pedro de, "Relación de la jornada de Cíbola conpuesta por Pedro de Castañeda de Naçera donde se trata de todos aquellos poblados y ritos y costumbres, la cual fue el año de 1540," Winship. French translation, Ternaux, vol. IX. English translations, Hammond and Rey; Winship (reprinted in *Journey of Coronado* and *Journey of*

Francisco Vázquez de Coronado, 1540–1542). See also, Hodge and Lewis. Cited as Castañeda.

Castaño de Sosa, Gaspár, "Memoria del descubrimiento que . . . hizo en el Nuevo México, siendo teniente del gobernador y capitan general del Nuevo-Reino de Leon," Pacheco y Cárdenas, vol. XV. *See also,* Hull.

Cervántes de Salazar, Francisco, *Crónica de la Nueva España.* Madrid, 1941.

Chávez Hayhoe, Arturo, "Guadalajara de 1542 a 1560," *Boletin de la Junta Auxiliar Jalisciense de la Sociedad Mexicana de Geografia y Estadistica,* vol. VII, 1941–1942.

Ciudad Rodrigo, Antonio de, "Certification of Fray Marcos's 'Relation,'" Pacheco y Cárdenas, vol. III. English translations, Baldwin; Hammond and Rey.

Colección de documentos inéditos para la historia de España (edited by Martín Fernández Navarrette *et al*), 113 vols. Madrid, 1842–1895. Cited as *Colección de España.*

Colección de documentos inéditos para la historia de Ibero-América, 2 vols. Madrid, 1927. Cited as *Colección Ibero-América.*

Colección de documentos inéditos para la historia de México. See, Garcia Icazbalceta.

Colección de documentos inéditos relativos al descubrimiento, conquista y organización de las antiguas posesiones españoles de América y Oceania. See, Pacheco y Cárdenas.

Conway, G. R. G., "A Scotsman in America in 1535," *Notes and Queries,* vol. CXLVIII.

Cornish, Beatrice Quijada, "The ancestry and family of Juan de Oñate," *The Pacific Ocean in History* (edited by H. M. Stephens and H. E. Bolton). New York, 1917.

Coronado, Francisco Vázquez de, "Absolutory sentence of Coronado," Hammond and Rey.

—————— "Appointment of Coronado as alderman of Mexico City [Toledo, March 29, 1539]." *See,* Bloom, "The Coronado-Bocanegra family alliance."

—————— "Appointment of Coronado as commander of the expedition to Cíbola, January 6, 1540," Hammond and Rey. For Spanish text, *see,* Aiton, "Coronado's commission."

—————— "Carta de Francisco Vázquez Coronado al emperador, dándole cuenta de la espedición á la provincia de Quivira, y de la inexactitud de lo referido á Fr. Marcos de Niza, acerca de aquel pais, desta provincia de Tiguex, 20 octubre, 1541," Pacheco y Cárdenas, vol. III, XIII. French translation, Ternaux, vol. IX. English translations, Hammond and Rey; Winship (reprinted in *Journey of Coronado, Journey of Francisco Vázquez de Coronado, 1540–1542,* and in *American History Leaflet,* no. 13).

—————— "Charges against Coronado resulting from the investigation into the management of the expedition, September 3, 1544," Hammond and Rey.

———— "Copia delle lettere di Francesco Vázquez di Coronado, gouernatore della Nuoua Galitia, al Signor Antonio de Mendozza, vicere della Nuoua Spagna, date in San Michiel di Culnacan, alli otto de marzo, 1539," Ramusio, III (ed. 1556). French translation, Ternaux, vol. IX. English translations, Hakluyt, III (ed. 1600); Hammond and Rey.

———— "Coronado's appointment as governor, April 18, 1539," Hammond and Rey.

———— "Coronado's testimony concerning the expedition," *ibid.*

———— "Coronado's testimony in the Viceroy Mendoza *residencia." See,* Aiton and Rey.

———— "Letter to the Emperor. From Compostela, December 15, 1538," Hammond and Rey. For Spanish text, *see,* Aiton, "Coronado's first report."

———— "Letter to the Emperor, July 15, 1539," Hammond and Rey. For extracts from this letter, *see,* Pérez Bustamante and Sauer, "Discovery of New Mexico reconsidered." *See also,* Wagner, "A 'Fray Marcos de Niza' note."

———— Relatione che mandò Francisco Vázquez di Coronado, capitano generale della gente che fu mandata in nome di Sua Maesta al paese nouamente scoperto, quel che successe nel viaggio dalli ventidua d'aprile di questo anno 1540, che parti da Culiacán per innanzi, & di quel che trouò nel paese doue andaua.—Dalla prouincia di Ceuloa & da questa città di Granata il terzo di agosto, 1540," Ramusio, III. English translations, Hakluyt, III (ed. 1600), (reprinted in *Old South Leaflet,* general series, no. 20); Hammond and Rey; Winship (reprinted in *Journey of Coronado* and *Journey of Francisco Vázquez de Coronado, 1540–1542).*

———— "Renunciation of grant of *regimiento* of City of Mexico in favor of Bernaldino de Bocanegra." *See,* Bloom, "The Coronado-Bocanegra family alliance."

———— "Residencia of Coronado—Charges brought against Francisco Vázquez de Coronado resulting from the investigation of his administration as governor of New Galicia conducted by Licentiate Lorenzo de Tejada, a member of the audiencia of New Spain, and visitador and juez de residencia in that province, together with Coronado's testimony refuting these charges. Guadalajara, September 1, 1544," Hammond and Rey (abridged).

———— "Sentence of Vázquez de Coronado on residencia charges," *ibid.*

Cortés, Hernando, *Cartas y relaciones de Hernán Cortés al emperador Carlos V,* edited by Don Pascual de Gayangos. Paris, 1866.

———— "Escritos sueltos de Hernan Cortes," *Biblioteca historica de la Iberia,* vol. XII. Mexico, 1871.

———— *The Letters of Cortés to Charles V,* translated and edited by F. A. MacNutt, 2 vols. New York and London, 1908.

Cuebas, Juan de, *The Muster Roll and Equipment of the Expedition of Francisco Vázquez de Coronado.* For Spanish text, *see,* Aiton, "Coronado's muster roll." Translated into English, with an introduction, by A. S. Aiton. Ann Arbor, 1939. English translation [with additions] from photostatic copy of original in Archivo General de Indias, Hammond and Rey.

Cuevas, Mariano, *Documentos inéditos del siglo XVI para la historia de Mexico.* Mexico, 1914.

────── *See,* Obregón.

Curtis, F. S., Jr., "Spanish arms and armor in the southwest," *New Mexico Historical Review,* vol. II, April, 1927.

Cushing, Frank Hamilton, "Outlines of Zuñi creation myths," *Thirteenth Annual Report, U. S. Bureau of American Ethnology, 1891–1892.* Washington, 1896.

────── *Zuñi Folk Tales.* New York, 1901. New edition, 1931.

Darton, Nelson H., "The Zuñi salt lake," *Journal of Geology,* vol. XIII, no. 3 (1905).

Davenport, Harbert, "The expedition of Panfilo de Narvaez by Gonzalo Fernandez Oviedo y Valdez," *Southwestern Historical Quarterly,* vol. XXVIII, October, 1924.

────── and Joseph K. Wells, "The first Europeans in Texas, 1528–1536," *ibid.,* vol. XXII, October, 1918, and January, 1919.

Day, A. Grove, *Coronado's Quest: The Discovery of the Southwestern States.* Berkeley and Los Angeles, 1940.

────── "Gómara on the Coronado expedition," *Southwestern Historical Quarterly,* vol. XLIII, January, 1940.

────── "Mota Padilla on the Coronado expedition," *Hispanic American Historical Review,* vol. XX, February, 1940.

Delanglez, Jean, "El Rio del Espiritu Santo," *Mid-America,* vol. XXV (n. s. vol. XIV), July, October, 1943; vol. XXVI (n. s. vol. XV), January, April, July, 1944. *See especially,* vol. XXVI.

Dellenbaugh, Frederick S., *The Romance of the Colorado River.* New York, 1902.

────── "The true route of Coronado's march," *Bulletin of the American Geographical Society,* vol. XXIX, December, 1897.

De Soto, Hernando, "Asiento y capitulación hechos por el capitán Hernando de Soto con el Emperador Carlos V para la conquista y población de la provincia de la Florida, y encomienda de la governación de la isla de Cuba, Valladolid, April 20, 1537," Pacheco y Cárdenas, vol. XV; also, Smith, *Colección.*

────── *Final Report of the United States De Soto Expedition Commission,* 76th Congress, 1st Session, House Doc. No. 71. Washington, 1939.

────── *Narrative of the Expedition of Hernando de Soto by the Gentleman of Elvas. See,* Smith, *Career of Hernando de Soto;* also, Robertson.

"Discurso y proposicion que se hace á Vuestra Magestad de lo tocante á los descubrimientos del Nuevo México por sus capítulos de puntos diferentes," Pacheco y Cárdenas, vol. XVII.

Documentos inéditos del siglo XVI para la historia de Mexico. See, Cuevas.

Documentos para la historia de Mexico, 20 vols. in 4 series. Mexico, 1853–1857.

Donoghue, David, "Coronado, Oñate, and Quivira," *Mid-America,* vol.

XVIII (n. s., vol. VII), April, 1936. Reprinted in *Preliminary Studies of the Texas Catholic Historical Society*, vol. III, April, 1936.

——— "The location of Quivira," *Panhandle Plains Historical Review*, vol. XIII, 1940.

——— "The route of the Coronado expedition in Texas," *Southwestern Historical Quarterly*, vol. XXXII, January, 1929. Reprinted in *New Mexico Historical Review*, vol. IV, January, 1929.

Dorantes de Carranza, Baltasar, *Sumario relación de las cosas de la Nueva España*. Mexico, 1902.

Emory, William H., *Notes of a Military Reconnoissance, from Fort Leavenworth, in Missouri, to San Diego, in California*, 30th Congress, 1st Session, House Ex. Doc. No. 41. Washington, 1848.

Espejo, Antonio, "Relación del viage, que yo Antonio Espejo, cuidadano de la ciudad de México, natural de Cordoba, hize con catorce soldados y un relijioso de la orden de San Francisco, á las provincias y poblaciones de la Nueva México, a quien puse por nombre, la Nueva Andalucia, á contemplacion de mi patria, en fin del año de mill e quinientos e ochenta e dos," Pacheco y Cárdenas, vol. XV. English translation, Bolton, *Spanish Exploration*.

Farnum, Mabel, *The Seven Golden Cities*. Milwaukee, 1943.

Fernández de Béthencourt, Francisco, *Historia genealógica y heráldica de la monarquía española*, 10 vols. Madrid, 1897–1920. For Coronado, see, vol. IX.

Fewkes, J. Walter, "A-wá-to-bi: An archaeological verification of a Tusayan legend," *American Anthropologist*, vol. XI, October, 1893.

——— "Pacific coast shells from prehistoric Tusayan pueblos," *ibid.*, vol. IX, November, 1896.

[Flores, Cristóbal], "Cuarta relación anónima de la jornada que hizo Nuño de Guzmán á la Nueva Galicia," Garcia Icazbalceta, *Colección*, vol. II.

Foik, Paul J., "Fray Juan Padilla; proto-martyr of the United States and Texas," *Mid-America*, vol. XIII (n. s. vol. II), October, 1930.

Freeman, Lewis R., "The conquistadores," *The Colorado River*. New York, 1923.

García, Genaro, and Carlos Pereyra. *Documentos inéditos ó muy raros para la historia de México*, 36 vols. Mexico, 1905–11.

García Icazbalceta, Joaquín, ed., *Colección de documentos inéditos para la historia de México*, 2 vols. Mexico, 1858, 1866.

——— *Don Fray Juan de Zumárraga primer obispo y arzobispo de México. Estudio biográfico y bibliográfico*. Mexico, 1881.

——— ed., *Nueva colección de documentos para la historia de México*, 5 vols. Mexico, 1886–92.

Garcilaso de la Vega, el Ynca, *La Florida del Ynca. Historia del Adelantado de Soto*. Lisbon, 1605. Various later editions.

Gayangos, Don Pascual de. *See*, Cortés.

Gentleman of Elvas. *See*, Smith, *Career of Hernando de Soto; also*, Robertson.

Gómara, Francisco López de, *Primera y segunda parte de la historia general de las Indias cõ todo el descubrimiento, y cosas notables que han *acaescido dende que se ganaron hasta el año de 1551. Con la conquista de Mexico, y dela Nueua España* (Medina del Campo, 1553 [1552]. Many editions, including Vedia, XXII). For Coronado, *see*, cap. 212-215. For English translation of this section, *see*, Hakluyt, III (ed. 1600). *See also*, Day, "Gómara."

Gould, Charles N., *The Geology and Water Resources of the Eastern Portion of the Panhandle of Texas*, U. S. Geological Survey Water Supply and Irrigation Paper No. 154. Washington, D. C., 1906.

―――― *The Geology and Water Resources of the Western Portion of the Panhandle of Texas*, U. S. Geological Survey Water Supply and Irrigation Paper No. 191. Washington, D. C., 1907.

Guzmán, Diego de, "Relación de lo que yo Diego de Guzmán he descobierto en la costa de la mar del Sur, por Su Magestad y por el ilustre señor Nuño de Guzmán, governador de la Nueva Galicia. Presentó en el Consejo de Indias, 16 marzo 1540," Pacheco y Cárdenas, vol. XV.

Guzmán, Nuño Beltran de, "Carta al emperador [Chiametla, January 16, 1531]," *ibid.*, vol. XIII.

―――― "Provanza ad perpetuan, sobre lo de la villa de la Purificación, de la gente que alli vino con mano armada.—En Madrid á 16 de marzo de 1540 la presentó en el Consejo de las Indias de Su Magestad, Nuño de Guzmán," *ibid.*, vol. XVI.

Hackett, Charles W., "The delimitation of political jurisdictions in Spanish North America to 1535," *Hispanic American Historical Review*, vol. I, February, 1918.

―――― ed., *Historical Documents Relating to New Mexico. See*, Adolph F. and Fanny Bandelier.

Hakluyt, Richard, *The Principal Navigations, Voiages, Traffiques and Discoueries of the English Nation*. London, 1598–1600. Many editions.

Hallenbeck, Cleve, *Álvar Núñez Cabeza de Vaca: The Journey and Route of the First European to Cross the Continent of North America, 1534–1536*. Glendale, Calif., 1939.

Hallenbeck, Cleve, and Juanita H. Williams. "La jornada del muerte," *Legends of the Spanish Southwest*. Glendale, Calif., 1938.

Hammond, George P., *Coronado's Seven Cities*. Albuquerque, 1940.

―――― *Don Juan de Oñate and the Founding of New Mexico*. Santa Fe, 1927.

―――― and Edgar F. Goad. *The Adventure of Don Francisco Vásquez de Coronado*. Albuquerque, 1938.

―――― and Agapito Rey. *Narratives of the Coronado Expedition 1540–1542*, Coronado Cuarto Centennial Publications, 1540–1940, vol. II. Albuquerque, 1940.

―――― and Agapito Rey, eds. *See*, Obregón.

Hanke, Lewis, *The Development of Regulations for Conquistadores*. Buenos Aires, 1941.

Hargrave, Lyndon L., "The Jeddito valley and the first pueblo towns in Arizona to be visited by Europeans," *Museum Notes* [Museum of Northern Arizona], vol. VIII, October, 1935.

Hazard, Daniel L., *Magnetic Declination in the United States in 1925*.

U. S. Coast and Geodetic Survey, Special Publication No. 126. Washington, 1926.

Herrera, Antonio de, *Historia general de los hechos de los castellanos en las islas y tierra firme del mar oceano.* Madrid, 1601–1615; reprinted [Barcia], 1730. French translation of three decades printed between 1659 and 1671; English translation of the same three decades, by Captain John Stevens, issued in London, 1725–26, and reissued, with arrangement altered, in 1740. For Coronado, *see*, Dec. VI, lib. V, cap. IX; lib. VII, caps. VII-VIII; lib. IX, caps. XI-XV.

Hewett, Edgar Lee, *Ancient Life in the American Southwest.* Indianapolis, 1930.

—— *See also*, A. F. Bandelier, and Hewett.

—— and Wayne L. Mauzy, *Landmarks of New Mexico*, Publication of the University of New Mexico and the School of American Research. Albuquerque, 1940.

Heylyn, Peter, *Cosmography in Four Books Containing the Geography and History of the Whole World.* Various editions.

Hodge, Frederick W., "Coronado's march to Quivira," Brower, *Harahey.*

—— "The first discovered city of Cíbola," *American Anthropologist*, vol. VIII, April, 1895.

—— *Handbook of American Indians North of Mexico*, 2 vols., Bureau of American Ethnology, Bulletin No. 30. Washington, 1907–10.

—— *History of Háwikuh, New Mexico, One of the So-called Cities of Cíbola.* Los Angeles, 1937.

—— "The six cities of Cíbola—1581–1680," *New Mexico Historical Review*, vol. I, October, 1926.

—— *See also*, Winship, *The Journey of Francisco Vázquez de Coronado.*

—— and Theodore H. Lewis, eds., *Spanish Explorers in the Southern United States, 1528–1543*, Original Narratives of Early American History, New York, 1907. Smith's translations of Cabeza de Vaca and the Gentleman of Elvas, and Winship's translation of Castañeda, with notes.

Hooton, Earnest Albert, *The Indians of Pecos Pueblo.* New Haven, 1930.

Hull, Dorothy, "Castaño de Sosa's expedition to New Mexico in 1590," *Old Santa Fe*, vol. III, October, 1916.

Icaza, Francisco A. de, *Diccionario autobiográfico de conquistadores y pobladores de Nueva España*, 2 vols. Madrid, 1923.

Icazbalceta. *See*, García Icazbalceta.

"Información de los méritos y servicios de los capitanes Andrés Dorantes y Don Sancho Dorantes de Carranza [Mexico, July 8, 1613]," Dorantes de Carranza.

"Información del virrey de Nueva España, D. Antonio de Mendoza, de la gente que va á poblar la Nueva Galicia con Francisco Vásquez Coronado, gobernador de ella [Compostela, February 21-26, 1540]," Pacheco y Cárdenas, vol. XIV. English translations, Hammond and Rey; Winship (abridged).

Ives, Joseph C., *Report upon the Colorado River of the West*, 36th Congress, 1st Session, Senate Ex. Doc. no. 90. Washington, 1861.

Ives, Ronald L., "Melchior Díaz—the forgotten explorer," *Hispanic American Historical Review*, vol. XVI, February, 1936. *See also,* Sauer, "Communication."

Jaramillo, Juan, "Relación hecha por el capitan Juan Jaramillo, de la jornada que había hecho a la tierra nueva en Nueva España y al descubrimiento de Cíbola, yendo por general Francisco Vázquez Coronado," Pacheco y Cárdenas, vol. XIV; Smith, *Colección*. French translation, Ternaux, vol. IX. English translations, Hammond and Rey; Winship (reprinted in *Journey of Coronado* and *Journey of Francisco Vázquez de Coronado, 1540–1542*).

Johnson, Willard D., "The high plains and their utilization," *Twenty-first Annual Report of the U. S. Geological Survey, 1899–1900*, Part IV.

Jones, Horace, "Quivira—Rice County, Kansas," *Collections of the Kansas State Historical Society, 1926–1928*, vol. XVII.

Jones, Paul A., *Coronado and Quivira*. Lyons, Kansas, 1937. An earlier publication entitled *Quivira* (Lyons, 1929) is reprinted here with an additional section.

Kelly, John Eoghan, *Pedro de Alvarado, Conquistador*. Princeton, 1932.

Keyes, Charles, "Quest of the Gran Quivira," *Arizona Historical Review*, vol. VI, July, 1935.

———— "Precursor of the Santa Fe trail," *El Palacio*, vol. V, July, 1918.

Kidder, Alfred V., *The Artifacts of Pecos*. New Haven, 1932.

———— *An Introduction to the Study of Southwestern Archaeology with a Preliminary Account of the Excavations at Pecos*. New Haven, 1924.

Kroeber, Alfred L., *Native Culture of the Southwest*. Berkeley, 1928.

Las Casas, Bartolomé de, *Breve relación de la destruccion de las Indias Occidentales*. Philadelphia, 1821.

———— *Historia de las Indias. Madrid*, 1875–76.

Leigh, Randolph, *Forgotten Waters: Adventure in the Gulf of California*. Philadelphia, 1941.

Leonard, Irving A. *Books of the Brave* (Being an account of books and of men in the Spanish conquest and settlement of the sixteenth century New World). Cambridge, Massachusetts, 1949.

López, Gonzalo, "Relación del descubrimiento y conquista que se hizo por . . . Nuño de Guzmán y su ejercito en las provincias de la Nueva Galicia," Pacheco y Cárdenas, vol. XIV.

López, Jerónimo, "Carta al rey dando algunos informes de la visita del licenciado Tello de Sandoval, de los sucesos del Perú y de otros particulares concernientes al buen gobierno de Nueva España [Mexico, March 1, 1547]," Paso y Troncoso, vol. V.

———— "Carta al rey dando noticia de haberse suspendido el envío de la armada al Perú y pidiendo se le cumplan las mercedes que le estaban hechas [Mexico, November 15, 1547]," Paso y Troncoso, vol. V.

López-Portillo y Weber, José, *La conquista de la Nueva Galicia*. Mexico, 1935.

Lowery, Woodbury, *The Spanish Settlements within the Present Limits of the United States, 1513–1561*. New York, 1901.

Lummis, Charles F., *The Spanish Pioneers*. Chicago, 1893. Several later editions.

Luxán, Diego Pérez de. *See*, Pérez de Luxán.

MacNutt, Francis A. *See*, Anghiera; *see also*, Cortés.

Mallery, Garrick, "Sign language among North American Indians compared with that among other peoples and deaf mutes," *First Annual Report, U. S. Bureau of American Ethnology, 1879–80*. Washington, 1881.

Marcos de Niza, Fray, "Relación del descubrimiento de las siete ciudades," Pacheco y Cárdenas, vol. III. Italian translation, Ramusio, III. French translation, Ternaux, vol. IX. English translations, Hakluyt, III (ed. 1600); Baldwin, *New Mexico Historical Review*, vol. I; F. Bandelier; Hammond and Rey.

——— *See also*, Zumárraga.

Martyr, Peter, *See*, Pietro Martire d' Anghiera.

Maynard, Theodore, *De Soto and the Conquistadores*. New York, 1930.

Mecham, J. Lloyd, "Antonio de Espejo and his journey to New Mexico," *Southwestern Historical Quarterly*, vol. XXX, October, 1926.

——— *Francisco de Ibarra and Nueva Vizcaya*. Durham, N. C., 1927.

——— "The northern expansion of New Spain, 1522–1822: A selected descriptive bibliographical list," *Hispanic American Historical Review*, vol. VII, May, 1927.

——— "The second Spanish expedition to New Mexico," *New Mexico Historical Review*, vol. I, July, 1926.

——— "Supplementary documents relating to the Chamuscado-Rodríguez expedition," *Southwestern Historical Quarterly*, vol. XXIX, January, 1926.

Mendieta, Gerónimo de, *Historia eclesiástica indiana, obra escrita á fines del siglo XVI . . . la pública por primera vez Joaquín García Icazbalceta*, 2 vols. Mexico, 1870.

Mendoza, Antonio de, "Asiento y capitulaciones, etc." *See*, Pedro de Alvarado.

——— "Carta á la emperatriz, participando que vienen a España Cabeza de Vaca y Francisco Dorantes, que se escaparon de la armada de Pánfilo de Narvaez, á hacer relación de lo que en ella sucedió [Mexico, February 11, 1537]," Pacheco y Cárdenas, vol. XIV.

——— "Carta al emperador [Jacona, April 17, 1540]," Pacheco y Cárdenas, vol. II. French translation, Ternaux, vol. IX. English translations, Hammond and Rey; Winship (reprinted in *Journey of Coronado* and *Journey of Francisco Vázquez de Coronado*).

——— "Carta al emperador, dándole cuenta de varios asuntos de su gobierno [Mexico, December 10, 1537]," Pacheco y Cárdenas, vol. II; Smith, *Colección*.

——— "Carta al muy noble señor Gonçalo Hernández de Oviedo, October 6, 1541," Oviedo, vol. III.

——— "Fragmento de la visita hecha a Don Antonio de Mendoza," Garcia Icazbalceta, *Colección de documentos*, vol. II. For replies to this *interrogatorio, see*, Aiton and Rey.

———— "Instruccion de don Antonio de Mendoza, visorey de Nueva España (al Fray Marcos de Niza)," Pacheco y Cárdenas, vol. III. French translation, Ternaux, vol. IX. English translations, Baldwin, *New Mexico Historical Review*, vol. I; Bandelier, *Contributions;* Hammond and Rey.

———— "Instruccion que debia observar el capitan Hernando de Alarcon en la expedicion á la California que iba á emprender de órden del virrey D. Antonio de Mendoza," Smith, *Colección*. English translation, Hammond and Rey.

———— "Lettere scritte dal illvstrissimo signor don Antonio di Mendozza, vice re della Nuoua Spagna, alla maesta dell' Imperadore. Delli cauallieri quali con lor gran danno si sono affaticati per scoprire il capo della terra ferma della Nuoua Spagna verso tramontana, il gionger del Vazquez con fra Marco à San Michiel di Culnacan con comissione à quelli regenti di assicurare & non far piu schiaui gli Indiani [1539]," Ramusio, III. French translation, Ternaux, vol. IX. English translations, Hakluyt (ed. 1600); F. Bandelier; Hammond and Rey.

———— *Residencia*. For questions [in Spanish], *see*, García Icazbalceta, *Colección de documentos*, vol. II; for Coronado's answers [in English], *see*, Aiton and Rey.

———— and Pedro de Alvarado. "Instructions to López de Zuñiga," Wagner, *Spanish Voyages to the Northwest Coast.*

Mindeleff, Victor, "A study of pueblo architecture: Tusayán and Cíbola," *Eighth Annual Report, U. S. Bureau of American Ethnology, 1886–87.* Washington, 1891.

Mooney, James, "Quivira and the Wichitas," *Harper's Monthly Magazine*, vol. XCIX, June, 1899.

Morales, Francisco, "Carta al Rey Don Felipe II, defendiéndose de ciertos cargos y dando curiosísimas noticias de Mejico," *Colección de documentos de Ibero-América*, vol. I. English translation [excerpt], Bloom, "Coronado-Bocanegra family alliance."

Morgan, Lewis Henry, "The seven cities of Cíbola," *North American Review*, vol. CVIII, April, 1869.

Mota Padilla, Matías Angel de la, *Historia de la conquista de la provincia de la Nueva Galicia, escrita en 1742*, Boletín de la Sociedad Mexicana de Geografía y Estadística. Mexico, 1870. Issued with "Noticias biográficas" by Joaquin García Icazbalceta (Mexico, 1872). *See also*, Day, "Mota Padilla on the Coronado expedition."

Moya de Contreras, Pedro, "Carta del arzobispo de México al presidente del Consejo de Indias . . . recomendando a Pedro de Ledesma [Mexico, October 30, 1580]," Paso y Troncoso, vol. XII.

Navarette, Martín Fernández de, *Colección de los viages y descubrimientos que hicieron por mar los Epañoles desde fines del siglo XV*, 5 vols. Madrid, 1825–37.

———— *See, Colección de documentos inéditos para la historia de España.*

Obregón, Baltazar de, *Historia de los descubrimientos antiguos y modernos de la Nueva España* [written in 1584. Edited by Mariano Cuevas]. Mexico, 1924. English translation by G. P. Hammond and A. Rey, under title *Obregón's History of Sixteenth Century Exploration in Western America*. Los Angeles, 1928.

—— "Carta al Consejo de Indias, en la que suplica se vea la obra que tiene escrita sobre descubrimientos en el Nuevo-México . . . [Mexico, April 17, 1584]," Paso y Troncoso, vol. XII.

—— "Carta al rey . . . en la que éste encarece sus servicios; suplica que se vea la crónica que ha escrito de los descubrimientos antiguos y modernos de la mayor parte de las Indias, y que se le hazan mercedes [New Spain, April 26, 1584]," Paso y Troncoso, vol. XII.

Oviedo y Valdés, Gonzalo Fernández de, *La historia general de las Indias*. Seville, 1535; reprinted, Salamanca, 1547; Madrid, 1851–55. The Madrid edition is in four volumes, the fourth volume not having been printed hitherto.

—— *See*, Davenport.

Pacheco, Joaquín F., Francisco de Cárdenas, Luís Torres de Mendoza, eds. *Colección de documentos inéditos relativos al descubrimiento, conquista y organización de las antiguas posesiones españoles de América y Oceania*, 42 vols. Madrid, 1864–84. *See*, vol. XXXIII for Index to vols. I-XXXII. Cited as Pacheco y Cárdenas.

Pacheco de Córdova y Bocanegra, Francisco, "Brief of petition to His Majesty [1605]." *See*, Bloom, "The Coronado-Bocanegra family alliance."

Paso y Tronsoco, Francisco del, compiler, *Epistolario de Nueva España, 1505–1818*, 16 vols. Mexico, 1939–42.

Peralta, Juan Suarez, *Noticias históricas*. Madrid, 1878.

Peramíldez, "Carta al secretario Juan de Sámano, dando aviso del alzamiento de la Nueva Galicia y de la muerte de don Pedro de Alvarado; que algunos solicitaban la governación de Guatemala y que el virrey había recibido noticias de la tierra en que estaba Francisco Vázquez Coronado y no había querido divulgarlas [Mexico, July 28, 1541]," Paso y Troncoso, vol. IV.

Perca, Pedro de, "Una relación pienso," from no. 3 of "Punctos sacados," Archivo General de Mexico, Misiones, vol. XXV; Sauer, *Road to Cíbola*.

Pérez Bustamante, C., Carlos Pereyra, and Luís Blanco Rivero. *Don Antonio de Mendoza, primer virrey de la Nueva España (1535–1550)*, Annales de la Universidad de Santiago, vol. III. Santiago de Galicia, 1928.

Pérez de Bocanegra, Hernán, "Probanza started before Audiencia of Mexico on November 9, 1554." *See*, Bloom, "The Coronado-Bocanegra family alliance."

Pérez de Luxán, Diego, *Expedition into New Mexico Made by Antonio de Espejo, 1582–1583*, translated, with introduction and notes, by G. P. Hammond and A. Rey, Quivira Society Publications, vol. I. Los Angeles, 1929.

Pilar, García del, "Relacion de la entrada de Nuño de Guzmán," Garcia Icazbalceta, *Colección*, vol. II.

Ponton, Brownie, and Bates H. M'Farland, "Alvar Nuñez Cabeza de Vaca:

A preliminary report on his wanderings in Texas," *Texas Historical Association Quarterly*, vol. I, January, 1898.

Preciado, Francisco, "Relatione dello scoprimento che nel nome di Dio va à far l'armata dell' illustrissimo Fernando Cortese, Marchese di Valle con tre naui, chiamata l'una Santa Agata, di grandezza di dugento quaranta botte, l'altra, la Trinita, di grandezza di settanta, & la terza san Tomaso, di quaráta, dellaquale armata fu capitano il molto magnifico caualiero Francesco di Vlloa habitator della città di Merida," Ramusio, III (ed. 1556). English translation, Hakluyt, III (ed. 1600.)

Prescott, William Hickling, *History of the Conquest of Mexico, with a Preliminary View of the Ancient Mexican Civilization, and the Life of the Conqueror, Hernando Cortés*. New York, 1843; many editions.

―――― *History of the Conquest of Peru, with a Preliminary View of the Civilization of the Incas*. New York, 1847; many editions.

Priestley, Herbert Ingram, editor and translator, *The Luna Papers: Documents relating to the Expedition of Don Tristán de Luna y Arellano for the Conquest of La Florida in 1559–1561*, 2 vols. De Land, Florida, 1928.

―――― *Tristan de Luna, Conquistador of the Old South*. Glendale, California, 1936.

"Proceso del Marqués del Valle y Nuño de Guzmán y los adelantados Soto y Alvarado, sobre el descubrimiento de la tierra nueva, en Madrid, 3 marzo, 1540; 10 junio, 1541," Pacheco y Cárdenas, vol. XV.

Ptolemy, C., *La geografia di Clavdio Ptolemeo, con alcuni comenti & aggiunti fatteui da Sebastiano munstero, con le tauole non solamente antiche & moderne solite di stāparsi, ma altre nuoue*. Venice, 1548. "The maps in this edition of Ptolemy's *Geography* for the first time present the results of Coronado's explorations"—Winship.

Purchas, Samuel, *Purchas, His Pilgrimage. Or, Relations of the World and the Religions Observed in All Ages and Places Discovered . . .*, several editions. For Coronado, *see* Part 2, Book 8, chapter 3.

Ramusio, Giovanni Battista, *Terzo volvme delle navigationi et viaggi*. Venice, 1556. Various later editions.

Reed, Erik K., "Southwestern Indians in Coronado's time," *National Park Service, Region III Quarterly*, vol. II, July, 1940.

"Relación del suceso de la jornada que Francisco Vázquez hizo en el descubrimiento de Cíbola, año de 1531 [1541]," Pacheco y Cárdenas, vol. XIV; Smith, *Colección*. English translations, Hammond and Rey; Winship (reprinted in *Journey of Coronado* and *Journey of Francisco Vázquez de Coronado, 1540–1542*. *See also*, "Coronado's journey to New Mexico").

"Relación postrera de Sivola," Winship. English translations, Hammond and Rey; Winship (reprinted in *Journey of Coronado* and *Journey of Francisco Vázquez de Coronado, 1540–1542*).

Robertson, James A., *True Relation of the Hardships Suffered by Governor Fernando de Soto and Certain Portuguese Gentlemen . . . by a Gentleman of Elvas*, Publication of the Florida State Historical Society No. 11, 2 vols. De Land, Florida, 1932–33.

Robinson, Duncan, "Coronado and his army," *Panhandle Plains Historical Review*, vol. XIII, 1940.

Ross, Edith Connelly, "The Quivira village," *Collections of the Kansas State Historical Society, 1926–1928*, vol. XVII.

"Royal cédula—Barcelona, April 17, 1535," Hammond and Rey, n. 1. This document limited Cortés's claim to exclusive rights of exploration in the north.

Rudo ensayo. See, Smith.

Ruiz, Antonio, "Testimony from Historia, Archivo General de México, vol. 316," Sauer, *Road to Cíbola*.

Samaniego, Lope de, "Carta á Carlos V sobre la conveniencia de mudar de sitio la fortaleza de Méjico, 1537," *Colección Ibero-América*, vol. I.

Sauer, Carl O., *Aboriginal Population of Northwestern Mexico, Ibero-Americana*, no. 10. Berkeley, 1935.

——— "Communication," *Hispanic American Historical Review*, vol. XVII, February, 1937.

——— "The credibility of the Fray Marcos account," *New Mexico Historical Review*, vol. XVI, April, 1941.

——— "The discovery of New Mexico reconsidered," *ibid.*, vol. XII, July, 1937.

——— *The Road to Cíbola*, Ibero-Americana no. 3. Berkeley, 1932.

——— and Donald Brand, *Pueblo Sites in Southeastern Arizona*, University of California Publications in Geology, vol. III, No. 7. Berkeley, 1930.

Saunders, Lyle, *A Guide to Materials Bearing on Cultural Relations in New Mexico*, Albuquerque, 1944.

Scholes, France V., "Some aspects of the Jumano problem," *Carnegie Institution Publication 523*. Washington, 1940.

Schott, Charles A., "Letter on magnetic declination," Brower, *Quivira*.

Scisco, L. S., "Coronado's march across the high plains," *Americana*, vol. VI, March, 1911.

Simpson, James Hervey, "Coronado's march in search of the 'Seven Cities of Cíbola,' and discussion of their probable location," *Report of the Smithsonian Institution for 1869. Washington*, 1871.

Smith, T. Buckingham, *The Career of Hernando de Soto in the Conquest of Florida*. New York, 1866. This is a translation into English of "The Narrative of the Gentleman of Elvas." Edited and reprinted by Edward G. Bourne, *Narratives of the Career of Hernando de Soto*, vol. I. New York, 1904. *See also*, Hodge and Lewis.

Smith, T. Buckingham, *Colección de varios documentos para la historia de la Florida y tierras adyacentes*, vol. I [1516–1794]. London, Madrid, 1857). Only one volume published.

——— *Relation of Alvar Núñez Cabeça de Vaca* [translated from the Valladolid edition of 1555]. Washington, 1851. Revised and published in New York, 1871. This edition edited and reprinted in Hodge and Lewis. Also reprinted in a limited edition, without notes, San Francisco, 1929.

——— *Rudo ensayo, tentative de una prevencional descripcion geographica de la provincia de Sonora . . . compilada así de noticias adquiridas por el colector en sus viajes por casi toda ella, como subministradas por los padres missioneros y practicos de la tierra.* St. Augustine, Florida, 1863. English translation, by Eusebio Guitéras, *Records of the American Catholic Historical Society,* Philadelphia, 1894.

Sotelo de Betanzos, Antonio, "Carta al rey, de Antonio Sotelo de Betanzos, maestre de campo del gobernador Francisco de Ibarra, dando algunos informes sobre la jornada que hizo el gobernador hasta Copala [Mexico, June 5, 1566]," Paso y Troncoso, vol. X.

———— "Carta al rey, hablando de las riquezas de las minas de Indehe y de otras que se habían descubierto, y de la rebelión de México [Temazcaltepeque, December 9, 1567]," *ibid.,* vol. X.

Sotelo de Betanzos, Antonio, "Relación informando al rey sobre las riquezas de la tierra descubierta en la jornada del gobernador Francisco de Ibarra, expresando su deseo de hacer nuevos servicios y suplicando que se le concedan algunas mercedes [Temazcaltepeque, December 9, 1567]," Paso y Troncoso, vol. X.

Spell, Lota, "The first philanthropic organization in America," *American Historical Review,* vol. XXXII, April, 1927.

Stevens, Captain John, translator. *See,* Herrera.

Stevenson, Matilda Coxe, "The Zuñi Indians: Their mythology, esoteric fraternities, and ceremonies," *Twenty-third Annual Report of the U. S. Bureau of American Ethnology, 1901–1902.* Washington, 1904.

Strickland, Rex W., "Moscoso's journey through Texas," *Southwestern Historical Quarterly,* vol. XLVI, October, 1942.

Suárez de Peralta, Joan, *Tratado del descubrimiento de las Yndias y su conquista, y los ritos . . . de los yndios; y de los virreyes y gobernadores . . . y del principio que tuvo Francisco Draque para ser declarado enemigo* [edited by Justo Zaragoza]. Madrid, 1878. Written in the last third of the sixteenth century.

Swanton, John R., *The Indians of the Southeastern United States,* Bulletin 137, Bureau of American Ethnology. Washington, 1946.

Sykes, Godfrey G., *The Colorado Delta.* Washington, 1937.

Tejada, Lorenzo de, "Appointment of Licentiate Tejada as judge of residencia for New Galicia," Hammond and Rey.

———— "Carta al principe del licenciado Tejada, oidor de la Audiencia de México, diciendo que había escrito enviando la residencia tomada a Francisco Vázquez de Coronado: que había necesidad de proveer á la Nueva Galicia de audiencia y prelado, y que dió cumplimiento á las cédulas que había recibido [Mexico, August 31, 1545)," Paso y Tronsoco, vol. IV.

———— "Carta al príncipe don Felipe del licenciado Tejada, avisando haber recibido los despachos de la comisión que se le confiaba en la Nueva Galicia y que de acuerdo con el virrey había demorado el viaje hasta que terminase la residencia que está dando: que después no había partido por una enfermedad que sufrio [Mexico, May 24, 1544]," Paso y Troncoso, vol. IV.

———— "Carta al rey del licenciado Tejada oidor de la Audiencia de

Mexico haciendo relación de todo lo que había proveído en la visita hecha á la Nueva Galicia, para tomar residencia al gobernador Francisco Vázquez Coronado, y a los capitanes, oficiates y justicias de dicha provincia [Mexico, March 11, 1545]," *ibid.*, vol. IV. *See also,* Pérez Bustamante.

Tejada, Lorenzo de, "Tejada's commission to investigate the cruelties on the expedition to Cíbola, September 7, 1543," Hammond and Rey.

Tello, Antonio, "Fragmentos de una historia de la Nueva Galicia, escrita hácia 1650," García Icazbalceta, *Colección,* vol. II.

—— *Libro segundo de la Cronica miscelanea, en que se trata de la conquista espiritual y temporal de la Santa provincia de Xalisco.* Guadalajara, 1891. Written c. 1650.

Ternaux-Compans, Henri, *Voyages, relations et mémoires originaux pour servir à l'histoire de la découverte de l'Amérique publiés pour la première fois, en français,* 20 vols. Paris, 1837–1841. Cited as Ternaux. *See,* vol. IX for Coronado documents.

"Testimonio dado en Méjico sobre el descubrimiento de doscientas leguas adelante, de las minas de Santa Bárbola, governación de Diego de Ibarra," Pacheco y Cárdenas, vol. XV. English translation of many of these documents in Bolton, *Spanish Exploration.*

Thomas, Alfred B., *After Coronado: Spanish Exploration Northeast of New Mexico, 1696–1727.* Norman, Okla., 1935.

Torquemada, Juan de, *Los veynte i vn libros rituales y monarchia yndiana, con el origen y guerras de los Yndios Occidentales. Compvesto por Fray Ivan de Torquemada, ministro prouncial de la orden de S. Francisco en Mexico, en la Nueba España.* Seville, 1615. Reprinted in an improved edition by Barcia, 3 vols. Madrid, 1723. New edition, 2 vols. Mexico, 1943.

"Traslado de las nuevas y noticias que dieron sobre el descobrimiento de una cibdad, que llamaron de Cibola, situada en la tierra nueva, año de 1531 [1541]," Pacheco y Cárdenas, vol. XIX. English translations, Hammond and Rey; Winship (reprinted in *Journey of Coronado* and *Journey of Francisco Vázquez de Coronado, 1540–1542).*

Troyano, Juan, "Carta al rey en que trata de sus largos servicios y de la conveniencia de poblar la tierra descubierta por Francisco Vázquez de Coronado: pide que se le envíe persona á quien dar noticias de varias cosas que conviene remediar, las cuales indica en quince capítulos [Mexico, December 20, 1568]," Paso y Troncoso, vol. X.

Twitchell, Ralph E., *Leading Facts of New Mexican History,* 5 vols. Cedar Rapids, Ia., 1911.

Ulloa, Francisco de, "Record and narrative of the voyage and discovery which, in the name of Our Lord, was made after this, your lordship's armada had left the port of Acapulco, July 8, 1539; as far as this Cedros island, where I now am, on April 5, 1540" [translated by Irene A. Wright], Wagner, *California Voyages* (also *California Historical Society Quarterly,* vol. III, December, 1924); Wagner, *Spanish Voyages.*

—— "Relación del armada, etc." *See,* Alarcón.

——— *See also,* Preciado.

Undreiner, George J., 'Fray Marcos de Niza, His Journey to Cíbola," *The Americas*, vol. III, April, 1947.

Vetancurt, Augustin de, *Teatro mexicano. Descripción breve de los sucessos exemplares, historicos, politicos, militares, y religiosos del nuevo mundo occidental de las Indias*, 2 vols. Mexico, 1698; 4 vols. Mexico, 1870–71. [Vol. IV, "Menologio Franciscano."]

Villagra, Gaspár Pérez de, *Historia de la Nueva Mexico*. Alcala, 1610. Reprinted in Mexico, 1900. Facsimile reproduction with prose translation into English by Gilberto Espinosa and notes and introduction by F. W. Hodge. Quivira Society Publications no. 4. Los Angeles, 1933.

Wagner, Henry R., *California Voyages, 1539–1541* San Francisco, 1925. Also in *California Historical Society Quarterly*, vol. III, December, 1924.

——— *The Cartography of the Northwest Coast of America to the Year 1800*, 2 vols. Berkeley, 1937.

——— "Fr. Marcos de Niza," *New Mexico Historical Review*, vol. IX, April, 1934.

——— "A 'Fray Marcos de Niza' note," *ibid.*, vol. IX, July, 1934.

——— *The Rise of Fernando Cortés*. Los Angeles, 1944.

——— *The Spanish Southwest, 1542–1794: An Annotated Bibliography*. Berkeley, 1924. Also published in 2 vols. as Quivira Society Publications No. 7, Albuquerque, 1937.

——— *Spanish Voyages to the Northwest Coast of America*. San Francisco, 1929.

——— "The voyage of Hernando de Alarcón," *California Historical Society Quarterly*, vol. III, December, 1924.

Waters, Frank, *The Colorado*. New York, 1946.

Wedel, Waldo R., *Archaeological Remains in Central Kansas and Their Possible Bearing on the Location of Quivira*, Smithsonian Miscellaneous Collections, CI, No. 7. Washington, 1942.

——— "In search of Coronado's province of Quivira," *Explorations and Field-work of the Smithsonian Institution in 1940*. Washington, 1941.

Williams, J. W., "Moscoso's trail in Texas," *Southwestern Historical Quarterly*, vol. XLVI, October, 1942.

Winship, George Parker, "The Coronado expedition, 1540-1542," *Fourteenth Annual Report of the U. S. Bureau of American Ethnology, 1892–93*, Part I. Washington, 1896. Cited as Winship.

——— *The Journey of Coronado*. Trail Makers Series. New York, 1904.

——— *The Journey of Francisco Vázquez de Coronado, 1540–1542*. San Francisco, 1933. A limited edition of translations of Castañeda and other Coronado documents, with additional notes and an introduction by F. W. Hodge.

——— "Why Coronado went to New Mexico in 1540," *Annual Report of the American Historical Association*, 1894. Washington, 1895.

Wynkoop, Frank M., "Journey of conquest," *New Mexico*, vol. XVIII June, 1940.

Ximénez de San Estéban, Jerónimo, "Carta á Santo Tomás de Villanueva

[Acapichtla, October 9, 1539]," García Icazbalceta, *Nueva Colección,* vol. I,

Zarate Salmeron, Gerónimo de, "Relaciones de todas las cosas que en el Nuevo Mexico se han visto y sabido . . . desde el año de 1538 hasta el de 1626," *Documentos para la historia de México,* Third series.

Zimmerman, James F., "The Coronado cuarto centennial," *Hispanic American Historical Review,* vol. XX, February, 1940.

Zumárraga, Juan de, "Carta al emperador [Mexico, April 17, 1540]," Cuevas, *Documentos inéditos.*

——— "Carta á un eclesiástico desconocido [Mexico, April 4, 1537]," *ibid.*

——— "Tres cartas familiares de Fr. Juan de Zumárraga, primer obispo y arzobispo de México; y contestación á otra que le dirige Fr. Marcos de Niza," García Icazbalceta, *Nueva colección,* vol. II.

——— *See also,* Carreño, "Nuevos documentos."

LOST DOCUMENTS

In various sources relating to the Coronado expedition references are made to items which have not come to light, but which may appear at some later time. They are listed here to tantalize scholars forever.

Alvarado, Hernando de, Map of the Río Grande Pueblos. See chapter XVI.

Cabeza de Vaca—"Certified statement of the date—year, month and day" requested by Vaca of the four Spaniards whom he met first.

Cabeza de Vaca—Account of journey prepared for the viceroy and forwarded by him to the crown.

Cabeza de Vaca—Map prepared by Cabeza de Vaca and Dorantes, at the request of Mendoza, showing their travels from Florida to Mexico.

Mendoza's letter to Dorantes at Vera Cruz, asking him to return to Mexico City. [Mentioned in Mendoza's letter of December 10, 1537.]

Mendoza's letter to King, giving Coronado's history and qualifications. [Mentioned in letter from Mendoza to King, December 10, 1537.]

King's order to Coronado to hold Residencia of de la Torre. [Mentioned in letter from Coronado to King, December 15, 1538—Compostela.]

Petition and report of solicitor concerning conditions at San Miguel in province of Culiacán. [Enclosed with letter from Coronado to King, December 15, 1538—Compostela.]

Coronado's letters to the viceroy from Compostela which included reports concerning Fray Marcos de Niza. [Mentioned in letter from Coronado to Mendoza, March 8, 1539.]

Coronado's letter to the viceroy from San Miguel concerning Indians and Fray Marcos. [Mentioned in letter of March 8, 1539.]

Fray Marcos de Niza's letter to the viceroy. [Mentioned as enclosed with letter from Coronado to the viceroy, March 8, 1539.]

Order and letter from King to Coronado decreeing that all Spaniards in

Nueva Galicia should build houses of stone or adobe. [Mentioned in letter from Coronado to King, July 15, 1539—Compostela.]

Decree from King ordering checking of accounts of administrators of the estates of deceased persons. [Mentioned in letter from Coronado to King, July 15, 1539—Compostela.]

Mendoza's letter to King telling of sending of "two Franciscan friars to discover limits of mainland in the region across the mountains." [Mentioned in letter from Mendoza to King, 1539.]

Fray Marcos de Niza's letters to the viceroy and to Father Fray Antonio de Ciudad-Rodrigo, written at Compostela following his return from the north. [Mentioned in Niza's "Report."]

Fray Marcos de Niza's record of names of islands and settlements on his journey. [Mentioned in Niza's "Report."]

Coronado's appointment as Captain general by Mendoza. [Mentioned in Appointment by the King, January 6, 1540.]

Oñate's letter to Samaniego telling him of the gift of the two horses to Coronado. [Mentioned in Coronado's "Residencia."]

Instructions from the viceroy to Alarcón regarding first expedition to establish communication with Coronado.

Mendoza's letter to the King written in February, 1540, at Compostela. [Mentioned in letter from Mendoza to King, April 17, 1540, at Jacona.]

Melchior Díaz's letter to Mendoza, received by Mendoza on March 20, 1540. The portion making up his report on the route to Cíbola is copied into Mendoza's letter of April 17, 1540, to the King.

Coronado's letters to Mendoza which Zaldívar may have carried south with Díaz's report.

Mendoza's letter to the King written "a few days" before letter of April 17. [Mentioned in Mendoza's letter of April 17, 1540—Jacona.]

Mendoza's message to Coronado, ordering him to send an advance guard from Culiacán ahead of the main army. [Mentioned in Zaldívar's testimony, *Información contra Coronado*.]

Coronado's message, left at Culiacán, addressed to Zaldívar, ordering him to take charge of his own company and join the main army under Arellano. [Mentioned in Zaldívar's testimony, *Información contra . . . Coronado*.]

Letters of the friars on the expedition to their convents, telling of the Trujillo affair.

Coronado's letter from Cíbola. "For, as I wrote to your Lordship, I made the trip from Culiacán in eighty days' travel. . . ." [Therefore, this letter was probably written in July. Mentioned in Coronado's letter to Mendoza, August 3, 1540—Cíbola.]

Coronado's letter to Mendoza. "On the 22nd of last April, I set out from the province of Culiacán with part of the army, following the arrangements of which I wrote to your Lordship. . . ." [Mentioned in letter from Coronado to Mendoza, August 3, 1540—Cíbola. Is this the same as the letter written, probably in July, from Cíbola, or did the letter concerning "arrangements" precede the trip?]

Drawing of route to Cíbola sent to Mendoza by Coronado. [Mentioned in letter of Coronado to Mendoza, August 3, 1540–Cíbola.]

Sketch of towns of Cíbola painted on a skin. [Mentioned in Coronado's letter to Mendoza, August 3, 1540–Cíbola.]

Sotomayor's report of the Cárdenas expedition to the Grand Canyon. [Mentioned by Castañeda.]

Alarcón's "acts of possession." [Mentioned in Alarcón's report.]

Alarcón's book about his expedition. [Mentioned in Alarcón's report.]

Alarcón's letter left "at the foot of this tree" and found by Díaz. [Mentioned by Castañeda.]

Map of the Alarcón expedition sent to Fernández de Oviedo by Nicolás Zamorano.

Alvarado's report on Tiguex. [Mentioned in "Account of What . . . Alvarado and . . . Padilla Discovered."]

Letters to Coronado from Diego de Alarcón [Alcaraz] telling of death of Melchior Díaz. [Mentioned by Castañeda.]

Coronado's letter to the King, dated April 20, 1541, at Tiguex, "giving detailed report and account of this expedition." [Mentioned in letter from Coronado to the King, October 20, 1541–Tiguex. This is probably the same report mentioned by Castañeda, and by Peramíldez in his letter of July 28, 1541.]

King's letter to Coronado, written at Madrid, June 11, 1540. The above letter dated April 20, 1541, is in answer to this. [Mentioned in letter from Coronado to the King, October 20, 1541–Tiguex.]

King's letter to Coronado, dated June 21, 1540, thanking him for his services and commanding him to continue them. [Mentioned, in brief, of petition to his Majesty by Francisco Pacheco de Córdova y Bocanegra, 1605. Is this the same letter which Coronado mentions as dated June 11?]

Coronado's letters sent from Tiguex to Don Pedro de Tovar to be received at Cíbola on his return from Soñora, directing Tovar to follow the army. [Mentioned by Castañeda.]

Coronado's letters left under crosses to direct Tovar from Tiguex to the army. [Mentioned by Castañeda.]

Mendoza's letters brought by Tovar to Tiguex. [Mentioned by Castañeda.]

Letter from Mendoza and Pedro de Alvarado, about April 29, 1541, instructing Coronado to aid López de Zuñiga, should he have need of help. [Mentioned in Mendoza's and Alvarado's "Instructions to . . . Zuñiga." Is this one of the letters brought by Tovar, or would the time be too short?]

Petition sent by army to Coronado when he was traveling with Chosen Thirty to Quivira, requesting him to permit them all to go on to Quivira. [Mentioned by Castañeda.]

Letter to Cárdenas, brought by Tovar to Tiguex, telling of death of brother. [Mentioned by Castañeda].

Coronado's letter to the governor of Harahey and Quivira. [Mentioned by Jaramillo.]

Relación Postrera appears to be based on a report written at Tiguex after

Arellano had returned there from the plains, but before Coronado arrived from Quivira.

Coronado's report to Mendoza concerning Quivira. [Mentioned in Coronado's letter to the King, October 20, 1541—Tiguex.]

Request by Padilla's Indian servants to return to New Spain and authorization to do so. [Coronado's testimony in the Mendoza "Residencia."]

Petition, "signed by many of the principal persons," presented to Coronado requesting that the army return to New Spain from Cíbola. [Testimony of Pedro de Castro and Hernando del Valle in the *Proceso de pleito . . . por parte de . . . Coronado.*]

Report telling of Coronado and the death of the Turk. [Mentioned by Sotelo de Betanzos in his letter to the King, June 5, 1566—Mexico.]

Letter written by Mendoza, and reported by "a gentleman" as having been seen by him at the Emperor's court in Flanders. This letter stated that Coronado had discovered the Seven Cities and had gone on to the northwest till he reached the sea.

Coronado's record of those who died on the expedition. [Coronado's testimony in the Mendoza "Residencia."]

Coronado—*Información de parte* heard before Doctor Antonio Rodríguez de Quesado, oidor of Mexico, in 1545, setting forth expenses incurred in conquests and journeys. [Mentioned in Pacheco de Cordova y Bocanegra, "Brief of Petition to His Majesty."]

Tovar's papers used by Castañeda in writing his history.

Book and small old trunk left by Coronado at Zuñi. [Mentioned by Luxán in his narrative.]

INDEX

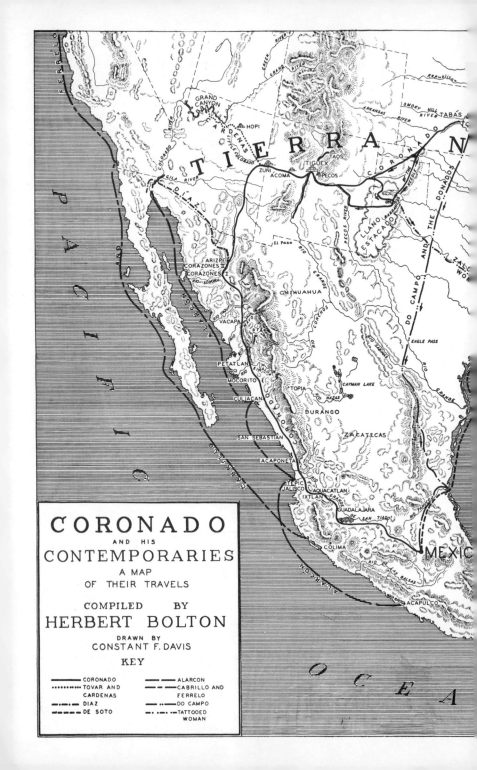

CORONADO

AND HIS

CONTEMPORARIES

A MAP
OF THEIR TRAVELS

COMPILED   BY
HERBERT BOLTON

DRAWN BY
CONSTANT F. DAVIS

KEY

CORONADO	ALARCON
TOVAR AND CARDENAS	CABRILLO AND FERRELO
DIAZ	DO CAMPO
DE SOTO	TATTOOED WOMAN

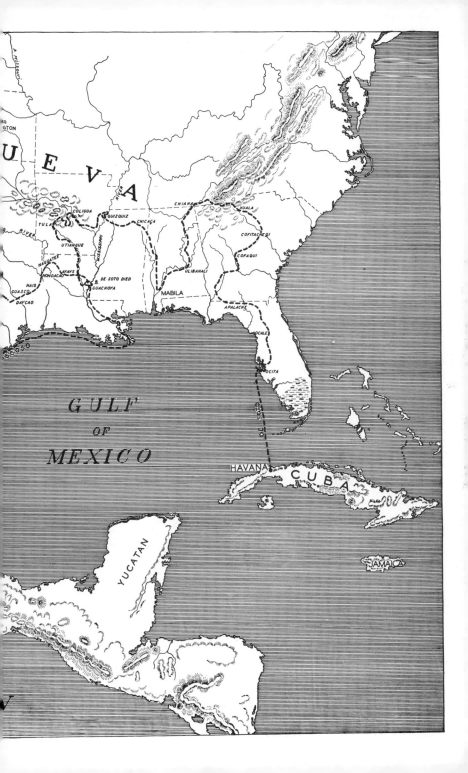

U E V A

CHIAHA
YUALA
COLIGUA
QUIZQUIZ
CHICACA
COFITACHEQI
TULA
UTIANGUE
COPAQUI
NAGUITEX
XAYAYS
NONDACAO
ULIBANALI
HAIS
DE SOTO DIED
GUASCO
GUACHOYA
MABILA
DAYCAO
APALACHE

RIVER
MISSISIPPI
RIVER
MISSOURI
GTON
KG TON

OCALE

OCITA

GULF

OF

MEXICO

HAVANA
CUBA

YUCATAN

JAMAICA